Sex Roles and Psychopathology

Sex Roles and Psychopathology

Edited by

Cathy Spatz Widom

Indiana University
Bloomington, Indiana

Plenum Press • New York and London

Library of Congress Cataloging in Publication Data

Main entry under title:

Sex roles and psychopathology.

Includes bibliographical references and index.
1. Psychology, Pathological. 2. Sex role. I. Widom, Cathy Spatz, date–   . [DNLM:
1. Identification (Psychology) 2. Psychopathology. WM 100 S518]
RC455.4.S45S48   1984   616.89   83-24774
ISBN 0-306-41406-6

©1984 Plenum Press, New York
A Division of Plenum Publishing Corporation
233 Spring Street, New York, N.Y. 10013

Printed in the United States of America

To the memory of my father, Jack Spatz,
to my mother, Paula, and
to the future of my daughter, Rebecca

Contributors

Mary Ellen Colten • Study Director, Center for Survey Research, 100 Arlington Street, Boston, Massachusetts 02116

Sue Cox • Research Associate, Langley–Porter Neuropsychiatric Institute, University of California-San Francisco, 564 30th Street, San Francisco, California 94131

Nancy Datan • Professor of Psychology and Co-Director, West Virginia University Gerontology Center, Morgantown, West Virginia 26506

Ellen Dwyer • Assistant Professor of Forensic Studies, Indiana University, 302 Sycamore Hall, Bloomington, Indiana 47405

Robert F. Eme • Clinical Child Psychologist, Forest Hospital and Foundation, Des Plaines, and private practice, 731 Grey Street, Evanston, Illinois 60202

Linda Fidell • Professor of Psychology, California State University, Northridge, California 91330

Stephen Finn • Graduate Student in Clinical Psychology, University of Minnesota, N438, 75 East River Road, Minneapolis, Minnesota 55455

Linda Holt • Graduate School of Psychology, West Virginia University, Morgantown, West Virginia 26506

Ronald A. LaTorre • Research Associate, Program Resources, Vancouver School Board, 1595 West 10th Avenue, Vancouver, British Columbia V6J 1Z8, Canada

Gloria R. Leon • Associate Professor of Psychology and Psychiatry, and Associate Director, Clinical Psychology Training Program, University of Minnesota, 75 East River Road, Minneapolis, Minnesota 55455

David Lester • Professor of Psychology, Stockton State College, Pomona, New Jersey 08240

Jeanne C. Marsh • Assistant Professor, School of Social Service Administration, University of Chicago, 969 East 60th Street, Chicago, Illinois 60637

Jane E. Platt • Assistant Professor of Psychiatry, Millhauser Laboratories HN 404, New York University Medical Center, 550 First Avenue, New York, New York 10016

Lenore Sawyer Radloff • Research Psychologist, Statistician, and Psychiatric Epidemiologist, National Institute of Mental Health, Center for Epidemiological Studies, Division of Biometry and Epidemiology, Room 18C-05, 5600 Fishers Lane, Rockville, Maryland 20857

Wendy E. Stock • Therapist and Research Assistant, Sex Therapy Center, Department of Psychiatry and Behavioral Science, Health Science Center—School of Medicine, State University of New York, Stony Brook, New York 11794

Cathy Spatz Widom • Chairperson and Associate Professor of Forensic Studies, and Associate Professor of Psychology, Indiana University, 302 Sycamore Hall, Bloomington, Indiana 47405

Barbara Ann Winstead • Assistant Professor of Psychology, Old Dominion University, 1410 West 48th Street, Norfolk, Virginia 23508

Barry E. Wolfe • Assistant Chief, Psychosocial Treatments Research Branch and Chief, Outcome Studies Section, Division of Extramural Research Programs, National Institute of Mental Health, Room 10C-18, Parklawn Building, 5600 Fishers Lane, Rockville, Maryland 20857

Peter B. Zeldow • Assistant Professor, Department of Psychology and Social Sciences, and Director of Education, Rush Presbyterian-St. Luke's Medical Center, 1753 West Congress Parkway, Chicago, Illinois 60612

Preface

Psychopathology is the science of deviant behavior. However, as psychopathologists, our explanations of deviant behavior are not developed in a sterile, laboratory environment. Abnormality is a relative concept, and the labeling of someone or some behavior as abnormal is inextricably linked to a particular social context. In the United States, for example, a woman reporting vivid hallucinations is likely to be committed to a mental hospital and the behavior considered maladaptive. In other cultures, the same behavior may be interpreted as reflecting magical, healing powers, and the woman honored and revered.

An explicit assumption underlying this book is that elements of social causality influence the development and maintenance of psychopathology. While the chapters emphasize environmental influences, this is not intended to negate the importance of physiological, biological, genetic, or hormonal factors in relation to psychopathology.

The purpose of this book is to examine the impact of sex role stereotypes on the occurrence and distribution of specific forms of psychopathology. In contrast to prior work, which emphasizes sex differences (e.g., Franks and Gomberg's *Gender and Disordered Behavior*) these are not the primary focus of this volume. *Sex Roles and Psychopathology* analyzes the extent to which cultural norms about the sexes, societal expectations and values about sex-typed behavior and sex differences, and professional biases influence the development, manifestation, and maintenance of abnormal behavior among men and women.

We hope to stimulate researchers to ask further questions about the relationship between sex roles and specific kinds of psychopathology. For example, to what extent are diagnostic criteria influenced by variables that may be theoretically *ir*relevant to a diagnosis? To what extent are similarities in the behavior of males and females interpreted differently in the context of psychiatric diagnoses?

Sex Roles and Psychopathology should be of interest to a wide audience. Professionals and students alike in psychology, psychiatry, community psychology, evaluation research, epidemiology, mental-health service fields, social work, women's studies, and sociology should find these chapters informative and, in some cases, quite provocative.

This book contains chapters that synthesize the results of empirical research, as well as chapters representing original theoretical analyses focusing on specific forms of psychopathology. Some chapters represent "state-of-the-art" reviews, particularly on topics where extensive research has been done and conceptual models developed. Other chapters break new ground and encourage the emergence of new approaches to research.

We begin with a historical review of psychiatric theory and practice in the 19th century and conclude with a discussion of contemporary medical practices. In between, chapters are organized into four major sections: Neurotic, Affective, and Schizophrenic Disorders; Social Deviation and Sexual Dysfunction; Age-Related Disorders, and Societal Management and Control.

As was evident in the 19th century, medical and psychiatric theory and practice were not sex blind. Some would argue that contemporary psychology and psychiatry cannot and should not be sex blind. However, this book draws attention to the ways in which definitions, diagnostic criteria, study designs, and conclusions are influenced by sex-role stereotypic assumptions. It is hoped that recognition of the biases inherent in our theory and practice will lead to further research and understanding of the role of sociocultural factors in the etiology, diagnosis, and treatment of a variety of forms of psychopathology.

Acknowledgments

As editor, I want to express my appreciation to the authors of the chapters. Their excitement and enthusiasm about the book and their interest and cooperation kept my spirits buoyed at difficult times. To Mary De-Shong, my secretary in the Department of Forensic Studies, my sincere thanks for patience and good humor in typing and retyping chapter drafts. I am most appreciative of the advice and insightful, critical, and constructive comments of Michael G. Maxfield. Without his constant encouragement and emotional support, this book would never have been completed. Finally, to Rebecca, Michael, and Mary, I want to express my gratitude for tolerating my "craziness" during the final stages in the preparation of this volume.

Contents

I

Introduction

Sex Roles and Psychopathology

Cathy Spatz Widom

1. Psychopathology in a Social Context

Psychopathology and deviance cannot be understood in the abstract. Rather, definitions of deviance and mental illness depend on cultural norms, societal expectations and values, individual differences, professional biases, and the social-political climate of the time. *Sex Roles and Psychopathology* analyzes the extent to which cultural norms about the sexes, societal expectations and values about sex-typed behavior, sex differences, and professional biases influence the development, manifestation, and maintenance of abnormal behavior among men and women.

Although people may be described and categorized along a variety of dimensions, few appear as salient as gender. Knowing whether someone is male or female provides us with basic information, expectations, and shared cultural assumptions about that individual. It is these psychological and cultural components of sex or gender that are generally conceptualized as *sex roles* (Katz, 1979).

The purpose of this book is to examine the impact of sex role stereotypes on the occurrence and distribution of specific forms of psychopathology. The chapters in this volume describe how cultural roles for each sex influence the development of psychopathology and how they in turn reflect underlying assumptions about etiology and diagnostic criteria.

Cathy Spatz Widom • Departments of Forensic Studies and Psychology, Indiana University, Bloomington, Indiana 47405.

An explicit assumption underlying this book is that elements of social causality influence the development of psychopathology. The rationale for each chapter is to explore how differential patterns of socialization, shaped by sex role stereotypes, influence the experiences of boys and girls. The book also seeks to elaborate how parents, teachers, and sociocultural institutions differentially reward or punish, provide opportunities or erect barriers that lead to sex-typed psychopathological behavior in males and females. While the same general factors influence the development of behavior, the strength, direction, and timing of socialization experiences often differ by sex.

Numerous studies have noted that females have higher overall rates of mental illness than males, but there remains some dispute as to the clarity, consistency, and meaningfulness of the findings (Dohrenwend and Dohrenwend, 1976; Gove, 1980; Radloff, 1980). Although some discussion of sex differences is therefore necessary to understand the impact of sex role stereotypes on specific forms of psychopathology, sex differences *per se* are *not* the primary focus of this volume.

The chapters in this book emphasize environmental influences. This is not intended to deny the importance of physiological, biological, genetic, or hormonal influences on the development and maintenance of psychopathological behavior. Rather, this decision reflects the objective of this volume to call attention to and sensitize researchers, clinicians, and practitioners to the sometimes subtle contribution that sex role stereotypes make toward diagnosis, definition, and disposition of a variety of disordered and deviant behaviors. Hence, it is not the intention of this volume to ignore or reject the contribution of biological factors. While sexual dimorphism indicates the existence of clear differences, the interpretation of these differences is determined by culture. It is the elaboration of these social and cultural influences on psychopathology that is the goal of this volume.

2. Sex, Roles, and Psychopathology

2.1. From Gender to Behavior: Some Basic Concepts

Interest in sex roles has mushroomed over the past 15 years. Along with this surge of interest, we have seen a variety of terms and concepts come into use. As the reader will see, while some authors use terms interchangeably, others have distinct preferences and take great pains to define their particular use. Some chapters discuss gender or gender roles, whereas others may refer to sex or sex roles. No attempt has been made to ensure consistent usage across the volume, but there are important distinctions in terminology that need to be emphasized before we begin. For example, one's self-definition as male or female (gender identity) is quite different from what we mean when we describe the influence of sex role stereotypes on one's behavior. However, these normative expectations, part of society's stereotypes, may ultimately become part of one's gender identity. It is therefore necessary to differentiate several related but distinct concepts.

Sex or *gender* simply refers to the biological sex of the individual— male or female. In contrast, *sex* or *gender identity* concerns the individual's awareness and acceptance of her/his biological sex. *Psychological masculinity/femininity* includes clusters of socially desirable attributes stereotypically considered to differentiate males and females. These attributes are also used to define the psychological characteristics of the masculine and feminine personality (Spence and Helmreich, 1978, p. 3). However, these psychological dimensions are not necessarily related to the broad spectrum of sex role behaviors.

Sex roles are those behaviors commonly understood to characterize a person of a given biological sex within a particular society. These behaviors typically correspond with societal stereotypes for males and females. *Sex role expectations* and *stereotypes* refer to the shared expectations and beliefs about appropriate behavior and characteristics for men and women in a given society. *Sex-typed* behaviors are those stereotyped behaviors commonly associated with being a biological male or female. Male-related behaviors are sex-typed as masculine; female-related behaviors are sex-typed as feminine.

It is important to differentiate these terms in order to understand the ways in which biological, psychological, and social differences between the sexes may be related to psychopathology. These definitions imply that sex or gender may influence the development of psychopathology in several different ways. Discussion of these influences is organized to correspond with the sex role concepts delineated above.

2.1.1. Influence of Biological Sex or Gender.   The identification of a biological effect is a complex issue (Parsons, 1980). Biological processes can influence gender dimorphism directly (through primary sexual dimorphism differences) or indirectly (through maturation rates or body size). Although we recognize the importance of biological influences, such hormonal, physiological, or genetic contributions are not central to the focus of this book. Nevertheless, this perspective is implicit in several chapters. For example, Eme (Chapter 12) argues that males are biologically more vulnerable from birth. Leon and Finn (Chapter 13) acknowledge that metabolic differences may partially explain the development of eating disorders. Similarly, males have body characteristics that may suit them better than females for physical aggression (bigger, more muscle mass, higher metabolism rates, more androgens, and a higher proportion of red blood corpuscles (Scheinfeld, 1958)). Biological and hormonal differences in levels of aggressiveness are related to predispositions to antisocial and criminal behavior (Chapter 9).

2.1.2. Gender Identity Disturbances. At a very simple level, gender identity disturbances may lead to the development of psychopathology. Such disturbances can also reflect symptoms of disordered behavior. With rare exceptions, humans are classified as male or female at birth or before, and gender remains constant throughout one's lifetime. The notion that biological sex or gender is constant is learned fairly early in life (Slaby and Frey, 1975) and is maintained. While individuals may vary in the extent to which they like or dislike their bodies, the vast majority do not want to change their sex. Among the rare exceptions are transsexuals, who feel that their physical body does not match their psychological sex. They are prisoners in a body of the wrong sex. Transvestites, on the other hand (Chapter 9), have no desire to change their sex, but rather wish to assume the feelings of the opposite sex through the process of cross-dressing. Despite vivid clinical accounts of body image distortions, hallucinations, and delusions, LaTorre concludes (Chapter 8) that there is little direct evidence that schizophrenia is related to impaired gender identity or body image. Male schizophrenics may, however, overadopt psychological characteristics associated with females and may prefer opposite sex roles.

2.1.3. Psychological Masculinity and Femininity. Is there any relationship between traditional masculine or feminine personality attributes and specific forms of psychopathology? For a number of disorders discussed here, psychological characteristics associated with traditional notions of femininity play a critical role in explanatory theories. Wolfe (Chapter 3) implicates the fearful and dependent personality, lacking in autonomy, in the development of phobias. These traditional characteristics associated with femininity lead to increased vulnerability of women to phobias. Cox and Radloff (Chapter 6), pointing to the similarities between depression and femininity, suggest that both may result from feelings of relative powerlessness and learned helplessness. Excessive masculinity was once thought to be causally related to female criminality and deviance (Chapter 9); however, little empirical support for this proposition currently exists.

2.1.4. Sex Roles: Socialization, Stereotypes, and Expectations. By far the strongest and most pervasive influence on psychopathology is found in the socialization experiences, stereotypes, and attitudes linked to sex roles. Several authors describe how differences in the socialization of males and females relate to differences in their behavior, which in turn may influence the development of various forms of psychopathology. By setting boundaries for acceptable behavior, sex roles act to place constraints on growing children, and these constraints are linked to psychopathology. Restrictions in access and opportunities to varied experiences in part shape the particular nature and extent of disorders among males and females.

For example, sex role socialization exerts a direct influence on eating habits (Chapter 13). Cultural roles for each sex prescribe notions of ideal body size and shape, emphasize the differential importance of physical attractiveness, and therefore influence the development of eating disorders through direct effects on eating habits. To the extent that sex roles prevent or promote certain behaviors, they influence the rates of psychophysiological disorders such as coronary heart disease (Chapter 5). Traditional sex role socialization also limits the range of females' sexual experiences throughout childhood and adolescence, providing rigid norms with detailed "sexual scripts" for appropriate male and female behavior (Chapter 11). The socialization of males and females in our culture makes women more susceptible to depression (Chapter 6) and makes adoption of hysterical traits more acceptable for females than for males (Chapter 4).

Experiences related to sex role socialization also influence rates of substance abuse and patterns of use and abuse development (Chapter 10). Access and opportunities again shape the nature of drug use for women. If consistent with her expected social role, certain forms of drug use by women are tolerated and indirectly encouraged; amphetamines for weight control and tranquilizers for increased quietude and passivity are common examples.

Sanctions and restraints, however, are not always harmful. Even though constraints on women's behavior act in deleterious ways, there are, in other cases, advantages resulting from such limitations. Traditional restrictions in the socialization of women have most likely resulted in the lower incidence of coronary heart disease, drug and alcohol abuse, and some forms of criminal behavior.

Sex role stereotypes influence assumptions and perceptions of disordered behavior, and can affect ultimate treatment and outcome. This is illustrated in several chapters. For example, the sexually active, assertive male corresponds to the ideal masculine stereotype, whereas a female of the same description would be labeled deviant and unnatural (Chapter 11). Female addicts are seen as sicker, more deviant, more reprehensible, and less treatable than male addicts (Chapter 10). Both men and women condemn drunkenness in women more than in males (Chapter 10), and female patients encounter harsher judgments than males when they engage in norm-deviant behavior (Chapter 15).

Sex role attitudes and stereotypes influence definitions of psychopathological behavior, diagnostic criteria, psychological assessments, and patient management. In some cases, diagnostic criteria are explicitly sex-linked; in other cases, males are excluded from eligibility (Chapter 4). Sex also interacts with other variables to influence clinical assessments and judgments, so that behavior that is within acceptable boundaries is condoned, whereas behavior that exceeds those limits is severely stigmatized (Chapters 9 and 15).

Historically, stereotypes about the nature and temperament of women influenced medical treatment and practice (Chapter 2). Contemporary sex role stereotypes continue to influence medical behavior, expectations, and treatment (Chapter 16). On the other hand, Zeldow (Chapter 15) warns that simple sex bias in clinical judgments is less pervasive than previously thought and that the evidence for *global* sex discrimination is weak.

2.2. Sex, Vulnerability, and Marital Status: A Paradox

That there are clear sex differences in rates of specific forms of psychopathology cannot be denied. Personality disorders, alcohol and drug abuse, and suicide are more common among males. Females are predominant in phobias, hysteria, psychophysiological disorders, and depression. In childhood disorders, males are predominant; only in the childhood *emotional* disorders do females achieve parity with males (Chapter 12). Following Eme's argument that males are genetically more vulnerable, it appears that females are favored from birth. However, if males are biologically more vulnerable, what happens to prevent their higher prevalence in adult forms of psychopathology? Why do studies of mental illness typically show higher overall prevalences in women? What happens to women to account for their catching up with and surpassing males?

Since endowment and experience influence behavior and shape lives, and endowment seems to favor females, the most likely explanation lies with experience. Indeed, sex role socialization experiences may prime women *more than men* to develop psychological disorders. Sex role norms sometimes protect women by limiting their behavior, but at the same time, sex role attitudes can act to predispose, prime, and promote certain forms of psychopathological behavior. How?

The traditional role for women involves marriage and motherhood. Yet marriage and motherhood are associated with increased psychiatric stress for women, but not for men. Thus, marital status appears to exert a critical influence on the development and extent of psychopathology. Marriage is associated with increased rates of depression, phobias, coronary heart disease, suicide, and drug and alcohol abuse for women, but with decreased rates for the same disorders for men. Apparently, being married exacerbates problems for women but buffers life's experiences for men. Over 100 years ago, Disraeli quipped, "Every woman should marry—and no man."* Perhaps the epigram should now read, "Every man should marry—and no woman."

2.3. Implications for Research Design, Treatment, and Management

Caution must be exercised in explaining the predominance of males or females in the various forms of psychopathology or in interpreting research findings. Definitions and connotations may artifically increase particular prevalence rates in males or females in different disorders. The relative incidence of males to females, then, may depend to a large part on whether the definition or diagnostic criteria explicitly incorporate characteristics possessed only by one sex (e.g., disorders of menstruation or pregnancy), or more likely found in females (e.g., sexy, provocative) or males (e.g., poor occupational performance as one of the criteria for antisocial personality).

Decisions in research design may influence the prevalence of one sex or the other. For example, by choosing to study suicide attemptors or psychotropic drug users, rather than completed suicides or heroin and marijuana users, one can implicitly affect the sex ratio of the sample.

Drawing information from institutional records for research on various forms of psychopathology may misleadingly favor one sex over the other. Colten and Marsh (Chapter 10) discuss how samples based on the general population tend to underrepresent young males, whereas estimates of drug use based on accidents or arrest rates overestimate males. On the other hand, studies of drug users seeking treatment at medical facilities are overrepresentative of females. The same kinds of problems affect studies of criminality (Chapter 9), where naïveté about the workings of the criminal justice system may produce erroneous conclusions.

What does an understanding of the influence of sex roles on particular forms of psychopathology contribute to the treatment and management of these disorders? First, as researchers and clinicians, we find that such an awareness of the kinds of influences attributed to sex roles increases our sensitivity in our work. Second, awareness of potential biases in diagnostic criteria or modes of treatment may be one step toward the elimination of such biases. Third, there are implications for treatment paradigms, clinical interventions, and public health education efforts.

Recognizing the contribution that sex role stereotypes or expecta-

*Thanks to Barry E. Wolfe for bringing this quotation to my attention.

tions make toward the etiology of disorders allows us a certain optimistism about the efficacy of treatment. If some portion of particular forms of psychopathology are learned, they surely can be unlearned. If we determine that critical elements in various disorders are sex role-related (e.g., feelings of powerlessness and helplessness in women), then appropriate treatment paradigms can be designed and implemented.

Furthermore, recognizing the kinds of external constraints on behaviors is important for designing treatment programs. As Dwyer notes in her analysis of 19th-century psychiatric practice and thought, the personal, political, and economic stresses on patients' lives were often overlooked (Chapter 2). Currently, external constraints in the form of major family responsibilities influence the incidence of coronary heart disease in women (Chapter 5). The performance ethic affects the sexuality of men and detracts from their feelings of intimacy. Awareness of such external contingencies is critical to the treatment of dysfunctional sexual behavior (Chapter 11). Children learn to evaluate themselves and to match their performance, preferences, attitudes, behaviors, and personal attributes against sex role stereotypes promulgated by society. It is possible that changes in child-rearing, educational practices, and societal expectations will lead to decreases in sex-typed behavior and to diminished sex differences in psychopathology.

3. Overview of the Chapters

While it is possible to organize a book on sex roles and psychopathology in a number of different ways, this volume is divided into five main parts: I. Introduction; II. Neurotic, Affective, and Schizophrenic Disorders; III. Social Deviation and Sexual Dysfunction; IV. Age-Related Disorders; and V. Societal Management and Control. The chapters in each section examine the extent to which sex roles and gender influence various forms of psychopathology, the particular nature of the influences, and the possible mechanisms whereby the influence occurs.

Because no single diagnostic system was chosen to structure the volume, its organization displays some familiar groupings and some that are perhaps not so familiar. It is, however, important to stress that diagnostic categories are not clear or discrete entities, neatly orthogonal and nonoverlapping with one another. It is quite common, for example, to find depression categorized with neurotic disorders as well as with functional psychoses.

Part I begins with this introduction by the editor where the purpose, nature, and scope of the book have been described. To place this contemporary work in perspective, Chapter 2 by Dwyer discusses insantiy from a historical perspective and examines the extent to which psychiatric diagnoses, commitment rates, and medical practices differed as a function of sex. Using American and English 19th-century treatises and archival institutional records to examine medical practice and psychiatric theorizing, Dwyer finds that medical theory was sex-specific and subject to then-current stereotypes about female temperament. Not surprisingly, given an emphasis on physiological symptoms, medical doctors often overlooked the personal, political, and economic stresses in their patients' lives. Dwyer concludes by noting a marked resemblance between 19th-century and contemporary psychiatric views.

Part II focuses on neurotic, affective, and schizophrenic disorders and begins with Chapter 3, "Gender Ideology and Phobias in Women." Social phobias are relatively equally distributed between sexes, whereas there are marked sex differences in agoraphobia, the focus of Wolfe's chapter. Wolfe asserts that normative expectations regarding gender may act as moral imperatives and as such may control behavior. He proposes that personal limitations and the constraints of traditional female roles combine to corrode women's capacity for achievement and autonomy in life situations. This places women at greater risk for the development of phobias. Specifically, he argues that internal and external constraints experienced by women help to produce a fearful and dependent personality, a gender identity of diminished personhood, and a behavioral style characterized by avoidance of difficult situations. These deficiencies, an example of what Wolfe terms the "gender imperatives," result in the development of phobias under conditions of severe stress.

Winstead begins Chapter 4 by calling attention to the fact that hysteria is not a unidimensional diagnosis. She asserts that traditional socialization experiences make the adoption of hysterical traits more acceptable for females than for males in our society. Not surprisingly, then, despite its various meanings and diagnostic criteria, hysteria is consistently associated with females. The relative incidence of males to females depends to a large extent on whether the diagnostic criteria explicitly incorporate characteristics possessed only by women, or those more likely to be found in women. For example, the predominance of females receiving the diagnosis Briquet's syndrome is misleading because many of the necessary symptoms involve disorders of menstruation and sexual problems found only in women. After reviewing psychoanalytic, sociocultural, interpersonal, and biological explanations for the predominance of women, Winstead suggests that efforts to understand hysteria may be seriously confounded by biased perceptions and sex role-stereotypic assumptions.

In Chapter 5, Platt focuses on coronary heart disease (CHD) to examine the relationship between sex roles and psychophysiological disorders. Unitary risk factors (cigarette smoking, oral contraceptives, and exercise), as well as more complex life-style variables (employment status, parity, stress, and Type-A behavior patterns), are discussed and evaluated as to their potential influence on the development of CHD. To the extent that sex role-related attitudes prevent or promote cigarette smoking, the use of oral contraceptives, and participation in strenuous sports or work activities, they influence the rates of CHD in women. Particular types of jobs (although not employment *per se*) and the interaction of employment with other factors (e.g., high levels of family responsibilities) are also associated with increased CHD in women. A variety of sex role-related attitudes affect the degree to which males and females differentially engage in behaviors that are risk factors, or that influence risk factors. These behaviors in turn affect rates of coronary heart disease and, presumably, other psychophysiological disorders. Furthermore, Platt argues that even if one sex is genetically primed or predisposed to a particular disorder, differential environmental reinforcement and exposure influence ultimate rates of development.

Cox and Radloff, in Chapter 6, propose that higher rates of depression in women are a function of social status differentiation and internalization of female sex roles. They present a sequential model of learned susceptibility and precipitating factors, hypothesizing that four types of symptoms in the syndrome (cognitive, behavioral, affective, and somatic) are linked in a causal and reinforcing sequence. Cox and Radloff suggest that there may be sex differences in exposure to precipitating events as well as both innate and learned susceptibility factors. Hence, depression may be a special problem for women not because they are biologically more predisposed, nor because they are exposed to more current stressors, but because they have learned through sex role socialization to be more susceptible to depression.

Beginning Chapter 7 with an explanation of why suicide statistics are difficult to obtain, Lester describes the consistent finding that males commit suicide, whereas females attempt it. Recently, however, sex differences in suicide rates have declined, apparently due to an increase in the rate for females. Marital status affects suicide rates (although in opposite ways for males and females), as does employment/career status. In reviewing possible explanations for the sex difference, Lester discusses choice of method, physiological variables (particularly hormonal factors), mental illness (psychosis), and a threshold model. None of these is supported by empirical data. Drawing upon sex role-related concepts, Linehan's (1973) model characterizes males as holding in problems until they reach crisis proportions, precipitating lethal actions. Females are characterized as using suicide attempts as a cry for help.

Despite these suggestions as to how sex roles might relate to suicidal behavior and the widespread recognition of the sex difference, the dearth of research or theory is depressing.

The last chapter in Part II examines the relationship between gender identity and sex roles and the diagnosis of schizophrenia. Vivid clinical accounts describe body distortions (hallucinations and delusions) in schizophrenic patients, but there is little direct evidence that schizophrenia is related to an impaired gender identity. Schizophrenics appear aware of expected sex roles, and appropriate sex role behavior has apparently been reinforced by parents. On the other hand, hospital staff were found to pressure patients to conform to traditionally "feminine" behavioral characteristics. LaTorre proposes a Diathesis-Gender-Stress model of schizophrenia, which involves inherited vulnerability and environmental factors that determine whether the disorder is manifested. He concludes that gender identity or role difficulties among schizophrenics are consistent with the literature and that such problems must be addressed in explanations of the disorder.

Part III focuses on social deviation and sexual dysfunction. Included are chapters on criminality, drug and alcohol use and abuse, and sexual dysfunction.

In Chapter 9, after describing the representation of females in crime statistics, Widom presents a heuristic biopsychosocial model, illustrating the factors that contribute to the development of criminal behavior and its definition as psychopathological. Using this framework, Widom examines the relationships between sex role stereotypes and criminality, describing how traditional assumptions about males and females influence theory, research, and the criminal justice system's response. Within the context of her model, she suggests that sex role stereotypes influence formal and informal definitions of what is criminal, that diagnostic criteria and clinical judgments differ by sex, and that boundaries of acceptable behavior influence the extent and form of criminal behavior in males and females. Widom discusses the relationship between psychiatric diagnosis and criminality and reviews the incidence of psychiatric disorder among prison populations. Although estimates of the extent of psychiatric disorder may vary, males are most frequently diagnosed as psychopathic or personality disorder. Drawing upon clinical observations and limited empirical evidence, Widom proposes that psychopathy and hysteria represent similar underlying disorders, which, as a result of different socialization experiences, opportunities, models, pressures, and situational factors, are manifested differentially in males and females in sex role-stereotypic ways. She concludes that sex role stereotypes exert a powerful effect on the definition, diagnosis, and disposition of criminal behavior.

Colten and Marsh begin Chapter 10 with a description of sex differences in the patterns of drug and alcohol use and abuse, and discuss the methodological difficulties in assessing prevalence statistics. They suggest that different role requirements for males and females affect the patterns of use and abuse. For example, women's drug use is more socially acceptable when the outcome of such behavior is consistent with appropriate social roles. Thus, women are encouraged to use prescription medications in ways that enforce stereotypic expectations. In sum, Colten and Marsh conclude that sex role norms and sex role socialization influence drug and alcohol use, produce different developmental patterns of substance abuse problems, and lead to sex differences in rates of substance abuse.

In Chapter 11, Stock begins her discussion of sexual dysfunction by asserting that sex roles affect all relationships and interactions between males and females. Sex roles may therefore determine, in part, the forms in which sexual dysfunction is manifested. After reviewing common forms of dysfunction in both males and females, she describes how traditional notions of sex roles limit the range of female sexual experiences throughout childhood and adolescence. Traditional sex roles establish rigid norms regarding appropriate social contexts for sexual conduct. Sexuality, she argues, is structured and patterned by learning and aimed at satisfying cultural expectations. Stock discusses female and male "sexual scripts," and how the internalization of expectations about sexuality affect sexual satisfaction, particularly in females. Relationship variables teach and reinforce sex role learning in sexuality, influencing the development and maintenance of sexual dysfunction. She singles out marriage as a situation in which sexual problems interact with relational problems. Finally, Stock stresses the importance of increasing awareness of oppressive external contingencies. She suggests that the effectiveness of therapy may be enhanced by recognizing the political, sociological, and economic forces that influence traditional sex role attitudes and behaviors.

Part IV includes three chapters focusing on age-related disorders. Here, the authors examine the extent to which sex roles and societal expectations at various points in the life cycle (childhood, puberty, and old age) influence the development and maintenance of disordered, maladaptive behaviors.

Eme has organized Chapter 12, "Sex-Related Differences in the Epidemiology of Child Psychopathology," according to DSM-III categories (intellectual, adjustment, behavioral, emotional, and developmental disorders). Although sex ratios vary across categories, males typically outnumber females. Only in the emotional disorders do females achieve parity with males. After examining a variety of biological and environmental theories in light of these differences, Eme suggests that males are more vulnerable to a host of pre-, peri-, and postnatal stresses and genetic anomalies that contribute to the development of these disorders. Thus, he argues that being male in childhood places one at risk for incurring mental disorder, and for this reason he urges that more attention be given to the special needs of male children.

In Chapter 13, Leon and Finn examine three eating disorders (anorexia nervosa, bulimia, and obesity) in the context of epidemiological and cross-cultural studies. They propose that cultural sex role stereotypes influence the development of eating disorders, and they describe some possible mechanisms involved in this process. *Direct* modes of cultural influence on eating patterns are illustrated by stereotypic expectations about table manners, appropriate styles of eating in public places, body size, sex differences in ideal body shape, and differences in the importance of physical traits. There are also *indirect* influences resulting from sex role-stereotypic attitudes and expectations about emotional expression and sexual behavior and conflict. Leon and Finn do not dismiss the possible contribution of biological variables related to endocrine functioning and hypothalamic regulatory factors. However, they suggest that recognition of the influence of sex role stereotypes on eating disorders has important implications for treatment paradigms and clinical interventions. They conclude with a plea for research that directly investigates the relationship between sex role stereotypes and eating disorders.

Holt and Datan present an overview of gender and aging in Chapter 14. They note that the elderly are probably more prone than other age groups to stressors of physical, emotional, and social origins. Using Antonovsky's (1979) salutogenic model of coping and stress, they suggest that the elderly lack resistance resources for coping with the stresses involved in aging, and that there are sex differences in access to these resources. Having spent a lifetime in traditional roles, older males have more access to the resistance resources that accompany work, whereas females may draw upon more social support resources. As people age, their resistance resources decline and feelings of powerlessness ensue. Holt and Datan suggest that efforts be directed toward increasing resistance resources as an antidote to some of the general problems associated with aging, and to the particular problems associated with senescence in women.

In the final section, two chapters focus on societal management and control. These chapters examine potential professional biases in patient management, clinical assessments, and medical treatment. The authors further discuss how these implicit biases may color our understanding of deviant and disturbed behavior.

In Chapter 15, Zeldow hopes to put the findings of Broverman *et al.* (1970) in proper perspective for the final time by raising doubts about the durability and robustness of the phenomenon. Zeldow finds that, although sex role stereotypes exist, a patient's sex is by itself rarely a factor in determining the degree of psychopathology, need for professional help, or prognosis. However, sex-related effects do occur and are embedded in complex contexts. Female patients risk harsher judgments than males when they engage in norm-deviant behavior. Attractiveness may interact with the sex of the patient to influence clinical judgments. Although Zeldow concludes that evidence for global sex discrimination is weak, he notes that complex and situation-specific effects are frequent and generally more prejudicial to women than to men. Studies of emergency room referral practices and drug-prescribing habits suggest that patient sex is a potent factor, alone and combined with variables such as race, work, and marital status. Zeldow stresses the need for further research, suggesting that such research become an integral part of routine program evaluations conducted by mental health organizations.

One of the first chapters in this volume was Dwyer's examination of medical practice and psychiatric theorizing during the 19th century. Chapter 16 by Fidell brings us full circle to *contemporary* medical practice. Fidell asserts that the general public probably underestimates the extent to which seeking and receiving medical care are influenced by social factors. In this chapter, she examines the impact of sex role stereotypes on health, medical behavior, and medical treatment, assessing the extent to which differences in treatment are a function of sex role stereotypes. She proposes two alternative hypotheses. The first states that sex differences in medical treatment are warranted because women are more disturbed. The other hypothesis proposes that doctors assess illness differently depending on one's sex, and that there is a tendency to ascribe psychogenic illness to women and organic illness to men. Fidell finds that sex differences in patient behavior exist and that these are consistent with sex role stereotypes. Numerous studies indicate that doctors tend to have stereotypic expectations regarding male and female patients. Fidell describes how these stereotypic notions are further reinforced in medical school training, textbooks, and advertising. Citing an earlier review documenting the presence of sex discrimination in medical treatment, she is careful to note that there is not enough compelling evidence to determine whether the sex differences in treatment are warranted. However, Fidell offers the reader an example from her personal experience to assist in reaching a tentative conclusion as to the validity of the two alternative hypotheses.

As in the 19th century, medical and psychiatric theory and practice are not sex blind. Some would argue that psychology and psychiatry should not and cannot be sex blind. This book draws attention to the ways in which definitions, diagnostic criteria, study designs, and conclusions are influenced by sex role-stereotypic assumptions. It is hoped that recognition of the biases inherent in our perceptions of these specific forms of psychopathology will lead to further research and ultimately to further understanding of the important role of sociocultural factors in the etiology, diagnosis, and treatment of psychopathology.

4. References

Antonovsky, A. *Health, stress, and coping.* San Francisco: Jossey-Bass, 1979.

Broverman, I. K., Broverman, D. M., Clarkson, F., Rosenkrantz, P. S., and Vogel, S. R. Sex role stereotypes and clinical judgments of mental health. *Journal of Consulting and Clinical Psychology*, 1970, *34*, 1–7.

Dohrenwend, B. P., and Dohrenwend, B. S. Sex differences and psychiatric disorders. *American Journal of Sociology*, 1976, *81*, 1447–1454.

Gove, W. Mental illness and psychiatric treatment among women. *Psychology of Women Quarterly*, 1980, *4*, 363–371.

Katz, P. A. The development of female identity. *Sex Roles*, 1979, *5*, 155–178.

Linehan, M. Suicide and attempted suicide. *Perceptual and Motor Skills*, 1973, *37*, 31–34.

Parsons, J. E. (Ed.). *The psychobiology of sex differences and sex roles.* New York: Hemisphere, 1980.

Radloff, L. S. Depression and the empty nest. *Sex Roles*, 1980, *6*, 775–781.

Scheinfeld, A. The mortality of men and women. *Scientific American*, 1958, *198*, 22–27.

Slaby, R. G., and Frey, K. S. Development of gender constancy and selective attention to same-sex models. *Child Development*, 1975, *47*, 849–856.

Spence, J. T., and Helmreich, R. L. *Masculinity and femininity: Their psychological dimensions, correlates, and antecedents.* Austin: University of Texas Press, 1978.

2

A Historical Perspective

Ellen Dwyer

1. Introduction

In September of 1888, a 36-year-old woman was brought to the New York State Lunatic Asylum at Utica by her father. According to the doctors who signed her commitment papers, she was greatly excited and used improper language. Her brother reported that 6 years earlier her husband had run off to Canada after embezzling some money. After he remarried, the patient became involved with a married man who used a ladder to her window to visit her almost every night. When her family discovered this liaison and attempted to cut it off, she responded with anger, threatening family members and pretending to attempt suicide through a drug overdose. At this point, the family brought her to the asylum, where she was diagnosed as a nymphomaniac. While there, she wrote numerous letters of complaint to friends and to asylum physicians. After a frantic letter to her father about the horrors of life in a madhouse, in which she promised never to see her lover again, her father came to take her home.

From the perspective of the 20th century, this case is a classic example of the ease with which 19th-century lunatic asylums could be used to control the behavior of deviant members of society, particularly females. Although families initiated the institutionalization process in most cases, the writings of medical doctors on madness and its treatment clearly justified such actions. As early as 1910, an experimental psychologist scathingly attacked the late Victorian literature on sex roles and psycho-

Ellen Dwyer • Department of Forensic Studies, Indiana University, Bloomington, Indiana 47405.

pathology. "There is no field aspiring to be scientific," she claimed, "where flagrant personal bias, logic martyred in the cause of supporting a prejudice, unfounded assertions, and even sentimental rot and drivel, have run riot to such an extent as here" (Woolley, 1910, p. 340). To many critics of the antifemale biases of contemporary psychology, her remarks have a continuing relevance. But, however justified their conclusions about their pre-Freudian counterparts, few contemporary psychologists look critically at the value systems that underlie their work or at the intellectual roots that have fed it. While 19th-century texts may easily be dismissed as quaint relics, those 19th-century doctors who studied, wrote about, and cared for their mentally ill contemporaries struggled with questions about the causes and treatment of insanity that have yet to be answered. But, in their very turmoil, their writings and debates offer material for thought and discussion even in the mid-20th century.

The best starting place for an overview of 19th-century psychiatric theory to 1865 is Norman Dain (1964). That for the rest of the century must be patched together from a wide range of books and articles. Several scholars have studied specific 19th-century syndromes (e.g., Carlson and Simpson, 1971; Rosen, 1975; Sicherman, 1980), and others have looked at the overall connections in 19th-century medicine between theories of sexuality and reproductive biology (e.g., Smith-Rosenberg, 1972, 1973, 1974a, 1974b, 1978, Smith-Rosenberg and Rosenberg, 1973).

Still to be written is a comprehensive overview of 19th-century American views of the influence of sex and sex roles on mental illness. The following pages are a modest beginning to that history, providing a précis of 19th-century doctors' views on sex roles and psychopathology, as expressed both in American writings and in those English treatises that were widely reprinted in the United States. In addition, the social impact of this theory is measured in terms of the medical practice and patient populations at New York's first two mental hospitals, the New York State Lunatic Asylum at Utica and the Willard Asylum for the Chronic Insane. I hope they will provoke thought about the resemblances between 19th- and 20th-century perspectives on sex roles and psychopathology, and about the reasons for the differences.

2. Nineteenth-Century Psychological Thought

2.1. The Differences Between the Sexes: An Early Nineteenth-Century View

Like their 20th-century counterparts, 19th-century doctors offered two kinds of explanation for the impact of sex differences on psychopathology: somatic (which emphasized the impact of sex-specific physiological problems on mental health) and environmental (which stressed the different life situations of men and women). The first 19th-century American medical text to deal at length with insanity was that of Benjamin Rush (1812). Although Rush paid little attention to the relative liability of men and women to insanity, his insistence that insanity was a physical disease, to be treated by medical means, laid the foundation for later analyses of the relationship between uterine malfunctions and female insanity. Rush's arguments for the more humane care of the insane helped attract attention to their plight and eventually contributed to the success of campaigns for the building of public and private lunatic asylums. The heads of these asylums, men such as Pliny Earle of Massachusetts, Thomas Kirkbride of Pennsylvania, and Amariah Brigham of New York, were to gain fame not only as institution-builders but also as major theoreticians on the question of insanity. Their writings appeared in books, annual reports, and journals such as the *American Journal of Insanity* (the official organ of the Association of Medical Superintendents of American Institutions for the Insane).

Brigham, the first editor of the journal, as well as the first superintendent of the New York State Lunatic Asylum at Utica, in 1833 published what was to become an often-cited book, *Remarks on the Influence of Mental Cultivation and Mental Excitement upon the Health* (1833/1865). Concerned about the seemingly rapid increase of insanity in 19th-century America, Brigham found a major source of this to be "the general and powerful excitement of the female mind," produced by the excessive development of intellectual powers in a sex whose "natural sensibilities" needed to be protected and nurtured (1833/1865, p. 5). Isaac Ray also shared Brigham's concern about the unhealthy lives of many American women, but he attributed the problem to a deficit of activity rather than to an excess (Ray, 1863, p. 215). Women (like men) who lacked regular, useful employment were driven to a "habitual vacuity" that sometimes ended in insanity. Ray's analysis of the debilitating consequences of the ornamental status of wealthy Victorian women anticipated George Beard's somewhat later emphasis on neurasthenia, the archetypal nervous disease of late 19th-century upper-class women (Rosenberg, 1962).

In contrast to Brigham, Ray also looked at the unhealthy situations of working-class women. Like many of his contemporaries, Ray was concerned about the apparent decline in the general health of American women, and he pointed out that married working-class women were particularly vulnerable to insanity because of the endless hardships of their daily lives (1863, p. 293). Emphasizing moderation as the key to mental health, Ray prescribed work to upper-class women and "cheap and innocent amusements" to working-class women (1863, p. 219).

In 1850 Edward Jarvis, a Massachusetts doctor and the initiator of the best 19th-century census of the insane, published an article that, after summarizing the somewhat contradictory 19th-century statistics on male and female insanity, asserted that most of these statistics were unreliable because they failed to take into consideration the relative numbers of men and women at risk to be institutionalized in the population as a whole. Recalculating the 1840 census on this basis, he found that, in the United States, there were 100 insane females to every 115 insane males. However, in Paris, Belgium, and among the paupers of England and Wales, the proportion of males to females was reversed. Thus, Jarvis concluded, the relative susceptibilities to insanity of men and women varied in different countries and at different periods of time (1850, pp. 147–149). Anatomical and physiological investigations of male and female brains, he felt, had not uncovered structural or functional differences sufficient to explain variations in susceptibility to insanity. Whatever their position on the functional importance of skull-size differentials, most 19th-century doctors agreed with Jarvis that there were major differences in temperament between the sexes. However, no sooner had he dismissed sex-specific anatomical and physiological arguments about the brain than Jarvis offered an archetypal summary of Victorian sexual stereotypes:

> The temperament of females is more ardent and more frequently nervous than that of males. Women are more under the influence of the feelings and emotions, while men are more under the government of the intellect. Men have stronger passions and powerful appetites and propensities.
>
> Women are more hopeful and confiding, especially in that which regards the affections, but they are less given to sensual indulgence. Men are more cautious in regard to matters of a social nature. But in regard to the affairs that affect the intellect, they are more bold and less cautious. Their intellectual functions are oftener exercised without reference to the power of the physical organ. Their inclinations and propensities . . . are more powerful and uncontrollable, and they are more likely to over-work and disturb the brain than women. (1850; pp. 150–151)

When these temperamental differences between the sexes were combined with differences in education and position, Jarvis added, they produced differential exposures to mental illness. For example, although physiological disturbances affected the brains of both sexes, women were more exposed to health risks because of the ease with which their reproductive systems became "deranged." Ill health also plagued more women than men, because of their relative lack of exercise in the fresh air. On the other hand, overambition and excess mental activity caused insanity more frequently in men, not because men were more susceptible to such forces but because of their greater exposure to them (1850, pp. 153–162). Overall, Jarvis concluded, contrary to popular belief, men were more exposed to, fell victim to more frequently, and were less often cured of insanity than women (1850, p. 163).

Although Jarvis argued his position carefully and with much supporting evidence, only parts of it were widely accepted. Asylum reports suggest that many doctors continued to believe in the greater female susceptibility to insanity, in part because they subscribed to those stereotypes about the female temperament that Jarvis summarized so well (e.g., Willard Asylum, 1872, p. 13, 1879, p. 9; Letchworth and Carpenter, 1882, p. 65).

2.2. Moral Causes of Insanity

2.2.1. Theory. Many of the factors described by Brigham and Jarvis as responsible for the alarming increase in insanity in 19th-century America fell into the category of what 19th-century doctors referred to as "moral causes." Moral causes were those that produced their effects by acting directly on the mind itself, in contrast to physical causes, which impaired mental activity as a secondary effect of physical impairment, disease, or the injury of bodily organs (Jarvis, 1850, p. 294; New York State Lunatic Asylum, 1864, p. 34). According to Brigham, the most important causes of insanity were the general excitement of civilized life and erroneous educational practices (1837, pp. 119–120). Bucknell and Tuke's list of major moral causes duplicated Jarvis's (Bucknell and Tuke, 1858, p. 256). All three claimed that women were most likely to be affected by domestic problems, loss of friends and disappointment in love, bodily disorders, and religious anxiety (in that order), whereas men were most susceptible to the debilitating effects of alcoholism, bodily disorders, and the reverse of fortunes.

As the century progressed, asylum superintendents increasingly stressed what they called the "predisposing" causes of insanity and deemphasized the "exciting" causes, those immediate stimuli that friends and neighbors frequently confused with the roots of insanity. As Isaac Ray commented in 1880, the exciting causes were but "the match which explodes the explosive material already existing" (1880, p. 169). This shift also was accompanied by greater stress on the physical origins of mental illness. Yet even the most avid asylum proponents of somatic explanations continued to show, in their discussions of specific cases, an understanding of the environmental stresses that so plagued women. For example, Dr. John Gray, the editor of the *American Journal of Insanity* for many years, and a man so devoted to a disease interpretation of insanity that his opponents accused him of refusing to print contrary interpretations, published in 1869 an article on nervous prostration in which the lonely life of a newly married farm woman was described in moving detail.

> Transferred to an isolated farmhouse, from a home in which she had enjoyed a requisite measure of social and intellectual recreation, she is subjected to a daily routine of very monotonous household labor. Her new home, if it deserves the name, is, by a strict utilitarianism, deprived of everything which can suggest a pleasant thought: not a flower blooms in the garden; books she has, perhaps, but no time to read them. Remote from neighbors, as in sparsely settled districts, for weeks together, she sees only her husband, and the generally uneducated man who shares his toil.
>
> The urgency of farm work necessitates hurried, unsocial meals, and, as night closes in, wearied by his exertions, the farmer is often accustomed to seek his bed at an early hour, leaving his wife to pass the long and lonely evening with her needle. Whilst the disposal of his crops, and the constant changes in the character of farm labor afford her husband sufficient variety and recreation, her daily life, and especially if she have also the unaided care of one or two ailing children, is exhausting and depressing to a degree of which but few are likely to form any correct conception. From this class come many applications for the admission of female patients. (Van Deusen, 1869, p. 447)

This article suggests that the 19th-century asylum sometimes served as a refuge for overworked, exhausted women, just as do clinics and psychiatric institutes today (Procek, 1980). Records from the New York State Lunatic Asylum confirm this view; not atypical was the case of a suicidal 20-year-old mother of two, who, after persuading her husband to take her to the lunatic asylum, exclaimed upon entering its doors, "Now I am home" (New York State Lunatic Asylum, 1870, p. 62). (That she died of pneumonia 3 weeks after entry suggests the therapeutic limitations of 19th-century asylums.)

2.2.2. Treatment. Since most of the moral causes of insanity were environmental, early 19th-century doctors and social reformers felt that the insane could best be treated by removal to asylums, where "quiet, silence, regular routine, take the place of restlessness, noise, and fitful activity" (Ray, 1863, p. 333). Moral treatment was also to include not merely the physical removal to an asylum but kind, individualized supervision by doctors and attendants, regular work for the willing and able-bodied, educational programs, and carefully chosen amusements (Savino and Mills, 1967; Dain, 1964, pp. 12–14; Grob, 1973, pp. 165–169; Bell, 1980, pp. 13–14). Thus, it resembled what today is called "milieu therapy" (Carlson and Dain, 1960, p. 519).

In theory at least, moral treatment was totally individualized, and asylum doctors treated each patient as a unique case, without regard to class, race, or ethnicity. In practice, the doctors' therapeutic prescriptions inevitably reflected the cultural values (including sexual stereotypes) of the larger society. For example, work programs differed for men and women; female patients devoted most of their time to laundry and sewing, while the men farmed and performed various mechanical tasks. At one asylum, the women produced everything from aprons and trimmed hats to tablecloths and shrouds (Willard Asylum, 1884, p. 31). When this same institution was criticized for its tendency to confine its female patients indoors, its superintendent responded that outdoor labor for women was generally impractical, despite the benefits to restless patients of light gardening (Willard Asylum, 1886, p. 23). Although the head of the New York State Lunatic Asylum declared in 1860 that many patients were unable to labor regularly (particularly the physically debilitated melancholics), 5 years later he reported that the average able-bodied male patient worked 6 hours a day, and the average female longer, because her work was less exhausting and could be performed in the house whatever the weather (New York State Lunatic Asylum, 1865, pp. 40–41). Although the New York doctors, like their compatriots elsewhere, insisted that work was a voluntary therapeutic option, one ex-patient claimed that able-bodied women who refused to work were punished (Davis, 1870, pp. 33–34, 49–50). The differences between the male and female work situations suggest one way in which that social ideology intended to protect women could be applied negatively, in this case keeping female patients confined to the asylum to work on menial domestic tasks for long hours.

According to Ray, the aim of moral treatment was to produce "quiet, self-control, orderly and respectful behavior, confidence in others, and submission to a higher will" (1863, p. 330). The similarity between such behavior and that prescribed for all 19th-century women may help to explain the higher female cure rates mentioned by Jarvis. Presumably, it was easier for even an institutionalized female to reassume stereotypic female behavior than it was for a male in the same situation to replace his learned sex roles with behavior associated with dependent females.

Several moral therapists tried to persuade state legislators to build separate lunatic asylums for men and women, arguing that these would facilitate classification, save money, and protect female patients from the sexual depredations of male patients and staff (Brigham, 1837, p. 115; New York State Lunatic Asylum, 1853, p. 12; Galt, 1855). Despite such arguments, few sex-segregated institutions were built, perhaps because they were perceived as unnecessary and therefore avoidable tax burdens. For despite their professed belief in the basic differences between the sexes, 19th-century doctors never attempted to develop psychiatric syndromes sufficiently sex-specific so as to justify radically distinct systems of psychiatric treatment.

2.3. Somatic Causes of Insanity

2.3.1. Theory. Probably the largest body of 19th-century writing on female psychopathology focused on the relationship between female mental and reproductive disorders (Bucknell and Tuke, 1858, p. 240; MacDonald, 1847; Churchill, 1851; Sims, 1883; Farnham, 1887; Clark, 1888). According to the medical theory of the day, the female reproductive cycle, from puberty to menopause, was easily "deranged" and its natural fluctuations dominated the emotional and physical lives of even healthy women (e.g., Bullough and Vogt, 1973b; Smith-Rosenberg and Rosenberg, 1973; Smith-Rosenberg, 1972, 1973, 1974a, 1978; Tyor, 1977; Skultans, 1979, pp. 77–97). The following passage summarizes many of these ideas:

> Under the influence of the female sexual organs, the strong characteristically become weak; fickleness supervenes upon a judgment previously calm and clear; indecision upon resolution; pusillanimity upon fearlessness and courage; deceitfulness upon a frank, open manner. We believe that the habits of truth-telling and fidelity in the social and domestic relations are more frequently broken up by irritable ovaries than by a native tendency to depravity in the female sex. Here, for example, is a young lady with an irritable ovary, who previously was fond of kittens, but who now falls into a swoon at the sight of one; then, here is another lady who was formerly very fond of society, but who now, from a familiar cause, has a dread of it, and prefers solititude; then again, another, who, for the same proximate reason, dislikes, repels, and finally leaves, the man whom she has solemnly sworn to love. . . . (Gorton, 1890, pp. 228–229)

By equating dislike of a kitten with that of a spouse, such writings used 19th-century stereotypes about the female temperament to trivialize major domestic conflict. Their authors resemble those English physicians who, according to Showalter, consistently ignored the content of female complaints, so that "expressions of unhappiness, low self-esteem, helplessness, anxiety, and fear were not connected to the realities of women's lives, while expressions of sexual desire, anger, and aggression were taken as morbid deviations from the normal female personality" (1980, p. 169). Whatever the sensitivity of individual doctors, undeniably much of the literature on uterine-derived insanity moved quickly past the patients' immediate situations to their supposed underlying uterine disorders (considered a more appropriate focus for medical/psychiatric attention).

Despite the primitive state of gynecological theory, doctors no doubt found it easier to look at physiological disorders than to treat complex problems, many of which had developed out of family dynamics. For example, not uncommon were cases in which newly married women expressed intense dislike for husbands whom they had married with great affection. While admitting that some had been shocked to learn at marriage of spouses' earlier sexual experiences and that others found marital coitus so painful that they developed vaginismus, doctors attributed the underlying cause of their "insane" anger to "cerebral irritations," exacerbated by the excitement of marriage (Storer, 1871, pp. 121–122).

Storer presented a highly influential and controversial summary of how these gynecological observations related to psychiatric theory. According to Storer (1871), while most male insanity resulted from lesions in the brain, in women disturbances of the brain were primarily sympathetic responses to irritations in the reproductive system that appeared first at puberty and persisted until after menopause (pp. 30, 155). The mere onset of puberty in women, Storer argued, arouses emotions in young girls that can only be compared to "the smoldering fires of a volcano, ready to burst forth at any exciting moment" (1871, pp. 78–79). Other physicians agreed with Storer that puberty and menstruation were common predisposing causes of insanity, but they looked to specific disorders and events to explain why only certain women succumbed to the stresses they induced. As Ray noted, the nervous impact of puberty alone was not insufficient to produce the partial mania so often exhibited by female adolescents, and he found the connection between the two events to be in physiological and functional disorders of the reproductive system, such as dysmenorrhea and amenorrhea (Ray, 1853, p. 200; Tuke, 1853, p. 60; "Female Diseases and Insanity," 1887, pp. 406–407; Clark, 1888, p. 293). In his study of adolescent female pyromaniacs, Ray observed that most were under the influence of the "constitutional disturbances" of puberty, aggravated by amenorrhea or the retarded evolution of the sexual organs (1853, pp. 197–200). Clark also felt that abnormal or retarded sexual development of the female reproductive organs triggered female insanity, for he had found that a number of insane women had such problems as infantile or excess sexual organs, small pelvises, and asymmetrical pelvic and mammary development (Clark, 1888, pp. 292–293). Clearly Clark identified female mental health with conformity to a narrow physical ideal, for he also commented on the frequency with which insane women had shoulders broader than the pelvis and "a masculine figure and carriage" (p. 293).

Considered even more threatening to female health than puberty and menstruation were the psychic and physical stresses of pregnancy. Lacking endocrinological theory, 19th-century doctors attributed the mood swings and depression of pregnancy to "sympathetic nervous irritation" in the brain, caused by an "excited uterus" (Storer, 1871, p. 148; MacDonald, 1847, pp. 114–115; Churchill, 1851, pp. 262–263). Typical was a lengthy article on puerperal insanity that appeared in the

American Journal of Insanity (MacDonald, 1847). During early pregnancy, its author argued, all women suffered from "cerebral disturbance," but only those with a hereditary predisposition to insanity or with excitable personalities actually went insane. During childbirth, temporary insanity was common and often manifested itself in the form of obscene and lewd language (uttered, he noted with horror, by women who were ordinarily very modest and might be expected to be ignorant of such words) (p. 119). Most dangerous of all was the period immediately after childbirth, when, exhausted by anxiety, overwork, poor nutrition, and a lack of exercise in the fresh air, many women succumbed to depression. When exacerbated by lactation, this postpartum debility sometimes led to melancholy and then to suicide or homicide (pp. 139–141).

Menopause, or the climacteric, also was considered responsible for some female insanity, although 19th-century doctors were more interested in the beginning than in the end of the reproductive cycle. (Farnham, 1887, p. 536). Predictably, Storer did not ignore menopause, repeating with approval the folk saying that old women become "either angels or devils" (1871, p. 111); but by the end of the 19th century, some doctors had begun to argue that the climacteric produced as many problems for males as for females (Clouston, 1898, pp. 617–618).

2.3.2. Treatment.   Most doctors agreed that the insanity produced by uterine disorders was easily cured (an optimistic conclusion in light of their primitive knowledge of female physiology). As early as 1847, the English doctor MacDonald explained the medical techniques most commonly used for curing those uterine disorders that caused puerperal insanity (1847, pp. 152–163). More harmful than helpful, he claimed, were such strategies as general bloodletting (which only exacerbated the existing exhaustion), excessively harsh emetics, and blisters. In their place, he suggested localized bleeding (in cases of "cerebral congestion"), a mild purging of the stomach and bowels (but only if they were irritated), and the use of devices such as warm baths, cold applications to the head, and mild opiates to soothe and to induce sleep. In chronic cases, small doses of tonics and outdoor exercise such as horseback riding helped restore health. In addition, many insane mothers benefitted from the quiet, orderly routines and nourishing meals characteristic of asylum life. MacDonald's stress on the need for good diet and plenty of rest was a common prescription; John Gray went further to recommend the establishment of organizations that would assist new mothers with domestic help, child care, and supplementary foods.

In Gray's writings can be found an early expression of the fear that the Anglo-Saxon race was headed for extinction because of its women's unwillingness to reproduce, for he heartily condemned the popular but "horrid belief that home life can be happier and more comfortable without children" (New York State Lunatic Asylum, 1886, p. 68). Whatever their efficacy, there were more treatments for puerperal mania than for the disorders associated with menstruation (perhaps because of the dramatic urgency of postpartum needs). Some doctors tried to cure dysmenorrhea with bloodletting; others used the same technique for amenorrhea. They also prescribed better diet and rest. If the quiet and routine of the asylum did not induce sleep, the doctors ordered soporifics, such as opium (Farnham, 1887, pp. 537–542).

After the Civil War, certain gynecologists also began to experiment with surgical and electrical treatments for amenorrhea, dysmenorrhea, and related disorders. The way in which surgical techniques like clitoridectomies and the removal of normal ovaries, a procedure known as Battey's operation (Longo, 1979), could be used to "cure" manifestations of inappropriate sexuality, as well as uterine disorders, is illustrated by Storer's example of how he treated "reflex insanity" in one of his patients (1871, p. 14). The patient, a young unmarried woman, came to him complaining of painful dysmenorrhea and of what she described as attacks of overwhelming sexual desire, which accompanied her menstrual periods. At such times, she could barely keep herself from soliciting the attention of young men, and she turned for relief to masturbation. Her "disgusting propensities," Storer declared, were merely the symptoms of physical problems, and he treated them by cutting the cervix and dilating the uterine canal. Although the erotic feelings returned once more (after the young woman had "indulged in" some pepper tea), Storer then banished them permanently, along with the dysmenorrheal pain, by applying a cauterizing chemical to the cervix. He concluded with the comment that, even if such treatment had not been justified on medical grounds, it would have been permissible "as a defence to female chastity" (a not atypical 19th-century medical fusion of science and religion).

Despite the large body of writings by the late 19th century on the relationship between gynecological disorders and female insanity, physicians complained that large lunatic asylums frequently failed to offer gynecological treatment to their patients ("Gynecological Examinations in Asylum," 1883, pp. 169, 337). One way to improve this situation, some argued, was to add female physicians to asylum staffs, for females need not worry that their gynecological examinations would sexually excite patients or offend family members, friends, and newspapers. In addition, the female physicians themselves argued, they could more easily understand the mental anguish of other women (Cleaves, 1879). Yet, in practice, only a few female physicians were added to asylum staffs, and those found career advancement difficult (McGovern, 1980).

Not surprisingly, male doctors' attitudes towards female physicians reflected the conservative values of late-Victorian America. When the New York State legislature proposed in 1879 to add female physicians to all state asylum staffs, John Chapin of the Willard Asylum wrote a 21-page letter of opposition to it (Willard Asylum, 1879). Two of his friends, also asylum superintendents who had had female physicians on their staffs, complained about these women's unwillingness to take orders, love affairs with male doctors, and stubborn insistence on unrelenting hard work. Their tone suggests that such doctors, "headstrong, arbitrary" females, were not true women, and one superintendent argued that, while he could conceive that a female assistant with "good common sense, good executive capacity, etc., etc." was a theoretical possibility, such women "don't study medicine and would be spoiled if they did" (Superintendent XXX, 1879).

2.3.3. **Debate over Gynecological Theories and Techniques.** Despite the large number of articles on the female reproductive system and its fragility, a substantial minority of the medical profession did not agree that female physiological problems directly caused insanity or that gynecological surgery was useful to cure mental illness. In the 1880s and 1890s, narrowly gynecological explanations were attacked bitterly by neurologists, who preferred to attribute mental illness to disturbances of the nervous system (Quen, 1977). Even earlier, however, a number of asylum superintendents had suggested that doctors like Storer were overstating their argument (Storer, 1871, pp. 16–17). Challenged by what she considered to be an overemphasis on uterine disease in the work of alienists, an assistant physician at the Willard Asylum compared the sexual organs of 30 female patients at Willard with those of 30 sane women of approximately the same age and social class (Farnham, 1887, pp. 543–544). She found that only 4 of the sane and 6 of the insane women had what she would consider healthy pelvic organs, and she concluded that, if uterine disease were this prevalent in the general population, it was surprising that so few women showed signs of major nervous disorders. Like several other female doctors, she felt that, in many instances, uterine disease furnished " 'the straw that broke the camel's back,' " rather than an inexorable impulse toward insanity (1887, p. 544). Farnham also commented rather pointedly that, while puberty was indubitably a difficult period for human beings, there was no evidence to prove that adolescent females were more prone to insanity than adolescent males (p. 534).

Equally controversial were such surgical procedures as Battey's operation, particularly by the end of the 19th century. In an article entitled "The Laparotomy Epidemic" (1886, p. 326), neurologists attacked the tendency of many doctors to remove normal ovaries. They also noted the frequency with which ovariotomies and similar treatments for female uterine disorders failed to restore sanity ("Insanity in Hysterical Women," 1880; "Ovariotomy in Insanity," 1887; "Female Diseases and Insanity," 1887; Leszynsky, 1887, pp. 1–7; "The Climacteric in Its Relation to Insanity," 1890). They even pointed to instances in which insanity followed (and, by implication, was caused by) gynecological operations ("Insanity after Gynecological Operations," 1895). As the debate between medical specialists became increasingly heated, some neurologists went so far as to suggest that gynecology for the most part could be replaced with neurology ("The Laparotomy Epidemic," 1886), a proposal that left troubled women buffeted between two equally limited sources of help: gynecological specialists, who felt that most of women's psychological problems were due to uterine disease, and neurologists, who argued that their physical problems were psychological in origin.

Allied to these criticisms was an increasing recognition of the complexity of sexuality. For example, *The Alienist and Neurologist* used the case of a nymphomanic woman without ovaries and uterus who had only a 2-inch vagina to point out the often ignored role of the cortical factor in orgasm ("Oophorectomy and Sexual Appetite," 1895). It also commented on the frequent failure of clitoridectomies to stop constant masturbation and suggested that in such cases the source of sexual excitement must be psychic rather than physical ("Clitoridectomy in Insanity," 1895).

The neurologists were not the only 19th-century doctors to challenge gynecological conventions; a number of gynecologists themselves disagreed with what they regarded as overly simplistic formulations of the psychic implications of the female reproductive system. A small number directly attacked the common assumption that menstruation and reproduction were debilitating experiences for women. For example, the physician Sarah Hackett Stevenson used Mary Putnam Jacobi's menstruation research to argue that menstrual periods are times of strength, not of depression, because they increase the quality and tension of the blood (Stevenson, 1880, p. 38). Stevenson went on to comment on the misogyny of textbooks on nervous disease that spoke of conditions of general nervousness as if they afflicted only women, despite contradictory evidence. When migraines and epilepsy attack men, Stevenson claimed, they are called by their proper names and treated as diseases, whereas the same symptoms in women are explained immediately as reflex responses to the uterus and ovaries (p. 52). Such bias is so blatant in medical writings, she claimed, that "no impartial judge can fail to recognize the truth that the element of sex has been assigned too much importance in the diseases of women, and not enough in the diseases of men" (p. 52).

Other female doctors (including Jacobi) were less willing than Ste-

venson to dismiss the notion of a connection between pelvic and cerebral problems, but Blackwell, for example, claimed that scientists lacked
sufficient knowledge about male and female physiology to justify their
generalizations about sex-based differentials (1875, p. 232). In her essays
on hysteria, Jacobi recounted with approval cases in which surgery was
used to remove healthy pelvic organs in order to alleviate hysteria (1888,
pp. 13, 37, 38), but she also acknowledged the influence of environmental factors on mental illness. Thus, she followed her discussion of female
physiology with a description of how the repressive social condition of
19th-century women increased their susceptibility to hysteria (1888, p.
66). Her prescription for treatment of hysterical women would have
been recognized immediately by early 19-century doctors as moral therapy: change of scene, occupation, and interest (pp. 66–67).

Many male doctors also refused to accept wholeheartedly such theories as Storer's reflex action. For example, after Skene had studied
some 400 female patients at a county lunatic asylum, he concluded that
in many cases puerperal insanity was produced not by the reproductive
experience but by poor diet and overwork (1880, p. 4). He also argued
that the insanity occurring at menopause is more often the result of
general physical problems connected with aging than of a reflex response to changes in the reproductive system. Unlike Storer, he distinguished between sexual promiscuity and pelvic disease and did not
attribute the first to the second (Skene, 1880, p. 7). While they acknowledged the need to look after the gynecological problems of insane wom-
en, the struggle of doctors like Blackwell, Jacobi, and Skene to untangle
the relationship between mind and body in insanity is in many ways as
typical of 19th-century psychiatry as is the unrelenting somaticism of
men like Storer.

3. Specific Syndromes

In general, 19th-century doctors (like those of the 20th) had difficulty making clear the differences between an exaggerated nervous state
and insanity. For example, while they could describe in great detail the
mood shifts of the newly pregnant woman, her irritability, and her
propensity to morbid fantasies, they were unable to pinpoint the dividing line between such common symptoms and pregnancy-induced insanity (MacDonald, 1847, pp. 114–119; Churchill, 1851, pp. 256–266).
Equally nonspecific were descriptions of the insanity of puberty, although the doctors described adolescence itself vividly: a time when
once-lively young girls became inactive and withdrawn, ignoring the
pursuits that had formerly fascinated them and showing indifference to

the feelings of family and friends (Churchill, 1851, p. 262). Inevitably, by their inability to distinguish conventional adolescent turmoil from insanity, postpartum fatigue from major depression, the doctors made easier the social definition of a wide range of behavior as insane.

With the exception of conditions such as senility, epilepsy, syphilis, and congenital imbecility, 19th-century medical theorists did not find consistent relationships between specific causes of insanity and forms of mental illness. Rather than rely on *ex post facto* analyses of their patients' outbreaks of insanity, they preferred to talk of "predisposing causes," such as heredity and physical disease, which could be used to explain everything from severe depression to chronic dementia.

3.1. Hysteria

Since the Greeks, hysteria has been considered an archetypal female affliction. The attitude of early 19th-century doctors toward it was ambivalent at best. Some considered it a kind of "feigned insanity," affected in order to attract attention (Bucknell and Tuke, 1858, p. 302), although they conceded that it often degenerated into mania (Churchill, 1851, p. 264). It was considered to afflict most often women under 30 whose health was delicate and habits indolent (Brigham, 1840, pp. 239–240). Easily excited, they overresponded to the slightest emotion, first weeping and sobbing and then laughing. They also showed a variety of physical symptoms, such as choking, coughing, and heart palpitations (Carlson and Simpson, 1971, p. 297). Many doctors felt that hysteria was the result of the basic instability of the female disposition, aggravated by the unhealthy inactivity of many middle-class women (Brigham, 1840, p. 241). In perhaps the most complete medical treatise on hysteria, Laycock tied hysteria to both the female reproductive system and the general female nervous system (Laycock, 1840). Both systems were so constituted that almost every female fell victim to the "disease" of hysteria at some point in her life (p. 59), and the menstrual flow itself, he argued, could be regarded as a type of "hysterical" hemorrhage. In a classic "double-bind" description of the female personality, Laycock argued that the fragile female nervous system accounted both for women's mental weakness and for their physical and psychic beauties. Later in the century, doctors further explored the connection of hysteria to the female reproductive system and concluded that uterine "vascular turgescence" produced hysteria in those women who had overindulged in "injudicious culture or perversion, or the improper excitement of the imagination" (Kellogg, cited in Storer, 1871, pp. 86–87; Sims, 1883). Others attributed hysteria to malfunctions in the central nervous system or cerebral cortex (Smith-Rosenberg, 1972, p. 666) and prescribed both moral and medical treatments. The frequent harshness of these (which ranged from icy baths to electric shock treatment and clitoridectomies) suggested doctors' impatience with this peculiarly female form of unhappiness (Smith-Rosenberg 1972, pp. 674–676). Even Brigham, who advised a careful investigation of hysterics' physical complaints, argued that often only the threat of a painful treatment (and he suggested burning the feet with a poker) deterred adolescent girls from recurrent binges of hysterical emotion (1840, p. 248).

3.2. Mania

Nineteenth-century doctors applied the label "mania" to a wide variety of conditions of nervous excitement. Typically, the manic insane were restless and changeable; many also had delusions of self-importance and wealth (Bucknell and Tuke, 1858, pp. 282–308; Ray, 1853, pp. 129–141; Mann, 1883, pp. 70–71; New York State Lunatic Asylum, 1885, p. 51). Although both males and females fell victim to mania, females generally were considered more liable to erotomania, moral mania, and hysteria. One doctor also noted that female manics outnumbered male in many public asylums but added that they had been driven there by a combination of physical and mental stresses (ranging from poor diet and excessive childbearing to seduction and neglect by husbands). Among the wealthy, he pointed out, men and women seemed equally susceptible to mania (Spitzka, 1883, pp. 138–139).

   3.2.1. Erotomania, Nymphomania, and Homosexuality. Perhaps the most threatening forms of mania for Victorian women were erotomania, nymphomania, and homosexuality. Discussions of hysteria frequently warned of the ease with which emotional excitement, particularly in young unmarried women, degenerated into such sexual perversions as erotomania (a cerebral condition in which the patient is ruled by sexual delusions [Mann, 1883, p. 22]), nymphomania (a uterine-derived disease often associated with masturbation), and homosexuality, frequently described as a likely outcome of masturbation (Churchill, 1851, p. 264; Kellogg, cited in Storer, 1871, pp. 86–87; Bullough and Vogt, 1973a). In their assertion that women were particularly susceptible to both erotomania and nymphomania (Mann, 1883, p. 23; Bullough and Vogt, 1973b), Victorian doctors expressed their basic ambiguity toward women, seeing them simultaneously as sensitive, spiritual creatures and as the prisoners of their uncontrolled and animal-like reproductive cycle (Rosenberg and Smith-Rosenberg, 1973, pp. 24–25).

   Given the generally repressive (although far from monolithic) nature of Victorian sexual ideology (e.g., Haller and Haller, 1974; Degler, 1974), the 20th-century observer may well be surprised by the extent to which early 19th-century doctors ignored (relatively speaking) the role of sexuality in producing mental illness (Dain, 1964, p. 91). Masturbation was a major exception. Because it physically exhausted those who practiced it, masturbation was considered to increase their susceptibility to both physical and mental illness (e.g., Dain, 1964, p. 91; Englehardt, 1978; Gilbert, 1975). Although writers such as Storer sometimes excused female masturbation as an uncontrollable product of diseased reproductive systems (Storer, 1871, pp. 123–124; Workman, 1869, pp. 33–34), their examples reveal the limited extent to which they exercised such toleration, for they excused only good women supposedly driven to despair, and even to death, by their inability to control their "perverted" sexual desires. As Englehardt notes, medical theory about masturbation conveniently reinforced the dictates of morality (1974, p. 20); whether male or female, many 19th-century children were raised in fear of the insanity that threatened all masturbators (Bullough and Vogt, 1973a).

Of course, no matter what their views on female sexuality, the heads of 19th-century lunatic asylums could not ignore its reality. As those arguing for the addition of female physicians to asylum staffs pointed out, male physicians frequently aroused sexual delusions in female patients, especially when the latter required gynecological examinations (Paoli and Kiernan, 1887). In general, asylum superintendents expressed a commonsense attitude toward its manifestations in patients; they saw too many syphilitic prostitutes and masturbating female patients to share the exaggeratedly asexual view of the "true women" presented in the popular literature of the day. One superintendent described in a matter-of-fact way the frequent connection among religious melancholy, sexual excess, and sexual abnormalities in both sexes, and he warned his fellow superintendents to be particularly careful of decorum in treating highly religious female patients, for many of these had almost uncontrollable erotic tendencies (Workman, 1869:34). (He hastened to add that such erotomania was not freely chosen but was the result of somatic abnormalities.)

Same-sex love also was considered a form of insanity; one author called it "a reasoning monomania" because its subjects' intellects and reasoning faculties were unimpaired and they suffered no delusions. Despite such outward normality, he warned, they were insane and sooner or later would succumb either to maniacal excitement or to hopeless dementia (Mann, 1883, pp. 20–21). Discussions of lesbianism (invariably referred to as a "morbid perversion") were relatively rare in 19th-century medical literature, although one author referred briefly to an epidemic of same-sex love at a girls' boarding school (Mann, 1883, p. 26).

Another exception to the general silence was an asylum superintendent's lengthy description of a case of "sexual perversion" in a 56-year-old widow (Wise, 1883). Dressed in male attire and with apparently masculine features, this patient first identified herself as a married Methodist minister named Joseph Lobdell. In a state of "erotic excitement," on her way to the wards she accosted and nearly overpowered a female attendant. Several weeks later she became quiet and depressed, and willing to talk about her past history. She declared that from the time she was a young girl she had preferred masculine sports and work but felt repelled by male company. At 20 she married a man she did not like, to please her parents and friends. When he deserted shortly after the birth of their child, she resumed masculine dress and became known as the "Female Hunter of Low Eddy." After several years as a trapper in northern Minnesota, she published a well-known book about her experiences. Subsequently, she suffered financial reverses and ended up in an almshouse, where she became attached to a young girl whose husband had left her destitute. The attachment being mutual, they left the almshouse to live in the woods as husband and wife for the next 13 years, until "Joe" suffered the attack of maniacal excitement that led to her commitment.

While Lobdell's case history offers a rare view of the life of an overt lesbian in 19th-century America, its significance as an indicator of attitudes toward female deviance is difficult to assess. The almost voyeuristic detail with which Wise describes "Lobdell's" life suggests that he encountered at the asylum relatively few cases of public lesbianism. Because the case history fails to make clear who initiated the commitment procedures, we cannot assume that "Lobdell" was sent to the asylum for her homosexuality. In fact, that she lived happily and for so long without interference, supporting herself and her "wife" with such traditional masculine activities as hunting and fishing, supports Smith-Rosenberg's contention (1975) that, in many ways, 19th-century America was surprisingly tolerant of same-sex love.

3.2.2. Moral Mania. Perhaps the most controversial 19th-century syndrome was moral mania (also known as moral insanity). It was characterized by a paralysis of the moral faculties, in which its victims recognized the difference between right and wrong but could not control their impulses to evil. Women were considered to be particularly vulnerable to moral mania during menstruation and after childbirth, at which times they were particularly prone to acts of homicide and infanticide. Even those doctors who opposed the insanity defense for men were willing to excuse those female murderers whose lives had been upright and conventional before the homicide (e.g., Ray, 1853, pp. 166–186, 211–214; "Law Cases Bearing on the Subject of Insanity," 1854; Ray, 1866; "The Trial of Mary Harris," 1866; "Case of Mrs. Elizabeth Hegge," 1868; Johnson, 1869, pp. 54–55; Mann, 1883, pp. 23–24, 331–339; "Moral Insanity," 1887; "Insanity and Adultery," 1888). Such differential treatment paralleled stereotypes of popular fiction. While young women who, like Ophelia, suffered insanity in response to traumatic incidents were treated sympathetically, "the cunning [male] lunatic, whose lucid intervals were mistaken for sanity but whose fiendish plots and eventual deliriums gave proof of a wicked soul" was not (Davis, 1957, p. 85).

In cases of moral insanity, stereotypes about the weakness of the female will and women's vulnerability to emotional stress worked for rather than against women. The price of such toleration was high, however, for the domestic situations that produced suicides and homicides were tied closely to those same clichés. Storer's comparison of mothers who killed their children with dogs who destroyed their pups also suggests that the Victorians' perspective on female moral insanity, like their view of the reproductive cycle that so often triggered it, reflected once again their ambivalence toward "the female animal" (Smith-Rosenberg and Rosenberg, 1974).

Because moral insanity was easily confused with moral imbecility, 19th-century doctors warned against equating the two, for moral imbecility referred to the distinct syndrome today called psychopathy (Mann, 1883, p. 85; "Moral Insanity," 1887, p. 126). Then, as now, it was considered to be primarily, although not exclusively, a male problem. Tyor (1977) suggests that those 19th-century women, such as prostitutes, who violated sexual mores heedlessly were likely to find themselves labeled "moral imbeciles" and incarcerated in institutions for the mentally retarded. In a rare discussion of female psychopathy, the matron of a New York State prison discussed a young black female pyromaniac, whose actions were not considered to be merely a result of the storms of puberty (Farnham, 1846). Instead, the girl was characterized as a "snake in human form," in passages that suggest the impact of both racial and sexual stereotypes on psychiatric thought. At one point the matron left the girl gagged and straitjacketed for 36 hours without food, but she never succeeded in subduing her for long. Although the girl was described as "quick of perception," with a great love of painting and drawing, the matron felt that, "like the rest of her race," the girl was human in form only.

3.3. Melancholy

Unlike hysteria, melancholy (or depression) afflicted both sexes, but women were felt to be more susceptible, particularly at puberty, childbirth, and menopause, points of major social as well as physical change for most 19th-century women (Bucknell and Tuke, 1858, pp. 309–313;

Johnson, 1869, p. 72; Gray, 1890, pp. 1–2). According to John Gray, melancholy developed under conditions similar to mania, but in mania the increased activity of the brain was expansive and aggressive, while in melancholy it was introspective and limited in scope (New York State Lunatic Asylum, 1866, pp. 25–26). Since much female melancholy began as a result of ill health from overwork and anxiety, once the women received proper rest and nourishment, Gray felt their melancholy should lift. It had to be treated early, and its presence was often hard to detect, particularly in women whose self-abasement and withdrawal were often mistaken for thoughtfulness (New York State Lunatic Asylum, 1866, p. 36). Gray's own case studies suggested that, at least in institutionalized women, the disease was often not cured. For example, a women who had fallen ill while taking care of an invalid mother came to the asylum for help but committed suicide just when recovery seemed imminent (Gray, 1871, p. 257).

3.4. Dementia

Dementia differed from mania primarily in that it was considered to result from deterioration of the brain, rather than from an aberration. The demented could be recognized by their weak memories and attention spans. They also often abandoned habits of orderly dress and personal cleanliness (Bucknell and Tuke, 1858, pp. 189–288; Ray, 1853, pp. 291–298; Willard Asylum, 1870, p. 27; Mann, 1883, p. 71; New York State Lunatic Asylum, 1886, p. 51). Senility was the most common form of chronic dementia. Although dementia resulting from syphilis was more common in males, doctors did not consider dementia to have sex-specific forms, and they could recommend few specific treatments with confidence.

4. Nineteenth-Century Psychiatric Practice in Lunatic Asylums

For much of the 19th century, psychiatric theorizing was dominated by doctors who worked in lunatic asylums. These men also edited and wrote for the major journal of the day, *The American Journal of Insanity*. Not until late in the century, with the increasing power of specialists such as neurologists and gynecologists, was this hegemony seriously challenged. Yet even though these asylum doctors produced much of the theoretical literature on insanity, they were not always able to put their sex-specific theories into practice.

One way to measure the extent to which sex-specific medical theory affected practice is to compare that theory with the statistical tables on the causes and incidence of insanity in newly admitted patients, published in many asylum annual reports. At Utica, such tables, largely catalogs of what were considered to be "exciting" causes of insanity, reflected in a fashion impossible to disentangle both the assessments of patients' families and friends and the views of asylum doctors (New York State Lunatic Asylum, 1845, 1849, 1859, 1869, 1879, 1889). Consistent with the medical literature's increasing emphasis on the physical causes of insanity, as the century progressed, statistics for the New York State Lunatic Asylum at Utica attributed ever higher percentages of mental illness in both men and women to physical problems. For example, in 1844 21% of all male insanity and 37% of all female insanity was considered to have physical causes; by 1868 the relative ratios were 43% and 58.2%. The female lead was due to the frequency with which female uterine disorders were listed as a cause of insanity. For males, intemperance grew in importance between 1844 and 1888, an expansion particularly striking in view of the asylum superintendents' growing conviction that alcoholics did not belong in lunatic asylums. Also increasing (from 1% in 1844 to a peak of 15% in 1868) was the percentage of men institutionalized for "vicious habits," the most common of which was masturbation. Interestingly, the stress in the medical literature on female sexual perversions did not show up in the Utica statistics, for the incidence of women institutionalized for "vicious habits" was low, vacillating between 0.6% and 5%. (Possibly, female sexual deviance was subsumed into the "uterine disorder" category, of which it so often was considered a by-product.)

Women were consistently reported to have higher rates of melancholy. (Between 1868 and 1888 an average of 47% of the new female admissions to Utica were diagnosed as suffering from melancholy, in contrast to 33% of the male.) In contrast, syphilis was almost unknown among the Utica women, whereas 9% of the males, on average, were its victims. (That there were more female paretics at Willard suggests that such women were more likely to be diagnosed as chronically ill.) About 43% of both males and females suffered from mania. Unfortunately, since neither the aggregate statistics nor the individual casebook records use such subcategories as erotomania or hysteria, we cannot recover their relative incidence in the female population.

Thus, in a number of ways, official statistics from the New York State Lunatic Asylum support the tenets of sex-specific psychiatric theory. (This consistency may have been higher at Utica than at other institutions, because of the active involvement of its superintendents in formulating that theory.) Yet aggregate incidence and causality tables leave unanswered many questions about the effects of social values on psychiatric diagnoses. For example, why did the number of male masturbators and alcoholics increase over the course of the century? What kinds of female symptoms attracted the catch-all label of "uterine disorder?" Did the kinds of behavior for which women were institutionalized change between 1843 (when Utica opened) and 1890? Several recent articles and books have suggested that inmates of 19th-century lunatic asylums, particularly when female, were the victims of the century's narrowing boundaries of acceptable behavior and the concomitant expansion of the definition of insanity (Himmelhoch and Shaffer, 1979; Showalter, 1980; Tomes, 1981). Although memoirs of former female patients (e.g., Packard, 1866; Davis, 1870) support Showalter's claim that "madness was no longer a gross and unmistakable inversion of appropriate conduct, but a collection of cumulatively disquieting gestures and postures" (1980, p. 159), no one has yet tested such a hypothesis using casebook data. In order to do so, one must move beyond the aggregate statistics of annual reports and look at the individual patient records. In the case of 19th-century New York, a sample of the records for the years between 1845 and 1890 uncovers a slow but steady rise in the number of patients without what one contemporary psychiatrist has called "obvious, stereotyped, chronic symptomology" (Townsend, 1980). (This group included a wide range of people, but none who were physically dangerous to themselves or others. They varied from individuals with occasional hallucinations to depressed melancholics and disorderly, but not violent, alcoholics.) Most marked was the increase in the number of women committed for public acts of deviance, especially for relatively unthreatening behavior. In addition, even though most women, like men, were sent to lunatic asylums at the initative of their families, the probability of a female's being committed by a public official more than doubled over the course of the century. (Whether this shift was due to real changes in female behavior or to an increased willingness on the part of the state to intervene in public disorder incidents involving women, for which men may have been sent to jail, or to a combination of the two, is difficult to determine.) Thus, as the characteristics of mental health became more clearly defined in medical literature, the community's tolerance for deviation from these characteristics decreased, and their willingness to use lunatic asylums to control it increased. Since members of the community, and particularly families, typically initiated the commitment process, doctors cannot be blamed for the increasing numbers of men and women in lunatic asylums. Doctors' only control was over the ways in which deviance was labeled, once men and women were admitted to the asylum.

By the end of the century, substantially more than half of the female wards at the Utica asylum were filled with women who had posed no overt threat to their neighbors or communities. One of these women, a

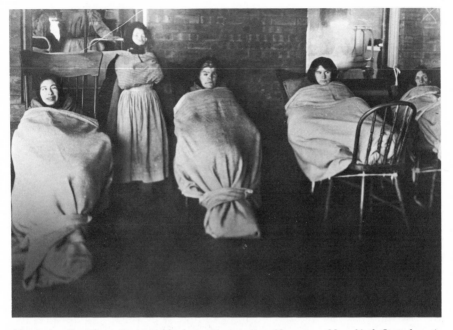

Figure 1.   Female patients in blanket restraints in a 19-century New York State lunatic asylum (Photo courtesy of the New York State Library archives).

young dressmaker named Phoebe Davis, was sent to Utica when she became depressed and misanthropic (Davis, 1870, p. 12). In an unusual memoir about her experience, she compared herself to "an old porcupine" (p. 42) and declared that, by the second half of the 19th century, asylums were filling up with troublesome women who were "superannuated beings but not crazy ones" (p. 29). Davis found life in the asylum often so frustrating that she could relieve the internal tension only by loud screaming. She also noted slyly that she sometimes disrupted her ward just to annoy a doctor with whom she had a disagreement (p. 15); she clearly felt that in such self-conscious sabotage lay her only power over those who ran the institution.

At the same time as the kinds of behavior for which men and women were institutionalized and the circumstances of commitment to Utica changed, the absolute number of women sent to lunatic asylums in New York State also increased. By 1888 there were only 83 men per 100 women in the New York State asylum population as a whole, an imbalance that is particularly striking given that, by 1890, probably as a result of renewed waves of immigration, the sex ratio among those aged 25 to 49, the group most at risk to be institutionalized, was 106 men to 100 women (Dwyer, 1983). Since women generally lived longer than men, some of this imbalance may have been due to the larger numbers of old women, particularly in county asylums, but the statistics easily convinced both the asylum superintendents and the State Commissioner in Lunacy of the need to increase the asylum space available for women. Inevitably, their belief in the greater susceptibility of women to insanity became a self-fulfilling prophecy, for no sooner were new wards built and new buildings constructed than they filled to overcrowding (e.g., Willard Asylum, 1871, p. 13, 1874, pp. 9, 11, 1877, pp. 9, 28, 1881, p. 8; Letchworth and Carpenter, 1882, p. 65; State of New York, 1882, p. 9).

5. Conclusion

Over the course of the 19th century, sex-specific theories of mental illness developed in a one-sided fashion. Although many doctors initially stressed the importance of the differing environments in which men and women operated, such moral theorists were eventually overwhelmed by the somaticists, who stressed the significance of female uterine disorders as the major source of female emotional instability. By 1873 even doctors such as Isaac Ray saw an "intimate sympathy between the uterine and cerebral systems" (Ray, 1873, p. 287). Although male masturbation aroused concern, there was no comparable body of writings about male reproductive organs. Asylum statistical reports also indicated a rise in the incidence of uterine-related diseases. Neither the theoretical writings nor the asylum doctors' diagnoses at Utica seemed much affected by the fact that female patients' case histories suggested a somewhat different picture. According to the case histories, the most dramatic shift in female insanity patterns between 1843 and 1890 was not in the number of women whose insanity had been precipitated by uterine disorders but in the number of women committed for relatively mild acts of deviance, precipitated by a wide range of environmental and physical stresses.

Although many 19th-century doctors hoped to liberate the mentally ill by stressing the physiological (instead of the moral) roots of their illnesses, their attempts to develop disease models of psychiatric syndromes, and to explore the physiological and neurological bases of mental illness, sometimes led them to overlook the personal and political stresses in their patients' lives, particularly the females'. Interestingly, asylum doctors were less likely than neurologists and gynecologists to lose sight of the role played by environmental stresses in producing insanity. Even such committed somaticists as John Gray of Utica complained of society's indifference to the plight of the working poor, particularly mothers. Their patients' casebook histories are filled with references to the travails of the poor, ranging from loss of employment and money to poor nutrition and inadequate sleep, as well as with descriptions of gastric and reproductive disorders.

Nineteenth-century psychiatric theory and practice were rooted deeply in the ideological, social, and economic relationships of the industrializing country. To blame asylum superintendents as a group or individuals such as Storer for the sexist and racist aspects of 19th-century psychiatric medicine is clearly inappropriate. The process of defining insanity was as intricate in the 19th century as it is today, the result of complex interactions among the individual, the community, and the medical world.

Many 20th-century physicians have maintained both their 19th-century predecessors' stereotypes about male and female temperament and their obsession with the physical bases of mental illness. At the same time, many have lost the concern expressed by the early asylum superintendents about the unhealthy social environment produced by the psychic and physical demands of life in a modern industrial state. Doctors still cannot define uterine normality, and many continue to assume that the female reproductive system is inherently unstable. Finally, the study of the relationship between the female reproductive cycle and female mental health continues to be complicated by emotions as strong as those that supposedly sway the fertile female (Parlee, 1973; Ruble, 1977; Abplanalp et al., 1979a, 1979b).

6. References

Abplanalp, J. M., Donnelly, A. F., and Rose, R. H. "Psychoendocrinology of the menstrual cycle: I. Enjoyment of daily activities and moods. *Psychosomatic Medicine*, 1979, 41, 587–604.(a)

Abplanap, J. M., Rose, R. M., Donnelly, A. F., and Livingston-Vaughan, L. Psychoendocrinology of the menstrual cycle: II, The relationship between enjoyment of activities, moods, and reproductive hormones. *Psychosomatic Medicine*, 1979, 41, 605–615. (b)

Blackwell, A. B. *The sexes throughout nature.* New York: Putnam's, 1875.

Brigham, A. *Remarks on the influence of mental cultivation and mental excitement upon health.* Boston: March, Cooper, and Lyon, 1835.

Brigham, A. Insanity and insane hospitals. *North American Review.* 1837, 44, 91–121.

Brigham, A. *An inquiry concerning diseases and functions of the brain.* New York: George Adlard, 1840.

Brigham, A. *Mental exertion: In relation to health.* London: John Camden, 1865. (Originally published, 1833.)

Brush, E. N. On the employment of women physicians in hospitals for the insane. *American Journal of Insanity*, 1891, 47, 323–330.

Bucknell, J. C., and Tuke, D. H. *A manual of psychological medicine: Containing the history, nosology, description, statistics, diagnosis, pathology, and treatment of insanity*. Philadelphia: Blanchard and Lea, 1858.

Bullough, V. L., and Vogt, M. Homosexuality and its confusion with the "secret sin" in pre-Freudian America. *Journal of the History of Medicine*, 1973, *28*, 143–155. (a)

Bullough, V. L., and Vogt, M. Women, menstruation, and nineteenth-century medicine. *Bulletin of the History of Medicine*, 1973, *1*, 66–82. (b)

Carlson, E. T., and Dain, N. The psychotherapy that was moral treatment. *American Journal of Psychiatry*, 1960, *117*, 519–524.

Carlson, E. T., and Simpson, M. M. Tarantism or hysteria? An American case of 1801. *Journal of the History of Medicine and the Allied Sciences*, 1971, *26*(3), 293–302.

Case of Mrs. Elizabeth Hegge. *American Journal of Insanity*, 1868, *25*(1), 1–51.

Channing, W. A consideration of the causes of insanity. *Journal of the American Social Science Association*, 1883, *18*, 68–92.

Chapin, John. Letter to New York State Senate, 1879.

Churchill, F. On the mental disorders of pregnancy and childbirth. *American Journal of Insanity*, 1851, *7*(3), 259–266.

Clark, A. C. Relations of the sexual and reproductive functions to insanity. *American Journal of Insanity*, 1888, *45*, 292–297.

Cleaves, M. A. The medical and moral care of female patients. In F. B. Sanborn (Ed.), *Proceedings of the Annual Conference of Charities, held at Chicago, June, 1879*. Boston: A Williams, 1879.

Clitoridectomy in insanity. *Alienist and Neurologist*, 1895, *16*(4), 478–479.

Clouston, T. S. *Clinical lectures on medical diseases* (5th ed.). Philadelphia: Lea Bros., 1898.

Condition of patients on admission to asylum. *Journal of Nervous and Mental Disease*, 1883, *10*(1), 169.

Dain, N. *Concepts of insanity in the United State, 1789–1865*. New Brunswick, N.J.: Rutgers University Press, 1964.

Davis, D. B. *Homicide in American fiction, 1798–1860: A study in social values*. Ithaca: Cornell University Press, 1957.

Davis, P. B. *Two years and three months in the New York lunatic asylum at Utica: Together with the outlines of twenty years' peregrinations in Syracuse*. Syracuse: Author, 1870.

Degler, C. N. What ought to be and what was: Women's sexuality in the nineteenth century. *American Historical Review*, 1974, *79*, 1467–1490.

Dwyer, E. "The Weaker Vessel": The law vs. societal realities in the commitment of women to nineteenth-century New York asylums. In K. Weisberg (Ed.), *Women and the law*. Cambridge: Schenkman, 1983.

Englehardt, H. T. The disease of masturbation: Values and the concept of disease. In J. W. Leavitt and R. L. Numbers (Eds.), *Sickness and health in America*. Madison: University of Wisconsin Press, 1978.

Farnham, A. M. "Uterine Disease as a Factor in the Production of Insanity. *Alienist and Neurologist*, 1887, *8*, 532–547.

Farnham, E. W. Case of destitution of moral feelings. *American Journal of Insanity*, 1846, *3*, 129–135.

Female diseases and insanity. *Alienist and Neurologist*, 1887, *8*, 406–407.

Galt, J. M. On the propriety of admitting the insane of the two sexes into the same lunatic asylum. *American Journal of Insanity*, 1855, *12*, 224–230.

Gilbert, A. N. Doctor, patient, and onanist diseases in the nineteenth-century. *Bulletin of the History of Medicine*, 1975, *49*, 217–234.

Gorton, D. A. Natural psychology. *Mental and Nervous Diseases*. Collected in New York State Commission in Lunacy, *Miscellaneous Documents*, 1890, *1*(37).

Gray, J. P. Insanity, its dependence on physical disease. *Transactions of the Medical Society of the State of New York*, 1871, pp. 240–264.

Gray, J. P. Responsibility of the insane-homicide in insanity. *American Journal of Insanity*, 1875, *31*, 1–57.

Gray, J. *Insanity: Some of its preventable causes.* Utica, New York: Ellis H. Roberts, 1885.

Gray, L. G. Three diagnostic signs of melancholia. *Journal of Nervous and Mental Disease*, 1890, *15*(1), 1–9.

Grob, G. N. *Mental institutions in America, social policy to 1875.* New York: Free Press, 1973.

Grob, G. N. Redefining the asylums: The unhistorical history of the mental hospital. *Hastings Center Report*, 1977, *7*(4), 33–41.

Gynecological examinations in asylums. *Journal of Nervous and Mental Disease*, 1883, *10*(2), 337.

Haller, J. S., and Haller, R. M. *The physician and sexuality in Victorian America.* Champaign: University of Illinois Press, 1974.

Himmelhoch, M. S., and Shaffer, A. H. Elizabeth Packard: Nineteenth-century crusader for the rights of women. *American Studies*, 1979, *13*(3), 343–375.

Insanity after gynecological operations. *Alienist and Neurologist*, 1895, *16*(4), 473–474.

Insanity and adultery. *American Journal of Insanity*, 1888, *44*, 532–34.

Insanity in hysterical women. *Alienist and Neurologist*, 1880, *4*(3), 499–500.

Jacobi, M. P. *Essays on hysteria, brain-tumor and some other cases of nervous disease.* New York: Putnam's, 1888.

Jarvis, E. On the comparative liability of males and females to insanity and their comparative curability and mortality when insane. *American Journal of Insanity*, 1850, *7*, 142–171.

Lasch, C. *The new radicalism in America, 1889–1963: The intellectual as a social type.* New York: Knopf, 1965.

Law cases bearing on the subject of insanity: Trial of Adeline Phelps, *alias* Bass, for the murder of her father, Elihu Phelps. *American Journal of Insanity*, 1854, *11*, 63–83.

Laycock, T. *A treatise on the nervous diseases of women.* London: Longman, Orme, Brown, Green, and Longmans, 1840.

Leszynsky, W. M. Insanity and oophorectomy. *New York Medical Journal*, 1887, June 25.

Letchworth, W. P. and Carpenter, S. M. Report on the carenic insane in certain counties, exempted by the State Board of Charities from the operation of the Willard Asylum Act. In the *Fifteenth Annual Report of the New York State Board of Charities.* Albany: Weed, Parsons, 1882.

Longo, L. D. The rise and fall of Battey's operation: A fashion in surgery. *Bulletin of the History of Medicine*, 1979, *53*, 244–267.

MacDonald, J. Puerperal insanity. *American Journal of Insanity*, 1847, *4*, 113–163.

MacMillan, M. B. Beard's concept of neurasthenia and Freud's concept of the actual neurosis. *Journal of the History of the Behavioral Sciences*, 1976 *12*(4), 376–390.

Mann, E. C. *A manual of psychological medicine.* Philadelphia: P. Blakiston, 1883.

McGovern, C. M. Doctors or ladies? Women physicians in psychiatric institutions, 1872–1900. *Bulletin of the History of medicine*, 1980, *55*(1), 88–109.

Johnson, D. E. *The question of insanity and its medico-legal relations considered upon general principles.* Raleigh, North Carolina: T. M. Hughes, 1869.

New York State Lunatic Asylum. *Second annual report of the managers of the state lunatic asylum.* Utica, 1845.

New York State Lunatic Asylum. *Sixth annual report of the managers of the state lunatic asylum, made to the legislature, February 1, 1849.* Albany: Weed, Parsons, 1849.

New York State Lunatic Asylum. *Tenth annual report of the managers of the state lunatic asylum.* Utica, 1853.

New York State Lunatic Asylum. *Sixteenth annual report of the managers of the state lunatic asylum, Utica, January 28, 1859.* State of New York, In Assembly, January 29, 1859.

New York State Lunatic Asylum. *Twenty-second annual report of the managers of the state lunatic asylum, for the Year 1864.* Albany: C. Van Benthuysen, 1865.

New York State Lunatic Asylum. *Twenty-third annual report of the managers of the state lunatic asylum, for the year 1865.* Albany: C. Wendell, 1866.

New York State Lunatic Asylum. *Twenty-sixth annual report of managers of the state lunatic asylum, for the year ending 30 November, 1868,* No. 21, In Senate, January 28, 1869.

New York State Lunatic Asylum. *Twenty-seventh annual report of managers of the state lunatic asylum, for the year 1869.* Albany: *Argus,* 1870.

New York State Lunatic Asylum. Thirty-sixth annual report of the managers of the state lunatic asylum, for the year ending November 30, 1878. Albany: C. Van Benthuysen, 1879.

New York State Lunatic Asylum. *Forty-second annual report of the managers of the state lunatic asylum, at Utica, for the year 1884.* Albany: Weed, Parsons, 1885.

New York State Lunatic Asylum. *Forty-third annual report of the managers of the state lunatic asylum at Utica, for the Year 1885.* Albany: Weed, Parsons, 1886.

New York State Lunatic Asylum. *Forty-sixth annual report of the managers of the state lunatic asylum at Utica, for the year ending September 30, 1888.* Albany: Troy Press, 1889.

Oophorectomy and sexual appetite. *Alienist and Neurologist,* 1895, *16*(4), 479–480.

Ovariotomy in Insanity. *Alienist and Neurologist,* 1887, 3(3), 405–406.

Packard, E. P. W. *Marital power exemplified in Mrs. Packard's trials, and self-defense from the charge of insanity; Or three years' imprisonment for religious belief, by the arbitrary will of a husband, with an appeal to the government to so change the laws as to afford legal protection to married women.* Hartford, Conn.: Lockwood, 1866.

Paoli, G. C., and Kiernan, J. G. Female physicians in insane hospitals. *Alienist and Nuerologist,* 1887, *8*(1), 21–29.

Parlee, M. B. The premenstrual syndrome. *Psychological Bulletin,* 1925, *80*(6), 454–465.

Proceedings of the association. *American Journal of Insanity,* 1880, 37(2), 139–223.

Procek, E. *Psychiatry and the social control of women.* Unpublished paper, Cropwood Round-Table Conference on Women and Crime, 1980.

Puerperal insanity. *American Journal of Insanity,* 1850, *7,* 374–375.

Quen, J. Asylum psychiatry, neurology, social work, and mental hygiene: An exploratory study in interprofessional history. *Journal of the History of the Behavioral Sciences,* 1977, *13*(1), 3–11.

Ray, I. *Treatise on the mental jurisprudence of insanity.* Boston: Little, Brown, 1853.

Ray, I. *Mental hygiene.* Boston: Ticknor and Fields, 1863.

Ray, I. The insanity of women produced by desertion and seduction. *American Journal of Insanity,* 1866, 23(2), 264–274.

Ray, I. *Contributions of mental pathology.* Boston: Little, Brown, 1873.

Ray, I. In *Proceedings of the Association,* 1880 (p. 169).

Romanes, G. J. Mental differences between men and women. *Nineteenth Century,* 1887, *21*(123), 654–672.

Rosen, G. Nostalgia: A "forgotten" psychological disorder. *Clio Medica,* 1975, *10*(1), 28–51.

Rosenberg, C. George M. Beard and American nervousness. *Bulletin of the History of Medicine,* 1962, *36*(2), 245–259.

Rosenkranz, B. G., and Vinovskis, M. A. The invisible lunatics: Old age and insanity in mid-nineteenth century Massachusetts. In S. F. Spicker, K. M. Woodward, and D. Van Tassel (Eds.), *Aging and the elderly, humanistic perspectives in gerontology.* Atlantic Highlands, N.J.: Humanities Press, 1978.

Ruble, D. N. Premenstrual symptoms: A reinterpretation. *Science,* 1977, *197,* 291–292.

Rush, B. *Medical inquiries and observations upon the diseases of the mind.* Philadelphia: Kimber and Richardson, 1812.

Savino, M. T., and Mills, A. B. The rise and fall of moral treatment in California psychiatry. *Journal of the History of the Behavioral Sciences,* 3(4), 359–369.

Showalter, E. "Victorian Women and Insanity. *Victorian Studies,* 1980, 23(2), 157–181.

Sicherman, B. The uses of a diagnosis: Doctors, patients, and neurasthenia. In J. Leavitt and R. Numbers (Eds.), *Sickness and health in America.* Madison: University of Wisconsin Press, 1980.

Sims, H. M. The prevention of hysteria in certain cases of nervous and hysterical women. *American Psychological Journal,* 1883, 1(1), 24–27.

Skene, A. J. C. Gynecology as related to insanity in women. *Archives of Medicine,* 1880, 3(1), 1–31.

Skultans, V. *English madness, ideas on insanity, 1580–1890.* London: Routledge and Kegan Paul, 1979.

Smith-Rosenberg, C. The hysterical woman: Sex roles and role conflict in nineteenth-century America. *Social Research,* 1972, 39, 652–678.

Smith-Rosenberg, C. The cycle of femininity: Puberty and menopause in nineteenth-century America. *Feminist Studies,* 1973, 1, 58–72.

Smith-Rosenberg, C. The female world of love and ritual: Relations between women in nineteenth-century America. *Signposts,* 1978, 1(1), 1–29.

Smith-Rosenberg, C. Puberty to menopause: The cycle of femininity in nineteenth-century America. In M. Hartman and L. W. Banner (Eds.), *Clio's consciousness raised: New perspectives on the history of women,* New York: Harper & Row, 1974. (a)

Smith-Rosenberg, C. Sex as symbol in Victorian purity: An ethnohistorical analysis of Jacksonian America. *American Journal of Sociology,* 1974, 84, 212–247. (b)

Smith-Rosenberg, C., and Rosenberg, C. The female animal: Medical and biological views of women's role in nineteenth-century America. *Journal of American History,* 1973, 60(2), 332–356.

Spitzka, E. C. *Insanity: Its classification, diagnosis, and treatment.* New York: Bermingham, 1883. 1883.

State of New York. No. 80. *Report of the Joint Committee of Senate and Assembly to Examine into the Management and Affairs of the State Lunatic Asylum at Utica.* In Senate, April 24, 1869.

State of New York. No. 13. *Seventh Annual Report of the State Commissioner on Lunacy.* In Senate, January 20, 1880.

State of New York. No. 175. *Report of the Committee of State Charitable Institutions in the Matter of the Asylum Investigation.* In Assembly, March 16, 1883.

State of New York. No. 164. *Report of the Special Committee of the Assembly, Appointed to Investigate the Affairs and Management of the State Lunatic Asylum at Utica.* In Assembly, April 30, 1884.

State of New York. *Report of the Investigation of the State Commission in Lunacy and the State Hospital for the Insane by the Subcommittee of the Senate Finance and Assembly Ways and Means Committees, Transmitted to the Legislature May 10, 1895.* Albany: James B. Lyon, 1895.

Stevenson, S. H. *The physiology of women, embracing girlhood, maternity, and mature age.* Chicago: Cushing, Thomas, 1880.

Storer, H. R. *The causation, course, and treatment of reflex insanity in women.* Boston: Lee and Shepard, 1871.

The climacteric in its relation to insanity. *American Journal of Insanity,* 1890, 47(1), 73.

The laparotomy epidemic. *Alienist and Neurologist,* 1886, 7(2), 325–329.

The trial of Mary Harris. *American Journal of Insanity,* 1866 22(3), 333–360.

Thompson, H. B. A review of the recent literature on the psychology of sex." *Psychological Bulletin*, 1910, 7, 335–342.

Tomes, N. *The burden of being their keepers: Patterns of commitment to a nineteenth-century mental hospital.* Unpublished manuscript, 1979.

Tomlinson, H. A. A case of acute melancholia, during the progress of which there appeared Argyle-Robertson pupil, with abolished patteglar reflex on one side and much diminished on the other. *Journal of Nervous and Medical Disease*, 1890, 15(1), 75–82.

Townsend, J. M. Psychiatry versus sociatal reactions: A critical analysis. *Journal of Health and Social Behavior*, 1980, 21(3), 268–278.

Tuke, D. H. *The insane in the United States and Canada.* London: H. K. Lewis, 1885.

Tyor, Peter L. "Denied the power to choose the Good: Sexuality and mental defect in American medical practice, 1850–1920. *Journal of Social History*, 1977, 10(4).

Tyor, P. L., and Zainaldin, J. S. Redefining the American asylum: A case-study approach. *Journal of Social History*, 1979, 13(1), 23–48.

Van Deusen, E. H. Observations on a form of nervous prostration (neurasthenia), culminating in insanity. *American Journal of Insanity*, 1869, 26, 446–461.

Webber, S. B. Causes of hysteria treated by hypnotism. *Journal of Nervous and Mental Disease*, 1890, 15(3), 585–596.

Wilbur, H. B. *Materialism in its relation to the causes, conditions, and treatment of insanity.* New York: D. Appleton, 1872.

Willard Asylum for the Insane. *First annual report of the trustees of the Willard asylum for the insane, for the year 1869.* Albany: Argus, 1870.

Willard Asylum for the Insane. *Second annual report of the trustees of the Willard asylum for the insane, for the year 1870.* Albany: Argus, 1871.

Willard Asylum for the Insane. *Third annual report of the Willard asylum for the insane, for the year 1871.* Albany: Argus, 1872.

Willard Asylum for the Insane. *Fifth annual report of the trustees of the Willard asylum for the insane, for the year 1873.* Albany, Weed, Parsons, 1874.

Willard Asylum for the Insane. *Eighth annual report of the trustees of the Willard asylum for the insane, for the year 1878.* Albany: Jerome B. Parmenter, 1877.

Willard Asylum for the Insane. *Tenth annual report of the trustees of the Willard asylum for the insane, for the year 1878.* Albany: Charles Van Benthuysen, 1879.

Willard Asylum for the Insane. *Twelfth annual report of the trustees of the Willard asylum for the insane, for the year 1880.* Albany: Weed, Parsons, 1881.

Willard Asylum for the Insane. *Fourteenth annual report of the trustees of the Willard asylum for the insane, for the year 1882.* Albany: Weed, Parsons, 1883.

Willard Asylum for the Insane. *Fifteenth annual report of the trustees of the Willard asylum for the insane, for the year 1883.* Albany: Weed, Parsons, 1884.

Willard Asylum for the Insane. *Seventeenth annual report of the trustees of the Willard asylum for the insane, for the year 1885.* Albany: Weed, Parsons, 1886.

Williams, J. H. *Unsoundness of mind in its legal and medical considerations.* New York: William Wood, 1892.

Wise, P. M. Case of Sexual Perversion. *The Alienist and Neurologist*, 1883, 4(1), 87–91.

Woolley, H. T. A review of the recent literature on the psychology of sex. *Psychological Bulletin*, 1910, 1(10), 335–342.

Worcester, W. L. Is puerperal insanity a distinct clinical form? *American Journal of Insanity*, 1890, 47(1), 52–58.

Workman, J. Insanity of the religious-emotional type and its occasional physical relations. *American Journal of Insanity*, 1869, 26(1), 33–48.

II

Neurotic, Affective, and Schizophrenic Disorders

3

Gender Ideology and Phobias in Women

Barry E. Wolfe

Every human being must solve two problems, the problem of economic security and the problem of self-esteem. Our culture assigns to men and women different ways and means for solving both.

Simone de Beauvoir,
The Second Sex

1. Introduction

In the last decade, a shift in perspective has occurred regarding the relationship between sex role behavior and mental health. Where once it was common knowledge that sex role conformity was prerequisite to mental health, some investigators now show an uncommon boldness in suggesting that a rigid conformity to one's "appropriate" sex role may provide fertile ground for the development of psychological maladjustments (Pleck, 1976). The limitations of a woman's traditional role, for example, have been thought to be significantly related to the etiology of a number of specific mental disorders, including depression, hysteria, anorexia nervosa, and phobias (Fodor, 1974; Frances and Dunn, 1975; Weissman and Klerman, 1977; Wolowitz, 1972).

We will explore the hypothesis that the limitations of a woman's traditional role and certain personal limitations, both mandated by the

Barry E. Wolfe • National Institute of Mental Health, Rockville, Maryland 20857.

traditional ideology of gender differentiation, combine to corrode a woman's capacity for achieving autonomy and mastery over her life situation. These external and internal constraints, in turn, help to produce—in a select group of women (i.e., those most committed to and influenced by the traditional gender ideology)—a fearful and dependent personality, a gender identity of diminished personhood, and a behavioral style characterized by the avoidance of difficult situations. These deficits, under conditions of severe stress, may result in the development of a phobia. This is an elaboration of a model first put forth by Fodor (1974). While this model has much to recommend it, particularly in relation to the etiology of agoraphobia, it also possesses many serious limitations. These too will be explored.

2. Phobias

A phobia is currently defined as an extreme and persistent fear of an object, event, or situation that objectively presents no real danger. While not unassailable, this definition has the decided virtue of providing a useful working description without contamination by unproven notions of etiology. At a descriptive level, the phenomenon of a phobic disorder can be separated into two components, phobic anxiety and phobic avoidance. Phobic anxiety is much like other forms of anxiety except that it occurs only in the presence of the phobic stimulus (Mavissakalian and Barlow, 1981).

A phobia also involves phobic avoidance of the feared stimulus, which serves as a defense against the painful experience of anxiety. Phobic avoidance may expand to the point that it severely encroaches upon the patient's daily life routine. Because of a terror of heights, for example, an acrophobic may deny him/herself a lucrative job offer that requires the individual to work in an office situated on an upper floor of an office building; the person in a panic over receiving a hypodermic injection may forgo much-needed medical attention; and the agoraphobic, desperate to avoid the pain and humiliation of an unpredictable panic attack, may cloister her/himself in the safety of house or apartment for many years.

Agoraphobia, incidentally, is the most common form of phobia seen in psychiatric practice, although other phobias appear to be more prevalent in the general population. As many as 60% of treated phobics suffer from agoraphobia (Marks, 1969). While almost any object, situation, or event may come to act as a phobic stimulus, most phobias—apart from agoraphobia—appear to cluster around three themes: "(1) monosymptomatic phobias of single situations or animals, (2) phobias of blood and injury and illness, and (3) phobias involving social situations" (Mavissakalian and Barlow, 1981, p. 4).

Information on the incidence and prevalence of the various phobias is sparse. Agras, Sylvester, and Oliveau (1969) carried out one of the few community studies on phobias in Vermont. Using a fear inventory, they interviewed a probability sample of the household population of greater Burlington. They estimated the total prevalence of phobia to be 77/1000 population. Slightly more than 2/1000 were receiving treatment for phobia. For agoraphobia, a prevalence rate of 6/1000 was found. As was suggested above, the prevalence of agoraphobia in the community seems to be much lower than the percentage of phobic patients who are treated for agoraphobia. Finally, phobic patients represent only 2–3% of all psychiatric patients who seek help (Marks, 1970; Terhune, 1949).

As can be seen, phobias represent a relatively rare disorder that afflicts a relatively small number of people. But within this circumscribed universe of phobics, there is a marked sex difference in the prevalence of this disorder. As many as 95% of animal phobics are female (Marks, 1969), while estimates of the percentage of female agoraphobics have ranged from 64% to 95% (Friedman, 1959; Marks and Herst, 1970). Only the social phobias reveal a relatively equal distribution between the sexes.

2.1. Agoraphobia

There is a good reason to consider agoraphobia separately from the other phobias. It is a more complex disorder that rarely begins in childhood. It is accompanied by much greater anxiety, which is unlikely to have developed in response to some trauma, and it bears, as we shall see, a debatable relationship to the defining characteristics of other phobias.

The phenomenon of agoraphobia has acquired many labels since Westphal coined the term in 1871: *Platzschwindel* (or dizziness in public places) (Benedikt, 1870), anxiety hysteria (Freud, 1959), and phobic anxiety depersonalization syndrome (Roth, 1959), among others. Westphal (1871) described a condition in which the most prominent feature was the anxiety that an individual suffered while walking across open spaces or through empty streets. Interestingly, particularly in light of the focus of this chapter, the three cases that Westphal described were all men. It must be remembered, however, that it was not the custom in the 19th century for women to travel outside of their homes alone. Thus, there was little opportunity for women to manifest the disorder.

Agoraphobia is typically accompanied by severe panic attacks. These terrifying and unpredictable attacks may be accompanied by shortness of breath, palpitations, feelings of depersonalization, dizziness, weakness in the limbs, and possibly bladder and bowel incontinence. Agoraphobics undergoing these attacks often feel a sense of impending doom, a fear that they may suffocate or die or perhaps go insane. They also fear that they may faint or lose control in a way that will humiliate them (Chambless, 1982). An agoraphobic's fears are much greater when he or she is alone. With a "phobic companion"—i.e., someone to accompany the phobic individual—some agoraphobics are able to venture forth a great distance beyond their zone of safety.

Agoraphobia is particularly distinguished from other phobias in the typical age of onset. Whereas most phobias appear to begin in childhood or adolescence, agoraphobia seems to develop in young adulthood. The modal ages of onset appear to be around 20 and from 30 to 35 (Mathews, Gelder, and Johnston, 1981). Its onset is not typically a response to a traumatic experience that subsequently becomes the focus for phobic behavior. Instead, the occurrence of a panic attack is usually preceded by a period of stress and anxiety, often associated with some critical developmental crisis (e.g., leaving home for the first time or contemplating leaving a bad marriage), and the pain and humiliation of the panic attack then lead to phobic avoidance (Chambless, 1982).

There is considerable debate in the literature regarding what is the most significant or central symptom of agoraphobia. Some of the possibilities include a fear of external situations such as shopping centers, fear of leaving the psychological safety of home, the anticipatory fear of panic attacks that usually accompany this disorder, and the panic attack itself (Goldstein and Chambless, 1978; Klein, 1981; Marks, 1970; Snaith, 1968).

Some investigators view the phenomenon of agoraphobia as so characteristically distinct from other phobias that they question whether it should be considered a phobia at all. Even here, however, there are differences of opinion. While all of these investigators agree that the term *agoraphobia* is a misnomer, there is no agreement on what the new "nomer" should be: an occasional manifestation of anxiety neurosis (Hallam, 1978), a separation-anxiety disorder (Bowlby, 1973; Frances and Dunn, 1975), nonspecific insecurity fears (Snaith, 1968), or a psychosomatic form of depression (Gardos, 1981). This chameleon of a disorder, as it did in the past, seems to gather new names faster than investigators can gather solid facts about it. Reading these reports and the etiological speculations of their authors is rather like encountering the proverbial blind men with the elephant. Each investigator seems to have grasped a vital truth about the disorder, but no one seems to have a monopoly on it. We are now about to investigate the elephant.

3. Sex Roles and the Ideology of Gender Differentiation

The concept of sex roles has been a useful construct employed by several different disciplines. A basic difficulty with the term, however, is that each discipline uses it to mean somewhat different things. Psychologists, for example, tend to focus on personality differences between the genders and the socialization practices that shape those differences, while sociologists concentrate on the sexual divisions of labor. Moreover, the concept of sex roles overlaps with the concept of gender identity, about which a separate clinical research literature has developed.

The three separate literatures on sex roles and gender identity that describe the evolution of differences between the genders in identity, personality, and social role have given little attention to the traditional ideology of gender differentiation that underlies their research assumptions, prompts their choice of methods, and, in large degree, determines the meaning of their findings (Wolfe, 1979). It is very evident, however, that what binds these literatures together is an androcentric ideology of gender differentiation. This ideology embodies a host of cultural norms and behavioral expectations that require differences between males and females across several domains of gender behavior. These norms are marked by a clear, cultural favoritism with respect to males. There are norms regarding the way men and women walk, talk, think, and dress. There are norms relating to differences in personality, erotic behavior, recreational activities, and the assignment of adult responsibilities.

These normative expectations in all of the domains of gender behavior become integral constituents of an individual's gender identity, that is, one's self-definition as male or female. While there is much variation in the specific expectations that are incorporated in any given person's identity or in the intensity with which these norms are held, they often have the force and grip of moral imperatives. Hence, instead of the term *sex role stereotypes*, we employ the construct *gender imperative*.

Much of the time we are hardly cognizant of the extent to which our behavior is controlled by gender imperatives. We become aware of their importance in our lives and in our self-definition only when there is an actual or threatened violation. When males show any sign of effeminacy or females give the impression, by word or by deed, that they do not need men, either sexually or economically (Keller, 1974), they are likely to be subjected to severe social censure (Wolfe, 1980).

4. Gender Ideology and Phobias

4.1. Gender Identity, Imperatives, and Phobias

The ideology of gender differentiation is apparent at birth. On the basis of an examination of the external genitalia, all newborn children are assigned to one sex or the other.* As soon as the infant's sex is known, parents begin to think of him or her in terms of the gender imperatives that they have incorporated about that particular sex. The fact that a parent's gender beliefs may bear only a casual acquaintance with reality was demonstrated by a rather ingenious study. Rubin, Provenzano, and Luria (1974) found that male infants were seen as stronger, larger, and more alert than female infants, while the latter were seen as smaller, weaker, and more delicate than their male counterparts, even though there were no actual differences between them.

Gender imperatives are incorporated by children at a very young age. By the time they are 3, children can identify the respective imperatives for boys and girls and are beginning to think of themselves as boys or girls on the basis of these imperatives (Thompson, 1975). At this age, hair and clothes are the most powerful cues children use to discriminate gender (Kessler and McKenna, 1978; Thompson and Bentler, 1971). Although children can distinguish one gender from another, they do not develop a sense of gender constancy until around age 6 or 7 (Kohlberg, 1966). Until that time, children often believe that they can change their gender merely by changing their clothes or the length of their hair.

Before puberty, much greater latitude is given to females with respect to their gender behavior. Violations do not bring the same painful consequences for females as they do for males (Hartley, 1959; Rekers and Lovaas, 1974). Studies have shown that both males and females indicate much greater disapproval of cross-gender behavior in boys than in girls (Feinman, 1974). After puberty, however, the pressures for girls to conform to feminine imperatives increases exponentially. If they have not begun to already, adolescent girls are encouraged by parents, peers, the media, the church, and the schools to adopt the characteristics that will allow them to successfully carry out the imperatives of the adult feminine role. The imperatives that they absorb typically include cultural ideas and ideals of femininity as soft, delicate, fearful, gentle, dependent, submissive, and passive. They are unlikely to receive the same

---

*The strength of the ideology is apparent in the fact that when children with ambiguous genitalia are assigned to the wrong sex, they eventually adopt the gender identity of the sex in which they have been reared (Money and Ehrardt, 1972; Money, Hampson, and Hampson, 1955).

encouragement as their brothers or other male associates for their achievement aspirations, and they may indeed come to fear success (Hoffman, 1972; Horner, 1969).

The imperatives that adolescent girls learn affect not only their behavior but also their sense of themselves and their capabilities. They cannot have failed to discern the frankly androcentric bias of their society, and they must therefore come to terms, in one way or another, with the different expectations that the culture generally has for their destiny. The implications for women of an androcentric culture are eloquently spelled out by Keller (1974):

> No matter what private advantages may be derived from a judicious manipulation of feminine opportunities in a culture overtly androcentric, the prevalent cultural favoritism is bound to undermine self-confidence and self-esteem in women. This is not to say that most men will have self-esteem in such a culture but only that their roles provide them with a pretext for it. (p. 428)

Later on Keller describes how women come to terms with the message of cultural bias and particularly the impact of that bias on their gender identities:

> Women come to terms with this message in a number of ways. For a few, this cultural slight is a spur to extraordinary efforts designed to prove their worthiness by conspicuous achievements. But most women, as indeed most men, will prune their ambitions to their opportunities. This leads to the familiar denial of self, of ambitions nipped in the bud, of projects abandoned, or of steps not taken. Initially the inhibition comes from a parent, teacher, or other social authority, but later one's inner arbiter takes over and what was once second nature becomes primary impulse to self-effacement. (p. 428)

Women reared under traditional imperatives are at risk of developing a gender identity that includes as integral elements of their self-concept a diminished sense of autonomy, a crippled potential for mastery, and an enduring hope of protection. With such a self-concept, it is easy to see why a woman may become extremely anxious when faced with difficult decisions, complex tasks, and the possibility of loss of primary loved ones.

4.2. Gender Imperatives and the Socialization of the Phobic Personality

If gender identity represents one's internal sense of oneself as male or female, then gender personality differences often represent the outward expression of the differences in gender identity. The literature on sex role socialization provides convincing evidence that males and females are reared differently and that those differences in child-rearing patterns are correlated with differences between men and women in personality characteristics and behavioral styles. Females are encouraged (by parent, peer, or pedagogue) to be more fearful, are less encouraged to display independent behavior, in fact are rewarded for being dependent, passive, and submissive rather than assertive and challenging. Males, by contrast, are encouraged to be independent, assertive, and achievement-oriented (Baumrind, 1980; Birns, 1977; Block, 1973; Eme, 1979; Hoffman, 1972).

A passel of theoretical mechanisms have been postulated to explain how these personality differences are socialized. Three major theories have received the most attention: social learning theory, cognitive-developmental theory, and the psychoanalytic theory of identification. Social learning theory actually embodies two different principles of learning: direct reinforcement of discrete behaviors and modeling and imitation (Mischel, 1966). The cognitive-developmental theory assumes that children move through a series of developmental stages and that what they learn depends on the stage of development they have reached. Identification theory also involves imitation, particularly of the same-sex parent. In addition, however, it assumes that because of the strength of the child's emotional tie with his or her same-sex parent, he or she will possess a much stronger emotional commitment to the relevant gender imperatives of that parent than to behavior that is not directly related to his/her masculinity or femininity. Baumrind (1980) has summarized a view of how females, by means of all three mechanisms but particularly through their close identification with their mothers, develop a deficit in autonomy and a corresponding penchant for unassertiveness and dependency:

> Girls develop their sense of what is right as well as what is feminine within the context of a concrete affective relationship with their mothers, who, because they are of the same gender, experience a strong identification and symbiosis with their daughters which the latter reciprocate (Dinnerstein, 1977; Chodorow, 1978). This diffuse personal identification of daughter with mother encourages the merging of the self with the perspective of the other and a consequent diffidence about asserting one's own perspective which can place women at a competitive disadvantage with men. In view of society's tolerance of female dependence throughout the life cycle, a gender identity defined by merging rather than by autonomy may also keep a daughter tied to the security of her home and the person of her mother, so that she fails to develop her full power and cognitive competence. (p. 643)

Baumrind suggests just how important a role social reinforcement plays in the imposition of the traditional gender ideology on females and males: "Whereas a girl, bribed by promises of love and approval, relinquishes her capacity for independence, a boy, bribed by promises of power and domination, prematurely relinquishes his dependence" (1980, 643). By whatever mechanism of learning, the message remains the same: Females do not need the same degree of independence training as boys, for eventually they will have a man to protect them and make decisions for them.

Females, in addition, are socialized to be more fearful than males, and they are not often rewarded for developing their mastery skills, which are effective antidotes to fear (Hoffman, 1972). Often a female's fearfulness is tied to the presumption of her delicacy. Because others think of her as delicate, she may be sheltered throughout her life from many of the rigors of life. Such overprotectiveness may lead to a pattern of avoidance, which, in turn, initiates a downwardly spiraling process in which she avoids situations that make her anxious. Her avoidance increases her anxiety whenever she faces the same situation again. The fear not only may grow in intensity but also may generalize to similar kinds of situations.

A woman who is presumed to be delicate, who is not rewarded for mastery and not allowed to be assertive, may develop special problems around her feelings of anger, particularly when that anger is directed toward the spouse on whom she depends. The fear of expressing her legitimate anger may lead a woman to avoid any confrontation with her spouse; the angrier she gets, the more anxious she becomes.

Indirect support for this formulation comes from the behavioral treatment of phobias. The guiding principle of the treatment known as prolonged exposure is that the phobic individual must confront the feared stimulus and find ways, during the course of exposure, to master the inevitable accompanying anxiety (Mavissakalian and Barlow, 1981). Exposure, in effect, represents an undoing of the aforementioned pattern of avoidance. Even Freud (1919/1959), in acknowledging the limits of psychoanalysis with phobics, contended that the patient must eventually confront the feared object if there is to be hope of the phobia's resolution.

The clinical literature on phobias also provides indirect support for the connection between female gender socialization and the development of a "phobic personality." The most explicit attempt to make such a connection was provided by Fodor (1974). In her view, a direct connection exists between the typical pattern of sex role socialization of women and their affinity to phobias.

Fodor (1974) endeavors to make her case by showing the correspondence between the characteristics associated with the typical development of women and the characteristics often observed among phobic patients. Thus, the literature on child development, particularly as it pertains to females, and the clinical literature on phobias are cleverly and effectively juxtaposed. From the phobia literature, we learn that phobic individuals typically are dependent and unassertive, possess a behavioral style of avoiding difficult situations, and are fearful of being alone and of functioning autonomously (Andrews, 1966). They have been overprotected or, in Terhune's quaintly macho phrase, "brought up soft" (1949, p. 172). As we can see, these are the same characteristics that women most influenced by the traditional gender ideology are likely to have.

Al-Issa (1980) echoes many of the same themes in his review of the literature on women and phobia. Phobias, according to him, are not related to specific stimulus situations. Phobias are better conceptualized as an avoidant-dependent response pattern that women learn—with the blessings of our culture—as a response to stress.

In their extensive clinical work with agoraphobics, Chambless and Goldstein (1981) most frequently have found the same premorbid personality of excessive dependency, high anxiety, low levels of self-sufficiency, and fear of autonomy. Like Fodor (1974) and Al-Issa (1980), they view agoraphobia as a reaction to stress in which the agoraphobic, partly due to gender-based personality and behavioral deficits, may begin to develop panic attacks in response to a crisis in her relationships. These panic attacks in conjunction with low levels of self-sufficiency increase her dependency on others.

The theme of deficient autonomy also appears in Seidenberg's (1972) case report of a 28-year-old agoraphobic housewife. He gives eloquent testimony to the phenomenological experience of this woman, who, because of the traditional gender imperatives operating in her family, had been denied all opportunity to develop a capacity for making her own choices about her life. What she experienced, in Seidenberg's words, was a "trauma of eventlessness," an awareness that nothing of her own accord had happened in her life and that nothing would happen. He dates her agoraphobic crisis to the moment of her crushing realization that "without some change or correction, her future life would be a continuum of a past which was characterized by submission to authority, absence of choice, and a general exclusion from the significant stimuli of life" (1972, p. 103).

There is suggestive evidence, then, that feminine gender imperatives may incline the susceptible woman toward the development of a "phobic personality," i.e., a set of characteristics that may serve as background mediator variables to the acquisition of a phobia. It is being argued that those imperatives that encourage women to avoid the development of autonomy, mastery, and assertiveness skills are the ones most likely to put her at risk for the development of a phobia.

4.3. Agoraphobia and a Woman's Marital Imperatives

Several investigators have pinpointed the marital relationship as being of special significance in the development of agoraphobia. Most of these reports have centered on the possible etiologic significance of a woman's conflict between her desire to leave an unsatisfactory relationship and her fear of being alone (Chambless and Goldstein, 1981; Fodor, 1974; Symonds, 1971). Fodor (1974) has emphasized that such a conflict might arise after a woman has been married for about 5 years. This may be the time when she feels the most trapped in a marriage, especially if there are young children requiring her care and attention. She cites several case histories to show just how "trapped" or "caged" agoraphobic women often say they feel (Friedman, 1959; Seidenberg, 1972; Sperling, 1974; Wolpe, 1970).

It is not the state of being married *per se* that Fodor believes is conducive to the development of a phobia but rather the persistent and enervating feeling that one is trapped in a debilitating relationship in which one is being dominated. Thus, the basic sex role-related conflict for the "coupled" woman, as Fodor sees it, is a conflict between the desire to be independent and free of domination and the fear of separating from a loved one and functioning on one's own. There is the additional implication in Fodor's perception of this conflict that the woman's fear of leaving also involves guilt over violating the imperatives of her feminine role. She is supposed to remain a wife and a mother. While Fodor's emphasis has been on married women or women involved in love relationships, a similar conflict is often experienced by younger agoraphobic women who feel controlled by their mothers (Chambless, personal communication).

Chambless and Goldstein (1981) see the same critical conflict in their agoraphobic patients. In their clinical experience, the majority of cases of agoraphobia have begun not after some traumatic conditioning event but in a climate of marital conflict. Most panic attacks occurred only after some troubling spousal interaction in which the patient had not asserted herself and had permitted herself to be badly mistreated. The panic attack then becomes the focus of this disorder and a conditioned distraction from the problems of the marriage:

> When this interpersonal conflict situation persists long enough or is worsened by other events such as illness or death of a significant other, the preagoraphobic person is likely to experience sharp outbreaks of very high anxiety-panic attacks.
>   The panic attack is a terrifying experience which, when paired with a low level of self-sufficiency, reinforces the agoraphobic person's belief that someone must take care of her or him. This sets off a self-defeating feedback loop in which panic attacks increase dependency and feelings of helplessness

which in turn increase the likelihood of remaining in the conflict which generates further panic attacks. Instead of focusing on resolving the conflictive situation, these clients begin to avoid situations where they feel panic attacks may occur. These are generally places where they feel trapped in some way. . . . (pp. 54–55)

Symonds (1971) also focuses on the impact of the marital relationship on phobias, but her clinical report represents a significant departure from the other accounts. Her patients did not appear to have the typical premorbid phobic personality. She describes 3 cases—and claims to have seen 20 similar cases in all—of women who appeared to be functioning self-sufficiently before marriage but who, once they were married, experienced a marked erosion of that independence, eventually becoming phobic. In one case, where once the woman could travel alone, drive a car, and hold a job, now all of these capabilities have disappeared: "She became fearful of travelling, especially by plane or subway. She may be afraid to be alone for a moment. She can no longer drive a car herself. . . . She clings to her husband for constant support, apparently changing from a capable, 'strong' person into a classically helpless female" (p. 144). A striking feature about all of Symonds's cases was the quality of their interpersonal relationships with their husbands. They appeared to avoid friction at all costs. They would not argue or fight; instead, they would abandon their point of view at the first sign of their husband's displeasure. "The phobias . . . seemed to immobolize them and prevent them from any act which might be interpreted as aggressive or self-assertive" (p. 145).

Symonds contends that these women all came from families where they were not allowed as children to be dependent. Marriage represented for them their socially sanctioned opportunity to be dependent without self-criticism or self-hate. The trouble comes, according to Symonds, when their dependency needs are frustrated in the marriage. These women develop an intense rage and subsequent panic over the seemingly threatening power of that rage. The panic, in turn, makes them cling all the more to their spouses.

Feminine gender imperatives associated with marriage may be phobia-inducing for reasons other than by shaping a dependent personality, which then makes it difficult for a woman to leave or stay in a bad relationship. The power structure within a traditional marriage also contributes to her difficulties. If a woman has sufficiently absorbed the ideological message of dependency and diminished autonomy by the time of her marriage, she is ready for someone else to take control of her life. She is quite ready to assume a supportive-subordinate role in relation to her husband, who is placed in charge not only of their combined economic fate but also of the most important decisions of their joint life.

The woman exchanges the power to determine her own economic fate for the promise of support from a husband, a bargain that echoes the one she may have made in childhood in which independence was exchanged for the promise of love and approval (Baumrind, 1980). If she is not working outside the home, she confines her attention to their home and their developing children. In these tasks, she does exercise much responsibility and decision-making authority, but she is like the mid-level manager in a huge bureaucracy in which her every decision is subject to veto from above. Longitudinal studies have shown, for example, that wives make many more concessions and changes in their values than do husbands (Barry, 1970).

The economic dependency of women in marriage not only introduces a disturbing inequality in marital interaction but, combined with an already developing dependent personality, may also shape a sense of inner helplessness and a growing fear that she cannot exist on her own resources. When the marriage turns sour, a woman's desire to leave may be accompanied by the contravening fear of being alone. Her own sense of personal inadequacy is reinforced by her very real economic dependency. Having perhaps sacrificed her own ambitions in order to further those of her spouse, she is not prepared to move out into the economic world on her own. Her fear of confronting her husband with her justifiable anger may have as much to do with the realities of her economic dependency as it does with a deeply ingrained personal diffidence.

Thus, women who adopt the traditional feminine role that makes marriage and the family their fundamental project in life (de Beauvoir, 1952) may be unable to leave a bad situation not just because they are emotionally dependent on their men but because they are financially dependent as well. This perilous synergism between what women are encouraged to avoid by custom and what they come to avoid by habit makes it doubly difficult for them to develop the kind of mastery of their situation that will eradicate their fearfulness.

5. Current Limitations of the Gender Ideology Model of Phobias

5.1. Pathways to Phobias

Any theory that links traditional gender socialization to phobias, in order to be complete, must include a theory of how specific phobias are acquired and maintained. The gender ideology model provides an explanation of how a certain group of women may receive encouragement

and sanction from the culture to develop certain personality traits conducive to the acquisition of a phobia, but it lacks a specific theory of
phobia acquisition. The only exception is in the case of agoraphobia,
where we have made an attempt to elucidate a specific mechanism of
phobia acquisition. Part of the difficulty in developing an adequate
etiological model of phobia is that a diverse collection of pathways to
phobia already has been identified. According to various investigators,
phobias may be acquired as a response to trauma, may represent a
symbolic transformation of an internal conflict, may be vicariously acquired, may develop through a process of information transmission, or
may be an irrational elaboration of a rational fear (Rachman, 1977; Salzman, 1978; Wolpe, 1958). Moreover, these pathways may not be mutually exclusive. Early traumas, for example, may take on odd symbolic
meanings for phobic individuals (Cameron, 1963).

   5.1.1. Phobias as Symbolically Transformed Conflict. A major
unresolved issue regarding the nature of phobia concerns whether to
interpret symbolically or directly the meaning of the phobic patient's
anxiety and avoidance behavior. Psychoanalysts have traditionally interpreted the phobic object as bearing a symbolic relationship to an
internal conflict, whereas behaviorists assume that the patient probably
experienced some trauma in relation to the object. Freud (1909/1925)
provided the first exposition of the symbolic view of phobias in his
analysis of Little Hans's horse phobia. Freud interpreted the boy's fear
of horses as a displacement of a threatening sexual wish for his mother
and an aggressive wish for his father's demise. Little Hans's fear of
being bitten by the horse represents a symbolic transformation of his
castration anxiety.

   According to the psychodynamic view, almost any object or situation, real or imagined, may become the source of a phobia. Psycho-
dynamicists therefore view the phobic stimulus as of secondary importance in the development of a phobia. The phobic stimulus serves as a
convenient catalyst for the phobic individual's symbolism through
which a satisfactory solution is created for an internal conflict.

   Children as well as adults constantly use symbols to represent their
experience, but the mind of a child may not be able to distinguish between real danger and cultural metaphor. Cameron (1963) shows with
great lucidity how the potential for acrophobia exists in how we learn
about the pain of real and metaphorical falls:

> While each of us is learning directly, early in childhood, to avoid the pain and
> fright of bad falls, we are also learning indirectly about symbolic and painful
> falls from high places. These the child at first symbolizes and represents to
> himself as being similar or identical in somewhat the manner that adults
> symbolize falling from grace or power in their allegorical speech and writing,

in poetry and in caricature. Humpty Dumpty had a great fall and no one could put him together again. Men tumble from high places—a workman is demoted, the grocer falls from favor, a policemen is broken, an official drops in everyone's estimation. It seems to the child that nobody wants to pick these people up. . . . Grownup talk makes it plain that bad people fall and deserve their fate. (pp. 280–281)

Cameron goes on to describe an actual case of acrophobia involving an unmarried woman who was jilted and left pregnant by her married lover. According to Cameron, the woman's suicidal impulses were managed by a symbolic transformation of the conflict—which involved, among other things, seeing herself as a fallen woman—into a fear of heights. Despite the intuitive appeal of this formulation, there is as yet little verifiable evidence that phobias develop in this manner. Nor are there studies available that provide some guidelines for distinguishing trauma-based from symbol-based phobias.

5.1.2. Phobia as a Trauma-Based Conditioned Fear. In the behavioral view, phobias and fears are assumed to be learned, acquired through a form of conditioning. Neutral stimuli that are associated with stimuli that ordinarily cause pain or fear themselves become the conditioned stimuli of pain or fear. The strength of a phobia is determined by the number of times an individual experiences an association between the experience of pain or fear and the phobic stimuli, as well as by the intensity of the fear or pain experienced in the presence of the phobic stimuli. Once situations and objects become capable of inducing fear, a secondary drive emerges, making an individual afraid of his or her fear. Thus, phobic individuals begin to avoid the feared object because such avoidance reduces the fear (Rachman, 1977). Kraft and Al-Issa (1965) describe the heat phobia of a 24-year-old patient that dates back to the age of 5:

When she was five years old, she witnessed a fire in which the charred bodies of two children were carried out of a burning house. . . . The patient developed phobic symtoms in relation to heat almost immediately after the traumatic incident. She showed great reluctance to put her hands into warm water and washed herself in . . . cold water. As a child, she was terrified of striking a match. . . . She also experienced difficulties in relation to drinking and eating hot foods. . . . She could not touch an electric hotplate either "on" or "off," and could not use a hot iron. (pp. 139–140)

Rachman (1977), a leading behavioral clinician, has recently published a reexamination of conditioning theory in which he points out a number of situations that conditioning theory cannot explain. Although, for example, people are repeatedly exposed to dangerous and stressful situations, they develop relatively few phobias. To give but one example, Rachman cites data on the impact of the German air raids on Great

Britain during World War II. In Bristol, which was subjected to some of the heaviest bombing, only 4% of 8000 school children developed symptoms of anxiety attributable to air raids. There were many short-lived fear reactions, to be sure, but surprisingly few protracted phobic reactions developed.

Another problem with the conditioning theory is that people more often fear objects with which they have had little experience and no pain than they do objects with which they have had a great deal of experience and, perhaps, a lot of pain. Agras *et al.* (1969), for example, found that the prevalence of fear of snakes was 390/1000 population while fear of dentists was only 198/1000. Recent data collected by Murray and Foote (1979) reveal a similar finding. On the basis of a questionnaire, their college students fell into phobic, high-fear, and low-fear groups with respect to snakes. All subjects in the study, it turns out, had very little experience or direct contact with snakes. Only 3 of the 117 subjects reported actually having been bitten by a snake, and all of these subjects were in the low-fear group.

5.1.3. The Vicarious Acquisition of Phobias. People sometimes acquire phobias by observing others becoming fearful in the presence of an object. In the Murray and Foote (1979) study, for example, one subject, recalling the earliest memories of his snake fear, described how his fear developed only after he witnessed grade-school colleagues scream and jump up on chairs at the sight of a harmless snake.

5.1.4. Phobias Transmitted by Means of Information and Instruction. Phobias may sometimes be transmitted by means of information and instruction. Fear is often communicated in our stories, in our myths, and in everyday conversation. It is the rare child who is not exposed by such means to fears of snakes, spiders, and many other common phobic stimuli. Fears acquired in this manner, however, are likely to be mild fears. Yet such a process of fear acquisition would explain why some individuals develop phobias concerning objects that they actually have never encountered (Rachman, 1977).

5.1.5. Phobia as the Irrational Elaboration of a Rational Fear. Finally, it needs to be pointed out that phobic objects differ in the extent of actual danger they do present. Fear of flying, for example, has a much greater basis in reality than does a fear of snakes or spiders. Yet even here, a rational fear can be made irrational by a process of elaboration. The irrational elaboration of fear most often is triggered by a fear of losing control. At the heart of a flying phobia is the phobic's awareness that his or her life is in someone else's hands. Similarly, acrophobics often are people who fear that if they approach a high place they will experience an uncontrollable urge to throw themselves over (Cameron, 1963).

With such a range of possible pathways to phobia—and we probably have not been comprehensive—it is unlikely that any one explanatory model will be able to account for all of the various ways in which phobias are acquired. The gender-imperative model appears to be particularly useful in explaining agoraphobia but less so in explaining the acquisition of other types of phobias. Much more needs to be known with respect to the relationship between a women's greater socialized fearfulness and the development of phobias before the gender-imperative model can contribute more to the understanding of phobias other than agoraphobia.

5.2. Other Limitations

A further difficulty with the gender-imperative model involves the choice of syndromes. The personality characteristics and role-related deficits hypothesized to make women more vulnerable to phobias also appear to make them more vulnerable to depression. This difficulty is compounded by the fact that some depressed women often suffer from phobias, and phobic women are often depressed (Bowen and Kohout, 1979). It has been suggested that the pure depressives may be distinguished from the pure phobics on the basis of the locus-of-control variable. Depressed individuals tend to be internalizers, whereas phobics more often view the responsibility for events as resting with the external environment (Beck and Rush, 1975; Emmelkamp and Cohen-Kettenis, 1975).

Another limitation of the gender-imperative model is the fact that to a greater or lesser degree, we are all exposed to the ideology of gender, yet there are in fact so few phobics. One would expect that there would be even more female phobics considering the strength of the gender influence that is hypothesized. Without more precise information, however, it is assumed that some women are more influenced by and committed to traditional gender imperatives, particularly those involving the cultural sanction of female dependency. These women appear to be at greater risk for phobias.

A final limitation to be mentioned involves the fact that there is a significant minority of men who are also phobic. We have even less information about male phobics and their backgrounds than we do about female phobics. What little information there is tends to suggest that male phobics possess the same kinds of predisposing personality characteristics as female phobics. Male phobics also have been characterized as overprotected, overly dependent, avoidant, and somewhat timid individuals. Such findings, if they hold up, suggest that the most likely role of the gender ideology may be to serve as a mediator variable, one that primes women more than men to develop phobic personality and behavioral predispositions.

6. Summary and Conclusions

The fact that we have presented a psychosocial model of the etiology of phobia does not mean that biological factors should be completely disregarded. There well may be genetic or physiological factors that predispose some individuals to phobias and other anxiety disorders (Carey and Gottesman, 1981; Torgersen, 1979). This may be true whether or not the sexes differ in terms of these phobia-inducing biological processes. To explain the sex difference in rates of phobias, biological hypotheses typically emphasize hormonal differences between men and women and therefore have centered upon a variety of endocrine-based disturbances (Asso and Beech, 1975; Zitrin, Klein, and Woerner, 1978). While data supporting biological suppositions currently are sparse, such explanations cannot be ruled out. Some pharmacotherapists, in fact, are so convinced of the biological origins of phobias—and therefore the necessity of drug therapy to treat them—that they look upon the misguided efforts of psychotherapists who treat phobias with psychotherapy alone as practicing license without a medicine (Klein, 1981; Sheehan, Ballenger, and Jocobsen, 1980; Wender and Klein, 1981).

In the model presented here, it is suggested that traditional gender imperatives may contribute to the increased vulnerability of women to phobias in a number of different ways. First, they may encourage a woman to think of herself as someone less capable for being female. A woman's oft-noted dependency is frequently connected to her diminished self-esteem, and her self-doubt may lead her to avoid competition, eschew assertiveness, and fear success. Not only is the press of reward and punishment designed to move her thinking in this direction but also her failure to develop assertiveness and a capacity for autonomy actually prepares her for the assumption of her adult role (Keller, 1974).

Second, differential gender socialization may produce in women a phobic personality, i.e., one that predisposes them to the development of a phobia. Once they enter a marriage relationship, such women may find their dependency needs frustrated, which inevitably leads to marital conflict. The combination of a phobic predisposition and prolonged interpersonal or marital conflict appears to put women at risk for agoraphobia. Finally, the power imbalance associated with the traditional marriage throws a somewhat different light on the oft-repeated fear of unhappily married agoraphobics of leaving their spouses. The combination of economic and emotional dependency makes it doubly difficult for the nonworking agoraphobic wife to leave, however bad a marriage.

Despite the fact that marriage represents the chief aspiration of the vast majority of women, the state of matrimony appears to be a troubling context for women. As we have seen, the majority of phobics are married women. In addition, married women appear to be at twice the risk for depression as married men (Weissman and Klerman, 1977). Moreover, there are data to suggest that married women have higher rates of mental illness in general than do married men (Gove, 1980; Gove and Tudor, 1973).100 years ago Disraeli quipped, "Every woman should marry—and no man." If these data on sex differences in mental health are accurate, the epigram now might better read: "Every man should marry—and no woman."

Researchers need to take a closer look at marriage and its relationship to phobias and other mental disorders. But this is only one of many areas for which we lack sufficient information. In fact, none of the elements within this theoretical net is firmly rooted in empirical investigation. It will be important to learn the following, for example:

1. Do phobic women differ from nonphobic women in the extent to which they are bound by traditional gender imperatives? If so, are the gender imperatives that augment a woman's dependency—as the clinical data suggest—the key phobia-inducing imperatives?
2. Are the identified background personality factors as strongly linked to phobias as the clinical evidence suggests?
3. Even if these personality factors are linked directly to phobias, do phobic women develop their timid, unassertive ways in a manner quite independent of any connection with traditional gender imperatives, as apparently men do?

Before our theorizing can advance, we need to achieve greater clarification about what phobias really are. Are there really several distinct pathways to phobias, or are they somehow interrelated? If there are several pathways to phobias, for which ones, if any, are traditional gender imperatives relevant?

These are some of the new questions that derive from this model. Regardless of the ultimate merit of the gender ideology model *per se*, one hopes it will sensitize investigators to issues relevant to phobias and other disorders that have not as yet been given their due.

7. References

Agras, W. S., Sylvester, D., and Oliveau, D. The epidemiology of common fears and phobias. *Comprehensive Psychiatry*, 1969, *10*, 151–156.

Al-Issa, I. *The psychopathology of women*. Englewood Cliffs, N.J.: Prentice-Hall, 1980.

Andrews, J. D. W. Psychotherapy of phobias. *Psychological Bulletin*, 1966, *65*, 455–480.

Asso, D., and Beech, H. R. Susceptibility to the acquisition of a conditioned response in relation to the menstrual cycle. *Journal of Psychosomatic Research*, 1975, *19*, 337–344.

Barry, W. A. Marriage research and conflict: An integrative review. *Psychological Bulletin*, 1970, *73*, 31–54.

Baumrind, D. New directions in socialization research. *American Psychologist*, 1980, *35*, 639–652.

de Beauvoir, S. [*The second sex*] (H. M. Parshley, Trans.). New York: Knopf, 1952.

Beck, A. T., and Rush, A. J. A cognitive model of anxiety formation and anxiety resolution. In I. Sarason and C. Spielberger (Eds.), *Stress and anxiety* (Vol. 2). New York: Halsted Press, 1975.

Benedikt, V. Über Platzschwindel. *Allgemeine Wiener Medzinische Zeitung*, 1870, *15*, 488.

Birns, B. The emergence and socialization of sex differences in the earliest years. In S. Chess and A. Thomas (Eds.), *Annual progress in child psychiatry and child development, 1977*. New York: Brunner/Mazel, 1977.

Block, J. H. Conceptions of sex role: Some cross-cultural and longitudinal perspectives. *American Psychologist*, 1973, *28*, 512–526.

Bowen, R. C., and Kohout, J. The relationship between agoraphobia and primary affective disorders. *Canadian Journal of Psychiatry*, 1979, *24*, 317–322.

Bowlby, J. *Separation: Anxiety and anger*. New York: Basic Books, 1973.

Cameron, N. *Personality development and psychopathology*. Boston: Houghton Mifflin, 1963.

Carey, G., and Gottesman, I. I. Twin and family studies of anxiety, phobic, and obsessive disorders. In D. F. Klein and J. Rabkin (Eds.), *Anxiety: New research and changing concepts*. New York: Raven Press, 1981. Pp. 117–136.

Chambless, D. L. Characteristics of agoraphobics. In D. L. Chambless and A. J. Goldstein (Eds.), *Agoraphobia: Multiple perspectives on theory and treatment*. New York: Wiley, 1982.

Chambless, D. L., and Goldstein, A. J. Clinical treatment of agoraphobia. In M. Mavissakalian and D. Barlow (Eds.), *Phobia: Psychological and pharmacological treatment*. New York: Guilford, 1981.

Chodorow, N. *The reproduction of mothering: Psychoanalysis and the sociology of gender*. Berkeley: University of California Press, 1978.

Dinnerstein, D. *The mermaid and the minotaur: Sexual arrangements and human malaise*. New York: Harper & Row, 1977.

Dohrenwend, B., and Dohrenwend, B. Sex differences in psychiatric disorders. *American Journal of Sociology*, 1976, *81*, 1447–1454.

Eme, R. F. Sex differences in childhood psychopathology: A review. *Psychological Bulletin*, 1979, *86*, 574–595.

Emmelkamp, P. M. G., and Cohen-Kettenis, P. T. Relationship of locus of control to phobic anxiety and depression. *Psychological Reports*, 1975, *36*, 390.

Feinman, S. Approval of cross-sex-role behavior. *Psychological Reports*, 1974, *35*, 643–648.

Fodor, I. G. The phobic syndrome in women. In V. Franks and V. Burtle (Eds.), *Women in therapy*. New York: Brunner/Mazel, 1974. Pp. 132–168.

Frances, A., and Dunn, P. The attachment-autonomy conflict in agoraphobia `.iternational Journal of Psychoanalysis*, 1975, *56*, 435–439.

Freud, S. Analysis of a phobia in a 5-year-old boy. In *Collected paper* ͺVol. 3). London: Hogarth Press, 1925. (Originally published, 1909.)

Freud, S. Turnings in the ways of psychoanalytic therapy. In *Collected papers* (Vol. 2). New York: Basic Books, 1959. (Originally published, 1919.)

Freud, S. Inhibitions, symptoms, and anxiety. In *Standard edition of the complete works of Sigmund Freud* (Vol. 20). London: Hogarth Press, 1959.

Friedman, P. The phobias. In S. Arieti (Ed.), *American handbook of psychiatry* (Vol. 1). New York: Basic Books, 1959. Pp. 292–306.

Gardos, G. Is agoraphobia a psychosomatic form of depression? In D. F. Klein and J. Rabkin (Eds.), *Anxiety: New research and changing concepts*. New York: Raven Press, 1981. Pp. 367–380.

Goldstein, A. J., and Chambless, D. L. A reanalysis of agoraphobia. *Behavior Therapy*, 1978, *9*, 47–59.

Gove, W. Mental illness and psychiatric treatment among women. *Psychology of Women Quarterly*, 1980, *4*, 345–362.

Gove, W., and Tudor, J. Adult sex roles and mental illness. *American Journal of Sociology*, 1973, *78*, 812–835.

Hallam, R. S. Agoraphobia: A critical review of the concept. *British Journal of Psychiatry*, 1978, *133*, 314–319.

Hartley, R. E. Sex-role pressures and the socialization of the male child. *Psychological Reports*, 1959, *5*, 457–468.

Hoffman, L. Early childhood experiences and women's achievement motives. *Journal of Social Issues*, 1972, *28*, 129–155.

Horner, M. S. Fail: Bright women. *Psychology Today*, November 1969, *3*, 36–38 ff.

Johnson, M. Mental illness and psychiatric treatment among women: A response. *Psychology of Women Quarterly*, 1980, *4*, 363–371.

Keller, S. The female role: Constants and change. In V. Franks and V. Burtle (Eds.), *Women in therapy*. New York: Brunner/Mazel, 1974. Pp. 411–434.

Kern, S. *Anatomy and destiny: A cultural history of the human body*. New York: Bobbs-Merrill, 1975.

Kessler, S. J., and McKenna, W. *Gender: An ethnomethodological approach*. New York: Wiley, 1978.

Klein, D. F. Anxiety reconceptualized. In D. F. Klein and J. Rabkin (Eds.), *Anxiety: New research and changing concepts*. New York: Raven Press, 1981. Pp. 235–262.

Kohlberg, L. A cognitive-developmental analysis of children's sex role concepts and attitudes. In E. E. Maccoby (Ed.), *The development of sex differences*. Stanford, California: Stanford University Press, 1966. Pp. 82–173.

Kraft, T., and Al-Issa, I. Behavior therapy and the recall of traumatic experience. *Behaviour Research and Therapy*, 1965, *3*, 55–58.

Marks, I. M. *Fears and phobias*. London: Heinemann, 1969.

Marks, I. M. Agoraphobic syndrome (phobic anxiety state). *Archives of General Psychiatry*, 1970, *23*, 538–553.

Marks, I. M., and Herst, E. R. A survey of 1,200 agoraphobics in Britain. *Social Psychiatry*, 1970, *5*, 16–24.

Mathews, A. M., Gelder, M. G., and Johnston, D. W. *Agoraphobia: Nature and treatment*. New York: Guilford, 1981.

Mavissakalian, M., and Barlow, D. *Phobia: Psychological and pharmacological treatment*. New York: Guilford, 1981.

Mischel, W. A social-learning view of sex differences in behavior. In E. E. Maccoby (Ed.), *The development of sex differences*. Stanford, California: Stanford University Press, 1966. Pp. 56–81.

Money, J. Nativism versus culturalism in gender-identity differentiation. In E. Adelson (Ed.), *Sexuality and psychoanalysis*. New York: Brunner/Mazel, 1975.

Money, J., Hampson, J., and Hampson, J. An examination of some basic sexual concepts: The evidence of human hermaphroditism. *Bulletin of the Johns Hopkins Hospital*, 1955, *97*, 301–319.

Murray, E. J., and Foote, F. The origins of fear of snakes. *Behaviour Research and Therapy*, 1979, *17*, 489–493.

Pleck, J. H. The psychology of sex roles: Traditional and new views. In *Women and men:*

Changing roles, relationships and perceptions. Aspen: Institute for Humanistic Studies, 1976.

Rachman, S. The conditioning theory of fear acquisition: A critical examination. *Behaviour Research and Therapy,* 1977, *15,* 375–387.

Rekers, G. A., and Lovaas, O. I. Behavioral treatment of deviant sex role behaviors in a male child. *Journal of Applied Behavioral Analysis,* 1974, *7,* 173–190.

Roth, M. The phobic anxiety depersonalization syndrome. *Proceedings of the Royal Society of Medicine,* 1959, *52,* 587–595.

Rubin, J. Z., Provenzano, F. J., and Luria, Z. The eye of the beholder: Parents views on sex of newborns. *American Journal of Orthopsychiatry,* 1974, *44,* 512–519.

Salzman, L. The psychotherapy of anxiety and phobic states. *Psychiatric Quarterly,* 1978, *50,* 17–21.

Seidenberg, R. The trauma of eventlessness. *Psychoanalytic Review,* 1972, *59,* 95–109.

Sheehan, D. V., Ballenger, J., and Jacobsen, G. Treatment of endogenous anxiety with phobic, hysterical and hypochondriacal symptoms. *Archives of General Psychiatry,* 1980, *37,* 51–59.

Snaith, R. P. A clinical investigation of phobias. *British Journal of Psychiatry,* 1968, *114,* 673–697.

Sperling, M. Somatic symptomatology in phobia: Clinical and theoretical aspects. *Psychoanalytic Forum,* 1974.

Symonds, A. Phobias after marriage: Women's declaration of dependence. *American Journal of Psychoanalysis,* 1971, *31,* 144–152.

Terhune, W. B. The phobic syndrome: A study of eighty-six patients with phobic reactions. *Archives of Neurology and Psychiatry,* 1949, *62,* 162–172.

Thompson, S. K. Gender labels and early sex role development. *Child Development,* 1975, *46,* 339–347.

Thompson, S. K., and Bentler, P. M. The priority of cues in sex discrimination by children and adults. *Developmental Psychology,* 1971, *5,* 181–185.

Torgersen, S. The nature and origins of common phobic fears. *British Journal of Psychiatry,* 1979, *134,* 343–351.

Weissman, M. M., and Klerman, G. L. Sex differences and the epidemiology of depression. *Archives of General Psychiatry,* 1977, *34,* 98–111.

Wender, P. H., and Klein, D. F. The promise of biological psychiatry. *Psychology Today,* February 1981, pp. 25–41.

Westphal, C. Die agoraphobie: Eine neuropathische erscheinung. *Archiv für Psychiatrie und Nervenkrankheiten,* 1971, *3,* 138–161.

Wolfe, B. E. Behavioral treatment of childhood gender disorders: A conceptual and empirical critique. *Behavior Modification,* 1979, *3,* 550–575.

Wolfe, B. E. *The imperatives of gender differentiation: Implications for psychotherapy research.* Talk presented at the annual meeting of the Society for Psychotherapy Research, Monterey, California, June 18, 1980.

Wolowitz, H. M. Hysterical character and feminine identity. In J. M. Bardwick (Ed.), *Readings on the psychology of women.* New York: Harper and Row, 1972. Pp. 307–313.

Wolpe, J. *Psychotherapy by reciprocal inhibition.* Stanford, California: Stanford University Press, 1958.

Wolpe, J. Identifying the antecedents of an agoraphobic reaction: A transcript. *Journal of Behavior Therapy and Experimental Psychiatry,* 1970, *1,* 299–304.

Zitrin, C. M., Klein, D. F., and Woerner, M. G. Behavior therapy, supportive psychotherapy, imipramine and phobias. *Archives of General Psychiatry,* 1978, *35,* 307–316.

4

Hysteria

Barbara Ann Winstead

1. Introduction

In an often-quoted statement, hysteria has been defined as "a picture of women in the words of men, and . . . what the description sounds like is a caricature of femininity" (Chodoff and Lyons, 1958, p. 739). Unfortunately, we cannot begin our exploration of sex roles and hysteria with a more objective definition of hysteria. No such definition exists. At best, we can search for an understanding of the ways in which the diagnosis "hysteria" has been used and of the relationship between its use and the gender of the person to whom the term has been applied.

The use of the term *hysteria* as a diagnosis has had an erratic history in American psychiatry: It was absent in the first edition of the *Diagnostic and Statistical Manual of Mental Disorders* (DSM), published in 1952; present in DSM-II (APA, 1968); and missing again in DSM-III (APA, 1980), which uses instead the diagnoses somatoform disorders, dissociative disorders, and histrionic personality disorder.

We begin with a review of current definitions and diagnostic criteria for hysteria. Following this, the research of epidemiological studies of the four primary types of hysteria [conversion disorder, dissociative disorder, somatization disorder (Briquet's syndrome), and hysterical personality] are presented, and then major explanations for the sex bias in the diagnosis of hysteria are discussed. We conclude with suggestions for improving current diagnostic practices.

Barbara A. Winstead • Department of Psychology, Old Dominion University, Norfolk, Virginia 23508.

2. Diagnosis

Despite its various historical uses, the term *hysteria* retains some communicative power. *The International Classification of Diseases,* 9th revision (ICD-9), published by the World Health Organization, defines hysteria, listed under neurotic disorders, as "a neurotic mental disorder in which motives, of which the patient seems unaware, produce either a restriction of the field of consciousness or disturbances of motor or sensory function which may seem to have psychological advantage or symbolic value" (WHO, 1978, p. 1101). It distinguishes between a *conversion* form of hysteria, which is characterized by a "psychogenic disturbance of function in some part of the body, e.g., paralysis, tremor, blindness, deafness, seizures," and a *dissociative* form, which is characterized by a "narrowing of the field of consciousness which seems to serve an unconscious purpose and is commonly accompanied or followed by a selective amnesia" (p. 1101). In the ICD-9 there is also a category for personality disorder, histrionic type, which is defined as "characterized by shallow, labile affectivity, dependence on others, craving for appreciation and attention, suggestibility and theatricality . . . and often sexual immaturity, e.g., frigidity and over-responsiveness to stimuli" (p. 1108).

In the third edition of the American Psychiatric Association's *Diagnostic and Statistical Manual* (DSM-III) "the concept and the term 'hysteria' have been avoided" (APA, 1980, p. 377). Disorders previously labeled hysterical neurosis have been assigned to two categories, somatoform disorders and dissociative disorders, and hysterical personality has become histrionic personality disorder. The somatoform disorders,* which include somatization disorder, conversion disorder, and psychogenic pain, are defined as disorders characterized by physical symptoms that have no demonstrable organic or physiological cause, i.e., appear to be psychogenic.

Distinctions among the other three subcategories depend on the number and type of symptom. Somatization disorder (referred to by others as Briquet's syndrome) is characterized by recurrent multiple physical symptoms without evidence of organic pathology. Conversion disorder is characterized by a disturbance in physical functioning, without evidence of organic pathology, that cannot be voluntarily corrected and is temporally related to some psychological conflict or need or a promise of relief or support as a consequence of symptom formation. Previous physical illness (often with similar symptoms) or exposure to

---

*Hypochondriasis, which is listed as a somatoform disorder, is not discussed here since it has not been regarded as a form of hysteria.

others with symptoms (real or hysterical) is a predisposing factor. Psychogenic pain disorder is essentially a conversion disorder in which the presenting symptom is pain.

The dissociative disorders* refer to psychogenically caused disruptions in memory (psychogenic amnesia), identity (multiple personality) or motor behavior, which are also accompanied by some disturbance in memory or identity (psychogenic fugue). Psychogenic amnesia and fugue are considered rare but are more prevalent during war or natural disasters. Multiple personality is extremely rare.

Histrionic personality disorder is characterized by dramatic, attention-seeking, and stimulation-seeking behaviors. In interpersonal relationships, individuals with this disorder tend to be seductive and charming at first, and later become dependent and demanding.

Empirical investigations of hysteria have yielded somewhat different diagnostic criteria. This is especially true for Briquet's syndrome. Briquet was the first to use hysteria to refer to a disorder that has many medically unexplained symptoms and is seen predominantly in females (with a female-to-male ratio of approximately 20:1; Woolsey, 1976). Following studies confirming the utility of a diagnostic category for cases with a history of multiple conversion symptoms (e.g., Purtell, Robins, and Cohen, 1951), Perley and Guze (1962) proposed a formal set of diagnostic criteria for hysteria: "a dramatic or complicated medical history beginning before the age of thirty-five; at least 25 symptoms in at least 9 of 10 symptom groups; and no other diagnosis could be made to explain the symptoms" (p. 423). In 1972 Feighner, Robins, Guze, Woodruff, Winokur, and Munoz included this system (lowering required age of onset to 30 years) as the diagnostic criteria for hysteria for use in psychiatric research. In order to avoid the confusion and prejudice associated with hysteria, Guze (1975) proposed referring to this polysymptomatic disorder as Briquet's syndrome. In this chapter, any diagnosis that follows the Perley-Guze or Feighner *et al.* criteria will be called Briquet's syndrome.

Clinicians with a psychoanalytic bent have provided detailed discussion of the hysterical personality (which is similar to DSM-III's histrionic personality disorder). For diagnosing this disorder, personality traits or cognitive style are more important than symptoms (Krohn, 1978). The hysterical style has been described as one characterized by vague, diffuse, emotion-laden impressions and memories. Hysterical

---

*Depersonalization disorder, which is listed as a dissociative disorder, is excluded from discussion here because depersonalization is rarely a patient's primary presenting complaint and appears to be associated more with schizophrenia or affective disorders than with hysteria (Brauer, Harrow, and Tucker, 1970).

individuals use "hunches" to solve problems, are highly suggestible and distractible, are attracted to romance and fantasy, and are, generally, uninterested in objective facts. Although they tend to appear emotional and are often prone to explosive emotional outbursts, their emotions are usually transient and not deeply felt. Emotional outbursts and somatic symptoms, if present, are regarded by these persons as visited upon them (Shapiro, 1965). Easser and Lesser (1965), in an often-quoted list of characteristics of the hysterical personality, include, in addition to some of the characteristics mentioned above, direct and active engagement with the human world; sexualized, romanticized relationships; and fear, anger, or anxiety in response to frustration or sexual excitement. A factor-analytic study of oral, obsessive, and hysterical personalities in female patients confirmed the presence of emotionality, exhibitionism, egocentricity, sexual provocativeness, and dependence as traits defining hysterical personality in women (Lazare, Klerman, and Armor, 1966). Suggestibility and fear of sexuality, however, did not load on the "hysterical" factor, whereas aggression and oral aggression did. The authors suggest that the appearance of these traits among those defining the hysterical personality is consistent with current rethinking of psychoanalytic concepts of hysteria. In recent years much has been written about the pre-oedipal, especially oral, characteristics of patients presenting with hysterical symptomatology or character styles (Easser and Lesser, 1965; Zetzel, 1968; Lazare, 1971). The concept that there are "good" (healthy, Oedipal) and "bad" (pathological, oral) hysterics is now an accepted one in psychoanalytic thought.

Krohn (1978) argues that any list of descriptors of surface behaviors will be inadequate for diagnosing hysteria because an individual with a hysterical personality adopts behaviors and characteristics that will allow him or her to place the self at the mercy of external forces, such as religious or medical authorities. The behaviors or personality traits displayed will depend on the specifics of the roles prescribed in a society or culture that are congruent with the hysteric's need for pseudopassivity.

Hysteria, clearly, is not a unidimensional diagnosis. The clearest lines of demarcation leave us with four separable entities: (1) conversion disorder/reaction/hysteria, (2) dissociative disorder/reaction/hysteria, (3) somatization disorder (Briquet's syndrome), and (4) hysterical personality/character disorder.

3. Incidence of Sex Bias in Diagnosis of Hysteria

To discover whether a sex bias in diagnosing hysteria exists, we turn to the results of epidemiological studies. Good epidemiological studies are rare, and the results of those that have been done may be incomparable because different researchers have often used different diagnostic criteria. A major source of information on the annual incidence of diagnoses of hysteria is the 1975 survey conducted by the National Institutes of Mental Health (NIMH, 1975). The diagnoses reported in the survey were based on DSM-II, which defines hysterical neurosis as "characterized by an involuntary psychogenic loss or disorder of function. Symptoms characteristically begin and end suddenly in emotionally charged situations and are symbolic of the underlying conflicts" (APA, 1968, p. 39). DSM-II encourages clinicians to make a distinction, when diagnosing hysterical neurosis, between conversion type, in which "the special senses or voluntary nervous system are affected" and which is often accompanied by "inappropriate lack of concern or *la belle indifférence*" (pp. 39–40), and dissociative type, in which "alterations may occur in the patient's state of consciousness or in his identity" (p. 40). Statistics in the NIMH survey* are reported for all three diagnoses: hysterical neurosis; hysterical neurosis, conversion type; and hysterical neurosis, dissociative type.

Based on data collected from four types of mental health facilities (private psychiatric hospitals, state and county psychiatric hospitals, inpatient psychiatric units in nonfederal public and private general hospitals, and outpatient services), Table 1 reports estimated annual percentages of admissions or discharges of patients with each of these diagnoses and the relative risk of receiving each of these diagnoses if the patient is female. In the following section, epidemiological information from this survey and other studies will be reviewed, organized according to the four subcategories of hysteria described above.

3.1. Conversion Disorder

A central controversy regarding conversion disorder is whether or not it has decreased in frequency since its supposed heyday in the late 19th and early 20th centuries. Concerning the prevalence of conversion disorder as defined therein, DSM-III states: "Although Conversion Disorder was apparently common several decades ago, it is now rarely

---

*Data were collected for 1 month on admissions to three sets of mental health facilities: 139 of 189 operating private psychiatric hospitals, all state and county psychiatric hospitals (returns from long-term leave were not included as admissions), and all organized outpatient services (both independent clinics and outpatient services affiliated with mental health facilities, but not federally funded community mental health centers). Data were also collected for 1 month on discharges from nonfederal general hospitals (both public and private) with a separate psychiatric inpatient service. Veterans Administration, Public Health Service, military, and territorial hospitals were not included in the survey. Figures from each sample month were inflated to represent 1 year (and figures from private psychiatric hospitals were additionally inflated to represent all hospitals). Calculations in Table 1 are based on the weighted (inflated) figures.

Table 1. Epidemidogical Data from 1975 NIMH Survey[a]

	Private psychiatric hospitals		State and county psychiatric hospitals		Nonfederal public and private general hospitals		Outpatient services		Total	
	Males (Wtd. N = 55,706)	Females (Wtd. N = 74,126)	Males (Wtd. N = 248,937)	Females (Wtd. N = 136,300)	Males (Wtd. N = 211,569)	Females (Wtd. N = 303,968)	Males (Wtd. N = 634,355)	Females (Wtd. N = 771,710)	Males (Wtd. N = 1,150,567)	Females (Wtd. N = 1,286,104)
Estimated annual percentage of admissions or discharges in 1 year with diagnosis of										
Hysterical neurosis	.14%	.39%	0	.06%	.27%	.57%	.22%	.51%	.17%	.47%
Conversion type	.08%	.27%	.01%	.06%	.10%	.60%	.03%	.17%	.04%	.27%
Dissociative type	.11%	.11%	.06%	.14%	.24%	.35%	.09%	.17%	.11%	.21%
Relative risk[b] of receiving diagnosis when patient is female										
Hysterical neurosis	1: 2.81				1: 2.15		1: 2.30		1: 2.64	
Conversion type	1: 3.39		1: 5.49		1: 6.22		1: 6.82		1: 7.08	
Dissociative type	1: 1.04		1: 2.45		1: 1.46		1: 1.95		1: 1.88	

[a] Source: National Institute of Mental Health 1975 Survey.

[b] Determined by calculating the odds ratio: $\dfrac{(N \text{ of females with diagnosis}) \times (N \text{ of males without diagnosis})}{(N \text{ of males with diagnosis}) \times (N \text{ of females without diagnosis})}$.

encountered. Most cases are seen on neurology or orthopedic wards and in military settings, especially in time of warfare" (APA, 1980, p. 245).

Many writers have held that the frequency of conversion disorder has decreased among medically knowledgeable populations (i.e., inhabitants of urban areas of industrialized countries) but has remained relatively steady among the less sophisticated (Abse, 1974; Chodoff, 1974; Chodoff and Lyons, 1958; Temoshok and Attkisson, 1977). Psychoanalytic writers usually append to this observation the view that dramatic conversion symptoms have been replaced by hysterical personality disorders (Blinder, 1966; Laplanche, 1974). Engel (1970) argues that no decline has occurred but that more sophisticated patients present with more sophisticated conversion symptoms. In fact, admissions to a psychiatric clinic showed no decline in diagnoses of hysteria between 1913 to 1920 and 1945 to 1960 (Stephens and Kamp, 1962), and relative frequency of diagnoses of hysteria in a general hospital did not change between 1953 and 1963 (Lewis and Berman, 1965). Others have pointed out that since patients with conversion disorders often present themselves to nonpsychiatrist physicians, especially neurologists, the "decline" in conversion symptoms observed by mental health professionals may be more apparent than real (Chodoff, 1974). An informative footnote to this argument is the reminder that Freud himself was a neurologist before he became a psychoanalyst (Laplanche, 1974).

The figures in Table 1 from the NIMH survey indicate that, while the incidence of hysterical neurosis, conversion type, is low, this disorder has not disappeared. It is also worth noting the relatively low rates of conversion hysteria in psychiatric hospitals and outpatient clinics compared with the rates in psychiatric units of general hospitals. Similarly, the rate of diagnoses of conversion reaction in a university general hospital was .36% (Lewis and Berman, 1965). As suggested above, the fact that conversion patients present with somatic complaints may mean that they are seen by nonpsychiatrist physicians or psychiatrists in medical settings more often than by professionals in mental health settings. In further substantiation of this phenomenon, rates of conversion symptoms among psychiatric consults in medical settings were 13.7% in one study (McKegney, 1967) and 13% in another (Ziegler, Imboden, and Meyer, 1960), and Weinstein, Eck, and Lyerly (1969) estimated the rate of conversion reactions among men admitted to a VA Neuropsychiatric Hospital in Appalachia to be as high as 25 to 30%.

Many studies give sex ratios or figures from which sex ratios for diagnoses of conversion reaction can be calculated. In epidemiological studies of conversion symptoms, the female to male ratios were 1:1 (Woodruff Clayton, and Guze, 1969), 1.5:1 (Carter, 1949), 2:1 (Ljungberg, 1957), 3:1 (McKegney, 1967), 4:1 (Lewis and Berman, 1965; Ziegler et al., 1960), and 5.2:1 (Gatfield and Guze, 1962). The higher figure in the last study probably reflects the exclusion in that sample of patients with pending monetary compensation. Studies collecting data on patients with conversion reactions for nonepidemiological purposes also provide information on sex ratios. Female to male ratios in these studies were 1.4:1 (Benedefeldt, Miller, and Ludwig, 1976), 1.75:1 (Horvath, Friedman, and Meares, 1980), 2.75:1 (Stern, 1977), and 4.56:1 (Merskey and Trimble, 1979). Finally, in a study using the new DSM-III criteria for conversion disorder and psychogenic pain disorder, the sex ratio was 2.5:1 for conversion disorder, 2.48:1 for psychalgia, and 2.13:1 for other neuroses (Bishop and Torch, 1979).

As the last study illustrates, the predominance of females among patients with a diagnosis of conversion reaction must be interpreted in the context of a general predominance of females among patients with other types of psychological disorders (Gove, 1979). Comparisons of sex ratios for conversion hysteria and other diagnoses and the relative risk figures presented in Table 1, however, make it clear that even among psychiatric patients females are relatively more susceptible than males to receiving a diagnosis of conversion reaction. On the other hand, the wide range of sex ratios for this diagnosis suggests that the criteria for diagnosis or the setting in which the diagnosis is made must affect sex differences in its frequency.

It has been argued that males are more likely to display conversion symptoms when there is a clear opportunity for secondary gain, such as monetary compensation, and indeed, *only* when there is secondary gain (Robins, Purtell, and Cohen, 1952). Data collected by Archibald and Tuddenham (1965), however, indicate that conversion symptoms in males can persist even when there is no hope of compensation. Furthermore, males are more likely than females to have employment that offers compensation. Therefore, as noted above, when cases with monetary compensation are excluded from studies of conversion hysteria, there is an increase in the female predominance of conversion symptoms. The reason for using monetary compensation as a criterion of exclusion is that the likelihood of malingering is greater when there is a possibility of monetary gain from the presence of symptoms. It is not clear, however, that VA or employment compensation has an effect that is fundamentally different from the relief from responsibility and household chores that many women experience or anticipate experiencing when they have conversion symptoms.

Although conversion symptoms were originally the hallmark of hysteria, several studies have shown that the relationship between conversion symptoms and hysterical personality is slight: Reported percentages of diagnoses of hysterical personality among conversion patients range from 18 to 25% (Chodoff and Lyons, 1958; Carden and Schramel, 1966; Mersky and Trimble, 1979; Ljungberg, 1957; Slater, 1965). In another study, however, 50% of the males received the diagnosis of both conversion hysteria and hysterical character disorder, and 60% of the females received both diagnoses (Lewis and Berman, 1965). In two studies with low percentages of hysterical personality, the percentages of conversion patients with passive-aggressive or passive-dependent personality were high: 41% (Chodoff and Lyons, 1958) and 58% (Carden and Schramel, 1966). But Merskey and Trimble (1979) report only 19% of their cases as "passive-immature-dependent" personality types. A striking difference between these studies is the high percentage of males in the former studies (88% in Chodoff and Lyons, 1958, and 100% in Carden and Schramel, 1966) and the high percentage of females in the latter (83%). Unfortunately, most studies do not report the association between conversion symptoms and personality type separately for males and females. It seems, however, that there may be a greater association between conversion symptoms and hysterical personality among women than among men and a greater association between conversion symptoms and passive-aggressive or passive-dependent personality among men than among women.

Given the "feminine" quality of the traits used to diagnose hysterical personality and the special qualities of the interaction between a male clinician and a female patient (e.g., patient is more likely to appear sexy or seductive), the question of a possible equivalence between passive-aggressive personality in males and hysterical personality in females arises. The characteristic feature of passive-aggressive personality is indirect resistance to social and occupational demands for adequate performance. As with monetary compensation, social and occupational demands against which resistance might occur are more likely to affect men than women. Furthermore, while an extremely helpless and dependent female may be considered a victim of mental illness, an extremely helpless and dependent male, because his deviation from the prescribed masculine role is more extreme, is more likely to be held responsible for his disorder and regarded as willfully or intentionally maladapted. It appears that, whereas women are perceived as passively succumbing to their hysterical symptoms, men are perceived as consciously deceiving (malingering) or intentionally resistant (passive-aggressive).* Any conclusion about an association between conversion

---

*The augmentation principle in attribution theory provides a possible explanation for this phenomenon. The augmentation principle states that "when there are known constraints, costs, sacrifices, or risks involved in taking an action, the action once taken is attributed more to the actor than it would be otherwise" (Kelley, 1973, p. 114). Out-of-role behavior is an example of potentially risky, costly behavior. Helpless, dependent, sickly behavior is much further from the male stereotype. Thus, for a male such behavior is more likely to be regarded as intentional and as his personal responsibility than it is for a female.

82   Barbara A. Winstead

symptoms and personality type should await further study of this phenomenon among males and females separately.

3.2. Dissociative Disorder

The NIMH survey of mental health facilities also includes statistics
on diagnosis of hysterical neurosis, dissociative type, as defined by
DSM-II. The estimated annual percentages of males and females receiving this diagnosis and the relative risks for females at four types of
mental health facilities are reported in Table 1 (see above for description
of NIMH survey). As with conversion disorder, dissociative disorder is
seen more frequently in the psychiatric units of general hospitals than in
psychiatric hospitals or outpatient clinics. The relative risk for females,
however, is substantially lower than for conversion symptoms.

Epidemiological studies of dissociative reactions are rare. There is
no evidence to suggest that the incidence of this disorder has declined
(Freedman, Kaplan, and Sadock, 1976), except perhaps for multiple personality, which is now considered to be extremely rare (Freedman *et al.*,
1976; APA, 1980). Kirshner (1973) reports a frequency for diagnosis of
"ego-alien behavior accompanied by varying degrees of amnesia" of
1.3% among males admitted to an Air Force medical center. In a study of
pseudoepilepsy (psychogenic seizures) in adolescents (no incidence rate
given), the ratio of females to males among 19 patients was 2.8:1 (Gross,
1979). On the other hand, a study of 22 adults with hysterical seizures
yielded a female to male ratio of 21:1 (Roy, 1979).

"Normal" dissociative states (e.g., trances, possession) may occur
frequently in certain religious or cultural groups either as an individual
or a group phenomenon. These experiences may be restricted to one
sex, for instance, trance among !Kung Bushmen (Lee, cited in Temoshok
and Attkisson, 1977) and possession cults among female Zulus (Bourguignon, 1974), or open to males and females, as is the trance among the
Spiritual Baptists on the island of St. Vincent (Henney, 1980). Examples
in the United States are glossolalia ("speaking in tongues") and snake
handling practiced by certain religious groups.

3.3. Somatization Disorder (Briquet's Syndrome)

As described above, Briquet's syndrome has been defined as a polysymptomatic disorder with early onset occurring predominantly among
women. Purtell, *et al.* (1951) confirmed this view of hysteria by comparing patients with hysteria, diagnosed "when there were many features
characteristic of the disease and when no other diagnosis, medical, neurological, or psychiatric, were present or would explain symptoms at the

time of the examination" (p. 902), with two control groups (healthy and chronically medically ill). All of the patients, in a general hospital sample, receiving a diagnosis of hysteria were female. A few men were diagnosed "compensation neurosis." The female-to-male ratio was 18.2:1. For purposes of comparison, men in service and VA hospitals with a diagnosis of hysteria were included in the study. The women with hysteria had an early age of onset (11 to 33 years) and had significantly more symptoms and surgical procedures than the healthy controls. Their presentations of symptoms distinguished them from the women with chronic medical illness by being vague, colorful, and dramatic. Compared with female hysterics, the male hysterics reported fewer somatic complaints, reported them in less dramatic ways, had no history of excessive surgery, and had, in 100% of the cases, an opportunity for compensation. Purtell et al. (1951) concluded that hysteria, defined as a disorder with early onset and a complicated history of numerous nonorganic physical symptoms presented in an exaggerated, dramatic fashion, is very rare, if not absent, in males.

Epidemiological studies of Briquet's syndrome in females suggest that its prevalence is 1 to 2% among normal postpartum women (1 certain and 1 possible case among 100 women [Farley, Woodruff, and Guze, 1968]) and 2% among women with medical illness (1 case among 50 patients [Woodruff, 1968]). In a series of 100 random admissions to a psychiatric clinic, Woodruff et al. (1969) found 8 cases of definite Briquet's syndrome (8%), all female. In a sample of female felons, the prevalence was as high as 41% (Cloninger and Guze, 1970).

A problem in interpreting the meaning of the predominance of females receiving a diagnosis of Briquet's syndrome is the definition of the disorder. To receive the diagnosis a patient must have symptoms in 9 of 10 symptom groups. One of these groups includes only disorders of menstruation. Therefore, to receive the diagnosis, a male would have to report symptoms in all of the 9 remaining groups. Another symptom group includes sexual indifference, frigidity, dyspareunia, other sexual difficulties, and vomiting or hypermesis gravidarum during pregnancy. Although males could report sexual indifference or other sexual difficulties, the symptoms listed are more relevant for diagnosing female sexual problems; impotence and premature ejaculation, for example, are not listed. It could be argued that the view of hysteria as a gynecological disorder has returned, even though it is given a new name.

Even so, the possibility of Briquet's syndrome occurring in males is confirmed by two case reports describing men who met all the diagnostic criteria and whose illnesses were not contingent on financial gain (Kaminsky and Slavney, 1976; Rounsaville, Harding, and Weissman, 1979). In a study of 50 men (alternate admissions to the psychiatric unit of a VA hospital), diagnostic interviews yielded no cases of Briquet's syndrome if the criteria were strictly applied (Kroll, Chamberlain, and Halpern, 1979). If the criteria were changed from 9 of 10 to 8 of 9 symptoms groups (excluding the group of menstrual disorders), 2 patients (4%) met the criteria. The authors argue, however, that these patients should be considered false positives because they "did not present with dramatic, complicated medical histories or multiple surgical interventions, and both had alternative clinical diagnoses which were more relevant to their psychiatric problems" (Kroll *et al.*, 1979, p. 173). One patient had a history of extensive drug usage; the other had possible borderline mental retardation and many depressive symptoms.

Interestingly, in a study conducted in a Greek hospital and unrelated to the issue of diagnosis (Rinieris, Stefanis, Lykouras, and Varsou, 1978), the subjects were diagnosed using the Feighner *et al.* (1972) criteria, and the female-to-male ratio was 3:1. This sex ratio is substantially lower than anything found in previous studies or predicted by the group responsible for most of the work on Briquet's syndrome.

For somatization disorder (see section 2 for differences between Briquet's syndrome and somatization disorder), DSM-III estimates a 1% prevalence rate among females. Given the less rigid criteria of DSM-III and the discrepant sex ratio in the Rinieris *et al.* (1978) study, the DSM-III statement that "this disorder is rarely diagnosed in males" (APA, 1980, p. 242) seems premature. The prevalence of Briquet's syndrome and somatization disorder among males needs further examination.

3.4. Hysterical Personality

The variety of definitions of hysterical personality make it the most difficult of the hysterias to study epidemiologically. Lindberg and Lindegard (1963) report a female-to-male ratio in a Swedish hospital sample of 3:2. For both males and females the frequency of diagnosis of hysterical personality was greater in younger patients. In a study of male admissions to a large federal psychiatric institution that includes a community mental health center, Luisida, Peele, and Pittard (1974) found an incidence of hysterical personality, explicitly including all characteristics in the DSM-II definition, of one per 1000. Consistent with the Lindberg and Lindegard (1963) study, men with hysterical personality (with one exception) were first treated between the ages of 15 and 25.

Although the diagnosis of the personality disorder (in all classification systems) relies mostly on the presence of certain personality characteristics, whereas the diagnosis of Briquet's syndrome relies on somatic complaints, Kimble, Williams, and Agras (1975) have demonstrated close agreement between the diagnoses of these two disorders. In a sample of 10 females with hysterical personality (diagnosed according to DSM-II) and 20 females with diagnoses of other neuroses or psychoses, they found that 9 of the 10 DSM-II hysterics met the Perley-Guze criteria for Briquet's syndrome. The other 2 patients who met the Perley-Guze criteria for Briquet's syndrome were diagnosed hysteria, conversion type, and schizophrenia rather than hysterical personality.

4. Explanations of Sex Bias in Diagnosis of Hysteria

The undeniable predominance of females among patients receiving a diagnosis of hysteria, of no matter which variety, can mean two things: (1) Females develop hysteria more often than males or (2) the definitions and connotations of the term *hysteria* cause it to be associated more often with females than with males. Those who have adopted the former view have proposed various explanations for this phenomenon. These can be roughly categorized as psychoanalytic, sociocultural, interpersonal, and biological. The following section will review these four perspectives on hysteria, as well as the ways in which definitions and perceptions of hysteria and of males and females contribute to the association between hysteria and being female.

4.1. Psychoanalytic Explanations

Psychoanalytic theory views hysteria as a neurotic disorder caused by fixation at and regression to the phallic stage of psychosexual development and, thus, failure to accomplish the major developmental task of this stage, i.e., the resolution of the oedipal complex. The oedipal complex involves a "genitalized" attachment to the parent of the opposite sex and feelings of jealousy and hostility toward the parent of the same sex. Male and female passages through this stage of development are necessarily different. A boy resolves the Oedipus complex by recognizing that his father is a powerful rival for his mother's love, by fearing retaliation from his father (castration fear), and, finally, by repressing his "sexual" desires for his mother and identifying with his father. For a girl the motive for overcoming her attachment to her father and identifying with her mother cannot be castration fear and is assumed to be loss of her mother's love, a weaker motive. This results in a weaker resolution of the Oedipus complex for females and weaker identification with the same-sex parent, which is the source of the superego. Since failures in development at the oedipal period are, according to psychoanalytic theory, the cause of hysteria, the girl is naturally more prone than the boy to developing hysteria.

Zetzel (1968) further suggests that any ambivalent feelings that the girl may have toward her mother before the oedipal phase could make it difficult for her to maintain a good relationship with her mother when they become rivals. A failure in the mother–daughter relationship then makes it difficult for the daughter to internalize a positive concept of her femaleness when she identifies with her mother, leading to the dependency and the feelings of powerlessness and weakness that characterize hysteria. Males are more likely to deal with dependency needs by reacting against them and thus adopting obsessional rather than hysterical defenses.

Lewis (1978, 1979) focused on sex differences in the superego and their relation to psychiatric illness. Sex differences in resolution of the Oedipus complex should result in sex differences in the superego. Lewis argues that shame and guilt are both aspects of superego functioning and that shame is more common in women and is associated with depression and hysteria, whereas guilt is more common in men and is associated with obsessions, compulsions, and schizophrenia. Shame occurs when a person experiences failure, rejection, feelings of inferiority, and fear of "loss of love"; guilt occurs when a person is aggressive and feels responsible for "bad" actions. In shame the person feels helpless, passive, and unhappy with him/herself; in guilt a person feels responsible but focuses more on the transgression than on the self.

According to Lewis (1979), women are more prone to shame and men to guilt for two reasons: (1) Women maintain anaclitic (loving) identifications and thus continue to fear "loss of love," whereas men must renounce these feminine identifications, and (2) cultural factors make women economically and socially inferior to men (evoking feelings of shame), while men are encouraged to be competitive and aggressive (evoking feelings of guilt). Lewis (1979) cites empirical research from two dissertations (Siebert, 1965; Binder, 1970) that demonstrates the expected sex differences in guilt and shame. The phenomenon of shame is similar in important respects to the phenomenon of hysteria. Dependency, feelings of inferiority and helplessness, fears of "loss of love," and concern about impressions made on others characterize both conditions.

4.2. Interpersonal Explanations

Celani (1976), presenting an interpersonal approach to hysteria, argues that "the communication and the impact on the receiver is the primary goal" (p. 1415) of the individual. For the hysteric, the message conveyed is one of frailty, helplessness, and weakness, which is intended to elicit interest and attention from others and to inhibit their aggression (Celani, 1976). This role is, in our culture, played more often by women, who direct their communication toward men.

Szasz (1961) agrees that the purpose of hysteria is to induce others to take care of the "patient" and absolve him or her of responsibility. He cites the role of the child in relation to parents as the prototype for the disorder. Others have also interpreted hysterical symptoms as the language of the powerless and helpless (Halleck, 1967; Hollender, 1972). Women are in many ways (e.g., physically, politically, economically) less powerful than men, so these complementary roles (i.e., female hysteric soliciting help from male through her self-presentation) are congruent with normal social roles. As Celani (1976) points out, Luisida *et al.* (1974) found that the most common symptom among the male hysterics whom they studied was suicidal thoughts. It could be that, in their effort to obtain the concern, attention, and help of others, males feel that they must make "louder," more serious gestures of need.

It is notable that both conversion and dissociative symptoms are far more common among men when they are soldiers in combat than in other settings. Robins *et al.* (1952) argued that males present with conversion symptoms *only* when there is an opportunity for secondary gain. Primary gain is the avoidance of anxiety, whereas secondary gain is some external reward (e.g., monetary compensation or time off from work). In a study of 12 cases of conversion reaction among enlisted men in Vietnam, Carden and Schramel (1966) found that these men did not experience alleviation of anxiety until they had been removed from combat. The authors suggest that the apparent secondary gain (i.e., removal from combat) should be considered primary gain in these cases. In any case, the symptoms are clearly (even if unconsciously) aimed at environmental manipulation. The more obvious factor contributing to the increase in the frequency of hysterical symptoms among men in combat is the presence of life-threatening circumstances.

A similarity between women and enlisted men is relative powerlessness and inability (actual or perceived) to do the things that they might find most life-enhancing. The military is one context in which nearly all males are in positions that are subordinate to some superior officer and are frequently without the power of self-direction, whereas in civilian life in Western industrialized societies men have at least the capacity to change their life circumstances, even when they cannot substantially improve them. Women in these societies generally have fewer opportunities. This analysis leads to the prediction that enlisted men in noncombat situations should have higher rates of conversion and dissociative symptoms than nonenlisted men and that, when women acquire greater social and economic power, they will have less need for the "language" of hysteria. Viewed from an interpersonal perspective, the question of primary versus secondary gain is moot. The important questions become: How and what do males and females communicate? Under what circumstances do they choose somatic complaints or dissociative experiences to communicate? Why do they make this choice?

4.3. Sociocultural Explanations

The roles that women are trained to fill and the models they imitate may contribute to their greater tendency to suffer from hysteria. Excluding diagnoses based on clinical symptoms associated with severe hysterical disorders, Lerner (1974) writes that "the diagnostic indicators of hysteria are very much in keeping with the media presentation of the female sex" (p. 159). Women are prepared, she continues, to make good wives and mothers by being taught to be attractive to men, to please and manipulate others, and to be intellectually dependent and docile. Men, on the other hand, are encouraged to be practical, efficient, logical, intellectually aggressive, and self-reliant. Lerner concludes that hysterical personality may reflect the effects of role pressures on women rather than the effects of psychopathology and that, if the diagnosis is defined as a list of personality traits, "then we may do well to discard the diagnostic category of hysterical personality . . . and simply speak of a feminine personality style that does not purport to be more than a description of certain female characteristics in the eyes of male diagnosticians" (p. 162). Wolowitz (1970) makes a very similar argument in terms of the socializing influences that press women to become dependent, emotionally responsive, and eager to please others rather than autonomous and masterful. His belief, however, in "the developmental appropriateness of an hysterical character in a nonpathological form in American women" (p. 307) suggests a rather different evaluation of the situation.

Many investigators have observed that women report more symptoms than men do (Guze, Woodruff, and Clayton, 1972; Phillips and Segal, 1969). In one study, when rates of reporting "medical" and "psychiatric" symptoms were compared, the only significant sex difference was for "medical" symptoms (Matarazzo, Matarazzo, and Saslow, 1961). Women also use health care services at a higher rate than men do. Mechanic (1978) has cogently discussed the enormous difficulties involved, when interpreting such sex differences, in distinguishing between subjects' perceptions and their responses to investigators, between illness and willingness to engage in illness behavior, and between subjective symptoms and actual disability. Possible explanations for the observed sex differences include women's greater interest in and knowledge about health, greater social tolerance for female complaints and lack of stoicism, enhanced perception of symptoms due to greater freedom to engage in sickness behavior (e.g., less social cost for staying at home in bed, more flexibility for scheduling visits to the doctor), more routine contact with physicians (for gynecological and obstetric examinations and for children's pediatric care), and fewer role obligations and thus greater freedom to adopt the sick role (Mechanic, 1978). Any of these factors could also influence the greater frequency of hysteria among women, since diagnosis of this disorder generally depends on the presence of somatic complaints and help-seeking behaviors.

4.4. Biological Explanations

More than with the other approaches to explaining sex differences in hysteria, the definition of hysteria is an important factor in interpreting the results of biological studies of hysteria. Most of these studies are of conversion or dissociative disorders. Recently a biological explanation of Briquet's syndrome has also been proposed (Cloninger, 1978). The major explanatory concepts in all cases have been attention, hemispheric asymmetry, and genetics.

4.4.1. Attention. Eysenck (1963) was among the first to specify biological mechanisms of attention as an explanation of hysteria. He viewed hysteria as a condition composed of high degrees of neuroticism and extraversion. According to Eysenck, neuroticism is accompanied by lability of the autonomic nervous system (ANS), and extraversion by central nervous system (CNS) inhibition. He characterized hysterics as individuals who have a constant need for external stimulation and who are highly distractible because they habituate rapidly to stimuli due to rapid buildup, relatively high levels, and slow dissipation of cortical inhibition.

Similarly, Ludwig (1972) considers attentional dysfunction as a central feature of hysteria. Like Eysenck, he argues that this dysfunction is a result of cortical inhibition of afferent stimulation. Reductions in awareness of bodily functions account for conversion symptoms, and not attending to symptoms accounts for *la belle indifférence* that accompanies these hysterical symptoms. The results of psychophysiological research cited by Ludwig (1972), however, are equivocal concerning the hysteric's tendency to suppress cortical or other physiological responses to stimulation. On the other hand, Bendefeldt *et al.* (1976), using a battery of psychological tests of attention and recent memory, confirmed Ludwig's predictions by finding greater impairment in vigilance-attention and recent memory, greater suggestibility, and greater field dependence in patients with conversion reactions than in a control group of nonpsychotic psychiatric patients.

Testing the hypothesis that the predisposing attentional deficit in hysteria is a failure in selective *inattention* (rather than impairment of attention), Horvath *et al.* (1980) demonstrated that patients who had recovered from conversion symptoms were significantly less likely than patients with free-floating anxiety to habituate (measured by galvanic skin response) to auditory tones. This demonstration involves the autonomic nervous system, not the central nervous system, but the indication of poor habituation is clearly opposed to Eysenck's notion of too rapid habituation.

The theorizing about an attentional deficit in hysteria is confusing because proponents of this view fail to focus on any single conception of attention and because research findings are contradictory and incomparable (e.g., ANS vs. CNS). In trying to make sense of these ideas and data, the meaning and significance of the stimulus that is being attended or ignored must not be overlooked. Eysenck's notion of one style of responding to stimulation (cortical inhibition) may be too global. Emotionally threatening stimuli should be more likely to be excluded from awareness than neutral stimuli (Ludwig, 1972), and hyperattention to trivial stimuli (as in Horvath *et al.*, 1980) may complement this effort. Differences between symptom-free and symptom-present conditions must also be taken into account. Although the assumption that there is a cognitive style with neurophysiological bases shared by individuals who have hysteria is central to this area of research, it may be that in symptom-free states the individual is constantly alert to potential danger, whereas with the development of symptoms, the potential danger is forestalled and inattention to threatening stimuli sets in.

None of these writers has speculated on the relationship between a possible attentional dysfunction and gender. Some evidence suggests that females are more sensitive to tactile, taste, and olfactory stimulation than males (Maccoby and Jacklin, 1974). Greater sensitivity could reasonably lead to different styles of coping with sensory input, possibly including greater preference among females for a style that incorporates massive efforts to exclude or dampen stimulation plus failure to do so for certain stimuli or at certain times. Clarification of the theoretical propositions linking attention to hysteria and empirical studies of these propositions and investigation of sex differences in relevant aspects of attention are needed.

4.4.2. Hemispheric Asymmetry.   Research on hemispheric asymmetry has demonstrated that the left hemisphere tends to be responsible for linguistic functions and logical, sequential operations, while the right hemisphere tends to be responsible for visuospatial functions, holistic operations, and emotion (Gainotti, 1972; Kimura, 1973; Levy, 1972). The overlap between characteristics of hysteria and functions of the right hemisphere is striking and has led several investigators to explore the connection between hemispheric asymmetry and hysteria.

As early as 1859, Briquet noted that unilateral hysterical paralysis occurred more often on the left side of the body (which, because of the crossing of the sensorimotor pathway, is connected to the right hemisphere). In five studies reviewed by Bishop, Mobley, and Farr (1978), 77% of 220 patients had left-sided symptoms. Other studies, however, have found a majority of patients with symptoms on the right side (61% of 31 cases reported by Stefansson, Messina, and Meyerowitz, 1976, and 54% of 277 cases reported by Kraepelin, cited in Bishop *et al.*, 1978) or on the dominant side, usually the right (88% of 33 cases reported by Fallik and Sigal, cited in Bishop *et al.*, 1978). Fallik and Sigal argue that choice of side for conversion symptoms is influenced by previous physical injury and thus is more likely to be on the dominant side of the body, where most physical injuries occur. Lateralization may also interact with gender. In some studies, when males are examined separately or when the sample studied is predominantly male, there is no significant difference in the numbers of left-sided and right-sided conversion symptoms, although Stern (1977) found a disproportionate number of left-sided symptoms in both males and females. In an effort to clarify the issue, Bishop *et al.*, (1978) examined an equal number of male and female patients with unilateral conversion symptoms. They found no significant lateralization of symptoms in either sex. Right hemisphere mediation of conversion symptoms clearly has not been proven.

An intriguing finding that lends support to the possibility of right hemisphere involvement in some cases of hysteria is the more frequent occurrence of indifference to or denial of symptoms in patients with right hemisphere damage than in patients with left hemisphere damage (Gainotti, 1972; Geschwind, 1975). The similarity of this response to *la belle indifférence* of some hysterical patients suggests the presence of right hemisphere dysfunction in hysteria.

Investigators of sex differences in hemispheric asymmetry have not come to consistent conclusions. Kimura (1973) found greater right-hemispheric specialization in males, but no correspondingly greater left-hemispheric specialization in females. Levy (1972) agrees that females have less hemispheric specialization than males. (On the other hand, Buffrey and Gray, 1972, argue that left-hemispheric specialization occurs earlier in females and probably persists into adulthood.) Another hypothesis is that hemispheric asymmetry is affected more by rate of maturation than by gender *per se*. Both male and female late maturers are better at spatial tasks, leading Waber (1977) to argue that late maturers develop greater hemispheric specialization, which improves performance on spatial tasks due to less interference from linguistic functions.

Since females mature earlier than males, they will, on the average, have less hemispheric specialization.

Applying these considerations to the sex differences in hysteria, one might hypothesize that less specialization is associated with the global, diffuse, and undifferentiated cognitive style that is characteristic of hysteria. Sex differences in hemispheric specialization would lead to sex differences in cognitive style and a greater prevalence of hysterical style among females, assuming that individuals develop symptomatology that is consistent with their cognitive style.

To make matters more complex, there is also a theory suggesting that hysteria results from a dysfunction in the dominant (usually left) hemisphere. Flor-Henry (1978) argues that there is "an impairment of understanding . . . of endogenous visceral signals and somatic sensory-motor integration in hysteria" (p. 159). In support of his theory he cites Ljungberg's (1957) finding of a significant decrement in verbal IQ (a dominant hemisphere function) in women with conversion symptoms. While drawing no connection between the two, Flor-Henry (1978) also suggests that "the prevalence of right hemisphere dominance is greater than has been assumed, *particularly in women*" (p. 155, emphasis added). To bring Flor-Henry's theory into line with other ideas about the connection between hemispheric asymmetry and hysteria, one might speculate that hysteria occurs when the dominant hemisphere is the *right*, rather than the left, and some dysfunction is present.

4.4.3. Genetics. Evidence for the heritability of conversion or dissociative disorders is sparse. The most that Rosenthal (1971) could state, after reviewing studies of the genetics of hysteria, was that "overall evidence points to the likelihood that heredity plays a role in the development of psychoneurotic symptoms" (p. 144). Family studies of Briquet's syndrome, however, suggest that there is a genetic predisposition for the disorder. There is an increased prevalence among first-degree female relatives of female hysterics: 14 to 26% as compared to 1 to 2% in the general population (Arkonac and Guze, 1963; Cloninger, Reich, and Guze, 1975; Guze, 1967; Woerner and Guze, 1968). Unfortunately, twin and adoptee studies of Briquet's syndrome are lacking, and the possibility that family environment rather than genetic factors is responsible for similarities among family members cannot be ruled out.

4.5. Hysteria and Sociopathy

Several investigators of hysteria have concluded that Briquet's syndrome is essentially the female version of a disorder that in males manifests itself as antisocial personality disorder, also referred to as sociopathy or psychopathy. As noted by Cloninger (1978), "the personality traits associated with Briquet's disorder and sociopathy largely overlap, differing primarily in their sex-related emphasis" (p. 194). Studies of female criminals have found a higher than expected proportion of women with hysteria or hysterical symptoms (Cloninger and Guze, 1970; Gibbens, 1969; Halleck, 1967). On the other hand, males with a diagnosis of hysteria have been found to have a higher than expected prevalence of criminal activity and drug or alcohol abuse (Luisida et al., 1974; Robins et al. 1952), and antisocial males have more somatic complaints than other males (Robins, 1966). In other words, while females are far more likely than males to receive a diagnosis of Briquet's syndrome and males are far more likely than females to receive a diagnosis of antisocial personality, there appears to be a high rate of co-occurrence of these disorders (or symptoms suggestive of these disorders), especially among female criminals and male hysterics.

The strongest support for the argument of a single disorder with different behavioral manifestations for males and females comes from family studies. Results of these have demonstrated that first-degree male relatives of females with Briquet's syndrome are more likely than other males to show signs of antisocial personality and alcoholism, and first-degree female relatives of males with antisocial personality are more likely than other women to have Briquet's syndrome (same-sex relatives have an even higher incidence of the proband's diagnosis) (Arkonac and Guze, 1963; Cloninger, 1978; Cloninger and Guze, 1970; Crowe, 1978; Woerner and Guze, 1968). There is also evidence that antisocial males and females with Briquet's syndrome mate assortatively (Guze, 1975; Woerner and Guze, 1968), but the reduction in calculated heritability necessitated by assortative mating does not completely account for the genetic factor in Briquet's syndrome and antisocial personality disorder. As noted above, because these are family studies, the possibility of environmental rather than genetic determinants of the higher incidence of these disorders cannot be ruled out.

Cloninger (1978) also points out that both hysterics and sociopaths tend to come from emotionally deprived and disharmonious low socioeconomic backgrounds. He argues that these environmental factors, a genetically determined physiological mechanism (specifically, low cortical activity and strong cortical inhibitory reactions), and drugs or trauma that affect frontal lobe activity all predispose an individual to impulsivity and stimulation-seeking or, when sufficient stimulation is not available, to distractibility and somatic anxiety. The different manifestations of the common underlying behavioral tendencies are the result of androgenization and the strength of the neurophysiological predisposition. Androgenization causes males to engage in more aggressive efforts at stimulation-seeking. Because aggression is biologically underdetermined and socially disapproved in females, cortical underarousal in females is more likely to lead to high somatic anxiety and a consequent tendency to experience somatic symptoms. Finally, whether male or female, individuals with more severely abnormal CNS functioning are likely to be antisocial and to engage in more extreme stimulation-seeking activities (Cloninger, 1978).

4.6. Hysteria in the Eye of the Beholder

Finally, the definition and connotations of the term *hysteria* may cause it to be associated more often with females than with males. The fact that most psychologists and psychiatrists, both those who create diagnostic criteria and those who use them, are male has also influenced the diagnosis of hysteria. Chodoff and Lyons (1958) concluded that most definitions of hysteria are "a picture of women in the words of men, and . . . what the description sounds like is a caricature of femininity" (p. 739).

The "maleness" of the clinician also contributes to the quality of the interaction between diagnostician and patient. Significantly, a central characteristic of hysterical personality is sexually provocative or seductive behavior. After reviewing criteria for diagnosing hysteria, Berger (1971) concluded that the definition that best reflects these criteria "would be: behavior or symptoms which arouse unconscious sexual feelings *in the observer*" (p. 283, emphasis in original). This is obviously much more likely to occur in heterosexual dyads. Since most diagnosticians are male, hysteria will necessarily be observed more often in females.

Support for the possibility that hysteria is in the eye of the beholder comes from the research conducted by Warner (1978, 1979). He presented a hypothetical clinical profile to 175 mental health professionals. "The profile referred to minor suicide attempts, failure to enjoy sexual relations, to sustain close relationships, or to feel affection for others. It detailed an immature, narcissistic, and self-centered disposition with lack of remorse for an illegal act and an excitable, self-dramatizing and flirtatious presentation. The sex of the patient so described was randomly designated as either male or female and subjects were given a choice of eight conditions, including anti-social and hysterical personality disorders, from which to make a diagnosis" (1978, p. 942). When the patient was female, the diagnoses were 76% hysterical personality disorder and 22% antisocial personality disorder; when the patient was male, the diagnoses were 49% hysterical personality disorder and 41% antisocial personality disorder. The degree of sex bias was statistically significant and present among all categories of mental health professionals, both male and female. The author concludes that "antisocial and hysterical personality disorders are essentially sex-typed forms of a single condition" (p. 839). Although male and female clinicians were equally likely to make sex-biased diagnoses in this study, they were given a written description of the patient, and, thus, impressions that occur in face-to-face interaction with a patient (e.g., seductiveness) did not contribute to diagnoses.

5. Conclusion

Hysteria has many meanings and diagnostic criteria, but its association with the female gender continues to be a reality. When the signs or symptoms on which diagnosis is based are necessarily more likely to be observed in women (e.g., sexy, seductive behavior in the patient when the doctor is male) or are restricted to women (e.g., problems related to menstruation or pregnancy), then women are more likely than men to recieve a diagnosis of hysteria merely because of the definition of the disorder. This is clearly an issue with the diagnoses of Briquet's syndrome and hysterical personality. Problems with definitions are not, however, restricted to these two hysterias. When unexplained medical symptoms provide a patient with the opportunity to receive monetary compensation, diagnosticians are likely to suspect malingering. Since detecting when the symptoms are consciously adopted (malingering) and when unconsciously (hysteria) is extremely difficult, some investigators have excluded cases from their studies of hysteria where monetary compensation is possible. In a society where a greater proportion of men than women work in jobs that offer monetary compensation for disability, this method of diagnosing hysteria (or malingering) leads, by definition of the disorder, to a predominance of women receiving the diagnosis. Cases of malingering, whenever they can be verified, should be excluded, but until it can be demonstrated that the possibility of monetary compensation *per se* alters the essential nature of the disorder, it should not be used as a criterion of exclusion.

In order for the question to be one of psychological interest, diagnostic criteria should permit men an opportunity to receive the diagnosis. When this is done, as is the case with dissociative disorder and frequently with conversion disorder, the predominance of women is less dramatic, although still present. Furthermore, for these disorders the influence of situational factors (e.g., military service and/or combat) gives us clues to the psychological functions of the symptoms, and these clues lead to hypotheses about the greater frequency of the disorders among women (e.g., women's relative lack of power of self-determination).

If women do, as the data suggest, complain more of and more often seek help for unexplainable physical symptoms, then this deserves examination. But as Mechanic (1978) has pointed out, the possible contributing factors to such a phenomenon are many and include variables in both the patient and the diagnostician. Psychosocial and biological explanations for individual differences in the experience and reporting of bodily symptoms and the use of such symptoms to alter life circumstances have been offered. Connections between these individual differences and gender have been explored.

Our efforts to understand hysteria, however, may leave us with perceptions and affects similar to those experienced by the hysteric him/herself: We have vague, global impressions, but few hard facts; we are prone to respond angrily to the lack of substantive research and the apparent biases in diagnosing hysteria; we have fantasies of a more ideal diagnostic system. But like the hysteric, we need to be conscious of the history of hysteria. We should take account of the ways in which it has matured from a gynecological disorder, in which a neglected uterus roamed about the body, to detailed descriptions of mental disorders that can apply (in some cases) to either males or females, and to more sophisticated theories that consider possible psychodynamic, social, and biological causes of hysteria. That there are still biases in diagnosing hysteria is true (Warner, 1978, 1979). It is also clear that socialization of males and females in our culture makes adoption of hysterical disorders more acceptable for females than for males. The awareness of our biases, however, may be one step toward their correction.

6. References

Abse, W. D. Hysterical conversion and dissociative syndromes and the hysterical character. In S. Arieti (Ed.), *American handbook of psychiatry* (2nd ed., vol. 3). New York: Basic Books, 1974.
American Psychiatric Association. *Diagnostic and statistical manual II.* Washington, D.C.: American Psychiatric Association, 1968.
American Psychiatric Association. *Diagnostic and statistical manual III.* Washington, D.C.: American Psychiatric Association, 1980.
Archibald, H. D., and Tuddenham, R. D. Persistent stress reaction after combat. *Archives of General Psychiatry,* 1965, *12,* 475–481.
Arkonac, O., and Guze, S. B. A family study of hysteria. *New England Journal of Medicine,* 1963, *268,* 239–242.
Bendefeldt, F., Miller, L. L., and Ludwig, A. M. Cognitive performance in conversion hysteria. *Archives of General Psychiatry,* 1976, *33,* 1250–1254.

Berger, D. M. Hysteria: In search of the animus. *Comprehensive Psychiatry*, 1971, *12*, 277–286.

Bishop, E. R., Mobley, M. C., and Farr, W. F., Jr. Lateralization of conversion symptoms. *Comprehensive Psychiatry*, 1978, *19*, 393–396.

Bishop, E. R., and Torch, E. M. Dividing "hysteria": A preliminary investigation of conversion disorder and psychalgia. *Journal of Nervous and Mental Disease*, 1979, *167*, 348–356.

Blinder, M. The hysterical personality. *Psychiatry*, 1966, *29*, 227–235.

Bourguignon, E. *Culture and the varieties of consciousness*. An Addison-Wesley Module in anthropology, No. 47, 1974.

Brauer, R., Harrow, M., and Tucker, G. J. Depersonalization phenomena in psychiatric patients. *British Journal of Psychiatry*, 1970, *117*, 509–515.

Buffrey, A. A. H., and Gray, J. A. Sex differences in the development of spatial and linguistic skills. In C. Ounsted and D. Taylor (Eds.), *Gender differences: Their ontogeny and significance*. London: Churchill Livingstone, 1972.

Carden, N. L., and Schramel, D. I. Observations of conversion reactions seen in troops involved in the Viet Nam conflict. *American Journal of Psychiatry*, 1966, *123*, 21–31.

Carter, A. B. Prognosis of certain hysterical symptoms. *British Medical Journal*, 1949, *1*, 1076–1079.

Celani, D. An interpersonal approach to hysteria. *American Journal of Psychiatry*, 1976, *133*, 1414–1418.

Chodoff, P. The diagnosis of hysteria: An overview. *American Journal Psychiatry*, 1974, *131*, 1073–1078.

Chodoff, P., and Lyons, H. Hysteria, the hysterical personality and "hysterical" conversion. *American Journal of Psychiatry*, 1958, *114*, 734–740.

Cloninger, C. R. The link between hysteria and sociopathy: An integrative model of pathogenesis based on clinical, genetic and neuro-physiological observations. In H. S. Akiskal and W. L. Webb (Eds.), *Psychiatric diagnosis: Explorations of biological predictors*. New York: Spectrum, 1978.

Cloninger, C. R., and Guze, S. B. Psychiatric illness and female criminality: The role of sociopathy and hysteria in the antisocial woman. *American Journal of Psychiatry*, 1970, *127*, 79–87.

Cloninger, C. R., Reich, T., and Guze, S. B. The multifactorial model of disease transmission: III. Familial relationship between sociopathy and hysteria (Briquet's syndrome). *British Journal of Psychiatry*, 1975, *127*, 23–32.

Crowe, R. R. Genetic studies of antisocial personality and related disorders. In R. L. Spitzer and D. F. Klein (Eds.), *Critical issues in psychiatric diagnosis*. New York: Raven Press, 1978.

Easser, B. R., and Lesser, S. R. Hysterical personality: A re-evaluation. *Psychoanalytic Quarterly*, 1965, *34*, 390–405.

Engel, G. L. Conversion symptoms. In C. M. MacBryde and R. S. Blacklow (Eds.), *Signs and symptoms: Applied pathologic physiology and clinical interpretation* (5th ed.). Philadelphia: Lippincott, 1970.

Eysenck, H. J. Biological basis of personality. *Nature*, 1963, *199*, 1031–1034.

Farley, J., Woodruff, R. A., Jr., and Guze, S. B. The prevalence of hysteria and conversion symptoms. *British Journal of Psychiatry*, 1968, *114*, 1121–1125.

Feighner, J. P., Robins, E., Guze, S. B., Woodruff, R. A., Jr., Winokur, G., and Munoz, R. Diagnostic criteria for use in psychiatric research. *Archives of General Psychiatry*, 1972, *26*, 57–63.

Flor-Henry, P. Gender, hemispheric specialization and psychopathology. *Social Science and Medicine*, 1978, *12B*, 155–162.

98 Barbara A. Winstead

Freedman, A. M., Kaplan, H. I., and Sadock, B. J. *Modern synopsis of comprehensive textbook of psychiatry* (2nd ed.). Baltimore: Williams and Wilkins, 1976.

Gainotti, G. Emotional behavior and hemispheric side of the lesion. *Cortex*, 1972, *8*, 41–55.

Gatfield, P. D., and Guze, S. B. Prognosis and differential diagnosis of conversion reactions. *Diseases of the Nervous System*, 1962, *23*, 623–631.

Geschwind, N. The apraxias: Neural mechanisms of disorders of learned movement. *American Scientist*, 1975, *63*, 188–195.

Gibbens, T. C. N. Psychosomatic aspects of the recidivist population. *Journal of Psychosomatic Research*, 1969, *13*, 253–256.

Gove, W. R. Sex differences in the epidemiology of mental disorder: Evidence and explanations. In E. S. Gomberg and V. Franks, *Gender and disordered behavior: Sex differences in psychopathology*. New York: Brunner/Mazel, 1979.

Gross, M. Pseudoepilepsy: A study in adolescent hysteria. *American Journal of Psychiatry*, 1979, *136*, 210–213.

Guze, S. B. The diagnosis of hysteria: What are we trying to do? *American Journal of Psychiatry*, 1967, *124*, 491–498.

Guze, S. B. The validity and significance of the clinical diagnosis of hysteria (Briquet's syndrome). *American Journal of Psychiatry*, 1975, *132*, 138–141.

Guze, S. B., Woodruff, R. A., Jr., and Clayton, P. J. Sex, age, and the diagnosis of hysteria (Briquet's syndrome). *American Journal of Psychiatry*, 1972, *129*, 745–748.

Halleck, S. L. Hysterical personality traits. *Archives of General Psychiatry*, 1967, *16*, 750–757.

Henney, J. H. Sex and status: Women in St. Vincent. In E. Bourguignon (Ed.), *A world of women*. New York: Praeger, 1980.

Hollender, M. H. Conversion hysteria. *Archives of General Psychiatry*, 1972, *26*, 311–314.

Horvath, T., Friedman, J., and Meares, R. Attention in hysteria: A study of Janet's hypothesis by means of habituation and arousal measures. *American Journal of Psychiatry*, 1980, *137*, 217–220.

Kaminsky, M. J., and Slavney, P. R. Methodology and personality in Briquet's syndrome: A reappraisal. *American Journal of Psychiatry*, 1976, *133*, 85–88.

Kelley, H. H., The processes of causal attribution. *American Psychologist*, 1973, *28*, 107–128.

Kimble, R., Williams, J. G., and Agras, S. A comparison of two methods of diagnosing hysteria. *American Journal of Psychiatry*, 1975, *132*, 1197–1199.

Kimura, D. The asymmetry of the human brain. *Scientific American*, 1973, *228*, 70–78.

Kirshner, L. A. Dissociative reactions: An historical review and clinical study. *Acta Psychiatrica Scandinavica*, 1973, *49*, 698–711.

Krohn, A. *Hysteria: The elusive neurosis*. New York: International Universities Press, 1978.

Kroll, P., Chamberlain, K. R., and Halpern, J. The diagnosis of Briquet's syndrome in a male population. *Journal of Nervous and Mental Disease*, 1979, *167*, 171–174.

Laplanche, J. Panel on "Hysteria today." *International Journal of Psycho-Analysis*, 1974, *55*, 459–469.

Lazare, A. The hysterical character in psychoanalytic theory. *Archives of General Psychiatry*, 1971, *25*, 131–137.

Lazare, A., Klerman, G. L., and Armor, D. J. Oral, obsessive, and hysterical personality patterns. *Archives of General Psychiatry*, 1966, *14*, 624–630.

Lerner, H. E. The hysterical personality: A "woman's disease." *Comprehensive Psychiatry*, 1974, *15*, 157–164.

Levy, J. Lateral specialization of the human brain: Behavioral manifestations and possible evolutionary basis. In J. A. Kiger, Jr. (Ed.), *The biology of behavior*. Corvallis, Ore.: Oregon State University Press, 1972.

Lewis, H. B. Sex differences in superego mode as related to sex differences in psychiatric illness. *Social Science and Medicine*, 1978, *12B*, 199–205.

Lewis, H. B. Shame in depression and hysteria. In C. Izard (Ed.), *Emotions in personality and psychopathology.* New York: Plenum, 1979.

Lewis, W. C., and Berman, M. Studies of conversion hysteria. *Archives of General Psychiatry,* 1965, *13,* 275–282.

Lindberg, B. U., and Lindegard, B. Studies of the hysteroid personality attitude. *Acta Psychiatrica Scandinavica,* 1963, *39,* 170–180.

Ljungberg, L. Hysteria. *Acta Psychiatrica Scandinavica,* 1957, *32*(Supplement 112).

Ludwig, A. M. Hysteria: A neurobiological theory. *Archives of General Psychiatry,* 1972, *27,* 771–777.

Luisida, P. V., Peele, R., and Pittard, E. A. The hysterical personality in men. *American Journal of Psychiatry,* 1974, *131,* 518–521.

Maccoby, E., and Jacklin, C. *The psychology of sex differences.* Stanford, Calif.: Stanford University Press, 1974.

Matarazzo, R., Matarazzo, J., and Saslow, G. The relationship between medical and psychiatric symptoms. *Journal of Abnormal and Social Psychology,* 1961, *62,* 55–61.

McKegney, F. P. The incidence and characteristics of patients with conversion reactions: I. A general hospital consultation service sample. *American Journal of Psychiatry,* 1967, *124,* 542–545.

Mechanic, D. Sex, illness, illness behavior, and the use of health services. *Social Science and Medicine,* 1978, *12B,* 207–214.

Merskey, H., and Trimble, M. Personality, sexual adjustment, and brain lesion in patients with conversion symptoms. *British Journal of Psychiatry,* 1979, *136,* 179–182.

National Institute of Mental Health 1975 Survey. Unpublished data, 1975. (Available from Survey and Reports Branch, Division of Biometry and Epidemiology, Alcohol, Drug Abuse, and Mental Health Administration, National Institute of Mental Health, Rockville, Maryland 20857.)

Perley, M. J., and Guze, S. B. Hysteria—The stability and usefulness of clinical criteria. *New England Journal of Medicine,* 1962, *266,* 421–426.

Phillips, D., and Segal, B. Sexual status and psychiatric symptoms. *American Sociological Review,* 1969, *34,* 58–72.

Purtell, J. J., Robins, E., and Cohen, M. E. Observations on clinical aspects of hysteria: A quantitative study of 50 hysteria patients and 156 control subjects. *Journal fo the American Medical Association,* 1951, *146,* 902–909.

Rinieris, P. M., Stefanis, C. N., Lykouras, E. P., and Varsou, E. K. Hysteria and ABO blood types. *American Journal of Psychiatry,* 1978, *135,* 1106–1107.

Robins, E., Purtell, J. J., and Cohen, M. E. "Hysteria" in men: A study of 38 patients so diagnosed and 194 control subjects. *New England Journal of Medicine,* 1952, *246,* 677–685.

Robins, L. *Deviant children grown up.* Baltimore: Williams and Wilkins, 1966.

Rosenthal, D. *Genetics of psychopathology.* New York: McGraw-Hill, 1971.

Rounsaville, B. J., Harding, P. S., and Weissman, M. M. Briquet's syndrome in a man. *Journal of Nervous and Mental Disease,* 1979, *167,* 364–367.

Roy, A. Hysterical seizures. *Archives of Neurology,* 1979, *36,* 447.

Shapiro, D. *Neurotic styles.* New York: Basic Books, 1965.

Slater, E. Diagnosis of hysteria. *British Medical Journal,* 1965, *1,* 1395–1399.

Stefansson, J. G., Medina, J. A., and Meyerowitz, S. Hysterical neurosis, conversion types. *Acta Psychiatrica Scandinavica,* 1976, *53,* 119–138.

Stephens, J. H., and Kamp, M. On some aspects of hysteria: A clinical study. *Journal of Nervous and Mental Disease,* 1962, *134,* 305–315.

Stern, D. B. Handedness and the lateral distribution of conversion reactions. *Journal of Nervous and Mental Disease,* 1977, *164,* 122–128.

Szasz, T. *The myth of mental illness*. New York: Dell, 1961.

Temoshok, L., and Attkisson, C. C. Epidemiology of hysterical phenomena: Evidence for a psychosocial theory. In M. J. Horowitz (Ed.), *Hysterical personality*. New York: Jason Aronson, 1977.

Waber, D. P. Sex differences in mental abilities, hemispheric lateralization, and rate of physical growth at adolescence. *Developmental Psychology*, 1977, *13*, 29–38.

Warner, R. The diagnosis of antisocial and hysterical personality disorders: An example of sex bias. *Journal of Nervous and Mental Disease*, 1978, 166, 839–845.

Warner, R. Racial and sexual bais in psychiatric diagnosis: Psychiatrists and other mental health professionals compared by race, sex, and discipline. *Journal of Nervous and Mental Disease*, 1979, *167*, 303–310.

Weinstein, E. A., Eck, R. A., and Lyerly, O. G. Conversion hysteria in Appalachia. *Psychiatry*, 1969, *32*, 334–341.

Woerner, P. I., and Guze, S. B. A family and marital study of hysteria. *British Journal of Psychiatry*, 1968, *11*, 161–168.

Wolowitz, H. M. Hysterical character and feminine identity. In J. Bardwick (Ed.), *Readings on the psychology of women*. New York: Harper & Row, 1970. Pp. 307–314.

Woodruff, R. A. Hysteria: An evaluation of objective diagnostic criteria by the study of women with chronic medical illnesses. *British Journal of Psychiatry*, 1968, *114*, 1115–1119.

Woodruff, R. A., Jr., Clayton, P. J., and Guze, S. B. Hysteria: An evaluation of specific diagnostic criteria by the study of randomly selected psychiatric clinic patients. *British Journal of Psychiatry*, 1969, *115*, 1243–1248.

Woolsey, R. M. Hysteria: 1875 to 1975. *Diseases of the Nervous System*, 1976, *37*, 379–386.

World Health Organization. *The international classification of diseases, 9th revision, Clinical modification*. Ann Arbor, Mich.: Edwards Brothers, 1978.

Zetzel, E. The so-called good hysteric. *International Journal of Psycho-Analysis*, 1968, *49*, 256–260.

Ziegler, F. F., Imboden, J. B., and Meyer, E. Contemporary conversion reactions: A clinical study. *American Journal of Psychiatry*, 1960, *116*, 901–910.

5

Sex Roles and Psychophysiological Disorders

Coronary Heart Disease

Jane E. Platt

Psychophysiology, as defined in the dictionary, is "the science of the relation between psychological and physiological processes." Psychophysiological disorders, therefore, are those in which psychological factors make a direct or indirect contribution to etiology. The issue that will be addressed in this chapter is the relationship between psychophysiological disorders and a particular set of psychological factors, those related to sex role. This relationship is of particular interest at this juncture in history for two reasons. First, it has become increasingly clear in recent years that psychological factors influence the development and treatment of numerous diseases including ulcers (Ackerman, Manaker, and Cohen, 1981), cancer (Shekelle, Raynor, Ostfeld, Garron, Bieliauskas, Liu, Maliza, and Paul, 1981), asthma (Teiramaa, 1979), and coronary heart disease (CHD) (Friedman and Rosenman, 1959). Second, sex roles, i.e., the behaviors, thoughts, or attitudes deemed appropriate to a person by virtue of his or her sex, have undergone rapid change in many segments of the population during the past 15 years and are continuing to change. The health consequences of these changes are not yet apparent, but there is concern, to cite one example, that changes in the social roles of women may increase their cardiovascular morbidity and mortality (see, e.g., Garbus and Garbus, 1980).

Jane E. Platt • Department of Psychiatry, Millhauser Laboratories, New York University Medical Center, New York, New York 10016.

1. Reasons for Studying Coronary Heart Disease in Women

Because of this specific concern, and for other reasons that will be discussed shortly, this chapter will focus on possible relationships between CHD and sex roles, with particular emphasis on factors that may influence CHD in women. There are several reasons why CHD is particularly well suited for developing a model of the potential relationships between sex roles and psychophysiological disorders and why women are a useful population to study. A primary reason is the existence of a sex difference in rates of CHD that shows evidence of being influenced by nongenetic as well as genetic factors. Although women have a lower incidence of CHD than men in virtually all societies, the size of the difference varies across cultures and has changed over time in the United States (U.S. Bureau of the Census, 1981; Armstrong, Duncan, Oliver, Julian, Donald, Fulton, Lutz, and Morrison, 1972). In 1960 the age-adjusted ratio of male to female deaths from arteriosclerotic and degenerative heart disease in the United States was 3.74:1 for whites between the ages of 45 and 64 (Moriyama, Krueger, and Stamler, 1971). United States mortality statistics for 1978, the latest year available, continue to show approximately the same ratio (U.S. Bureau of the Census, 1981). In comparison, the ratio of male to female deaths from arteriosclerotic heart disease in Japan in 1960 was only 1.54:1 (Moriyama *et al.*, 1971). Earlier in this century the sex difference in cardiovascular-renal mortality was also much smaller in the United States. CHD death rates in American men and women began to diverge around 1920, when the rates for women began declining while those of men increased. This pattern continued until fairly recently, when the rates for men also began a decline (U.S. Bureau of the Census, 1981; Johnson, 1977; Moriyama, Woolsey, and Stamler, 1958). In 1940 the ratio of male to female deaths from CHD among white 40-year-olds was about 3.1:1. By 1960 it had reached 6:1 (Moriyama *et al.*, 1971). These changes in the male–female ratio of CHD have occurred too rapidly to be accounted for by genetic changes. Together with the cross-cultural differences cited above, they strongly suggest that sociocultural and environmental factors make a contribution to the sex difference in CHD. Attempting to identify these factors is a useful strategy for investigating the relationship between sex roles and CHD as long as it is recognized that some aspects of sex roles may influence rates of CHD within one sex without contributing to the rate difference between the sexes in an important way.

CHD is also well suited for developing a model of the relationships between sex roles and psychophysiological disorders because it is a well-investigated syndrome. Potential risk factors for CHD have been examined in several large-scale prospective studies such as the Framingham study (Haynes, Feinleib, Levine, Scotch, and Kannel, 1978; Haynes, Levine, Scotch, Feinleib, and Kannel, 1978) and the Western Collaborative Group study (Rosenman, Brand, Jenkins, Friedman, Strauss, and Wurm, 1975). These studies have identified a number of factors that appear to contribute independently to cardiovascular risk, including physiological factors such as blood pressure and serum levels of cholesterol, triglycerides, and beta lipoprotein; sociocultural and life-style factors such as smoking and level of education; and factors of a more psychological nature such as the Type-A behavior pattern (Rosenman *et al.*, 1975). Many of these risk factors were originally identified in exclusively male samples, but a number of them have also been validated as risk factors in women (Rosenman and Friedman, 1961). The existence of a well-documented set of CHD risk factors provides a starting point for inquiry since one way that sex role-linked behaviors may influence the risk of CHD is through relationships to known risk factors.

The reason women are a good population to study vis-à-vis the issue of sex roles and CHD is that female sex roles have undergone significant changes since the beginning of the century, especially during the past 15 years. Perhaps the best way to characterize these changes is in terms of a widening of acceptable roles. The more traditional female roles have not been eliminated, but women have expanded their roles to include activities that were formerly associated primarily with men. This situation is particularly opportune for investigating the contribution of sex role behaviors to the incidence of CHD—or to any other psychophysiological disorder—because it provides a degree of role variance that is generally not found in the male population. For example, the contribution of paid employment to CHD can be studied by comparing employed women to housewives. This type of comparison is not feasible in males because most adult males are employed and have no widely acceptable alternative role. Changes in female sex roles also provide the opportunity to correlate role changes with historical trends in the incidence of CHD in women. This strategy is less applicable to men because male sex roles have not changed to the same extent as those of women in this century.

2. Pathways of Risk

Risk factors for CHD can be divided into those that are behavioral or psychological in nature and those that are physiological, a distinction that may be useful in tracing pathways of risk. Since CHD is a physiologically defined condition, behavioral and psychological risk factors must eventually translate into physiological variables, albeit not necessarily ones that have been identified. This translation may occur at various removes from the observable or measurable behavior, but it must occur if a behavior contributes to risk. Consequently, sex roles will affect the risk of CHD to the extent that they affect the likelihood of engaging in behaviors that have risk-related physiological consequences.

Our current knowledge of the relationship between sex role-mediated behavior and the risk of CHD is rudimentary. The literature on risk, for the most part, has identified relationships between certain behaviors and the occurrence of CHD or between certain physiological factors (e.g., elevated serum cholesterol) and CHD. What has not been as well established are the links between behavioral risk factors and the physiological variables that mediate their relationship to CHD, on the one hand, and between behavioral risk factors and their relationship to sex roles, on the other. A useful strategy for developing knowledge in this area, therefore, is to begin with known behavioral risk factors and investigate their relationship to both sex roles and physiological variables. This strategy may uncover as yet unknown physiological risk factors. The converse strategy is to begin with known physiological risk factors and investigate how they are related, first, to behavior and, subsequently, to sex roles. Although many physiological risk factors may not be influenced by behavior, there are clearly others that are. A fuller understanding of the potential pathways between sex roles and CHD depends on these missing links being identified.

In the following part of the chapter, sex role-related demographic, behavioral, and psychological characteristics of women that may have an influence on the development of CHD will be examined. Unitary variables in which an easily identified behavior affects the risk of CHD will be considered first. This will be followed by an examination of more complex life-style variables.

3. Unitary Risk Factors

3.1. Cigarette Smoking

Cigarette smoking is a behavior historically linked to sex role that has been shown unequivocally to increase the risk of CHD. In a number of prospective studies it has been found that men who smoke have higher rates of CHD than nonsmokers and that the increase in risk is dose-related (Doll and Peto, 1976; Rosenman et al., 1975; Doyle, Dawber, Kannel, Kinch, and Kahn, 1964). For example, in men who were 39 to 49 years old during the intake period for the Western Collaborative Group study, the rate of CHD rose from 6.0 cases per 1000 subjects per year among those smoking 1–15 cigarettes daily to 12.9 cases per year among those who smoked 26 or more cigarettes a day (Rosenman et al.,1975). The elevation in risk caused by smoking is greater among younger men: Death rates from CHD are elevated approximately 100% among middle-aged adults, but only about 20% at the oldest ages (Hammond, 1966).

Cigarette smoking has been found to be a risk factor in women as well as in men despite their overall lower rate of CHD. Slone and his colleagues (Slone, Shapiro, Rosenberg, Kaufman, Hartz, Rossi, Stolley, and Miettinen, 1978) examined the relationship between smoking and CHD in a population of women 49 years of age or younger who had survived a myocardial infarction (MI), but were otherwise healthy, and in matched controls. Women were excluded from the sample if they had a history of previous MI or if they were thought to be at high risk for CHD for other reasons. MI was strongly associated with cigarette smoking in this population. Eighty-nine percent of MI cases had been smokers, compared to 55% of controls, which resulted in a relative risk of 6.8. Furthermore, as in male samples, the relationship was dose-related: The estimated relative risk increased from 4.4 in women who smoked 1–14 cigarettes per day to 21 in those who smoked more than 35 cigarettes daily. On the basis of these data, 76% of MIs in women under the age of 50 who are not at high risk for other reasons are attributable to cigarette smoking. Similar findings have been reported in other morbidity and mortality studies that have examined the link between CHD and cigarette smoking in women (Mann, Doll, Thorogood, Vessey, and Waters, 1976; Oliver, 1974; Bengtsson, 1973a; Spain, Siegal, and Bradess, 1973). Although the physiological mechanisms by which smoking increases risk have not been clearly established, recent evidence suggests that levels of high-density lipoprotein in smokers are depressed compared to the levels found in nonsmokers, but they return to normal if a person stops smoking (Stubbe, Eskilsson, and Nilsson-Ehle, 1982). High-density liproprotein is thought to have a protective effect against CHD (see below).

Cigarette smoking was once a sex role-permissible behavior for men but not for women. Social mores have changed, however, a point made by the advertising campaign of a well-known brand of cigarettes targeted to the female market. Women now smoke in increasingly large numbers. Between 1935 and 1965 the percent of adult females who were regular cigarette smokers rose from 18.1 to 33.1 (U.S. Department of Health and Human Services, 1980, p. 23). By 1979 it had decreased slightly to 28.2%. The corresponding percentages for males are 52.2, 51.5, and 36.9, indicating that a sharp drop in the prevalence of cigarette smoking among men occurred between 1965 and 1979. As a result, the proportions of men and women who smoke are approaching one another. Among teenagers, in fact, a reversal appears to have taken place: More females than males smoke. Between 1968 and 1979 the percentage of females 17 to 18 years old who smoke rose from 18.6 to 26.2, whereas for males the percentages dropped from 30.2 to 19.3, figures that are based on nationwide surveys conducted by the National Clearinghouse for Smoking and Health and the National Institute of Education (U.S. Department of Health and Human Services, 1980, p. 36). Not only are more women smoking, they are smoking at younger ages and are smoking more heavily than they used to. For women born before 1900, the mean age of onset of smoking was 35 years, compared to 19 years for men, whereas in 1979 it was 16 years for both sexes (U.S. Department of Health and Human Services, 1980, p. 32). Furthermore, the percentage of female smokers smoking 25 or more cigarettes per day increased from 13.7 in 1965 to 22.4 in 1979 (U.S. Department of Health and Human Services, 1980, p. 27). Some of the relative freedom from CHD that women have enjoyed in comparison to men may have resulted from the fact that fewer women smoked in the past, and those who did smoked less than men. In people who have never smoked regularly, the ratio of male to female deaths from CHD is smaller than the ratio that results when smokers and nonsmokers are considered together. This is particularly true for younger age groups. In people aged 45–54, the sex mortality ratios for deaths from CHD are 4.5 in those who never smoked regularly compared to 7.5 for the total sample (Waldron, 1976). What this implies is that some portion of the excess of male over female deaths from CHD is due to the larger number of men who smoke. One might therefore expect the ratio of male to female deaths from CHD to decrease as the number of women who smoke increases and begins to equal the proportion of the male population that smokes. An effect of this nature has not been observed in the United States, where death rates from CHD have been falling for both men and women (U.S. Bureau of the Census, 1981), but it may yet appear in the future as the increasingly large part of the female population that smokes reaches an age where CHD is more common. In England and Wales the standardized mortality rates for ischemic heart disease in women aged 35–64 increased almost 50% between 1958 and 1970, which parallels an increase in cigarette smoking in those countries during the same period (Oliver, 1974; Todd, 1972).

Cigarette smoking represents a situation in which the relationship between sex role and a psychophysiological disorder, CHD, is direct and uncomplicated. Whatever the mechanism, smoking increases the risk of CHD. Cigarette smoking was formerly a behavior that was proscribed for women, whereas now it is accepted. The psychological contribution to etiology here is indirect in the sense that a set of attitudes determines the likelihood of engaging in a behavior, but it is the behavior, not the attitudes, that affects risk.

3.2. Oral Contraceptives

The use of oral contraceptives is another example of a risk factor for CHD where a set of sex role-related attitudes influences the likelihood of engaging in a behavior that has a fairly direct effect on risk. It is also the most obvious example of a risk factor that influences the incidence of CHD within the female population but has no relevance to the question of men's higher rates of CHD.

Increased risk of MI associated with the use of oral contraceptives is well established (Dalen and Hickler, 1981; Stadel, 1981; Mann and Inman, 1975; Mann, Vessey, Thorogood, and Doll, 1975; Radford and Oliver, 1973). Most cases, however, occur in women who also have other risk factors (Mann *et al.*, 1975; Radford and Oliver, 1973). The increase in risk appears to be multiplicative rather than additive, which indicates that there is a synergistic interaction between oral contraceptives and other risk factors (Stadel, 1981). The increased risk of MI that results from the use of oral contraceptives persists even after their use has been discontinued and is related to the number of years of prior exposure (Slone, Shapiro, Kaufman, Rosenberg, Miettinen, and Stolley, 1981).

The decision to use a contraceptive is affected by a number of factors, including attitudes about appropriate or desirable sex role behavior. In a society where a woman's primary role is to produce children, and as many as possible, contraceptive use of any type by married women is likely to be low. On the other hand, if a society frowns upon female premarital sexual activity, the use of contraceptives by women who break this taboo is likely to be high, and such women are likely to chose a very effective contraceptive method if one is available.

Control over pregnancy becomes an increasingly important factor in women's lives as they take on new roles in addition to or in place of their more traditional ones. Under such circumstances the demands of different roles such as mother and worker often compete. Even when a woman wants to have a child, she may have strong incentives to time her pregnancy to fit in with other demands in her life. When the negative consequences of an unplanned pregnancy are high, for whatever reason, a premium is likely to be placed on the use of a highly dependable contraceptive, particularly one whose use is controlled by the woman herself. For a woman who has chosen to use a female contraceptive, the choice between oral contraceptives and other reliable methods, however, is probably related more to issues of health and aesthetics than to sex role-related attitudes *per se.*

3.3. Exercise

Physical inactivity is a risk factor for CHD inasmuch as regular strenuous exercise is associated with lower rates of coronary disease (Paffenberger and Hale, 1975). To the extent that such activity is considered unfeminine it will influence CHD rates in women. In a study of longshoremen who were followed for 22 years, death rates for those whose daily work demanded repeated and sustained bouts of high energy output were about half the level of those whose work required medium or low energy expenditures (Paffenberger and Hale, 1975). The latter two groups had similar rates, which suggests that activity must be sufficiently vigorous and last long enough to produce a training effect before it will lower CHD risk. Other prospective studies have found lower rates of CHD in men whose leisure-time activities included regular vigorous exercise (Rosenman *et al.*, 1975; Morris, Chave, Adam, Sirey, and Epstein, 1973). Physical activity also affects CHD rates in women. In a community study in Göteborg, Sweden (Bengtsson, 1973b), women hospitalized for MI were significantly more likely than controls to have been relatively inactive, both at work and at leisure, at an earlier period in their life.

Exercise has numerous effects that may be responsible for lowering the risk of CHD. These include decreases in heart rate, blood pressure, platelet aggregation activity, and body weight, and increases in oxygen consumption and fibrinolysis (Fletcher, 1981; Clausen, 1977). Exercise can also decrease Type-A behavior (Blumenthal, Williams, Williams, and Wallace, 1980) and increase levels of high-density lipoprotein cholesterol (HDL-C). High levels of HDL-C have been reported to be inversely related to the incidence of CHD in both men and women, which suggests that they have a protective effect against CHD (Miller, 1978; Gordon, Castelli, Hjortland, Kannel, and Dawber, 1977). It has been hypothesized that HDL-C facilitates the egress of cholesterol out of the artery wall, allowing it to be transported to the liver, where it is metabolized (Miller and Miller, 1975).

Regular strenuous exercise increases HDL-C levels without changing levels of total plasma cholesterol, although some of this effect may be due to reductions in body weight and changes in body composition (Moffat and Gilliam, 1979). Levels of HDL-C in male and female Olympic athletes are about 20% higher than those typical of the general population of North America of the same age (Deshaies and Allard, 1982). Positive correlations between physical activity and HDL-C levels, and between maximum aerobic capacity and HDL-C levels, have also been found in more typical populations (Williams, Robinson, and Bailey, 1979; Miller, Rao, Lewis, Bjorsvik, Myhre, and Mjos, 1979). Women generally have higher levels of HDL-C than men, but they too respond to physical training with increases in HDL-C concentration. Men and women who participated in a 10-week training program that included warm-up exercises and walking or jogging three times a week both increased their levels of HDL-C significantly above pretraining levels (Blumenthal *et al.*, 1980).

Activities that involve regular vigorous physical activity, such as participation in strenuous sports or heavy occupational labor, are traditionally associated with the male sex role in our society. Women are considered the weaker sex: Muscles and sweat are regarded as unfeminine. Although jobs that require high levels of physical exertion are disappearing from our economy for both sexes, women are still less likely than men to engage in this type of occupation. Furthermore, from an early age, girls are less strongly encouraged than boys to develop their athletic abilities. Sports and exercise programs for schoolgirls and for college women are generally not as well supported as those for males, which affects rates of participation and makes it less likely that girls will develop lifetime habits of regular exercise. Although there are signs that this pattern may be changing, it is still the norm. To the extent that sex role-related attitudes prevent or promote participation in strenuous sports or work activities, they are likely to influence rates of CHD in women.

4. Complex Risk Factors

The examples examined up to this point are cases in which sex role-related attitudes influence the likelihood of engaging in easily identified unidimensional behaviors. These behaviors, in turn, have demonstrable physiological effects that contribute directly to raising or lowering the risk of CHD. In the remaining part of this chapter we will examine an interrelated and more complicated set of sex role-influenced factors that affect coronary risk. These factors are employment status, parity, stress, and the Type-A behavior pattern. Although employment status and parity are easily ascertained, their relationship to CHD is likely to occur through the presence of intervening variables such as stress. It is to be expected, therefore, that relationships between employment and CHD and parity and CHD will not be unitary but will depend on job or family characteristics. Stress and the Type-A behavior pattern are more complicated than the previous variables that have been examined because they are psychological constructs whose presence has to be inferred from a combination of psychological characteristics, behaviors, situational variables, and the interactions between them. They present problems of definition and measurement. In addition, their relationship to the physiological variables that ultimately determine risk is less well understood.

One of the more obvious sex role differences between men and women in Western industrialized societies is that men have traditionally held paying jobs outside the home, whereas women, unless forced by economic necessity, have not. Throughout this century, but particularly since World War II, women have been entering the paid labor force in increasingly large numbers. According to statistics from the United States Department of Labor (U.S. Department of Labor, Bureau of Labor Statistics, 1978; U.S. Department of Labor, Women's Bureau, 1954), the percentage of women in the labor force increased from 28% in 1950 to 42% in 1978, and it continues to rise. Moreover, women have been increasing their representation in job categories traditionally dominated by men.

The contribution of occupationally related factors such as job stress to the sex difference in rates of CHD is an area that has not been sufficiently explored. However, if factors related to employment increase the risk of CHD, the increase in the number of women who work should eventually be reflected in a relative increase in the rate of CHD among women compared to men. In 1971 Moriyama et al. reported that death rates for white women aged 35 to 54 were rising while those for white males had leveled off, whereas more recent statistics show proportionally equivalent decreases in CHD death rates for men and women (U.S. Bureau of the Census, 1981). Since CHD is a chronic disease that develops over a long period of time, a rise in the proportion of women affected by CHD relative to men may still appear at some time in the future.

Employment *per se* does not appear to influence rates of CHD in women. Particular types of jobs, however, and the interaction of employment with other factors have been associated with increased CHD in female populations. Rosenman and Friedman (1961), using a sample of women chosen for fitting the Type-A or Type-B behavior pattern, found that housewives were as likely to have CHD as women who worked. But the nature of the job had an effect. While 35% of study participants were in professional or executive occupations, they accounted for 62% of the cases of clinical coronary disease identified in the study. This finding suggests that the job pressures associated with certain types of employment may increase coronary risk. An alternative explanation, however, is that coronary-prone women self-select themselves into high-pressure occupations, an issue that will be discussed later in the chapter with respect to the prevalence of the Type-A behavior pattern. Several papers emanating from the Framingham study, which is based on a more representative sample, have also reported that the incidence of CHD among employed women is no higher than among housewives (Haynes and Feinleib, 1980; Haynes, Feinleib, and Kannel, 1980; Haynes, Feinleib, Levine, Scotch, and Kannel, 1978). Here too, however, women in certain occupational groupings had an elevated risk of CHD, and other factors interacted with job category to affect risk. Women clerical workers were twice as likely as white- or blue-collar workers or housewives to develop CHD. Moreover, clerical workers who developed CHD were likely to suppress hostility and to have nonsupportive bosses, variables that may contribute to job-related stress. Among working women, but not among housewives, the incidence of CHD increased with the number of children. Working women who had three or more children were significantly more likely to develop CHD (11%) than were childless working women (6.5%) or housewives with three or more children (4.4%). The excess risk previously noted among female clerical workers was found only in those with children (15.4% vs. 6.3%). Those who had children and were also married to a blue-collar husband were over three times more likely to develop CHD than were nonclerical mothers, 21.3% versus 6.0%, respectively.

What these findings suggest is that employment combined with a high level of family responsibilities, as represented by three or more children, produces stress. This stress is more extreme if a woman is also under economic pressure. The effect of parity on CHD in employed women does not appear to be a biological consequence of a large number of pregnancies since housewives with the same number of children did not show elevated rates of CHD. Bengtsson, Hällström, and Tibblin (1973) have reported that women with MI are more likely than controls to have four or more children, but they did not distinguish between and nonworking women in their analysis.

The results of studies that have attempted to assess stress directly and to examine its relationship to CHD have not been consistent (see reviews by Jenkins, 1971, 1976). This lack of consistency is not surprising because stress is hard to define and to measure objectively. Its sources are to be found both externally, in the environment, and internally, in a person's emotional makeup. That the causes of stress are subjective and vary from person to person is a truism, but it makes the measurement of stress difficult. Furthermore, the relevant factor in CHD is likely to be the overall level of stress in a person's life. For some people, high levels of stress may be concentrated in one particular life area, while for others there may be several sources of stress that summate. Results of studies may vary depending on which areas of life stresses are evaluated, how many different areas are included, and of course, how stress is operationally defined.

Jenkins (1971), who has reviewed the literature on psychological and social precursors to CHD, reports that various stressful life conditions have been implicated as raising the risk of coronary disease. These include death of a close relative, work overload, and life dissatisfaction. Self-ratings of stress by patients and clinical judgments by physicians have also been positively associated with CHD. But most of these studies are retrospective and therefore methodologically flawed by potential problems with selective recall and by the confounding of preexisting and illness-induced stress. Jenkins (1976) also reported on studies that used summary measures of life change as an index of stress. Here too there are methodological problems, particularly the lack of adequate control groups. Although the results of studies on life change and CHD are inconsistent, Jenkins found that the methodologically stronger studies were the ones that tended to find no relationship. It should be noted, however, that life change scales are based on a definition of stress that includes positive as well as negative events. This differs from more typical definitions of stress that include primarily negative events and emotions. Life change scores, therefore, may not show the same relationship to CHD as other indices of stress.

With respect to the issue of sex roles, the majority of studies that have considered the relationship between stress and CHD have examined only men. Although the generalizability of their findings to women cannot be automatically assumed, the few studies that have examined women are in general accord with those employing all-male samples. Bengtsson and her colleagues (Bengtsson et al., 1973), who did a retrospective study of women with ischemic heart disease, found that women who had suffered an MI had experienced a significantly greater number of negative stressful events such as divorce or severe illness of the husband in the year preceding their attack than had women in the control group. Subjective feelings of stress were also assessed in this study. Women with a diagnosis of MI or angina pectoris reported feeling stressed significantly more often than controls. This was particularly true for the two most severe categories of stress, which were defined as continuous feelings of stress in the year or the 5 years preceding the acute illness.

The effect of stress on the incidence of CHD in women has also been examined in several reports issuing from the Framingham study. In a cross-sectional study of men and women from the Framingham sample (Haynes, Feinleib, Levine, Scotch, and Kannel, 1978), CHD cases of both sexes below the age of 65 scored significantly higher on an aging worries scale, which assessed concerns about things like growing old, retirement, sickness, death, and loneliness. Women over 65 with angina reported significantly more marital disagreements and personal problems involving sex, money, and family than did noncases. A prospective study that was also based on Framingham data found different sets of behaviors associated with CHD in working women and housewives, but in both cases these behaviors could be considered causes or signs of stress. In working women, suppressed hostility was associated with CHD, whereas in housewives CHD was associated with increased tension, emotional liability, anger, and anxiety (Haynes et al., 1980).

While the few studies that have been conducted to date suggest a relationship between stress and CHD in women, more studies are needed before definite conclusions can be drawn. The variables that need to be assessed in order to identify such a relationship may differ in men and women because of sex differences in sources of stress and in how different sources of stress interact. For example, the finding that working women with children are more likely to suffer from CHD than those without children is not likely to generalize to men since the responsibility and attendant stresses of raising children still fall largely upon women. Moreover, potential external sources of stress may not have the same impact on men and women because of sex differences in certain personality or behavioral patterns, namely, in the prevalence of what has been labeled Type-A or coronary-prone behavior.

Coronary patients have frequently been observed to have a characteristic personality and style of interacting with their environment. As long ago as 1910 Sir William Osler noted that patients suffering from angina tended to be intense, robust, and vigorous men who were highly involved in their work, people whose engines were always at "full speed ahead" (1910, p. 839). More recently, Friedman and Rosenman (1959) introduced the concept of Type-A behavior to describe a pattern of behavior they found typical of coronary patients. The Type-A behavior pattern is characterized by high levels of aggressiveness, ambitiousness, and competitive drive, an excess of hostility, overcommitment to work, and a chronic sense of time urgency (Jenkins, 1976; Rosenman et al., 1975; Rosenman and Friedman, 1961; Friedman and Rosenman, 1959). It is usually assessed either through a standard interview in which both the content and nonverbal style of response are taken into account, or by a self-administered questionnaire, the Jenkins Activity Survey (JAS) (Jenkins, Zyzanski, and Rosenman, 1971; Jenkins, Rosenman, and Friedman, 1967). A relationship between Type-A behavior and increased risk of CHD has been found for both men (Haynes, Feinleib, Levine, Scotch, and Kannel, 1978; Rosenman et al., 1975; Kenigsberg, Zyzanski, Jenkins, Wardwell, and Licciardello, 1974; see also reviews by

Harlan, 1981; Jenkins, 1971, 1976) and women (Haynes *et al.*, 1980; Hay-nes, Feinleib, Levine, Scotch, and Kannel, 1978; Kenigsberg *et al.*, 1974; Bengtsson *et al.*, 1973; Rosenman and Friedman, 1961). The increase in risk is independent of the standard risk factors since it remains even after correlations between Type-A behavior and those factors have been taken into account using multivariate statistical techniques (Orth-Gomer, Ahlbom, and Theorell, 1980, Rosenman *et al.*, 1975).

As noted by Jenkins (1976, p. 1034), Type-A behavior is not the same as stress but is "a style of behavior with which some persons habitually respond to circumstances that arouse them." The behavior pattern results from an interaction between a predisposed personality and environmental conditions. While it is not properly considered stress because the conditions that elicit it are not inherently stressful to the majority of people, it may be considered as the result of self-imposed stress. Data relevant to the issue of the mechanisms mediating the relationship between Type A and increased coronary risk are instructive on this point. Type-A people have been reported to respond to challenging situations with greater signs of sympathetic nervous system activation than those who are Type B (the opposite of Type A). It has been suggested that this tendency may be partially responsible for the increased risk of CHD found in this population (Friedman, Byers, Diamant, and Rosenman, 1975; Carruthers, 1969). Friedman and his colleagues (Friedman *et al.*, 1975) found that under resting conditions plasma nor-epinephrine (NE) concentrations were equal in Type-A and Type-B men. However, under conditions of competition involving the completion of a puzzle more quickly than an opponent, NE levels in Type-A men rose 30%, whereas those of Type-B men remained unchanged. Nocturnal urinary excretion of NE is the same in Type-A and Type-B men, but levels of NE in urine formed during working hours shows a much greater increase in those who are Type A (Friedman, St. George, Byers, and Rosenman, 1960). Heart rate and blood pressure responses also show greater increases in Type-A men compared to Type-B men under conditions of challenge (Dembroski, MacDougall, and Lushene, 1979). Since increased release of NE and an increase in heart rate and blood pressure normally result from exposure to stress (Gray, 1971, pp. 57–61), it is not unreasonable to argue that Type-A people respond to many situations in such a way as to put themselves under physiological stress, even if the situation does not call for it.

Men and women, on average, differ in the degree to which they manifest Type-A behavior. Most studies that have compared them find that women score lower than men on assessments for the Type-A behavior pattern (Blumenthal *et al.*, 1980; Haynes, Levine, Scotch, Feinleib, and Kannel, 1978; Waldron, 1978a). This sex difference in the prevalence of Type-A behavior may make an important contribution to the sex difference in CHD. Waldron (1976), reanalyzing data from studies by Rosenman and Friedman, has found that the prevalence of CHD is approximately equal in Type-B men and women. Furthermore, the prevalence among Type-B men is considerably lower than among women who are Type A. Among Type-A men and women in younger (<50) age groups, however, there is still a substantial elevation of male CHD rates. The persistence of the sex differences in CHD in younger Type-A persons, together with the lack of a sex difference in those who are Type B, suggests that the lower prevalence of Type-A behavior among women accounts for only part of the sex difference in rates of CHD.

What, however, accounts for the lesser prevalence of Type-A behavior in women? Evidence for a genetic contribution to Type-A behavior within sex is weak to negative. Rahe and Rosenman (1975) studied male monozygotic (MZ) and dizygotic (DZ) twin pairs and found that A–B behavior, based on the standard interview, showed no heritability. In a study of male and female MZ and DZ twins assessed on the JAS, scores on a previously identified factor "Hard-driving competitiveness" did show evidence of heritability, but overall Type-A scores did not (Mathews and Krantz, 1976). The overall A–B score was more highly correlated in the MZ than DZ twin pairs, but the difference was not statistically significant.

Heritability within same-sex pairs, however, is not directly relevant to the issue of sex-linked, biologically influenced differences in Type-A behavior. On the basis of a review of a large number of studies that examined sex differences in behavior, Maccoby and Jacklin (1974) concluded that males show more aggressiveness and competitiveness than females. These two traits are both important components of Type-A behavior. Moreover, the evidence that they reviewed suggests that these differences are biologically based and are mediated by pre- and postnatal exposure to sex hormones. This should not be taken to mean that the environment has no influence on aggression and competitiveness. As they are careful to point out, "an individual's aggressive behavior is strengthened, weakened, redirected, or altered in form by his or her unique pattern of experiences. All we mean to argue is that there is a sex-linked differential readiness to respond in aggressive ways to the relevant experiences" (p. 247).

Regardless of whether or not there is a biological component to the sex difference in Type-A behavior, it is clear that such behavior can be influenced by learning. The influence of cultural conditioning on Type-A behavior in both sexes is supported by the observation that such behavior is uncommon in nonindustrialized societies (Rosenman, 1974) and may be less common in rural as compared to urban areas of the

United States (Butensky, Faralli, Heebner, and Waldron, 1976). Although the observation was based on a small and not necessarily representative sample, rural working-class students have been found to be less Type A than their suburban middle-class counterparts, which suggests the presence of subcultural or social class influences on the development of Type-A behavior (Butensky et al., 1976). Interpretation of this type of data with respect to social class or rural/urban differences within the United States must be made with caution, however, because of the possibility of sample bias resulting from upward mobility of Type-A parents or from out-migration of Type-A-headed families from rural to urban areas. These same investigators also failed to find sex differences in Type-A behavior among the 5th-, 9th-, and 12th-graders who composed their sample, a finding they attribute to a shared school environment.

Although they too must be interpreted with caution, data on female employment and the presence of Type-A behavior suggest the importance of sex role-related environmental influences on the development of the Type-A behavior pattern. As previously noted, women on average show less Type-A behavior than men. Working women, however, show more Type-A behavior than housewives (Haynes et al., 1980; Haynes, Feinleib, Levine, Scotch, and Kannel, 1978; Rosenman and Friedman, 1961), and full-time working women with some college education have higher Type-A scores than those who work part time (Waldron, 1978b). Mean Type A scores for working women, in fact, have been reported to be the same as those for men (Haynes, Feinleib, Levine, Scotch, and Kannel, 1978; Shekelle, Schoenberger, and Stamler, 1976). Moreover, women in high-status occupations have higher Type-A scores than those in occupations with lower status (Waldron, 1978b). One interpretation of these findings is that employment, particularly high-status employment, sets up situations that encourage and reward Type-A behavior, thereby increasing its occurrence. Competitiveness and devotion to work are generally valued within the occupational world and they are rewarded accordingly. Furthermore, it is precisely those high-status jobs that most encourage Type-A behavior that in the past have been most closed to women. The roles of housewife, wife, and mother, on the other hand, do not encourage or reward Type-A behavior. If anything, they tend to reward its opposite. Type-A behavior is not related to success with members of the opposite sex or to success in social relationships generally, two types of achievement valued within the traditional female role (Waldron, Hickey, McPherson, Butensky, Gruss, Overall, Schmader, and Wohlmuth, 1980). Since women are less likely than men to work outside the home, and when they do are less likely to hold high-status jobs, women on average are less likely to be reinforced for Type-A behavior, which may account in part for the sex difference in its prevalence.

Although employed women may show more Type-A behavior than housewives because work environments reinforce it, Type-A women may also be more likely than those who are Type B to self-select themselves into work environments and to remain in them despite marriage and children. Waldron and her colleagues (Waldron, Zyzanski, Shekelle, Jenkins, and Tannenbaum, 1977) found that in a sample of employed women, those between the ages of 30 and 35 had the highest Type-A scores, an age pattern that was not found among men. Scores for women in this age group were equivalent to those of men the same age. Type-A scores for younger employed women, however, were lower than those of their male counterparts. In explanation, these authors suggest that Type-A women are more likely to seek paid employment and are less likely to give up their jobs when they have children. Since the majority of women 30–35 have at least one child, women who are Type B and who can afford to are likely to have absented themselves from the paid labor force by this time, accounting for the high Type-A scores among those who are still employed.

Data on college students also support the idea that Type-A women self-select themselves into the paid labor force and into higher pressure jobs. In a sample of male and female undergraduates from a selective eastern university, women who had specific career goals had higher Type-A scores than those without such goals. The Type-A scores of those who were aiming for a professional career were considerably higher than those of employed white women the same age. Type-A students also spent more time studying, had higher grades, and took more courses, which indicates that they were seriously pursuing their goals (Waldron *et al.*, 1980). These findings suggest that even before they enter the paid labor force, women who intend to work, and particularly those who intend to have professional careers, are already showing more Type-A behavior than women without these goals. There is no reason, however, why self-selection and learning must necessarily be mutually exclusive explanations. Women who are Type A may initially self-select themselves into the labor market, but having a job or a career may nevertheless reinforce and increase Type-A behavior. Since men, in general, do not have the option of not working, almost all adult males will be put in situations that reinforce Type-A behavior. Women, on the other hand, who have the housewife role potentially available to them, will enter or remain in the work environment only if they are already prone to Type-A behavior. Thus, the majority of men will be exposed to environments that reinforce Type-A behavior, whereas only some women will be. Even if there is a genetic contribution to the higher preva-

Jane E. Platt

lence of Type-A behavior among males, this type of differential exposure to Type-A-reinforcing environments would tend to increase its size. Conversely, as more women enter the occupational world and are also reinforced for Type-A behavior, its incidence in the female population should increase and with it the rates of CHD among women.

5. Conclusions

The potential set of relationships between sex roles and CHD is complex. Any sex role-related attitude or behavior that affects the degree to which men and women engage in behaviors that are risk factors themselves or which have an effect on risk factors should influence rates of CHD. As more is learned about the physiological precursors of CHD and how they are affected by behavior, the pathways between behavior and CHD will become better understood. It is from this knowledge that a fuller understanding of the relationship between sex roles and CHD will be developed. The relationship between sex roles and CHD will never be static, however, for as sex roles change, the relationship between them and CHD will necessarily change, not in form but in content.

6. References

Ackerman, S. H., Manaker, S., and Cohen, M. I. Recent separation and the onset of peptic ulcer disease in older children and adolescents. *Psychosomatic Medicine*, 1981, *43*, 305–310.

Armstrong, A., Duncan, B., Oliver, M. F., Julian, D. G., Donald, K. W., Fulton, M., Lutz, W., and Morrison, S. L. Natural history of acute coronary heart attacks: A community study. *British Heart Journal*, 1972, *34*, 67–80.

Bengtsson, C. Smoking habits in a population sample of women and in women with ischaemic heart disease. *Acta Medica Scandinavica (Supplementum)*, 1973, *549*, 60–64. (a)

Bengtsson, C. Physical activity in a population sample of women and in women with ischaemic heart disease. *Acta Medica Scandinavica (Supplementum)*, 1973, *549*, 93–96. (b)

Bengtsson, C., Hällström, T., and Tibblin, G. Social factors, stress experience, and personality traits in women with ischaemic heart disease compared to a population sample of women. *Acta Medica Scandinavica (Supplementum)*, 1973, *549*, 82–92.

Blumenthal, J. A., Williams, R. S., Williams, R. B., and Wallace, A. G. Effects of exercise on the Type A (coronary-prone) behavior pattern. *Psychosomatic Medicine*, 1980, *42*, 289–296.

Butensky, A., Faralli, V., Heebner, D., and Waldron, I. Elements of the coronary-prone behavior pattern in children and teenagers. *Journal of Psychosomatic Research*, 1976, *20*, 439–444.

Carruthers, M. E. Aggression and atheroma. *Lancet*, 1969, *2*, 1170–1171.

Clausen, J. P. Effects of physical training on cardiovascular adjustments to exercise in man. *Physiological Reviews*, 1977, *57*, 779–815.

Dalen, J., and Hickler, R. B. Oral contraceptives and cardiovascular disease. *American Heart Journal*, 1981, *101*, 626–639.

Dembroski, T. M., MacDougall, J. M., and Lushene, R. Interpersonal interaction and cardiovascular response in Type A subjects and coronary patients. *Journal of Human Stress*, 1979, *5*, 28–36.

Deshaies, Y., and Allard, C. Serum high-density lipoprotein cholesterol in male and female Olympic athletes. *Medicine and Science in Sports and Exercise*, 1982,*14*, 207–211.

Doll, R., and Peto, R. Mortality in relation to smoking: 20 years' observations on male British doctors. *British Medical Journal*, 1976, *2*, 1525–1536.

Doyle, J. T., Dawber, T. R., Kannel, W. B., Kinch, S. H., and Kahn, H. A. The relationship of cigarette smoking to coronary heart disease. *Journal of the American Medical Association*, 1964, *190*, 886–890.

Fletcher, G. F. Exercise and coronary risk factor modification in the management of atherosclerosis. *Heart and Lung*, 1981, *10*, 811–813.

Friedman, M., Byers, S. O., Diamant, J., and Rosenman, R. H. Plasma catecholamine response of coronary-prone subjects (Type A) to a specific challenge. *Metabolism*, 1975, *24*, 205–210.

Friedman, M., and Rosenman, R. H. Association of specific overt behavior pattern with blood and cardiovascular findings: Blood cholesterol level, blood clotting time, incidence of arcus senilus and clinical coronary artery disease. *Journal of the American Medical Association*, 1959, *169*, 1286–1296.

Friedman, M., St. George, S., Byers, S. O., and Rosenman, R. H. Excretion of catecholamines, 17-ketosteroids, 17-hydroxy-cortoids and 5-hydroxyindole in men exhibiting a particular behavior pattern (A) associated with high incidence of clinical coronary artery disease. *Journal of Clinical Investigation*, 1960, *36*, 758–764.

Garbus, S. B., and Garbus, S. B. Will improvement in the social status of women increase their cardiovascular morbidity and mortality? *Journal of the American Women's Medical Association*, 1980, *35*, 258–261.

Gordon, T., Castelli, W. P., Hjortland, M. C., Kannel, W. B., and Dawber, T. R. High density lipoprotein as a protective factor against coronary heart disease. *American Journal of Medicine*, 1977, *62*, 707–714.

Gray, J. *The psychology of fear and stress*. London: Weidenfeld and Nicolson, 1971.

Hammond, E. C. Smoking in relation to the death rates of one million men and women. *National Cancer Institute, Monograph*, 1966, *19*, 127–204.

Harlan, W. Physical and psychosocial stress and the cardiovascular system. *Circulation*, 1981, *63*, 266A–271A.

Haynes, S., and Feinleib, M. Women, work and coronary heart disease: Prospective findings from the Framingham heart study. *American Journal of Public Health*, 1980, *70*, 133–141.

Haynes, S. G., Feinleib, M., and Kannel, W. B. The relationship of psychosocial factors to coronary heart disease in the Framingham study. *American Journal of Epidemiology*, 1980, *111*, 37–58.

Haynes, S. G., Feinleib, M., Levine, S., Scotch, N., and Kannel, W. B. The relationship of psychosocial factors to coronary heart disease in the Framingham study II. Prevalence of coronary heart disease. *American Journal of Epidemiology*, 1978, *107*, 384–402.

Haynes, S. G., Levine, S., Scotch, N. A., Feinleib, M., and Kannel, W. B. The relationship of psychosocial factors to coronary heart disease in the Framingham study I. Methods and risk factors. *American Journal of Epidemiology*, 1978, *107*, 362–383.

Jenkins, C. D. Psychologic and social precursors of coronary disease (second of two parts). *New England Journal of Medicine*, 1971, *284*, 307–317.

Jenkins, C. D. Recent evidence supporting psychologic and social risk factors for coronary disease (second of two parts). *New England Journal of Medicine* 1976, *294*, 1033–1038.

Jenkins, C. D., Rosenman, R. H., and Friedman, M. Development of an objective psychological test for the determination of the coronary-prone behavior pattern in employed men. *Journal of Chronic Diseases*, 1967, *20*, 371–379.

Jenkins, C. D., Zyzanski, S. J., and Rosenman, R. H. Progress toward validation of a computer-scored test for the Type A coronary-prone behavior pattern. *Psychosomatic Medicine*, 1971, *33*, 193–202.

Johnson, A. Sex differentials in coronary heart disease: The explanatory role of primary risk factors. *Journal of Health and Social Behavior*, 1977, *18*, 46–54.

Kenigsberg, D., Zyzanski, S. J., Jenkins, C. D., Wardwell, W. I., and Licciardello, A. T. The coronary-prone behavior pattern in hospitalized patients with and without coronary disease. *Psychosomatic Medicine*, 1974, *36*, 344–351.

Maccoby, E. E., and Jacklin, C. N. *The psychology of sex differences*. Stanford, Calif.: Stanford University Press, 1974.

Mann, J. I., Doll, R., Thorogood, M., Vessey, M. P., and Waters, W. E. Risk factors for myocardial infarction in young women. *British Journal of Preventive and Social Medicine*, 1970, *30*, 94–100.

Mann, J. I., and Inman, W. H. W. Oral contraceptives and death from myocardial infarction. *British Medical Journal*, 1975, *2*, 245–248.

Mann, J. I., Vessey, M. P., Thorogood, M., and Doll, R. Myocardial infarction in young women with special reference to oral contraceptive practice. *British Medical Journal*, 1975, *2*, 241–245.

Mathews, K. A., and Krantz, D. S. Resemblance of twins and their parents in pattern A behavior. *Psychosomatic Medicine*, 1976, *38*, 140–144.

Miller, G. J., and Miller, N. E. Plasma high density lipoprotein concentration and the development of ischaemic heart disease. *Lancet*, 1975, *1*, 16–19.

Miller, N. E. The evidence for the antiatherogenicity of high density lipoprotein in man. *Lipids*, 1978, *13*, 914–919.

Miller, N. E., Rao, S., Lewis, B., Bjorsvik, G., Myhre, K., and Mjos, O. D. High-density lipoprotein and physical activity. *Lancet*, 1979, *1*, 111.

Moffat, R. J., and Gilliam, T. B. Serum lipids and lipoproteins as affected by exercise: A review. *Artery*, 1979, *6*, 1–19.

Moriyama, M., Krueger, D. E., and Stamler, J. *Cardiovascular disease in the United States*. Cambridge: Harvard University Press, 1971.

Moriyama, M., Woolsey, T. D., and Stamler, J. Observation on possible factors responsible for the sex and race trends in cardiovascular-renal mortality in the United States. *Journal of Chronic Disease*, 1958, *7*, 401–412.

Morris, J. N., Chave, S.P.W., Adam, C., Sirey, C., and Epstein, L. Vigorous exercise in leisure-time and the incidence of coronary heart disease. *Lancet*, 1973, *1*, 333–339.

Oliver, M. F. Ischaemic heart disease in young women. *British Medical Journal*, 1974, *4*, 253–259.

Orth-Gomér, K., Ahlbom, A., and Theorell, T. Impact of pattern A behavior on ischaemic heart disease when controlling for conventional risk indicators. *Journal of Human Stress*, 1980, *6*, 6–13.

Osler, W. The Lumleian lectures on angina pectoris. *Lancet*, 1910, *1*, 697–702.

Paffenbarger, R. S., Jr., and Hale, W. E. Work activity and coronary mortality. *New England Journal of Medicine*, 1975, *292*, 545–550.

Radford, D., and Oliver, M. F. Oral contraceptives and myocardial infarction. *British Medical Journal*, 1973, *3*, 428–430.

Rahe, R., and Rosenman, R. H. Heritability of Type A behavior. *Psychosomatic Medicine*, 1975, *37*, 78–79. (Abstract)

Rosenman, R. H. The role of behavior patterns and neurogenic factors in the pathogenesis of coronary heart disease. In R. S. Eliot (Ed.), *Stress and the heart*. Mount Kisco, N.Y.: Future Publishing, 1974.

Rosenman, R. H., Brand, R. J., Jenkins, C. D., Friedman, M., Strauss, R., and Wurm, M.

Coronary heart disease in the Western Collaborative Group study. *Journal of the American Medical Association*, 1975, 233, 872–877.

Rosenman, R. H., and Friedman, M. Association of specific behavior pattern in women with blood and cardiovascular findings. *Circulation*, 1961, 24, 1173–1184.

Shekelle, R. B., Raynor, W. J., Ostfeld, A. M., Garron, D. C., Bieliauskas, L. A., Liu, S. C., Maliza, C., and Paul, O. Psychological depression and 17-year risk of death from cancer. *Psychosomatic Medicine*, 1981, 43, 117–125.

Shekelle, R. B., Schoenberger, J. A., and Stamler, J. Correlates of the JAS Type A behavior pattern score. *Journal of Chronic Disease*, 1976, 29, 381–394.

Slone, D., Shapiro, S., Kaufman, D. W., Rosenberg, L., Miettinen, O. S., and Stolley, P. D. Risk of myocardial infarction in relation to current and discontinued use of oral contraceptives. *New England Journal of Medicine*, 1981, 305, 420–424.

Slone, D., Shapiro, S., Rosenberg, L., Kaufman, D. W., Hartz, S. C., Rossi, A. C., Stolley, P. D., and Miettinen, O. S. The relation of cigarette smoking to myocardial infarction in young women. *New England Journal of Medicine*, 1978, 298, 1273–1276.

Spain, D. M., Siegal, H., and Bradess, V. A. Women smokers and sudden death. *Journal of the American Medical Association*, 1973, 224, 1005–1007.

Stadel, B. V. Oral contraceptives and cardiovascular disease (second of two parts). *New England Journal of Medicine*, 1981, 305, 672–677.

Stubbe, I., Eskilsson, J., and Nilsson-Ehle, P. High density lipoprotein concentrations increase after stopping smoking. *British Medical Journal*, 1982, 284, 1511–1513.

Teiramaa, E. Psychic factors and the inception of asthma. *Journal of Psychosomatic Research*, 1979, 23, 253–262.

Todd, G. F. (Ed.). *Statistics of smoking in the United Kingdom.* London: Tobacco Research Council, 1972.

U.S. Bureau of the Census. *Statistical abstract of the United States: 1981* (102d ed.). Washington, D.C.: U.S. Government Printing Office, 1981.

U.S. Department of Health and Human Services, Public Health Service: *The health consequences of smoking for women, a report of the surgeon general.* Washington, D.C.: U.S. Government Printing Office, 1980.

U.S. Department of Labor, Women's Bureau. *Changes in women's occupations 1940–50.* Washington, D.C.: U.S. Government Printing Office, Women's Bulletin 253, 1954.

U.S. Department of Labor, Bureau of Labor Statistics. *Employment and earnings.* Washington, D.C.: U.S. Government Printing Office, December 1978.

Waldron, I. Why do women live longer than men? Part I. *Journal of Human Stress*, 1976, 2, 2–13.

Waldron, I. Type A behavior pattern and coronary heart disease in men and women. *Social Science and Medicine*, 1978, 12B, 167–170. (a)

Waldron, I. The coronary-prone behavior pattern, blood pressure, employment and socioeconomic status in women. *Journal of Psychosomatic Research*, 1978, 22, 79–87. (b)

Waldron, I., Hickey, A., McPherson, C., Butensky, A., Gruss, L., Overall, K., Schmader, A., and Wohlmuth, D. Type A behavior pattern: Relationship to variation in blood pressure, parental characteristics and social activities of students. *Journal of Human Stress*, 1980, 6, 16–27.

Waldron, I., Zyzanski, S., Shekelle, R. B., Jenkins, C. D., and Tannenbaum, J. The coronary-prone behavior pattern in employed men and women. *Journal of Stress*, 1977, 3, 2–18.

Williams, P., Robinson, D., and Bailey, A. High-density lipoprotein and coronary risk factors in normal men. *Lancet*, 1979, 1, 72–75.

6

Depression in Relation to Sex Roles

Differences in Learned Susceptibility and Precipitating Factors

Sue Cox and Lenore Sawyer Radloff

1. Introduction

There is a considerable body of research comparing rates of mental illness for the two sexes. When all categories are combined, it is unclear that either sex has an overall rate greater than the other (Gove, 1980), though there are clear differences in rates for specific forms of psychopathology. Indeed, a current trend is to analyze particular psychopathologies in terms of sex roles in order to better understand and treat them. For example, suggestions have been made that personality disorders, alcohol and drug abuse, and unlawful behaviors may be ways in which men exhibit their emotional distress and psychopathology based on the male sex role (Johnson, 1980; Weissman and Klerman, 1979). In addition, many researchers have interpreted higher rates of depression in women in terms of various aspects of the female sex role (Radloff, 1975; Weissman and Klerman, 1977, Radloff and Cox, 1981).

Depression is an entity that is included in both categories, neurotic disorders and functional psychoses. When these two categories are used

Sue Cox • Langley Porter Neuropsychiatric Institute, San Francisco, California. Lenore Sawyer Radloff • Center for Epidemiologic Studies National Institute of Mental Health. Reprinted, in part, from Radloff and Cox (1981).

as criteria of mental illness, women have been shown to have higher rates according to extensive reviews of community surveys, first admissions to psychiatric hospitals, psychiatric care in general hospitals, and psychiatric outpatient care in private and public clinics (Gove and Tudor, 1973; Gove, 1979, 1980). Although these criteria include much more than the entity of depression, the findings are interpreted in terms of the female sex role, and these interpretations have been used to account for higher rates of depression in women (Radloff, 1975).

These interpretations will be discussed later but may be briefly summarized as follows: The female sex role contains only one source of gratification, the home; the work performed in this sphere is assumed to have many frustrating aspects and is considered by society to have a low status. It is unstructured and invisible, allowing the opportunity for brooding on emotional discomfort, thereby worsening it. When a woman is employed outside the home, the female sex role entails working in a lower-status and less-satisfying job, working under the double strain of household chores and a job, and working in an environment where there are strains due to uncertainty and the role conflict arising from the fact that some aspects of the worker role are different from or incompatible with those of the sex role. In addition, as a result of the industrialization of the 20th century, the value and meaningfulness of the female sex role have declined, and this may be reflected in the fact that women have a more negative self-concept compared to men (Gove, 1973; Radloff, 1975).

That depression in particular is more common among women than among men has been established not only in studies of psychiatric patients but also in household surveys of random samples of the general population using self-report measures of depressive symptoms. In their extensive review of this evidence, Weissman and Klerman (1977) conclude that patterns of sex differences cannot be entirely explained by sex biases in symptom reporting and help seeking, or by genetic and endocrine factors alone. They suggest that the effects of social roles and social stresses are also important in relation to sex differences in depression, and these are promising areas of research. In a later paper, Weissman and Klerman (1979) suggest that higher rates of depression in women may be based on both the long-standing social status differences, including social, economic, and legal discriminations against women, and women's internalization of the female sex role, including "femininity" and learned helplessness.

Learned helplessness in relation to the female sex role was originally advanced as an explanation for depression in women by Radloff (Radloff and Monroe, 1978). Since then, the model of learned helplessness has been expanded to further define possible sex differences in learned susceptibility and precipitating factors for depression by integrating several cognitive and behavioral models (Radloff and Rae, 1979). This chapter will present this model of depression, and data on depression that have been presented elsewhere (Radloff, 1975, 1980a,b; Radloff and Rae, 1979, 1981) will be discussed in terms of the model and in terms of other related work. Before this, however, theories of depression that could be relevant to sex differences, and in particular to depression in women, are presented. By now it should be clear that the focus of this chapter will be on the psychosocial aspects of depression and only certain selected theories of depression. (For a review of the biological basis of depression and other psychological theories, see Williams, Katz, and Shield, 1972; Akiskal and McKinney, 1975; Friedman and Katz, 1974.)

2. Definitions and Symptoms of Depression

There are a variety of definitions of depression and its symptoms; a diagnosis of clinical depression depends on the pattern of symptoms as well as on their severity and duration. One way of classifying the symptoms of depression, and one that is most useful to the focus of this chapter, is into a syndrome of four dimensions (e.g., see Beck, 1967). The *cognitive dimension* includes hopeless, helpless beliefs and the conviction that nothing will ever get better. The *motivational/behavioral dimension* includes reduced activity and feeling apathetic and lacking in energy. Depression often interferes with normal activities and especially disrupts interpersonal relationships. The *affective dimension* includes feeling sad, "blue," depressed, and unable-to-enjoy. The depressed person may also feel irritable and anxious, even quite openly angry and hostile, especially with the people closest to her/him (Weissman and Paykel, 1974). This anger is apparently not used to communicate and solve problems but rather simply to express distress. The so-called *vegetative dimension* includes disturbances of appetite and sleep. Most commonly, depressives have insomnia and a loss of appetite, but some sleep much more than usual, and/or overeat. These symptoms usually appear only in fairly severe depression (McLean, 1976).

The most widely accepted description of clinical depression is the DSM III (American Psychiatric Association, 1980) criteria for a major depressive episode. These are prominent and persistent depressed mood and/or lack of enjoyment along with at least four of the following, for at least 2 weeks: eating disturbance, sleep disturbance, psychomotor agitation or retardation, loss of interest, loss of energy, worthlessness, guilt, trouble concentrating, suicidal thoughts or actions.

3. Theories of Depression

3.1. Psychoanalytic Theories—Object Loss and Aggression Turned Inward

According to psychoanalytic theory, depression results from object loss, or the withdrawal of emotional energy from an object. Here, an object refers to the internal psychological representation of an external person or thing. Since external object loss usually elicits secondary intrapsychic object loss, the term *object loss* has been used somewhat loosely to apply to both the social event and the psychological process envolved. Intrapsychic loss or withdrawal of emotional energy from an internal object may occur, however, even when the external person or thing still exists. Some examples of object loss might be the loss of an important relationship, a job, a social role, or an activity.

Object loss could be used to explain sex differences in depression in the following manner: The female sex role has been theorized to involve stronger attachment bonding (Chodorow, 1976, 1978), so that when there is a disruption in the attachment, greater object loss and therefore greater depression would result (Weissman and Klerman, 1979). In addition, the female sex role includes being more "people"-rather than "thing"-oriented, so that a greater proportion of emotional energy would be invested in internalized person rather than thing objects. Since personal relationships are more vulnerable to fluctuations and uncertainties, women would be more vulnerable to object loss and therefore depression. Indirect evidence for this is that depressed women have been found to be less maladjusted in instrumental roles than in expressive ones (Klerman and Weissman, 1980). Depression has also been related to the degree of object loss in the form of social role loss specific to sex roles. Depression in women has been related to loss of the role of mother when children leave home and in men to the loss of the worker role upon retirement (Bart, 1971).

The aggression-turned-inward hypothesis was originally proposed by Abraham (1911/1927) and Freud (1917/1957) and was elaborated upon by other psychoanalytic theorists. (See Mendelson, 1960, for a summary and review of these theories.) For Abraham, aggressive impulses toward a love object became redirected toward the self upon the loss of the object. In contrast, Freud assumed that the aggression toward another person became directed against the self by means of object identification, a more primitive process occurring before a relationship to an object is established. It is unclear how these relate specifically to sex roles except that most psychoanalytic theories include in their formulations of depression extreme oral dependency, intense narcissistic needs, low self-esteem, a severe and punishing superego, and feelings of guilt in relation to aggression turned inward—traits also attributed to the "feminine" personality (see below).

3.2. Critique of Psychoanalytic Theories

Psychoanalytic theories have been presented because of their historical importance and to provide a context for the theories that follow. Unfortunately, psychodynamic formulations are seldom stated in ways amenable to empirical testing and are therefore beyond the usual empirical research methods that would allow these theories to be confirmed or disconfirmed.

It is interesting, however, that there are parallels between psychoanalytic descriptions of depressives and those of the "feminine personality." This similarity has also been noted by Weissman and Klerman (1977, 1979), and they credit recent feminist critique with the linking of these two aspects of psychoanalytic theories, which had existed and remained unconnected for 50 years.

According to psychoanalytic theory, the *normal* "feminine personality" is characterized by narcissism, masochism, low self-esteem, excessive dependency, and inhibited hostility as a result of the female resolution of the oedipal situation. This could be seen as indirect validation of these psychoanalytic theories since the higher rates of depression in women may be related to female psychological development within psychoanalytic terms. However, according to psychoanalytic theory, the etiology of depression lies within the oral and anal stages of psychosexual development, whereas the origins of the "female personality" are presumed to occur in the phallic stage. Furthermore, there is empirical support for only very limited aspects of the psychoanalytic descriptions of both the depressed and the female personalities (e.g., see Chodoff, 1972). A more psychosocial explanation for the similarities between depression and "femininity" is that both may be the result of relative powerlessness and helplessness.

3.3. Learned Helplessness Theory

In an interpretative review of research studies on depression, Weissman and Klerman (1977) suggest that "elements of the traditional female role *either through learned or real helplessness,* may contribute to depression" (italics added). In discussing depression in the context of powerlessness, Bart (1975) also suggests that the learned helplessness model of depression (Seligman, 1975) is useful in understanding the "depressenogenic" features of the traditional female role.

The experimental paradigm for learned helplessness is a dog strapped in a harness who receives traumatic and uncontrollable electrical shocks. When the animal is no longer harnessed and receives electrical shocks, it will typically sit or lie, quietly whining until the shock terminates, making no attempt to cross a barrier and thus escape shock. An animal not previously subjected to inescapable and uncontrollable shocks will typically run and howl, quickly learning to cross the barrier to escape the pain. The first animal, by contrast, seems to give up and passively accept the pain.

What is crucial about learned helplessness is the extent to which having no control over traumatic events in the *past* leads a person to believe that nothing that she or he does matters, and further leads to failure to act or to try to respond in adaptive ways to *current* trauma. By passive acceptance of current trauma, the person continues to experience that she/he has no control over the pain, which leads to further development of negative expectations and a sense of helplessness, hopelessness, and powerlessness.

3.4. Reinforcement Theory

Behavioristic theory of human behavior and behavior modification as a psychotherapeutic method had their beginnings in controlling the behavior of animals by means of reinforcement. Behavioral approaches to depression (e.g., Lewinsohn, 1975) suggest that depression is related to a loss of major sources of positive reinforcement, and to low rates of reward or rewarded behavior. In addition, the "sick role" or certain depressive behaviors may be positively reinforced.

According to reinforcement theory, depression can be seen as a "vicious cycle," similar to learned helplessness. A lack of rewards can lead to fewer initiated responses and more passivity, which results in even fewer rewards.

3.5. Cognitive Theory

Cognitive theories of depression focus on the thoughts of the depressed person that begin with a sense of loss. Low self-esteem, self-reproaches and self-criticisms, pessimism, and hopelessness also pervade the cognitive processes of the depressed person. The "cognitive triad" (Beck 1967) refers to a negative view of the self, the outside world, and the future. The negative attitudes described by this theory predispose a person to depression and maintain it, though the actual occurrence of depression also depends on precipitating events. The cognitive view is that cognitions determine affect, so that events will be interpreted pessimistically and will lead to further depressed affect.

3.6. Stress and Life Events Theory

The relationship of the life events (often interpreted as stressors) to the onset of illness has been established (Holmes and Masuda, 1973; Paykel, 1973). Such stressors may increase susceptibility to depression as well as other forms of illness. The work of Brown and Harris (1978) on life stresses and depression presents an analysis of depression in terms of life events and conditions as provoking agents that interact with individual vulnerability factors such as those related to socioeconomic status and mastery. There is some evidence that women do not have more stressful life events, nor do they judge life events as more stressful. However, given the same level of stress, women have more symptoms than men, suggesting that women may experience life stresses differently than men, perhaps having lower thresholds or greater vulnerabilities (Weissman and Klerman, 1979; Klerman and Weissman, 1980).

3.7. A Sequential Model of Learned Susceptibility and Precipitating Factors

Previous work (Radloff and Rae, 1979, 1981) presents a sequential model of susceptibility and precipitating factors in depression that combines features of several other theories of depression (the reinforcement model, Lewinsohn, 1975; the learned helplessness model, Seligman, 1975; the attribution model, Abramson, Seligman, and Teasdale, 1978; the cognitive model, Beck, 1976; and the sequential model, McLean, 1976). This model suggests that the four types of symptoms in the syndrome of depression (cognitive, behavioral, affective, and somatic) are logically linked together in a causal sequence. Furthermore, the symptoms are of such a nature that they reinforce each other so that the sequence can become a vicious cycle.

The epidemiologic (or "disease") model assumes that the probability that an individual will develop a given disease depends on that individual's *susceptibility* to the disease and the *exposure to the precipitating factors* that initiate the disease. In the case of depression, both susceptibility and precipitating factors may include both social and biological factors. It is here suggested that there is a component of susceptibility that is a learned habit, which could be called a "helpless style of coping," and that the precipitating factors activating this kind of susceptibility would be problems or stresses with which an individual must cope.

General learning theory has shown that in the presence of a goal (to achieve a reward or avoid a punishment), the response that succeeds in reaching the goal (i.e., is reinforced) will be "learned" (i.e., will be more likely to occur again in similar circumstances). Learning will not occur if any part of the sequence is absent, i.e., if there is no goal or response, no reinforcement, or no contingency between response and reinforcement. A person may fail to learn to cope if one or more of these factors is consistently missing. For example, extremely overprotected or "spoiled" children may learn as little as children in an extremely deprived environment. People cannot learn to obtain rewards by their own responses if rewards are either always or never available regardless of their actions (lack of contingency). They may also fail to develop goals if they never lack anything, or if they never have anything. Learning will also fail if the person cannot or does not make the responses that would succeed in reaching a goal (lack of appropriate skills). If rewards or punishments are completely independent of a person's responses, this is what Seligman (1975) has called an "uncontrollable situation." It has been found that experiences in such situations may lead the person to generalize this helplessness to new situations, and that this generalized "learned helplessness" is related to depression.

It is possible that a person can also learn to *not cope* (as well as fail to learn to cope). If successful responses that are rewarded are also consistently punished, the person will be in conflict and may try to solve it by avoiding the situation entirely (e.g., giving up the goal). It is also possible that people can be directly taught not to cope by instruction or example (e.g., discouragement or disparagement by significant others). Whatever its origin, failure to cope may become a generalized habit of not responding even when there is a goal that could be reached by some possible response. It may also be verbalized in helpless cognitions ("nothing I do matters," "I can't cope," "I can't do anything right"), which are characteristic of depression.

It is suggested here that the cognitive dimension of depression (the expectation that goals cannot be reached by any responses available to the person) is a basic factor in learned *susceptibility* to depression. Depression itself will not occur unless a goal situation occurs. In other words, the precipitating factors that activate this type of susceptibility are goals (rewards desired or punishments to be escaped or avoided). Given a goal situation and the expectation that nothing the person can do will influence the outcome, then the person is unlikely to try to do anything. This lack of activity is like the motivational/behavioral dimension of depression. Depending on the environment and the generality of the helpless cognitions, such a person would be faced with more and more inescapable punishments and fewer and fewer rewards. This would result in pain, anxiety, sadness, and lack of enjoyment (the affective dimension of depression). There is speculation and some evidence (e.g., Brenner, 1979) that the vegetative dimension of depression may follow from severe and prolonged affective disturbance.

Theoretically, then, depression develops sequentially, but in real life it is, no doubt, a vicious cycle. The lack of coping would strengthen the helpless cognitions (and also contribute to low self-esteem). The sleep and appetite disturbances would reduce energy level and aggravate the motivational/behavioral deficit. The sadness and apathy would interfere with social relationships, thereby reducing reinforcements still further. The depression would continue to deepen unless the cycle were interrupted. For treatment, intervention at any point in the cycle might be effective. Reduction in precipitating factors may also be necessary in cases where they are abnormally numerous or stressful.

3.8. Learned Susceptibility and Sex Roles

It is helpful to distinguish susceptibility from precipitating factors in interpreting the sex difference in depression. There could be a sex difference in susceptibility, in exposure to precipitating factors, or both. Precipitating factors are generally assumed to be outside environmental "insults." If men and women differ in the degree of *exposure* to these factors and if these factors affect men and women in the same way, then this might contribute to the sex difference in depression. The longstanding social, economic, and legal discriminations against women have already been suggested as real, external, environmental events that lead to depression in women (Weissman and Klerman, 1979). There may also be a sex difference in various *susceptibility* factors, both innate and learned. Sex-linked biological factors may exist but have not yet been identified. There is fairly strong evidence that the learning history of women is more likely to lead to the type of learned susceptibility to depression described above (i.e., lack of instrumental coping). Since this has been reviewed elsewhere (Radloff and Monroe, 1978), only a brief summary and a few examples will be given here.

The most plentiful evidence comes from studies of sex role stereotypes. Stereotypes reflect what we expect from people. Studies have consistently found that people expect females (even healthy newborn babies) to be weaker, less able to get what they want by their own actions, and therefore more in need of help and protection than males (Block, 1975; Rubin, Provenzano, and Luria, 1974). There is evidence that people are more likely to do things for girls, while boys are shown how to do things for themselves (Latane and Dabbs, 1975; Unger, 1976).

In the studies of child-rearing practices reviewed by Maccoby and Jacklin (1974), only one consistent sex difference was found: The actions of boys more frequently *have consequences* than do the actions of girls. Granted, boys are often punished (especially for agression), but both rewards and punishments depend on the boys' behavior. Boys can therefore learn to control rewards and punishments by their own actions. In contrast, an observational study of nursery schools (Serbin, O'Leary, Kent, and Tonick, 1973) found that girls got fewer reactions than did boys from adults for all behaviors, including aggression. The authors describe, for example, a small girl who struck out aggressively in anger and was totally ignored. Even her best temper tantrum had no effect on her environment. That is the ultimate in helplessness, and it is reminiscent of the clinical descriptions of the impotent rage of the angry depressive.

For males in our culture, achievement and competence are clearly rewarded. For females, they have mixed results. Some studies have found that females who displayed competence were simply ignored (Wolman and Frank, 1975). For example, studies of small group problem-solving found that females were less listened to, were more often interrupted, and had less influence on the group decisions. An extreme example is the study in which females were given the right answer ahead of time but still could not get the group to accept it (Altemeyer and Jones, 1974). Other studies found that competent females sometimes got rewards but were often also punished, especially by social rejection. The "fear of success" studies (Horner, 1968; Winchel, Fenner, and Shaver, 1974; Feather and Raphelson, 1974) illustrate this: When a female was portrayed as successful, especially in achievement-oriented ways, people predicted many bad consequences of her success. In another study, male and female actors portrayed assertive and nonassertive roles. The assertive females were rated by observers as less likable and more in need of psychotherapy than nonassertive females; the reverse was true for the male actors (Costrich, Feinstein, Kidder, Marecek, and Pascale, 1975). In reviewing such studies, Unger (1976) pointed out the parallel between the treatment of women and that of low-status individuals.

Other studies found that females who succeeded on a task were more likely than males to attribute their success to luck or other factors that would not allow them to take credit for their success. This could produce a cognitive barrier to learning by blocking the effectiveness of positive reinforcement. It was also found that females were less likely than males to expect to succeed in the future, and were less likely to *attempt* to succeed in the future (Feather and Simon, 1975; Frieze, Fisher, McHugh, and Valle, 1975). Recently, it has been found that depressed people were likely to have similar "attribution style"; namely, when they did well at something, they attributed it to luck, but when they failed, they took all the blame (Rizley, 1978). This attribution could be described as a generalized expectancy of failure to cope.

Many studies have found that work produced by females was rated as less significant (Goldberg, 1968; Lavach and Lanier, 1975) and was less rewarded by pay, promotions, and status than comparable work produced by man. "Women's work" is sometimes defined as "pleasing other people." Success at this would be unpredictable, and the rewards very intangible.

In summary, for "competent behavior," which, in our culture, is highly praised, females (compared with males) have been found to get fewer rewards, to have less control over their rewards, and to have more of their rewards accompanied by punishment. Women have also been instructed by the stereotypes that competent instrumental behavior is not expected of them. That this "training in helplessness" has been effective is shown by their attribution style (taking less personal credit for success) and their low expectations of success. The behavioral effect is seen in their reduced rates of attempting to solve problems.

In conclusion, it is suggested that depression is a special problem for women not because they are biologically female, nor only because they may be exposed to more current stressors, but also because they have learned through sex role socialization to be more susceptible to depression. While there may be many sources of learned susceptibility that would affect the two sexes equally, stereotyped sex role socialization is an added source of susceptibility to depression for women.

4. Some Data on Sex Differences in Depression

The data presented here came from a mental health interview survey sponsored by the Center for Epidemiologic Studies at the National Institute of Mental Health, conducted in Kansas City, Missouri, in 1971–72 and Washington County, Maryland, in 1971–73. Individuals aged 18 years and over were randomly selected for interview from a representative sample of households. Response rates were 74.8% in Kansas City, 80.1% in Washington County.

The racial compositions of the samples reflected those of the populations: There were about 24% nonwhite in Kansas City and only 2% in Washington County. Preliminary analyses suggested that the whites and nonwhites should not be combined because they may differ in relationships among some variables. The number of nonwhites were too small to analyze separately in detail, so the present findings cover analyses of whites only, with a sample size of 2515 whites (876 in Kansas City, 1639 in Washington County).

In the data reported here, degree of depression is operationally defined as the score on the CES-D Scale (Center for Epidemiologic Studies-Depression Scale). The score consists of the number of symptoms of depression experienced during the past week, weighted by frequency/duration of each symptom. A higher score indicates a higher level of depression. (For more information about this scale, see Radloff, 1977.)

The questionnaire used in this survey included over 300 separate questions, including the CES-D scale. The present analyses cover only the CES-D scale and some of the more objective sociodemographic factors that have previously been found to relate to depression (Silverman, 1968). (See also Radloff, 1975, 1980a; Radloff and Rae, 1979, 1981, for further details.)

Overall, the average scores on the depression scale were higher for women than for men. However, this was true only among the married, the divorced/separated, and the never-married who were not living in their own households (mostly young people living with parents). Among the widowed and the never-married living in their own households, the men were as high as or higher than the women.

Other social factors associated with more depression for both sexes included youth (those aged 18–24 were more depressed than all other age groups), low education, low income, low-status employment, and physical illness (current or recent). Among males, but not females, currently employed workers were less depressed than others. For both males and females, those who have had children but were not living with them ("empty nest" parents) were less depressed than others. The average depression scores for females were higher than those for comparable males in all subgroups of these factors *except* in the high-level professionals. In some cases, however, the sex difference was quite small and not statistically significant (see Radloff and Cox, 1981, for details).

Returning to the sex–marital status interaction, the social factors were analyzed by sex separately for each marital status, to determine whether the interaction might be due to differences in these other factors. However, none of them seemed to account for the sex–marital status pattern. Even when matched on several of these factors at a time, the married and divorced/separated women were more depressed than comparable men, but the widowed and never-married (living in their own households) were not (Radloff, 1975, 1980a).

It has been suggested that having a job outside the home might help the mental health of married women. In these data, however, among the married, the working wives were not significantly different from the housewives. Both were significantly more depressed than the working husbands. This held even when controlled for total family income, amount of time spent doing housework, and presence and ages of children (Radloff, 1975). This finding should be interpreted with caution, however. The measure of housework may not have been adequate to reflect the strain of double duty for employee wives. It also fails to take the quality of the wife's employment into account. The married women were working at much lower-level jobs than the men. Those few who were working at professional or managerial jobs had very low depression scores (even lower than comparable husbands). Interestingly, the unemployed husbands were more depressed than unemployed wives, while in the *non*married groups (including never-married, widowed, and divorced/separated) the unemployed women were much more depressed than the unemployed men.

Regarding the effects of children, three groups have been compared: those who had never had children, those who had children living with them at the time of the interview, and those who had children but were not living with them (the "empty nest" group). Among the married, this last group ("empty nest") was significantly *less* depressed than the other groups (Radloff, 1975). This held even when controlled for age, income, and age of youngest child (Radloff, 1980b). The presence of children and the absence of money helps to explain the very high depression scores of the divorced/separated women. The divorced/ separated women were more likely to be living with children and to have income of less than $4000, compared with divorced/separated men. Controlling on these factors reduced but did not completely eliminate the sex difference in this group. The women were still more depressed (Radloff, 1980a).

Overall, a large variety of social and demographic risk factors have been examined and found to relate to CES-D sources in the same direction for both men and women. However, simply matching on these factors did not eliminate the sex difference in depression. Furthermore, there was some indication that the relationship of depression to the risk factors was somewhat stronger for women than for men. That is, matching men and women on these variables resulted in quite similar levels of depression at low (more favorable) levels of the variables; as factors associated with depression increased, the discrepancy between men and women's depression scores increased (Radloff and Rae, 1981).

5. Discussion

The model of learned susceptibility to depression (described above) is helpful in explaining the empirical patterns of relationships of depression to other social variables. The most consistent of these are higher levels of depression associated with youth, low education, low income, physical illness, and life events losses. Some of the variables seem related to learned susceptibility, some to presence of precipitating factors, and some to both. Some may also be related to innate susceptibility or to selective factors.

This kind of learning history that would lead to learned susceptibility (the helpless-hopeless cognitive component) has already been shown to be more common for women than for men. Seligman (1975) had discussed a variety of other risk factors for depression, especially poverty and school failure, in terms of learned helplessness. "A child reared in . . . poverty will be exposed to a vast amount of uncontrollability" (p. 159). A background of poverty and/or poor education would reduce a person's chances of learning effective coping habits and would leave the person more vulnerable to depression. Since past poverty and poor education are often correlated with current poverty and low-status occupations (including unemployment), the high levels of depression in these groups may be at least partly due to learned susceptibility. If the high level of depression in the young is a fairly recent development, it might be partly due to a misguided application of permissive or "child-centered" philosophies. If parents are afraid to deprive a child of any pleasures, regardless of the child's own behavior, the child may never learn to cope. It may also be that increased competence and therefore decreased susceptibility may come with age from experience and maturity.

The variables may also be associated with higher levels of precipitating factors. Poverty, low education, unemployment, youth, life changes (especially marital separation and bereavement), and physical illness are all likely to present a person with many and difficult problems to be solved. They may also often be accompanied by a lack of or a reduction in supportive resources that normally help people to solve their problems. If such conditions persist, or if the problems they create are actually unsolvable, learned susceptibility may be increased as well. An excess of such stressful conditions may contribute to the high depression in the young, who have higher rates of life changes as well as high unemployment rates and low income. Women, on the average, also have lower income and education than men and are more likely to be responsible for young children.

The present findings on the effects of children are in contrast to Bart's (1971) study of middle-aged women in psychiatric hospitals. She found depression to be associated with "the empty nest" particularly in women who had been overinvolved in the mother role and who were not employed outside the home. However, the present results are consistent with other studies where it has been found that the presence of children in the home is associated with more symptoms of distress (Bernard, 1975) and lower life satisfaction (Campbell, Converse, and Rodgers, 1976). Pearlin and Lieberman (1977) found that married people who reported that their last child had left home and/or married within the past 4 years were (nonsignificantly) lower on a measure of psychological distress (anxiety and depression symptoms) than parents who did not report these events. It is possible that the group studied by Bart represent a minority who are faced with severe problems when their children leave home. Perhaps the other studies represent the majority of whom the presence of children causes persistent but less severe problems.

Explanations of the sex–marital status interaction are more complex and involve social roles and selectivity in marriage patterns as well as learned susceptibility and precipitating factors. Gove (1972) reviewed studies of mental illness that reported marital status as well as sex. All studies agreed in finding higher rates among women than men among the married. In other marital status categories, however, the results were less consistent, with a majority showing higher rates for men than women among the never-married, the divorced, and the widowed. The studies with age adjustment supported this result. The results of the present study agree with these findings, except with respect to the divorced.

Speculation about the effects of marriage on women by Gove (1972) and by Bernard (1973) emphasized the female sex role of housewife. The assumption was that the married man has two major sources of satisfaction (job and family) but that the married women has only one (family). Further, the role of the housewife plays in the family may be a source more of frustration than of satisfaction. The effects of small children on the mother's lack of control over her own life were pointed out by Bernard. Since the female sex role includes responsibility for household duties, if the married woman has a job outside the home, she is likely to have the stress of overwork. In addition, her job is likely to be of lower income and status, and less a source of satisfaction than her husband's. Finally, another set of investigators (Weissman and Klerman, 1979) suggest that the features of experimentally induced boredom in animals resemble caricatures of lonely, depressed housewives. This may remind us that the "spoiled" and overprotected may be as vulnerable to depression through helplessness of too few goals as those who may be overwhelmed by the demands of coping with too many goals.

Another possible explanation for the sex difference in depression could be that men (or married men) might experience the same distress but manifest it in different ways, including alcoholism, physical illness, and denial of symptoms. Studies (Gove, 1973; Clancy and Gove, 1974) have shown that although nonmarried men do manifest these problems, married men do not. Research has consistently confirmed the good health (mental and physical) of *married* men. Additional evidence is available from the present study for the many scales used in the interview, including use of medications, disability days, a short "aggression scale," problems due to drinking (slightly modified Mulford Scale), and the Crowne-Marlowe Scale for Social Desirability. The married men were low on all items, compared with married women and nonmarried men.

Another alternative explanation discussed by Gove (1972), Bernard (1973), and others is differential selectivity in marriage. Psychological problems may be cause or effect of marital status. The selective pattern suggested is that mental illness may prevent men from marrying but may not prevent women from marrying. It takes a certain degree of mental health to fulfill the male sex role—to live up to the tradition to initiate the decision to marry and be prepared to support oneself, a wife, and possibly children. Bernard (1973) also points out that the tradition for a woman to "marry a man she can look up to" means that women who remain single may be the "cream of the crop," while men who remain single may be the "bottom of the barrel." Specific to depression, it is very likely that the learned susceptibility factor described above (helpless, hopeless, inability to cope) would make a man *less* likely to marry. However, such a style is compatible with traditional views of "femininity" and might make a woman *more* likely to marry. In fact, to be "feminine" and helpless is a more "adequate" fulfillment of the female sex role than to be not feminine and not helpless. Men may actually prefer more "feminine" and helpless women as marriage partners (see Belote, 1981), possibly because of the male sex role requirement, i.e., that he is expected to "take care of" his family. If there is a tradition for a women to "marry a man she can look up to," it implies a tradition for a man to "marry a woman he can look down to." The data presented here are consistent with the notion that the less helpless women and the more helpless men may be most likely to stay unmarried long enough to be heads of their own households. There is some indirect evidence that the more passive/dependent women do not consider any life-style except marriage, while more active women can tolerate the single life (Bernard, 1973, pp. 35–39).

The sex–marital status interaction can be better understood by combining this notion of selectivity (more susceptible men and less susceptible women are likely to stay unmarried) with the learned susceptibility and precipitating factors model of depression. The overall sex difference in learned susceptibility would predict that women would be more depressed than men in all groups. Precipitating factors, however, would vary by marital and parental status, with the divorced/separated living with children under most stress and the married whose children have become independent under least stress. The multiplicative relationship of susceptibility and precipitating factors suggests that the sex difference would be greater in groups under greater stress.

First, consider the "ever-married." On the average, due to differential selectivity in marriage, the women would have higher susceptibility to depression. In the currently married, with relatively low levels of stress, both sexes should have relatively low levels of depression, with the women somewhat higher than the men. This is what has been empirically found. Assuming that the divorced/separated are exposed to more precipitating factors, both men and women should have higher levels of depression than the married, with the increase larger for women. The women do follow this pattern, but the divorced/separated men have very low depression scores. This can be partly explained by income and responsibility for children. The few men who are like the women on these factors have higher depression scores than married men. There may also be some bias in the sample of divorced/separated men; the less mentally healthy may be living in transient situations, in group quarters, or with families of origin, so that they would be less likely to be interviewed. Some may also be in the armed services, jails, or mental institutions. This bias would be counterbalanced by any tendency for the more healthy men to remarry.

The widowed should be similar to the married in susceptibility but have higher depression and a larger sex difference because of increased precipitating factors. The fact that widowed men are *more* depressed than the women may be partly because widowhood is less common, therefore less expected and therefore more stressful for men than for women. It may also be that many men are literally "helpless around the house." Selective factors may also be involved: More men than women remarry after being widowed. If we assume that the less depressed men are the more likely to remarry, then those men who remain widowed would be the more depressed.

To explain the pattern of findings in the never-married, we may consider those who were not living in their own households as "not-yet married" and assume that their susceptibility to depression was similar to that of the married. Their relative youth and lack of independence would predict overall higher depression than in the married for both sexes, with the women higher than the men, as was observed.

The never-married who *were* heads of their own households would be the only group where susceptibility to depression is predicted (by selectivity in marriage) to be higher in the men than in the women. Assuming a level of precipitating factors similar to that of the married would predict the pattern of depression scores that were observed.

In conclusion, it should first be emphasized that the learned factors in depression discussed here are only part of the picture: the part that is most relevant to associations of depression with sex roles and social factors. There are genetic and biochemical factors in depression that may also be correlated with some of these factors and therefore contribute to the findings. It must also be noted that the data reported here are based on self-reported symptoms, *not* on a clinical diagnosis. These symptoms are associated with a variety of types of depression as well as other mental health problems and also occur to some extent in healthy people. Therefore, the results as well as the theoretical speculations should be interpreted with caution.

With these cautions in mind, it can be suggested that the learned susceptibility-precipitating factors model of depression deserves further study. It does provide a plausible explanation of empirical findings that cannot comfortably be explained by genetic and biochemical factors alone. Particularly for women, this is an encouraging note since, if susceptibility to depression is partly learned, then perhaps it can be unlearned. Research can be designed to test the efficacy of methods predicted by the model to reduce susceptibility to depression (e.g., Beck, 1976). The model also calls attention to the role of life stresses and could guide service providers toward more effective outreach and early intervention programs. The integration of experimental research, epidemiologic studies, and treatment outcome evaluation with theoretical models can improve our understanding of the nature of depression and eventually lead to more effective prevention and control.

6. References

Abraham, K. Notes on the psycho-analytic investigation and treatment of manic-depressive insanity and allied conditions. In *Selected papers on psycho-analysis.* London: Hogarth Press and the Institute of Psycho-analysis, 1927. (Originally published, 1911.)

Abramson, L. Y., Seligman, M. E. P., and Teasdale, J. D. Learned helplessness in humans: Critique and reformulation. *Journal of Abnormal Psychology,* 1978, *87,* 49–74.

Akiskal, H. S., and McKinney, W. T., Jr. Overview of recent research in depression. *Archives of General Psychiatry,* 1975, *32,* 285–305.

Altemeyer, R. A., and Jones, K. Sexual identity, physical attractiveness and seating position as determinants of influence in discussion groups. *Canadian Journal of Behavioral Science,* 1974, *6,* 357–375.

American Psychiatric Association. *Diagnostic and statistical manual of mental disorders* (3rd ed.)—*DSM III.* Washington, D.C.: APA, 1980.

Bart, P. B. Depression in middle-aged women. In V. Gornick and B. K. Moran (Eds.), *Women in sexist society.* New York: Basic Books, 1971. Pp. 163–186.

Bart, P. B. *Unalienating abortion, demystifying depression and restoring rape victims.* Paper presented at the meeting of the American Psychiatric Association, Anaheim, 1975.

Beck, A. T. *Depression.* New York: Harper & Row, 1967.

Beck, A. T. *Cognitive therapy and the emotional disorders.* New York: International Universities Press, 1976.

Belote, B. Masochistic syndrome, hysterical personality, and the illusion of the healthy woman. In S. Cox (Ed.), *Female psychology: The emerging self* (2nd ed.). New York: St. Martin's Press, 1981.

Bernard, J. *The future of marriage.* New York: Bantam Books, 1973.

Bernard, J. *The future of motherhood.* Baltimore: Penguin, 1975.

Block, J. H. *Another look at sex differentiation in the socialization behaviors of mothers and fathers.* Paper presented at the Conference on New Directions for Research on Women, Madison, Wisconsin, May 1975.

Brenner, B. Depressed affect as a cause of associated somatic problems. *Psychological Medicine*, 1979, 9, 737–746.

Brown, G. W., and Harris, T. *Social origins of depression.* New York: Free Press, 1978.

Campbell, A., Converse, P., and Rogers, W. *The quality of American life.* New York: Russell Sage Foundation, 1976.

Chodoff, P. The depressive personality: A critical review. *Archives of General Psychiatry*, 1972, 27, 666–673.

Chodorow, N. Oedipal asymmetries and heterosexual knots. *Social Problems*, 1976, 23, 454–468.

Chodorow, N. *The reproduction of mothering: Psychoanalysis and the sociology of gender.* Berkeley: University of California Press. 1978.

Clancy, K., and Gove, W. Sex differences in mental illness: An analysis of response bias in self reports. *American Journal of Sociology*, 1974, 80, 205–216.

Costrich, N., Feinstein, J., Kidder, L., Marecek, J., and Pascale, L. When stereotypes hurt: Three studies of penalties for sex-role reversals. *Journal of Experimental Social Psychology*, 1975, 11, 520–530.

Feather, N. T., and Raphelson, A. C. Fear of success in Australian and American student groups: Motive or sex role stereotype? *Journal of Personality*, 1974, 42, 190–201.

Feather, N. T., & Simon, J. G. Reactions to male and female success and failure in sex-linked occupations: Impressions of personality, causal attributions, and perceived likelihood of different consequences. *Journal of Personality and Social Psychology*, 1975, 31, 20–31.

Freud, S. Mourning and melancolia. In *The standard edition of the complete psychological works of Sigmund Freud* (Vol. 14). London: Hogarth Press and The Institute of Psycho-analysis, 1957. (Originally published, 1917.)

Friedman, R. J., and Katz, M. M. (Eds.). *The psychology of depression: Contemporary theory and research.* Washington, D.C.: Winston, 1974.

Frieze, I. H., Fisher, J., McHugh, M. C., and Valle, V. A. *Attributing the causes of success and failure: Internal and external barriers to achievement in women.* Paper presented at the Conference on New Directions for Research on Women, Madison, Wisconsin, May 1975.

Goldberg, P. A. Are women prejudiced against women? *Transaction*, 1968, 5, 28–30.

Gove, W. R. The relationship between sex roles, marital status, and mental illness. *Social Forces*, 1972, 51, 34–44.

Gove, W. R. Sex, marital status and mortality. *American Journal of Sociology*, 1973, 79, 45–67.

Gove, W. Sex differences in the epidemiology of mental disorder: Evidence and explanations. In E. Gomberg and V. Franks (Eds.), *Gender and disordered behavior.* New York: Brunner/Mazel, 1979.

Gove, W. Mental illness and psychiatric treatment among women. *Psychology of Women Quarterly*, 1980, 4(3), 363–371.

Gove, W. R., and Tudor, J. Adult sex roles and mental illness. *American Journal of Sociology*, 1973, 78, 812–835.

Holmes, T. H., and Masuda, M. Life changes and illness susceptibility. In J. P. Scott and E. C. Senay (Eds.), *Separation and depression: Clinical and research aspects.* Washington, D.C.: AAAS Publication No. 94, 1973. Pp. 161–186.

Horner, M. S. *Sex differences in achievement motivation and performance in competitive and noncompetitive situations.* Unpublished doctoral dissertation, University of Michigan, 1968.

Johnson, M. Mental illness and psychiatric treatment among women: A response. *Psychology of Women Quarterly*, 1980, 4(3), 363–371.

Klerman, G., and Weissman, M. Depressions among women: Their nature and causes. In M. Guttentag, S. Salasin, and D. Belle (Eds.), *The mental health of women*. New York: Academic Press, 1980.

Latane, B., and Dabbs, J. M. Sex, group size and helping in 3 cities. *Sociometry*, 1975, *38*, 180–194.

Lavach, J. F., and Lanier, H. B. The motive to avoid success in 7th, 8th, 9th, and 10th grade high-achieving girls. *Journal of Educational Resources*, 1975, *68*, 216–218.

Lewinsohn, P. M. The behavioral study and treatment of depression. In M. Hersen, M. Eisler, and P. M. Miller (Eds.), *Progress in behavioral modification*. New York: Academic Press, 1975. Pp. 19–64.

Maccoby, E. E., and Jacklin, C. N. *The psychology of sex differences*. Stanford: Stanford University Press, 1974.

McLean, P. Therapeutic decision-making in behavioral treatment of depression. In P. O. Davidson (Ed.), *The behavioral management of anxiety, depression and pain*. New York: Brunner/Mazel, 1976. Pp. 54–83.

Mendelson, M. *Psychoanalytic concepts of depression*. Springfield, Ill.: Charles C Thomas, 1960.

Paykel, E. Life events and acute depression. In J. P. Scott and E. C. Senay (Eds.), *Separation and Depression: Clinical and research aspects*. Washington, D.C.: AAAS Publication No. 94, 1973. Pp. 215–236.

Pearlin, L. I., & Lieberman, M. A. Social sources of emotional distress. In R. G. Simmons (Ed.), *Research in community and mental health*. Greenwich, Conn.: JAI Press, 1977.

Radloff, L. S. Sex differences in depression: The effects of occupation and marital status. *Sex Roles*, 1975, *1*, 249–265.

Radloff, L. S. The CES-D scale: A self-report depression scale for research in the general population. *Applied Psychological Measurement*, 1977, *1*, 385–401.

Radloff, L. S. Risk factors for depression: What do we learn from them? In M. Guttentag, S. Salasin, & D. Belle (Eds.), *The mental health of women*. New York: Academic Press, 1980. (a)

Radloff, L. S. Depression and the empty nest. *Sex Roles—A Journal of Research*. 1980, *6*, 775–781. (b)

Radloff, L. S., and Cox, S. Sex differences in depression in relation to learned susceptibility. In S. Cox (Ed.), *Female psychology: The emerging self* (2nd ed.). New York: St. Martin's Press, 1981.

Radloff, L. S., & Monroe, M. M. Sex differences in helplessness: With implications for depression. In L. S. Hansen and R. S. Rapoza (Eds.), *Career development and counseling of women*. Springfield, Ill.: Charles C Thomas, 1978.

Radloff, L. S., and Rae, D. S. Susceptibility and precipitating factors in depression: Sex differences and similarities. *Journal of Abnormal Psychology*, 1979, *88*, 174–181.

Radloff, L. S., and Rae, D. S. Components of the sex difference in depression. In R. G. Simmons (Ed.), *Research in community and mental health* (Vol. 3). Greenwich, Conn.: JAI Press, 1981.

Rizley, R. Depression and distortion in the attribution of causality. *Journal of Abnormal Psychology*, 1978, *87*, 32–48.

Rubin, J. Z., Provenzano, F. J., and Luria, Z. The eye of the beholder: Parents' views on sex of newborns. *American Journal of Orthopsychiatry*, 1974, *44*, 512–519.

Seligman, E. P. *Helplessness: On depression, development and death*. San Francisco: W. H. Freeman, 1975.

Serbin, L. A., O'Leary, D. K., Kent, R. N., and Tonick, I. J. A comparison of teacher response to problem and preacademic behavior of boys and girls. *Child Development*, 1973, *44*, 796–804.

Silverman, C. *The epidemiology of depression.* Baltimore: Johns Hopkins Press, 1968.

Unger, R. K. Male is greater than female: The socialization of inequality. *Counseling Psychologist,* 1976, *6,* 2–9.

Weissman, M. M., and Klerman, G. Sex differences and the epidemiology of depression. *Archives of General Psychiatry,* 1977, *34,* 98–111.

Weissman, M., and Klerman, G. Sex differences and the epidemiology of depression. In E. Gomberg and V. Franks (Eds.), *Gender and disordered behavior.* New York: Brunner/Mazel, 1979.

Weissman, M. M., and Paykel, E. S. The depressed woman. Chicago: University of Chicago Press, 1974.

Williams, T. A., Katz, M. M., and Shield, J. A. (Eds.). *Recent advances in the psychobiology of the depressive illnesses: Proceedings of a workshop sponsored by the Clinical Research Branch Division of Extramural Research Programs, National Institute of Mental Health.* Washington, D.C.: Department of Health, Education and Welfare Publication #(HSM) 70-9053, 1972.

Winchel, R., Fenner, D., and Shaver, P. Impact of coeducation on "fear of success" imagery expressed by male and female high school students. *Journal of Educational Psychology,* 1974, *66,* 726–730.

Wolman, C., and Frank, H. The solo woman in a professional peer group. *American Journal of Orthopsychiatry,* 1975, *45,* 164–171.

7

Suicide

David Lester

1. Trends

One of the most consistent findings from research into suicidal behavior is that males kill themselves more than females. In contrast, females attempt suicide more than males. This sex difference has been found in almost all nations, in almost all eras, and in almost all subgroups of the population of a given nation (for example, in white and black Americans, in the single, widowed, married, and divorced, and in all age groups).

It is very difficult to trace all completed and attempted suicides in a community, and the most thorough effort to attempt this task remains the study by Farberow and Shneidman (1961), who focused on Los Angeles in 1957. They found 540 men but only 228 women who completed suicide. In contrast, they located 1824 women but only 828 men who had attempted suicide.

Interestingly, this sex difference is found in almost every other culture. For example, Yap (1958) studied Hong Kong, whose population is mainly Chinese. He located 145 men but only 118 women who had completed suicide, whereas he located 508 women but only 386 men who had attempted suicide.

The data for completed suicides are more easily obtained since these deaths are officially recorded with reasonable accuracy. Looking at mortality statistics, we find an excess of male suicides both across the United

David Lester • Department of Psychology, Stockton State College, Pomona, New Jersey 08240.

States and across nations. The ratio of the male suicide rate to the female suicide ranged from 2.5 in Delaware to 5.6 in Vermont during 1949–51 (Gibbs and Martin, 1964) and from 1.5 in Japan to 7.4 in El Salvador (Gibbs and Martin, 1964). (The ratio for the U.S. was 3.6.) The ratio of the male suicide rate to the female suicide rate for the United States in 1964 ranged from 2.1 for those aged 35–44 to 14.5 for those aged 85 and older (Lester, 1979).

Although the male–female ratio of suicides in the United States has remained fairly stable over the last 20 years (see Lester, 1979), the female suicide rate has been increasing recently at a proportionately higher rate than for males, though the females suicide rate remains only about one-third of the male suicide rate.

Burvill (1972) looked at nine nations and found that the female suicide rate had increased in all of them from 1955 to 1965, thereby causing the male–female ratio to decrease. It appears, therefore, that modern society is leading to more suicidogenic stress for females while having no ameliorative effect for males. Gove (1972) also has noted this phenomenon. From 1952–53 to 1962–63, the suicide rate for white males in the United States rose 10%, whereas the suicide rate for white females rose 49%. (The corresponding increases for black males and black females were 33% and 80%, respectively.) For nine western indus-trialized nations, the female suicide rate rose 18%, while the male sui-cide rate rose 2%.

This relatively higher increase in the female suicide rate is not, however, found in all age groups. Data reported by Metropolitan Life (1976) and presented in Table 1 show that suicide rates from 1963 to 1973

Table 1.   Mortality from Suicide 1963–64 to 1973–74 for the U.S. White Population[a]

| | Death rate per 100,000 | | | | | |
| | 1963–64 | | 1973–74 | | Percent change | |
Age	Male	Female	Male	Female	Male	Female
All ages	17.4	6.2	18.8	7.1	8.0	14.5
15–24	9.2	3.0	17.6	4.5	91.3	50.0
25–34	16.7	7.2	22.6	8.6	35.3	19.4
35–44	22.4	10.7	23.3	12.1	4.0	13.1
45–54	31.8	12.5	28.3	13.9	−11.0	11.2
55–64	38.6	11.0	32.3	11.5	−16.3	4.5
65–74	38.9	9.7	35.9	8.8	−7.7	−9.3
75 and over	52.4	6.7	47.1	6.8	−10.1	1.5

[a] Source: Metropolitan Life (1976).

have risen relatively more in females aged 35 and older, and in younger males aged 15 to 34.

Among professionals, the sex difference in suicide is much less. In some recent studies, females have been found to have a higher suicide rate than males. For example, female physicians have a higher suicide rate than male physicians (Ross, 1973). In other occupations, such as nurses, chemists, and psychologists, the female suicide rate is greater than for the general female population, though still less than the male suicide rate for those occupations.

This increased suicide rate among female professionals may be caused in part by the role conflicts created for females when they work. Furthermore, professional females may experience greater stress in their work (as a result of sexism) than do males. It also appears that stresses from a career may be more suicidogenic than stresses from other sources.

2. Marital Status and Suicidal Behavior

Gove (1972, 1979) has explored in detail the relationship between marital status and completed suicide for males and females. Since World War II, females have had higher rates of mental illness in the United States, and in particular, married women have higher rates of mental illness than married men. In contrast, never-married men have higher rates of mental illness than never-married women. Gove concluded that marriage reduces psychiatric stress for males but increases psychiatric stress for females. Marriage is more advantageous for men than for women.

Gove examined the ratio—suicide rate for never-married/suicide rate for married—an index called by Durkheim (1951) the coefficient of preservation. If Gove's hypotheses is correct, this ratio should be higher for males than for females. For the U.S. for 1959–61 the ratio for males aged 26–64 years of age was 2.0 and for females it was 1.5. Single males were 97% more likely to complete suicide than married males, while single females were 47% more likely to complete suicide than married females. (Divorce and widowhood also seems more disadvantageous for males than for females.) Gove also presented data to show that this same pattern appeared when rates of threatened and attempted suicide were examined. Durkheim's coefficient of preservation was consistently higher for males than for females. According to Gove, "there have been changes in the women's role that have been detrimental to (married) women and that, as marital roles are presently constituted in our society, marriage is more advantageous to men than to women while being single (widowed, divorced) is more disadvantageous" (1972, pp. 211–212).

Related to this, Bock and Webber (1972) have noted the extremely high suicide rate of the elderly widower as compared to the elderly widow. They attributed this to a greater social isolation (including more frequent absence of kin and of organizational memberships) among the widowers as compared to the widows, and they documented this with a survey of the elderly in a Florida county. The high incidence of suicide among widowers is very likely to be related to the changes in their roles associated with retirement, whereas there may be more continuity in the roles of the women as they age. (See Chapter 14 by Holt and Datan in this volume.)

Herman (1977) felt that suicide among divorced women was likely to be common because of their dependency role learned from their past life experiences and the difficulty in learning new roles as an adult, both of which would lead to feelings of helplessness.

3. Characteristics of Suicidal Individuals

Studies of suicidal individuals have found them to be less active in their social lives and to have poorer relationships with peers and superiors. Suicidal individuals have been found to resent those upon whom they depend, which inhibits straightforward discussions of personal and interpersonal problems and unfulfilled needs. They are also found to have less confidence in their ability to control their future, especially in interpersonal relationships, and to have less ability to use mature interpersonal strategies (Lester, 1972).

Seriously suicidal individuals have been found to have a lifelong inability to maintain warm and mutually interdependent relationships and to be interpersonally isolated and disengaged (even if married). They tended to make more efforts to change their role prior to their suicidal action than low-risk individuals and to communicate more to their significant others (Lester, 1972).

Clinical impressions of suicidal individuals have focused on difficulties in communicating to significant others just what they want from a relationship and on manipulative intent in the suicidal actions, coupled with frequent rejection from the spouse. It has been hypothesized that suicidal actions can result in part from conscious death wishes on the part of the significant other toward the suicidal partner. Suicidal individuals have been described as taking a demanding, passive-aggressive, and clinging role with their partner (Lester, 1972).

A study of married suicidal individuals (Hattem, 1964) concluded that these individuals were more emotionally unstable, more hypersensitive to rejection, and more critical of the world than their nonsuicidal spouse. They felt weak, dependent, and inferior. In contrast, the spouses felt more self-oriented, exploitive, and competitive, and recognized their need to have relationships with weak others. Hattem described these marriages as submissive-exploitive.

Are the characteristics described above more appropriate to the traditional female role or to the traditional male role? Perhaps females have felt less in control of their future than males, have been more likely to take a demanding, passive-aggressive clinging role, and have felt weaker, more dependent, and more inferior than males.

Wold (1971) proposed 10 types of suicidal individuals, based upon his experience with patients at the Los Angeles Suicide Prevention Center. Two types were characteristic only of women.

1. Discarded women had experienced repeated rejection by men and by their parents. They felt that they were failures as women, but assumed a facade of feminity and had hysterical personalities.
2. Harlequin women eroticized death, seeing death as peaceful and pleasurable. They were masochists and alienated, with a poor self-image and a facade of femininity.

Four other types were primarily women.

3. The chaotic type was psychotic, impulsive, and confused.
4. Middle-age depression characterized another type.
5. The "I can't live without you" type had a passive-dependent but stable life-style. She/he became suicidal in response to a rift in a symbiotic relationship.
6. The "I can't live with you" type was typically involved in a relationship with a person of the same type. Both partners were suicidal and harbored destructive wishes for the other.

Two types are found equally often among men and women.

7. Adolescents with problems in communication with their parents and identity and dependency problems often became suicidal. It was not unusual for the parents to have death wishes for their children.
8. The old-and-alone type was typically depressed, was in poor physical health, and had given up on life.

The final two types were characteristic of men.

9. The down-and-out type was a drug and alcohol abuser with a downwardly mobile life course. His self-esteem was low, his health poor, and his interpersonal relationships superficial.

10. The violent type experienced episodes of rage. He drank a lot but was able to hold a steady job and was rarely living alone. However, his rage often led to assaultive and self-destructive behavior.

Several studies have identified consistent differences between male and female suicides. Suicidal women tend to be diagnosed more often as neurotic and with affective disorders rather than as schizophrenic or psychopathic (Davis, 1968). Women tend to be suicidal more often in response to interpersonal problems, whereas men tend to be suicidal more often in response to intrapsychic conflicts and to commit suicide in response to job loss and legal problems (Beck, Lester, and Kovacs, 1973; Farberow, 1970).

4. Explanations for Sex Differences in Suicidal Behavior

4.1. Methods for Suicide

Women use different methods for suicide than those used by men. Men prefer active methods such as hanging and shooting. Women prefer passive methods such as drugs and poisons. More subtle differences exist. When suicide is committed by firearms, men are more likely to shoot themselves in the head. Lester (1969a) has speculated that women are more concerned with their physical appearance after death and so choose less disfiguring methods for suicide. Evidence exists for this notion in a study conducted by Diggory and Rothman (1961) on the consequences of death feared most. Women reported more concern with their physical appearance after death than did men.

Thus, one explanation for the sex difference in suicidal behavior is that women choose methods for suicide that are less likely to kill. For example, you are more likely to survive a shot in the body than one in the head, and you are more likely to survive a drug overdose than a bullet wound.

Lester (1969a) noted that this explanation, though possibly correct in part, was insufficient because within any method men die more often than women. For example, for those who jump to their death, a greater proportion of men die.

Perhaps women choose less lethal methods for suicide because they are less intent on dying. However, choice of method may be affected by socialization. For example, Marks and Stokes (1976) surveyed male and female students and found that males had much more familiarity with firearms when growing up than did females. Southern students had more early experience with firearms than northern students, and this was reflected in the finding that suicide was committed most often using firearms in the South, for both males and females. Perhaps these differences in socialization experiences affect the choice of a method for suicide?

4.2. Physiological Explanations

Several studies have explored the relationship between the incidence of suicidal behavior and the phase of the menstrual cycle. It appears that the incidence of completed suicide does not vary significantly over the menstrual cycle, but that attempted suicide is more common during the premenstrual and menstrual phases (Lester, 1979). Thus, it is possible that the higher incidence of attempted suicide in women is due to an excess of attempts made during these two phases of the menstrual cycle. (However, we must remember that we do not know whether there is an excess during these two phases or a deficit at the other phases of the menstrual cycle.) This has led to the suggestion that the level of the circulating sex hormones affects the incidence of suicidal behavior.

Pregnant women have been found to have a low rate of suicide. One estimate of the suicide rate for pregnant women was .03 (per 100,000 per year) compared to a rate of about 6 for women in general (Barno, 1967). However, attempted suicide seems to be as common in pregnant women as in nonpregnant women (Whitlock and Edwards, 1968). Clearly, changes in the likelihood of suicide during pregnancy can have many causes. However, since pregnancy does involve changes in the levels of circulating hormones, hormone levels have been suggested as a possible source of the lowered incidence of suicidal behavior in pregnant women.

Along these same lines, Kane, Daly, Wallach, and Keeler (1966) reported using Enovid to treat a suicidal woman, and Lester (1969b) has suggested that women using the birth control pill might have a different suicide rate from other women. This suggestion has not yet been empirically tested.

These reports by no means prove that the levels of circulating sex hormones affect the incidence of suicidal behavior in women. Psychological explanations of the associations can easily be provided. However, the reports do raise the possibility of a physiological influence on the suicidal behavior of women.

4.3. Psychosis and Mental Illness as an Explanation

Lester (1970) noted that psychotics have higher rates for completed suicide while neurotics have higher rates for attempted suicide. A review of community surveys revealed that males are more prone to psy-

chosis, whereas females are more prone to neurosis. A community survey of a county in Tennessee (Roth and Luton, 1943) and one of a section
of Baltimore (Lemkau, Tietze, and Cooper, 1942) both reported this sex
difference. Lester suggested that the sex difference in suicide may be a
result of this difference in the incidence of particular psychiatric disorders. Males are more likely to become psychotic and so may be more
likely to complete suicide. Females are more likely to become neurotic
and so may be more likely to attempt suicide. No adequate test of this
hypothesis has yet appeared.

4.4. Societal Explanations

There is one explanation of the sex difference in suicidal behavior that
has particular importance for a discussion of sex roles and suicidal behavior. Linehan (1973) felt that an important determinant of what happens when a person is in crisis is what alternatives are socially acceptable. She felt that attempted suicide was seen in our society as a weak
and feminine behavior, and less available to males. Males, therefore,
may be less able to communicate mild levels of distress, suppressing
their self-destructive impulses until they are so strong as to precipitate a
lethal suicide action.

Linehan tested her ideas by presenting to undergraduate students
case studies involving males and females in crisis and varying the characteristics of the patients so that some were portrayed as "masculine"
while others were portrayed as "feminine." She found that the students
predicted suicide as an outcome more often for males than for females,
and also that suicide was the predicted outcome more often for masculine patients than for feminine patients. The students predicted suicide 71% of the time for the masculine males, 62% of the time for masculine females, 43% of the time for feminine males, and 22% of the time
for feminine females.

This suggests that social sex role stereotypes, which are probably
based in part on differences in the social roles and the behavior of males
and females in the society, serve to perpetuate those stereotyped roles.

5. Female Suppression and Sex Differences in Suicide

A discussion of sex roles and their influence on the suicide rate has
to include the issue of female suppression in societies. Does the differential status of females in a society have any impact upon their suicide
rate?

Stewart and Winter (1977) attempted to explore the characteristics of nations in which females were suppressed and discriminated against. They used a sample of all modern countries and identified 25 possible indices of female suppression and/or discrimination, including such variables as the relative amount of education given to females and the length of time for which females have been able to vote. They used a differential measure of the male–female suicide rate by simply subtracting the female suicide rate from the male suicide rate (rather than using a ratio index). Their results showed that the differential suicide rate between the sexes was *not* related to the indices of female suppression/discrimination.

(Incidentally, Stewart and Winter did find that the male suicide rate was relatively higher in countries where the divorce rate was higher, where there was a relatively high number of teenage females married, where there were fewer illegitimate births, where the life expectancies of both sexes were more similar, and where the differences in the male and female homicide rates were less.)

Related to the concept of female suppression is that of ascribed status. Typically, those individuals discriminated against and oppressed in a society have their status ascribed to them. They are what they are and do what they do because of the social roles and societal status prescribed for them. In contrast, the roles of the elite in a society are determined to a large extent by what they themselves accomplish and achieve.

People in ascribed roles have more external constraints on their behavior. Henry and Short (1954) argued that strong external constraints provide a clear external source to blame for one's misery and so facilitate homicidal behavior and inhibit suicidal behavior. In contrast, those in achieved roles have weak external constraints on their behavior. Their failures cannot be blamed so easily on external agents. They themselves must bear the burden of responsibility. Thus, suicidal behavior is facilitated and homicidal behavior is inhibited.

If we view the traditional female role as an ascribed one and the traditional male role as an achieved one, then suicidal behavior should be more common in males, whereas homicidal behavior should be more common in females. Only the first of these predictions can be confirmed. In the United States, males show both more suicidal behavior and more homicidal behavior.

The traditional roles change somewhat during time of war. In times of war, when males are drafted into the armed forces, females take over many of the traditional male roles in society. They thus become more able to achieve a role in the society. Lester (1972) reviewed information on suicide rates during time of war and found some evidence for a relatively higher female suicide rate.

Several studies have looked at the association between the extent to which women are in the labor force and the overall suicide rate of a region. Newman, Whittemore, and Newman (1973) found in two U.S. cities (Atlanta and Chicago) that the suicide rate was higher in those census tracts with a higher proportion of females in the labor force. Although Lester (1973) failed to replicate this association using data from Buffalo, Stack (1978) replicated the association using a sample of 45 nations of the world.

The reasons for this association are far from clear, and none of the studies have tried to clarify them. It may be that more married and working females are committing suicide in areas where more females are in the labor force, possibly because of role strain. On the other hand, it may be that the participation of females in the labor force creates additional stress for men (both those in the labor force competing with the females and those married to the working females), thereby increasing their suicide rate. Or it may be that the association is a spurious one, resulting from the importance of some other major sociological variable that is also associated with the percentage of females in the labor force (for example, industrialization).

Cumming, Lazer, and Chisholm (1975) reported that married women who were employed in British Columbia, Canada, had a lower suicide rate than those who were not employed. They concluded that there was no evidence for the existence of role strain in married working women. Incidentally, the suicide rates for single, widowed, and divorced women who were employed were also lower than those of the unemployed. Thus, employment is associated with a lowered suicide rate for all women, regardless of marital status.

Future studies are necessary to explore why geographic regions with many working females have a higher suicide rate.

6. Final Comments

At a macroscopic level of analysis, there is some evidence for a relationship between sex roles and suicide. The effects of marital status on the suicide rates in males and females, the prediction by college students of suicide in masculine and feminine males and females, the sex difference in suicidal behavior, and the theoretical ideas of Henry and Short on ascribed versus achieved status all lend support to the notion that sex roles are related to suicidal behavior.

Sex roles also involve particular kinds of relationships between men and women. Two problems confront us here. What are the characteristics of the relationships between men and women—for example, between husbands and wives? What are the characteristics of the interpersonal relationships of those prone to suicide? Neither of these questions is easily answered.

Virtually no research has been conducted on the interpersonal relationships of those who complete suicide. Their death makes collection of data difficult. Interviews with the friends and relatives of the deceased person (often called psychological autopsies) yield some information, but it is generally unreliable. Informants often have a distorted perception of the deceased's behavior and personality, and their reports are not an adequate substitute for objective psychological test scores or the observations of expert clinicians. Thus, most of the information on the interpersonal relationships of suicidal individuals has been collected from studies of those who attempt suicide, and many suicidologists have argued that the study of attempted suicide can tell us little that is relevant to completed suicides (Lester, 1972).

At a microscopic level of analysis, where we explore the relationship between actual behavioral roles and the frequency and kind of suicidal behavior in individual people, we find little systematic research. It is, of course, easier to study distal variables (such as marital status) than to study proximal variables (such as the nature of an individual's role). The data are more readily available and distal variables are operationally defined more easily than proximal variables.

The result is that we have some interesting possibilities as to how and why sex roles might be related to suicidal behavior. But we have little concrete evidence from studies of individuals that sex roles *per se* are (or are not) related to suicidal behavior.

7. References

Barno, A. Criminal abortion deaths, illegitimate pregnancy deaths and suicides in pregnancy. *American Journal of Obstetrics and Gynecology*, 1967, *98*, 356–367.

Beck, A. T., Lester, D., and Kovacs, H. Attempted suicide by males and females. *Psychological Reports*, 1973, *33*, 965–966.

Bock, E. W., and Webber, I. L. Suicide among the elderly. *Journal of Marriage and the Family*, 1972, *34*, 24–31.

Burvill, P. Recent decreased ratio of male:female suicide rates. *International Journal of Social Psychiatry*, 1972, *18*, 137–139.

Cumming, E., Lazer, C., and Chisholm, L. Suicide as an index of role strain among employed and not employed married women in British Columbia. *Canadian Review of Sociology and Anthropology*, 1975, *12*, 462–470.

Davis, F. Sex differences in suicide and attempted suicide. *Diseases of the Nervous System*, 1968, *29*, 193–194.

Diggory, J. C., and Rothman, D. Values destroyed by death. *Journal of Abnormal and Social Psychology*, 1961, *63*, 205–210.

Durkheim, E. *Suicide*. New York: Free Press, 1951.

Farberow, N. L. Self-destruction and identity. *Humanitas*, 1970, *6*, 45–68.

Farberow, N. L., and Shneidman, E. S. *The cry for help*. New York: McGraw-Hill, 1961.

Gibbs, J., and Martin, W. *Status integration and suicide*. Eugene: University of Oregon Press, 1964.

Gove, W. Sex, marital status and suicide. *Journal of Health and Social Behavior*, 1972, *13*, 204–213.

Gove, W. Sex differences in the epidemiology of mental disorder. In E. S. Gomberg and V. Franks (Eds.), *Gender and disordered behavior*. New York: Brunner/Mazel, 1979. Pp. 23–68.

Hattem, J. V. Precipitating role of discordant interpersonal relationships in suicidal behavior. *Dissertation Abstracts*, 1964, *25*, 1335–1336.

Henry, A., and Short, J. *Suicide and homicide*. New York: Free Press, 1954.

Herman, J. Women, divorce and suicide. *Journal of Divorce*, 1977, *1*, 107–117.

Kane, F., Daly, R., Wallach, M., and Keeler, M. Amelioration of premenstrual mood disturbance with a progestational agent. *Diseases of the Nervous System*, 1966, *27*, 339–342.

Lemkau, P., Tietze, C., and Cooper, M. Mental hygiene problems in an urban district. *Mental Hygiene*, 1942, *26*, 100–119.

Lester, D. Suicidal behavior in men and women. *Mental Hygiene*, 1969, *53*, 340–345. (a)

Lester, D. The antisuicide pill. *Journal of the American Medical Association*, 1969, *208*, 1908. (b)

Lester, D. Suicide, sex and mental disorder. *Psychological Reports*, 1970, *27*, 61–62.

Lester, D. *Why people kill themselves*. Springfield, Ill.: Charles C Thomas, 1972.

Lester, D. Completed suicide and females in the labor force. *Psychological Reports*, 1973, *32*, 730.

Lester, D. Sex differences in suicidal behavior. In E. S. Gomberg and V. Franks (Eds.), *Gender and disordered behavior*. New York: Brunner/Mazel, 1979. Pp. 287–300.

Linehan, M. Suicide and attempted suicide. *Perceptual and Motor Skills*, 1973, *37*, 31–34.

Marks, A., and Stokes, C. Socialization, firearms and suicide. *Social Problems*, 1976, *23*, 622–629.

Metropolitan Life. Recent trends in suicide. *Statistical Bulletin*, 1976, *57*(May), 5–7.

Newman, J., Whittemore, K., and Newman, H. Women in the labor force and suicide. *Social Problems*, 1973, *21*, 220–230.

Ross, M. Suicide among physicians. *Diseases of the Nervous System*, 1973, *34*, 145–150.

Roth, W. F., and Luton, F. H. The mental health program in Tennessee. *American Journal of Psychiatry*, 1943, *99*, 662–675.

Stack, S. Suicide. *Social Forces*, 1978, *57*, 644–653.

Stewart, A., and Winter, D. The nature and causes of female suppression. *Signs*, 1977, *2*, 531–553.

Whitlock, F., and Edwards, J. Pregnancy and attempted suicide. *Comprehensive Psychiatry*, 1968, *9*, 1–12.

Wold, C. Subgroupings of suicidal people. *Omega*, 1971, *2*, 19–29.

Yap, P. Suicide in Hong Kong. *Journal of Mental Science*, 1958, *104*, 266–301.

8

Schizophrenia

Ronald A. LaTorre

1. Introduction

Of all the psychodiagnoses, schizophrenia has captured the lion's share of time, effort, financial support, and interest for the last half century (Arieti, 1974). The purpose of this chapter is to review clinical and empirical evidence regarding gender identity and gender roles of schizophrenics as well as to consider possible explanations for gender identity or role disturbances. Symptomatology and selected demographic characteristics are reviewed, as are studies that have directly assessed the gender identity and gender roles of schizophrenics. It is suggested that a gender identity or role difficulty is consistent with the literature on schizophrenia, and that gender identity or role problems must be included in any comprehensive theory of schizophrenia.

2. Clinical and Behavioral Symptoms

2.1. Hallucinations and Delusions

Anecdotal and clinical reports of schizophrenics have often described hallucinations and/or delusions suggestive of disturbed gender identities. For example, using the Schreber case as an illustration, Freud (1925) theorized that paranoia resulted from repressed homosexual ten-

Ronald A. LaTorre • Vancouver School Board and The University of British Columbia, Vancouver, British Columbia V6J 1Z8, Canada.

dencies. Schreber was a man who maintained the delusion that he was to give birth to a new humankind. Schreber's feminine and homosexual identifications were further expressed by his belief that the sun was to be father of the offspring. More recently, Arieti (1974) claimed that one of the "relatively common characteristics" of the self-image of pre-schizophrenic children is an uncertainty regarding their gender or sexual identification or both.

Genital hallucinations are perceptions that one's genitals have changed in size, shape, or other characteristics. Edie (1976) presents, as an example, the case of a 21-year-old unmarried male who suffered delusions of persecution and believed that his penis was shrinking into his abdomen. Researchers in England have reported that approximately one in three schizophrenics (both men and women) report genital hallucinations (Gittleson and Dawson-Butterworth, 1967; Gittleson and Levine, 1966).

Delusions of sex change may or may not coexist with genital hallucinations. Freud's (1925) analysis of the Schreber case suggested some delusion of sex change or doubt about sexual identity despite the absence of any clear genital hallucination. Krafft-Ebing (1933) referred to *metamorphosis paranoica sexualis*—the delusion of sex change that may appear in schizophrenia. An example of such a case is presented by LaTorre (1979). He reports the case of a middle-aged woman who complained that her family was putting testosterone into her food in order to turn her into a man. Such delusions are reported by approximately one in four schizophrenics and are more common among unmarried and male schizophrenics (Gittleson and Dawson-Butterworth, 1967; Gittleson and Levine, 1966).

The delusion of sex change may be so convincing that a schizophrenic will be misdiagnosed as a transsexual. Haberman, Hollingsworth, Falek, and Michael (1975) report the case of a 19-year-old male schizophrenic who was misdiagnosed and treated as a transsexual by a "well-known" gender identity clinic on the west coast, an internist in Atlanta, and an endocrine department of a southern university medical school. He claimed to have internal female sex organs and to menstruate from an area between his testes and his anus. He often produced stained underwear as evidence.

Another symptom suggesting gender identity/role confusion or ambivalence is autocastration or genital self-mutilation. Male schizophrenics have one of the highest rates of autocastration (Beilin, 1953, Blacker and Wong, 1963; Kushner, 1967; Mendez, Kiely, and Morrow, 1972; Shore, Anderson, and Cutler, 1978). Cases of genital self-mutilation have also been reported for schizophrenic women (Standage, Moore, and Cole, 1974). Except in the case of schizophrenia, genital self-mutilation by a woman is rare. Akhtar and Thomson (1980) maintain that self-induced genital injury and autocastration are almost pathognomonic of schizophrenia.

In delimiting the factors associated with genital self-mutilation, Blacker and Wong (1963) listed characteristics similar to those that are believed to be characteristic of the "schizophrenogenic" family: an over-controlling, dominant mother and the absence of a competent man with whom to identify. They also reported a repressed pathological feminine identification among their schizophrenic male autocastrators.

Kushner (1967) reported two cases of genital mutilation. One 37-year-old schizophrenic man performed an autopenectomy with an open razor subsequent to engaging in a homosexual relationship in which he played the "passive" role. A 41-year-old schizophrenic man performed bilateral autoorchidectomy after he felt his "soul" enter the body of a female co-worker. He felt and desired that the lodging of his soul in a woman's body should be his ultimate destiny. It is unnecessary to resort to complex psychoanalytic interpretations to realize the gender identity or role problems that these men suffered.

2.2. Sexuality

There are reports of higher incidences of homosexuality and masturbation and a lower incidence of heterosexuality among schizophrenic men than among nonpsychiatric controls (Akhtar and Thomson, 1980; Klaf and Davis, 1960; Nestoros, Lehmann, and Ban, 1981; Rossi, Delmonte, and Terracciano, 1971). Although Piron (1975) demonstrated that schizophrenic men responded favorably to erotic, overtly sexual, seductive pictures of women, showing a greater preference for these pictures than did alcoholics or normal controls, the male schizophrenic appears unable to perform the gender role behavior required to obtain the object of his desire. Henn, Herjanic, and Vandepearl (1976) relied on rape data to highlight the impaired masculinity and lesser aggressiveness of schizophrenic men. The percentage of schizophrenic men who commit rape is much lower than is the percentage of nonschizophrenic men who rape.

This inability to perform or behave appropriately translates to a fear of sex, which may precipitate schizophrenia (Pinderhughes, Grace, and Reyna, 1972). Kaplan (1974) has noted a related phenomenon in sex therapy where one partner is schizophrenic. Treating such a couple removes rationalization or other defenses and thus places pressure on the schizophrenic to perform sexually.

One might attribute these symptoms to non-gender-related factors such as hospitalization or medication, but this does not appear to be valid. The pattern of sexual behavior noted above exists in the premorbid (pre-hospital admission) state (Nestoros et al., 1981).

2.3. Marriage and Fertility

Problems with gender identity or gender role proposedly underlie the low marriage, high divorce, and low remarriage rates so consistently observed in schizophrenia (Bland and Orn, 1978; Dube and Kumar, 1972; Farina, Garmezy, and Barry, 1963; Klorman, Strauss, and Kokes, 1977; Turner, Dopheen, and Labreche, 1970; Watt and Szulecka, 1979). Single schizophrenics have a far worse prognosis and their hospital stay is approximately twice that of married schizophrenics (Farina *et al.*, 1963).

A sex difference in the marital status of schizophrenics has also been noted, with schizophrenic women more likely to be married than schizophrenic men (Klorman *et al.*, 1977; Watt and Szulecka, 1979). This sex difference would be expected if gender identity or role difficulties existed among schizophrenics and could become less obvious as gender roles change (Samuels, 1978). Our society has traditionally burdened the man with being the initiator and aggressor in courtship—a role that schizophrenic men may be unable to play with success. Because the woman's role in courtship has not been as crucial in establishing and supporting a family, one would expect that schizophrenic women's marital relations would be less affected than schizophrenic men's.

Another explanation for the lower marriage rates among female than among male schizophrenics is offered by Seyfried and Hendrick (1973). On the evidence that women prefer men who adopt masculine roles, they would not be attracted to schizophrenic men. Men, however, show no overall preference, being attracted to women regardless of the roles they adopt. So even if schizophrenic women did not display appropriate gender roles, they would still be capable of attracting a mate, unlike their male counterparts.

It is tempting to ascribe the lower marital rates in schizophrenia to some other factor such as psychopathology (Turner and Gartrell, 1978). However, sex differences in marital rates appear specific to schizophrenia and are not observed in other psychopathological states as affective disorders and anxiety states (Forrest and Hay, 1972).

Not only do schizophrenic men and women marry less often, when they do marry their marriages are often dysfunctional. Becker (1963) called attention to the observed gender role disturbances in seven schizophrenic women and their husbands. Alanen and Kinnunen (1975) reported that the most common type of marriage for a male schizophrenic was one in which the wife was dominant, aggressive, and narcissistic and displayed a masculine identification. The schizophrenic husband was passive and dependent and displayed a feminine identification.

The fertility of individuals labeled schizophrenic has also been reported to be lower than that of other individuals (Mai, 1972; Rimmer and Jacobsen, 1976; Slater, Hare, and Price, 1971). However, Bland and Orn (1978) attribute the lower fertility rate to the lower incidence of marriage, showing that among married schizophrenics fertility is comparable to that of the normal population. Lewine (1978), in contrast, questions such a heterogeneous control group, maintaining that any control should be as similar to the schizophrenics as possible. Using a "matched" control group, as opposed to "unmatched" census data, Rimmer and Jacobsen (1976) still found a lower reproductive rate among schizophrenics. However, even Rimmer and Jacobsen did not control or match for frequency of heterosexual behavior, reduced in schizophrenics, which may account for the lower fertility rates.

3. Empirical Assessments of Gender Identity and Gender Roles in Schizophrenia

3.1. Definitions of Gender Identity and Gender Role

The terms *gender identity* and *gender role* have had various connotations and denotations in the professional literature (LaTorre, 1979). Gender identity is here defined as a self-definition of being either a man or a woman (Green, 1974; LaTorre, 1979; Money, 1973). It is a deep belief that may, in some cases, be unconscious. That is, while most men would say, "I am a man," and most women would claim, "I am a woman," what they say to others may not be what they actually feel or believe. Gender roles are those characteristics such as traits, behavior, and appearance that differentiate men from women. Gender role includes both gender role *adoption* (i.e., those aspects of gender role that the individual has actually acquired) and gender role *preference* (i.e., person's preference for gender-typed objects or behaviors). (For more detail, see LaTorre, 1976, 1979.)

3.2. Gender Identity

The assessment of gender identity has plagued researchers for some time. Self-reports are vulnerable to deliberate distortion due to social desirability, lying, and faking, and to unconscious distortion. Since the development of one's gender identity is dependent on one's body image (self-perception of having a man's or a woman's body), most gender identity tests measure or assess some aspect of the body image.

One method of assessing gender identity is the Draw-A-Person

(DAP) test. Because people most often draw their own sex first, drawing the opposite sex first is taken as a sign of gender identity reversal. Schizophrenics do not draw the opposite sex first more often than do normal controls (Kokonis, 1972; Smith, 1953), although their drawings do show less sex differentiation (Biller and Poey, 1969; Burton and Sjoberg, 1964; Ries, Johnson, Armstrong, and Holmes, 1966). However, Strumpfer and Nichols (1962) have shown that various hospitalized groups (i.e., schizophrenics and surgical patients) respond by showing a lack of sex differentiation on the DAP.

When asked to enhance the sex differentiation of their figure drawings, schizophrenics, especially male schizophrenics, do not differentiate the sexes as well as do control groups (Biller and Poey, 1969). Also, when asked to verbally enumerate sex differences, schizophrenics omit some very obvious ones (e.g., genitalia, body shape, hair length, and cosmetics).

Using self-report questionnaires, Chapman, Chapman, and Raulin (1978) demonstrated that chronic male schizophrenics possessed more body-image aberration than did a control group of men enlisted at shopping centers and fire stations. Interestingly, there was an inverse correlation between length of hospitalization and the degree of body-image disturbance, which led the researchers to conclude that such a disturbance was specific to the early stages of schizophrenia. Unexplained by the researchers was the fact that a sample of 718 university men obtained an average body-image aberration score that was almost identical to that obtained by the schizophrenic men.

Fisher (1964), too, reported a greater body-image disturbance among male and female schizophrenics than among the immediate close relatives of psychiatric patients chosen to control for stress. However, hospitalized neurotic men and women also reported more body-image disturbance than did controls and were indistinguishable from the schizophrenic sample. Nonetheless, there were no differences among the groups in their responses to items dealing with the sexual aspects of their body image.

Erwin and Rosenbaum (1979) tested schizophrenic patients, normal controls, and organic patients. Taking into account the realistic problems with the organic group, schizophrenic men and women reported significantly more body-image disturbance than did the other groups. On the basis of the results of a weight-discrimination task, Erwin and Rosenbaum related the disturbance to impaired proprioceptive feedback.

Seruya (1977) also presented evidence of impoverished proprioceptive feedback. Schizophrenics were more inaccurate than normal controls in estimating their own body characteristics but displayed no deficit in estimating those of a neutral other person.

Although such "body-image disturbances" appear more often among those labeled schizophrenic, the inconsistency of some findings (Chapman *et al.*, 1978), the lack of specificity in regard to schizophrenia (Fisher, 1964), and the fact that items specifically dealing with the sexual aspect of body image are unaffected (Fisher, 1964) provide little concrete evidence that any self-reported body-image disturbance is related to an impaired gender identity in schizophrenia.

Another test of body image is the body satisfaction test. McClelland and Watt (1968) reported gender reversal in the body satisfaction of a chronic schizophrenic sample. Schizophrenic women reported satisfaction with more body parts and functions than did schizophrenic men. This finding was in contrast to the results of the normal controls, where the women reported satisfaction with fewer body parts and functions in contrast to the men.

Subsequent studies, using acute and outpatient samples, have failed to replicate the McClelland and Watt results (Ecker, Levine, and Zigler, 1973; Elfert, 1971). It is possible that the finding is specific to chronic cases and may be an artifact to prolonged stress or long-term hospitalization.

Rosenweig and Shakow (1937) used mirror gazing to determine body-image preoccupation. They found that hebephrenic schizo-phrenics spent more time looking into the mirror than did normal controls. More recently, Fisher (1973) remarked that mirror gazing as well as the insertion of objects into taboo body areas, wearing of bright or gaudy clothes, and exposing of genitalia are the schizophrenics' attempts to delineate a body boundary and to determine a body image.

LaTorre and Piper (1979) relied on the Embedded Figures Test (EFT) as a nontransparent test of body image. They found no indication that the sex difference in cognitive style was absent or reversed in schizo-phrenics (although their overall scores were more field-dependent than were the scores of either normal controls or those with affective dis-orders).

Thus, there is little direct evidence that schizophrenia *per se* is relat-ed to an impaired gender identity. Positive results of some studies are confounded by hospitalization or other stressors. Other studies do not clearly differentiate between paranoid and nonparanoid subsamples of schizophrenia. And body-image tests may be an invalid assessment of gender identity.

3.3. Gender Role Adoption

Gender role adoption consists of an individual's acquired charac-teristics and is more frequently assessed by self-report inventories. Until the mid-1970s, one of the most frequently used self-report measures of masculinity-feminity was the MMPI Mf scale. McClelland and Watt (1968) used a modified MMPI Mf scale and failed to detect a sex-by-diagnosis interaction, as did LaTorre and Piper (1979) when they used the standard Mf scale. Both schizophrenic and nonschizophrenic groups attained gender-differentiated scores. In a fascinating report of 11 monozygotic twins discordant for schizophrenia (Mosher, Pollin, and Stabenau, 1971), 7 of the 11 index cases attained more gender-inappropriate scores on the Mf scale than did their twin, 1 index case attained the identical Mf score, and 1 twin who obtained a more masculine score than did her index sister later developed schizophrenia herself.

Ishiyama and Brown (1965) relied on the Berdie Adjective Checklist to determine the self-concepts and ideal concepts of schizophrenics residing in both locked-door and open-door wards. The self- and ideal concepts were more feminine for women on open-door wards. In fact, the self-concept of schizophrenic women on open-door wards was more feminine than was the ideal concept of schizophrenic women on locked-door wards. Schizophrenic men from open- and locked-door wards had similar ideal concepts, but the self-concepts of the men on the open-door wards were more masculine than the self-concepts of those on the locked-door wards. Length of hospitalization was equated for all groups in their study.

Neurotics, paranoid schizophrenics, and nonparanoid schizophrenics have all scored higher on gender-inappropriate scales of the Adjective Checklist and lower on the gender-appropriate scales of the checklist in contrast to normal controls (Kayton and Biller, 1972). This suggests that pathology of any sort is related to impaired gender role adoption.

Sannito, Walker, Foley, and Posavac (1972) offer evidence that schizophrenic women take less delight in being feminine and enjoy less the homemaker role than do most normal controls.

McClelland and Watt (1968) reported that housewives and schizophrenic men exhibit a Deprivation-Enhancement pattern in their TAT stories. Schizophrenic women, employed men, and employed women show the more "masculine" Enhancement-Deprivation sequence in storytelling.

Using the Bem Sex Role Inventory (BSRI), LaTorre, Endman, and Gossmann (1976) found no interaction between sex and diagnosis. Nonschizophrenic psychiatric women obtained an average score more feminine than that obtained by schizophrenic women, who in turn showed higher femininity scores than control women. Psychiatric male patients (both schizophrenic and nonschizophrenic) obtained average scores indicative of androgyny (balance of masculine and feminine traits), while normal men obtained an average score reflecting greater masculinity than femininity. Unfortunately, the schizophrenic sample was the youngest group, and age correlates with femininity (LaTorre and Piper, 1978).

The study by LaTorre, Roozman, and Seltzer (cited in LaTorre, 1976) compared the BSRI results of four groups of men: schizophrenics, nonschizophrenic psychiatric patients, surgical patients, and nonpatient controls. Schizophrenic men showed greater femininity than either nonpsychiatric group. Nonschizophrenic psychiatric patients, in turn, showed greater femininity than did the surgical patients. All four groups were equated for age, and the three patient groups were equated for length of hospitalization (approximately 2 weeks). With age and hospitalization controlled, pathological men, especially schizophrenics, proved to be more feminine than did normal stressed controls.

In a subsequent study in which both men and women were administered the BSRI, LaTorre and Piper (1979) found sex differences in nonschizophrenic psychiatric patients and in normal controls but found no such differences in paranoid and nonparanoid schizophrenic patients. With masculinity and femininity scales considered separately, psychiatric groups exhibited an exaggerated femininity score, but no difference in masculinity.

To summarize, well-controlled studies show that schizophrenics adopt gender roles that are atypical for nonpathological groups. More recently developed tests (e.g., BSRI) that assess masculinity and femininity separately indicate that schizophrenic men and women overadopt feminine roles. This does not appear to be the result of stressful hospitalization or demographic differences (such as age differences) because such variables were controlled in those studies. It is noteworthy that more recently developed tests include items that are socially desirable attributes (Bem, 1974), in contrast to earlier gender role tests. Schizophrenics may be less concerned with providing socially desirable responses (Piron, 1975).

3.4. Gender Role Preference

Gender role preference refers to the preference one has for gender-typed objects or styles of behavior. The Personal Preference Scale (PPS), developed by Krout and Tabin (1954), contains one subscale that specifically deals with preferences for masculine activities or objects and another that specifically addresses feminine activities or object preferences. Using the masculine subscale, Kokonis (1973) found a significant difference in the preference scores of normal and schizophrenic men. The scores of his control group were identical to the scores obtained by the men in Krout and Tabin's standardization. The scores of his male schizophrenic group, however, were identical to the scores obtained by the women in Krout and Tabin's standardization.

Using the Role Preference Test (RPT), McClelland and Watt (1968) reported that schizophrenic men and women more often preferred opposite gender roles to those of normal men and women. Elfert (1971) found no difference in gender role choices between ambulatory schizophrenic and neurotic men but reported that ambulatory neurotic women chose more opposite gender roles than did ambulatory schizophrenic women. Ecker *et al.* (1973) also failed to replicate the McClelland and Watt results on samples of schizophrenic and surgical patients, although they did report a tendency for male schizophrenic patients to choose more opposite gender roles. LaTorre, Roozman, and Seltzer (cited in LaTorre, 1976) also reported a tendency for psychiatric groups to prefer the opposite gender role more frequently than did either surgical patients or nonpatient controls. Schizophrenics chose more than twice as many opposite gender roles as did the two normal control groups. LaTorre and Piper (1979) reported a tendency for schizophrenic men and women to prefer more opposite gender roles. They also reported that the RPT score significantly correlated with length of hospitalization— but only for female patients.

These studies show a trend for male schizophrenics to prefer opposite gender roles. The results for female schizophrenics are equivocal, but LaTorre and Piper's (1979) data showed that normal women frequently show a preference for opposite gender roles (e.g., control women in their study chose opposite gender roles in about 31% of the pairs presented to them; control men chose opposite gender roles only 11% of the time). This could reflect a greater societal freedom and tolerance for women to cross gender boundaries than for men, or it might simply reflect more desirability for typical male roles.

3.5. Reinforcement, Knowledge, and Ability to Differentiate Gender-Appropriate Roles

To test a variety of hypotheses about parental and hospital staff pressures to conform to gender-inappropriate roles, LaTorre and Piper (1979) asked schizophrenics and nonschizophrenics to complete the BSRI (consisting of 20 masculine and 20 feminine traits) under different instructions. The four areas assessed were parental reinforcement of masculine and feminine role behavior, hospital staff's desire for patients to display masculine and feminine behaviors, the ability of the patient to differentiate gender-related social roles, and the patient's gender-related knowledge. The results showed that all four groups (long-term schizophrenics, recently admitted schizophrenics, nonschizophrenic psychiatric patients, and nonpatient controls) could distinguish between the masculine and feminine items on the BSRI. Thus, schizophrenics appear to be aware of socially appropriate gender roles. Likewise, each of the groups noted that their parents would have been more pleased had they adopted those roles most socially appropriate for their own gender. That is, schizophrenics failed to report parental pressure to conform to anything but gender-appropriate roles.

The men and women of two groups (recently admitted schizophrenics and noninstitutionalized controls) believed that the staff preferred patients to display more feminine than masculine traits. This finding has been corroborated by Shulman (1978), who reported that recently admitted schizophrenic men, in contrast to nonpsychiatric controls, believed that desirable ward behavior was passive conformity. Those patients also identified their role with a greater need for succor, abasement, and defense and a lesser need for dominance, autonomy, aggression, and achievement. Of interest is Shulman's observation that while staff openly encouraged psychiatric patients to be independent, they covertly pressured them to submit to staff authority. Shulman's observation notwithstanding, we are puzzled why only recently admitted schizophrenics have detected or felt this feminizing effect, while the long-term schizophrenics and the affectively disordered have failed to note it. More research is needed to uncover the extent of staff pressure to "feminize" patients and the relationship this has to gender roles.

The fourth area assessed was gender-related knowledge. Long-term schizophrenics and the affectively disordered possessed a knowledge more typical for women than for men. The smallest sex difference in gender knowledge scores was between the recently admitted schizophrenic men and women. One interpretation of these results is that schizophrenics, by virtue of their greater preference for opposite gender roles, acquire knowledge more typical for the opposite sex, or that they lack the interest to actively seek knowledge useful in implementing same-sex gender roles. Another interpretation is that, having acquired knowledge less gender-typed or more gender-inappropriate, schizophrenics more often choose or prefer opposite gender roles.

In sum, schizophrenics seem to be aware of appropriate gender roles. They claim that their parents would have been most pleased had they adopted the roles appropriate for their sex. There is some evidence of staff pressure to make patients of both sexes adopt roles traditionally associated with the feminine role.

4. Premorbidity and Age at Onset

4.1. Premorbidity

In attempting to determine predictive factors in the development of schizophrenia, some researchers have resorted to a "follow-back" technique. With schizophrenic and nonschizophrenic samples defined, researchers delve into school and hospital records to determine differences in the premorbid characteristics of the two groups. Because personnel in schools and hospitals rarely address gender identity and role directly in their reports, few studies provide data useful to our concerns.

Two follow-back studies are relevant. Gardner (1967) followed back 165 individuals who had been referred to a guidance center as children. Preschizophrenic boys displayed significantly more neurotic symptoms than did control boys. No differences were observed between pre-schizophrenic girls and their controls. Relying on the assumption that neurotic symptoms are more typical of girls, Gardner suggested a gender role problem among preschizophrenic boys that resulted in societal rejection or ridicule and contributed to the eventual onset of schizophrenia.

Watt and Lubensky (1976), in the other relevant follow-back study, found that preschizophrenic girls obtained lower grades in high school mathematics than did control girls. The two groups of girls did not differ in high school English grades; preschizophrenic and control boys did not differ in either English or mathematics high school grades. Watt and Lubensky felt that their finding contradicted the "hypothesis of sex role alienation" in schizophrenia because "normal sex role development" is quantitative excellence for the man and verbal excellence for the woman. In their classic review of the sex-difference literature, however, Maccoby and Jacklin (1974) reported no studies where girls obtained better English grades in high school. Of the 19 studies testing verbal skills of high school-age subjects, the majority did not show sex differences. Further, the Watt and Lubensky (1976) control group seem atypical in their own gender role development because these control boys were reported significantly more passive than were control girls.

4.2. Age at Onset

The relationship between age at onset of schizophrenia and gender identity or role difficulties may not be readily apparent. Any comprehensive theory of schizophrenia, however, must be able to explain the early age of onset of this disorder because it is an integral part of the schizophrenic syndrome. Age at onset is so pathognomonic of schizophrenia that Penrose (1971) recommended that only cases of early onset should be diagnosed as schizophrenia. He further demonstrated a greater concordance for ages at onset of a disorder among family members than for the diagnoses given to those members.

Just as well documented is a sex difference in age at onset. That men develop "schizophrenia" at an earlier age than do women was suggested over a century ago—long before the term *schizophrenia* existed

(Jarvis, 1850). This same sex difference has been noted repeatedly (e.g., Kramer, 1978; Lewine, 1979; Lewine, Strauss, and Gift, 1981; Rosanoff, Handy, Plesset, and Brush, 1934; Watt and Szulecka, 1979). However, these reports have operationally defined age at onset as age at first hospitalization, which means that age at onset is really *earlier* than reported in the literature. This could call into question the previously observed sex differences if some factor (such as women's greater likelihood of marriage) protected women from hospitalization for a longer period.

Lewine (1980) found that duration of schizophrenic symptoms prior to hospitalization was similar for both sexes. Nystrup (1976) determined the actual age at onset and found that the sex difference, although lessened, still existed for age at onset. More men than women develop schizophrenia up to 24 years of age, and more women than men develop schizophrenia after the age of 35.

The earlier age at onset for men is not an artifact of a discriminatory or prejudicial diagnostic system because four different diagnostic systems (hospital's discharge diagnosis; DSM-II; a "flexible" system requiring the presence of six or more discriminating symptoms; and the New Haven Schizophrenia Index) yielded significant sex differences in age at onset, with men developing schizophrenia earlier in life than women (Lewine *et al.*, 1981).

Although the sex difference in the age at onset of schizophrenia is not generally addressed in major theories of schizophrenia, Lewine *et al.* (1981) offered a number of possible explanations that deserve review. They suggested, first, that men have a stronger "dose" of genetic predisposition. This is likely based on early reports that the concordance rate between men is higher than the concordance rate between women for schizophrenia (Lewine, 1979; Rosanoff *et al.*, 1934). However, Samuels (1979) reviewed this evidence and noted that the women in these risk studies had not always been followed through their risk period, and she concluded that such a sex difference in concordance rates does not exist. Further, it is unclear how a greater "dose" would affect the man, particularly in late adolescence and early adulthood. Another explanation proffered is that men are generally more vulnerable to diseases and disorders, and schizophrenia represents just one of the disorders to which they are more vulnerable. While that statement may be true, it does little to explain why an *age discrepancy* exists.

A third explanation is that men are more susceptible to stress. This is a generalization from animal studies. If man is more susceptible to stress, one would expect such a pattern for all such disorders. This is not the case. Women have an earlier age at onset for disorders such as depression and personality disorders (Lewine *et al.*, 1981).

The fourth explanation is that psychosocial stresses are greater for men during late adolescence and early adulthood than they are for women. It is this explanation that may be used to explain how a gender identity or role problem underlies the sex difference in the age at onset recorded for schizophrenia. The period of late adolescence and early adulthood is a critical period for gender identity and gender role consolidation. The adolescent is emerging from a period wherein different roles (including gender roles) were tested. Some adolescents are so attracted by opposite roles (or so repelled by same-sex gender roles) that they commit suicide while cross-dressed (Bakwin and Bakwin, 1966). The early acceptance and successful integration of gender identity and gender roles seem more important for later adjustment for men than for women (one reason for the sex difference in incidence of paraphilias). Hence, problems in this area will manifest themselves earlier in men than in women.

5. Explanations of Gender Identity and Gender Role Difficulties in Schizophrenia

5.1. Familial Basis

Parents may consciously and overtly indicate that they prefer their child to adopt gender roles appropriate for his or her sex, only to sabotage their own stated preference by not personally instructing the child, reinforcing him or her, or providing or allowing the child exposure to certain life events that may allow the child to learn about or appreciate those roles. For example, a father may desire a tough, athletic son yet never take the boy to athletic events, never teach him how to throw, kick, bat, or head a ball, never take time to explain the rules of the games, and even ignore (rather than praise) the child when he shows an interest in sports or displays a tough, athletic quality. The mother, too, may undermine the father's or even her own desires by never letting the child engage in rough-and-tumble play or take part in athletic events for fear he might be injured. Rather than encouraging the child to share manly activities with him, the father may exile the child into the house while performing such activities as chopping firewood. While indoors, the mother may have the child help her with such activities as cooking, setting the table, or cleaning the house. This interpretation is consistent with the "double-bind" theory of schizophrenia.

After observing the families of schizophrenic men and women, a group of researchers at Yale concluded that schizophrenic men came from a distinctly different familial background than did schizophrenic women. Beginning their studies over a quarter of a century ago, Fleck, Lidz, and Cornelison (1963) concluded that schizophrenic men most often grew up with skewed families and schizophrenic women most often grew up within schismatic families.

The overly protective, symbiotic mother in the skewed family (the infamous *schizophrenogenic mother*, believed at one time to be the cause of all schizophrenia) combined with a passive, ineffectual father is sure to impair a boy's gender identity or gender role development. From the analyst who could claim that such a child would not resolve the Oedipal complex or successfully experience ego differentiation from the mother to the behaviorist who could see the environment as one in which there are inappropriate gender models or as one in which there would be insufficient rewards for gender-typed behavior, all must acknowledge the potential harm such a family could have on a child's gender identity or gender role development. The same would be true for women raised in a schismatic family. This potential harm is demonstrated by Sathyavathi's (1979) finding that schizophrenics, but not neurotics, either identify with the cross-sexed parent or identify with neither parent.

5.2. Biological Basis

Gender identity may have a central nervous system basis, and problems in gender identity may result from bioanatomical disturbances. Fisher and Cleveland (1959) demonstrated that schizophrenics less often displayed a GSR pattern of left reactivity. Fisher (1960) later noted that individuals with a reduced left reactivity pattern were more field-dependent (which is also true of schizophrenics) and tended to have more body disturbances, more inabilities to incorporate both masculine and feminine roles, and less awareness of proper sexual roles and relationships, all suggesting a left hemisphere dysfunction.

Schizophrenics, especially male schizophrenics, performed better on verbal than on nonverbal tests (Flor-Henry, 1974), suggesting dominant left hemisphere supremacy. Left temporal lobe overactivation in schizophrenics was reported by Franzen and Ingvar (1975).

Schweitzer, Becker, and Welsh (1978) established a preferential use of the left hemisphere for normal women on the basis of lateral eye movement and demonstrated that both male and female schizophrenics displayed the usual female pattern of left hemisphere activation.

More evidence is clearly required to demonstrate a central nervous system site for gender identity and gender role encoding. However, if schizophrenics do suffer such a central dysfunction or overactivation, then it would not be surprising for them to show problems in gender identity or gender role development.

6. The Diathesis-Gender-Stress Model of Schizophrenia

The Diathesis-Gender-Stress Model of schizophrenia is an attempt to reconcile the genetic and environmental schools. One may inherit a vulnerability to schizophrenia (or to symptoms that result in one's being labeled schizophrenic), but nongenetic, environmental factors are required to make the disorder manifest (Gottesman and Shields, 1973; Kety, Rosenthal, Wender, and Schulsinger, 1971; Liem, 1980; Rosenthal, Wender, Kety, Welner, and Schulsinger, 1971).

The nongenetic component is typically conceived as some types of stress. However, Rabkin (1980) has recently reviewed the literature and failed to find a higher *overall* premorbid stress level specific to schizophrenia. If stress does contribute to schizophrenia, it must be a particular type of stress or stressors. The Diathesis-Gender-Stress Model proposes that a leading stressor, if not *the* leading stressor, in the development of schizophrenia is some difficulty in one's gender identity or gender-role development. The Diathesis-Gender-Stress Model of schizophrenia explains a number of facts for which other major theories of schizophrenia do not account.

The Diathesis-Gender-Stress Model proposes that a preschizophrenic child develops a faulty gender identity. The indirect evidence reviewed in this chapter supports this claim; the inability of the empirical evidence to fully support the claim is probably due to the poor state of the art of gender identity assessment rather than to an absence of the problem. Absence of evidence may not be used as evidence of absence (i.e., we are not allowed to affirm the null hypothesis). The exact cause of this problem is open to interpretation (e.g., left temporal involvement that is inherited, disturbed familial dynamics), but there is sufficient evidence to suggest that familial dynamics may at least be a contributing factor. This faulty or weak gender identity is worsened by parental noninvolvement or parental hostility, resulting in poor same-sex models and inadequate same-sex information sources.

The notion that disturbed familial dynamics undermine the gender role development of a particular sex is corroborated by the findings that the incidence of schizophrenia between members of the same sex is greater than between opposite-sex members within the same family and that same-sex siblings of schizophrenics are more psychologically disturbed than are opposite-sex siblings. Even among the well siblings of schizophrenics, those of the same sex as the index sibling display more emotionally intense reactions and express more guilt about being well (e.g., Samuels and Chase, 1979).

As the preschizophrenic begins school, the girl is exposed to same-sex models who reinforce her gender role behavior. The boy, unfortunately, continues without the appropriate role model and is reinforced more often for opposite-sex gender role behavior than for same-sex gender role behavior (Fagot and Patterson, 1969). This drives the preschizophrenic boy even further from an appropriate gender identity and role consolidation and may be why (a) "follow-back" studies are better able to detect preschizophrenic boys than preschizophrenic girls (Watt and Lubensky, 1976), (b) both male and female schizophrenics have a knowledge system traditionally associated with women (LaTorre and Piper, 1979), (c) female schizophrenics experience a better premorbid history (Klorman *et al.*, 1977; Zigler, Levine, and Zigler, 1977), and (d) there is a "buffer" that prevents the woman from developing symptoms for a longer period of time (Lewine, 1979; Lewine *et al.*, 1981; Watt and Szulecka, 1979).

As the preschizophrenic male, ill-equipped to seize his male role, approaches young adulthood with its pressures to find a mate and establish an occupation, his gender identity uncertainty and gender role inability exert sufficient pressure to precipitate the illness. His poor relations with the opposite sex are evidenced by lower marriage rates. The inability to form intimate relations with the opposite sex combines with "gonadal pressure," resulting in increased autosexual and homosexual relations—not because these men are homosexual but because they are unable to initiate heterosexual relations (Salzman, 1974).

The general disorientation and confusion in schizophrenia combine with a growing inability to cope with gender identity uncertainty and gender role inability to produce some of the more pathognomonic signs of schizophrenia such as genital hallucinations, delusions of sex change, and genital mutilation.

The female preschizophrenic's gender identity uncertainty or gender role inability is less debilitating in adolescence and early adulthood because our society has traditionally imposed the more aggressive role on the man. An inability to obtain a job is not as serious for a woman, and she is more likely to get married than is her male preschizophrenic counterpart. The marital relationship is sufficient to act as a psychological support and further shelter her from society, for however temporary it may be. Difficulties with the marital relationship, exemplified by one of the highest divorce rates among psychopathological groups and a higher divorce rate than among schizophrenic men (Nystrup, 1976), exacerbates any gender identity or role difficulty. Stresses eventually become too great and she is hospitalized, although at a later age than is her male schizophrenic counterpart.

7. Conclusion

Clinical and anecdotal evidence points to a problem of gender identity in schizophrenia. Symptoms often express negation of biological sex and, in some cases, a reversal of biological sex. Empirical evidence fails to provide strong support, but gender identity assessment techniques lack sufficient credibility and demonstrated validity.

There appears to be some disturbance in gender role adoption as male and female schizophrenics frequently fail to show the typical gender role scores attained by normal controls. There is also some indication that both male and female schizophrenics have adopted more feminine roles than have normal controls or other pathological groups. The disturbed family relationships of the preschizophrenic may force them to seek caring, reinforcement, and modeling from the elementary school—a very feminized environment (LaTorre, 1979). This could underlie the greater adoption of feminine role behavior. The "feminizing" effect of hospitalization cannot be ruled out as a contributing factor.

The few gender role preference studies are inconclusive, but there is evidence suggesting a preference for female roles in both male and female schizophrenics consistent with a feminine gender role adoption. As length of hospitalization is increased, the pattern changes to cross-sexed gender role preference. Whether hospitalization produces this effect or there is some differential bias in the selection of recently admitted and long-term schizophrenics is open to debate. The contradictory and inconsistent results might also be attributable to differences in the variables controlled or uncontrolled in studies of gender role preference. Some symptoms of schizophrenia support the hypothesis of a gender role preference disturbance in schizophrenics, but the majority of schizophrenics do not possess those symptoms.

Demographic data suggest lower marriage rates, a more passive and introverted approach to sexuality, and a poorer work history for male schizophrenics. Assessment of the female schizophrenic is more difficult as her role more often requires no response (e.g., passivity, shyness) in contrast to the male's required role (e.g., assertion, initiative).

The literature reviewed is consistent with the Diathesis-Gender-Stress Model of schizophrenia, which posits a gender identity and role disturbance as a leading stressor in the development of schizophrenia. Other models or theories of schizophrenia have not explained gender-related demographic characteristics, premorbid patterns, and symptoms found in schizophrenia.

Treatment of gender identity problems may change the symptomatic course of the illness. For example, Nell (1968) anecdotally reported on a residential treatment center that allowed and encouraged sexual relations among its young adult schizophrenics. The patients' therapists had the advantage of personal acquaintance with both partners, and were therefore able to respond in therapy to problems centering around sexual relations—an area directly and importantly related to gender roles. Within such a supportive environment, the training of this one gender role produced therapeutic gains.

8. References

Akhtar, S., and Thomson, J. A. Schizophrenia and sexuality: A review and a report of twelve unusual cases—Part II. *Journal of Clinical Psychiatry*, 1980, *41*, 166–171.

Alanen, Y. O., and Kinnunen, P. Marriage and the development of schizophrenia. *Psychiatry*, 1975, *38*, 346–365.

Arieti, S. Schizophrenia: The psychodynamic mechanisms and the psychostructural forms. In S. Arieti and E. B. Brody (Eds.), *American handbook of psychiatry (Vol. 3) Adult clinical psychiatry* (2nd ed.). New York: Basic Books, 1974. Pp. 551–587.

Bakwin, H., and Bakwin, R. *Clinical manifestations of behavior disorders in children.* New York: Saunders, 1966.

Becker, J. "Good premorbid" schizophrenic wives and their husbands. *Family Process*, 1963, *2*, 34–51.

Beilin, L. M. Genital self-mutilization by mental patients. *Journal of Urology*, 1953, *70*, 648–655.

Bem, S. The psychological measurement of androgyny. *Journal of Consulting and Clinical Psychology*, 1974, *42*, 155–162.

Biller, H. B., and Poey, K. An exploratory comparison of sex-role-related behaviors in schizophrenics and nonschizophrenics. *Developmental Psychology*, 1969, *1*, 529.

Blacker, K. H., and Wong, N. Four cases of autocastration. *Archives of General Psychiatry*, 1963, *8*, 169–176.

Bland, R. C., and Orn, H. 14-year outcome in early schizophrenia. *Acta Psychiatrica Scandinavica*, 1978, *58*, 327–338.

Burton, A., and Sjoberg, B., Jr. The diagnostic validity of human figure drawings in schizophrenia. *Journal of Psychology*, 1964, *57*, 3–18.

Chapman, L. J., Chapman, J. P., and Raulin, M. L. Body-image aberration in schizophrenia. *Journal of Abnormal Psychology*, 1978, *87*, 339–407.

Dube, K. C., and Kumar, N. An epidemiological study of schizophrenia. *Journal of Biosocial Sciences*, 1972, *4*, 187–195.

Ecker, J., Levine, J., and Zigler, E. Impaired sex-role identification in schizophrenia expressed in the comprehension of humor stimuli. *Journal of Psychology*, 1973, *83*, 67–77.

Edie, A. Karo in an Anglo-Saxon Canadian. *Canadian Psychiatric Association Journal*, 1976, *21*, 389–392.

Elfert, D. *Sex-role identification in ambulatory schizophrenics and neurotics: A comparative study of levels of sexual identity.* Unpublished doctoral dissertation, New York University, 1971.

Erwin, B. J., and Rosenbaum, G. Parietal lobe syndrome and schizophrenia: Comparison of neuropsychological deficits. *Journal of Abnormal Psychology*, 1979, *88*, 234–241.

Fagot, B. I., and Patterson, G. R. An *in vivo* analysis of reinforcing contingencies in the preschool child. *Developmental Psychology*, 1969, *1*, 563–568.

Farina, A., Garmezy, N., and Barry, B., III. Relationship of marital status to incidence and prognosis of schizophrenia. *Journal of Abnormal and Social Psychology*, 1963, *67*, 624–630.

Fisher, S. Right-left gradients in body image, body reactivity, and perception. *Genetic Psychology Monographs*, 1960, *61*, 197–228.

Fisher, S. Body image and psychopathology. *Archives of General Psychiatry*, 1964, *10*, 519–529.

Fisher, S. *Body consciousness: You are what you feel.* Englewood Cliffs, N.J.: Prentice-Hall, 1973.

Fisher, S., and Cleveland, S. E. Right-left body reactivity patterns in disorganized states. *Journal of Nervous and Mental Disease*, 1959, *128*, 396–400.

Fleck, S., Lidz, T., and Cornelison, A. Comparison of parent–child relationships of male and female schizophrenic patients. *Archives of General Psychiatry*, 1963, *8*, 17–23.

Flor-Henry, P. Psychosis, neurosis and epilepsy. *British Journal of Psychiatry*, 1974, *124*, 144–150.

Forrest, A. D., and Hay, A. J. The influence of sex on schizophrenia. *Acta Psychiatrica Scandinavica*, 1972, *48*, 49–58.

Franzen, G., and Ingvar, D. H. Abnormal distribution of cerebral activity in chronic schizophrenia. *Journal of Psychiatric Research*, 1975, *12*, 199–214.

Freud, S. Psycho-analytic notes upon an autobiographical account of a case of paranoia (dementia paranoides). In *Collected papers* (Vol. 3). Edinburgh: R. R. Clark, 1925.

Gardner, G. G. The relationship between childhood neurotic symptomatology and later schizophrenia in males and females. *Journal of Nervous and Mental Disease*, 1967, *144*, 97–100.

Gittleson, N. L., and Dawson-Butterworth, K. Subjective ideas of sexual change in female schizophrenics. *British Journal of Psychiatry*, 1967, *113*, 491–494.

Gittleson, N. L., and Levine, S. Subjective ideas of sexual change in male schizophrenics. *British Journal of Psychiatry*, 1966, *112*, 779–782.

Gottesman, I. I., and Shields, J. Genetic theorizing and schizophrenia. *British Journal of Psychiatry*, 1973, *122*, 15–30.

Green, R. *Sexual identity conflict in children and adults.* New York: Basic Books, 1974.

Haberman, M., Hollingsworth, F., Falek, A., and Michael, R. P. Gender identity confusion, schizophrenia and a 47 XYY Karyotype: A case report. *Psychoneuroendocrinology*, 1975, *1*, 207–209.

Henn, F. A., Herjanic, M., and Vandepearl, R. H. Forensic psychiatry: Profiles of two types of sex offenders. *American Journal of Psychiatry*, 1976, *133*, 694–696.

Ishiyama, T., and Brown, A. F. Sex role-conceptions and the patient role in a state mental hospital. *Journal of Clinical Psychology*, 1965, *21*, 446–448.

Jarvis, E. On the comparative liability of males and females to insanity, and their comparative curability and mortality when insane. *American Journal of Insanity.* 1850, *7*, 142–171.

Kaplan, H. S. *The new sex therapy.* New York: Brunner/Mazel, 1974.

Kayton, R., and Biller, H. B. Sex-role development and psychopathology in adult males. *Journal of Consulting and Clinical Psychology*, 1972, *38*, 208–210.

Kety, S. S., Rosenthal, D., Wender, P. H., and Schulsinger, F. Mental illness in the biological and adoptive families of adopted schizophrenics. *American Journal of Psychiatry*, 1971, *128*, 302–306.

Klaf, F. S., and Davis, C. A. Homosexuality and paranoid schizophrenia: A survey of 105 cases and controls. *American Journal of Psychiatry*, 1960, *116*, 1070–1075.

Klorman, R., Strauss, J. S., and Kokes, R. F. Premorbid adjustment in schizophrenia: Concepts, measures and implications. Part III. The relationship of demographic and diagnostic factors to measures of premorbid adjustment in schizophrenia. *Schizophrenia Bulletin*, 1977, *3*, 214–225.

Kokonis, N. D. Choice of gender on the DAP and measures of sex-role identification. *Perceptual and Motor Skills*, 1972, *35*, 727–730.

Kokonis, N. D. Parental dominance and sex-role identification in schizophrenia. *Journal of Psychology*, 1973, *84*, 211–218.

Krafft-Ebing, R. *Psychopathia sexualis*. New York: Physicians and Surgeons Book Co., 1933.

Kramer, M. Population changes and schizophrenias 1970–1985. In L. C. Wynne, R. L. Cromwell, and S. Matthysse (Eds.), *The nature of schizophrenia: New approaches to research and treatment*. New York: Wiley, 1978.

Krout, M. H., and Tabin, J. K. Measuring personality in developmental terms: The Personal Preference Scale. *Genetic Psychology Monographs* 1954, *50*, 289–335.

Kushner, A. W. Two cases of auto-castration due to religious delusions. *British Journal of Medical Psychology*, 1967, *40*, 293–298.

LaTorre, R. A. The psychological assessment of gender identity and gender role in schizophrenia. *Schizophrenia Bulletin*, 1976, *2*, 266–285.

LaTorre, R. A. *Sexual identity: Implications for mental health*. Chicago: Nelson-Hall, 1979.

LaTorre, R. A., Endman, M., and Gossmann, I. Androgyny and need achievement in male and female psychiatric inpatients. *Journal of Clinical Psychology*, 1976, *32*, 233–235.

LaTorre, R. A., and Piper, W. E. The Terman-Miles M-F Test: An examination of exercises 1, 2, and 3 forty years later. *Sex Roles*, 1978, *4*, 141–154.

LaTorre, R. A., and Piper, W. E. Gender identity and gender role in schizophrenia. *Journal of Abnormal Psychology*, 1979, *88*, 68–72.

Lewine, R. Choosing control groups in the study of schizophrenic patients. *Schizophrenia Bulletin*, 1978, *4*, 244–247.

Lewine, R. R. Sex differences in schizophrenia: A commentary. *Schizophrenia Bulletin*, 1979, *5*, 4–7.

Lewine, R. Sex differences in the age of symptom onset and first hospitalization in typical schizophrenia, schizophreniform psychosis and paranoid psychosis. *American Journal of Orthopsychiatry*, 1980, *50*, 316–322.

Lewine, R. R., Strauss, J. S., and Gift, T. E. Sex differences in age at first hospital admission for schizophrenia: Fact or artifact? *American Journal of Psychiatry*, 1981, *138*, 440–444.

Liem, J. H. Family studies of schizophrenia: An update and commentary. *Schizophrenia Bulletin*, 1980, *6*, 429–455.

Maccoby, E. E., and Jacklin, C. N. *The psychology of sex differences*. Stanford: Stanford University Press, 1974.

Mai, F. Fertility and psychiatric morbidity. *Australian and New Zealand Journal of Psychiatry*, 1972, *6*, 165–169.

McClelland, D. C., and Watt, N. F. Sex-role alienation in schizophrenia. *Journal of Abnormal Psychology*, 1968, *73*, 226–239.

Mendez, R., Kiely, W. F., and Morrow, J. W. Self-emasculation. *Journal of Urology*, 1972, *107*, 981–985.

Money, J. Gender role, gender identity, core gender identity: Usage and definition of terms. *Journal of the American Academy of Psychoanalysis*, 1973, *1*, 397–403.

Mosher, L. R., Pollin, W., and Stabenau, J. R. Families with identical twins discordant for schizophrenia: Some relationships between identification, thinking styles, psychopathology and dominance-submissiveness. *British Journal of Psychiatry*, 1971, *118*, 29–42.

Nell, R. Sex in a mental institution. *Journal of Sex Research*, 1968, *4*, 303–312.

Nestoros, J. N., Lehmann, H. E., and Ban, T. A. Sexual behavior of the male schizophrenic: The impact of illness and medications. *Archives of Sexual Behavior,* 1981, *10,* 421–442.

Nystrup, J. A hospital population of schizophrenic patients undergoing change. *Acta Psychiatrica Scandinavica,* 1976, *53,* 211–226.

Penrose, L. S. Critical survey of schizophrenia genetics. In J. G. Howells (Ed.), *Modern perspectives in world psychiatry.* New York: Brunner/Mazel, 1971.

Pinderhughes, C. A., Grace, E. B., and Reyna, L. J. Psychiatric disorders and sexual functioning. *American Journal of Psychiatry,* 1972, *128,* 1276–1283.

Piron, E. Assessment of the male alcoholic's response to women through the use of visual stimuli. *Dissertation Abstracts International,* 1975, *36,* 454B–455B.

Rabkin, J. G. Stressful life events and schizophrenia: A review of the research literature. *Psychological Bulletin,* 1980, *87,* 408–425.

Ries, H. A., Johnson, M. H., Armstrong, H. E., Jr., and Holmes, D. S. The Draw-A-Person test and process-reactive schizophrenia. *Journal of Projective Techniques,* 1966, *30,* 184–186.

Rimmer, J., and Jacobsen, B. Differential fertility of adopted schizophrenics and their half-siblings. *Acta Psychiatrica Scandinavica,* 1976, *54,* 161–166.

Rosanoff, A. J., Handy, L. M., Plesset, I. R., and Brush, S. The etiology of so-called schizophrenic psychoses. *American Journal of Psychiatry,* 1934, *91,* 247–285.

Rosenthal, D., Wender, P. H., Kety, S. S., Welner, J., and Schulsinger, F. The adopted-away offspring of schizophrenics. *American Journal of Psychiatry,* 1971, *128,* 307–311.

Rosenweig, S., and Shakow, D. Mirror behavior in schizophrenic and normal individuals. *Journal of Nervous and Mental Disease,* 1937, *86,* 166–174.

Rossi, R., Delmonte, P., and Terracciano, P. The problem of the relationship between homosexuality and schizophrenia. *Archives of Sexual Behavior,* 1971, *1,* 357–362.

Salzman, L. Other character-personality syndromes: Schizoid, inadequate, passive-aggressive, paranoid, dependent. In S. Arieti and E. B. Brody (Eds.), *American handbook of psychiatry (Vol. 3) Adult clinical psychiatry* (2nd ed.). New York: Basic Books, 1974. Pp. 224–234.

Samuels, L. Sex differences in concordance rates for schizophrenia: Finding or artifact? *Schizophrenia Bulletin,* 1978, *4,* 14–15.

Samuels, L. Reply to Lewin. *Schizophrenia Bulletin,* 1979, *5,* 8–10.

Samuels, L., and Chase, L. The well siblings of schizophrenics. *American Journal of Family Therapy,* 1979, *7,* 24–35.

Sannito, T., Walker, R. E., Foley, J. M., and Posavac, E. J. A test of female sex identification: The Thorne feminity study. *Journal of Clinical Psychology,* 1972, *28,* 531–539.

Sathyavathi, K. Parental identification in schizophrenics. *Indian Journal of Clinical Psychology,* 1979, *6,* 153–159.

Schweitzer, L., Becker, E., and Welsh, H. Abnormalities of cerebral lateralization in schizophrenia patients. *Archives of General Psychiatry,* 1978, *35,* 982–985.

Seruya, B. B. The effects of training on body-size estimation of schizophrenics. *Dissertation Abstracts International,* 1977, *38,* 1421B.

Seyfried, B. A., and Hendrick, C. When do opposites attract? When they are opposite in sex and sex-role attitudes. *Journal of Personality and Social Psychology,* 1973, *25,* 15–20.

Shore, D., Anderson, D. J., and Cutler, N. R. Prediction of self-mutilation in hospitalized schizophrenics. *American Journal of Psychiatry,* 1978, *135,* 1406–1407.

Shulman, M. D. The relationship of dogmatism to passive-conformist role behavior among hospitalized schizophrenic patients. *Dissertation Abstracts International,* 1978, *39,* 1501B–1502B. (No. 7814907)

Slater, E., Hare, E. H., and Price, J. S. Marriage and fertility of psychiatric patients compared with national data. *Social Biology,* 1971, *18*(Suppl.), 60–73.

Smith, E. A study of sex differentiation in drawings and verbalizations of schizophrenics. *Journal of Clinical Psychology*, 1953, *9*, 183–185.

Standage, K. F., Moore, J. A., and Cole, M. G. Self-mutilation of the genitalia by a female schizophrenic. *Canadian Psychiatric Association Journal*, 1974, *19*, 17–20.

Strumpfer, D. J., and Nichols, R. C. A study of some communicable measures for the evaluation of human figure drawings. *Journal of Projective Techniques*, 1962, *26*, 342–353.

Turner, R. J., Dopheen, L. S., and Labreche, G. P. Marital status and schizophrenia: A study of incidence and outcome. *Journal of Abnormal Psychology*, 1970, *76*, 110–116.

Turner, R. J., and Gartrell, J. W. Social factors in psychiatric outcome: Toward the resolution of interpretive controversies. *American Sociological Review*, 1978, *43*, 368–382.

Watt, D. C., and Szulecka, T. K. The effect of sex, marriage and age at first admission on the hospitalization of schizophrenics during 2 years following discharge. *Psychological Medicine*, 1979, *9*, 529–539.

Watt, N. F., and Lubensky, A. W. Childhood roots of schizophrenia. *Journal of Consulting and Clinical Psychology*, 1976, *44*, 363–375.

Zigler, E., Levine, J., and Zigler, B. Premorbid social competence and paranoid-non-paranoid status in female schizophrenic patients. *Journal of Nervous and Mental Disease*, 1977, *164*, 333–339.

III

Social Deviation and Sexual Dysfunction

9

Sex Roles, Criminality, and Psychopathology

Cathy Spatz Widom

1. Introduction

A 65-year-old white woman applied to the state police for a gun permit. On her application she said she was an ordained minister, that she was being followed, and that she needed protection. Two weeks later, she shot and killed two elderly gentlemen, claiming that she "didn't know what came over her."

This example illustrates one way in which assumptions held by criminal justice agencies influence behavior and responses. If a 19-year-old male had applied for a permit, in the above incident, a "red flag" would have gone up immediately for the state police.

Over 30 years ago, Lemert (1951) pointed out:

> Fairly reliable data tells us that there are fewer female criminals, hobos, radicals, and gamblers. While this can be explained partly as being due to internal limits which make certain roles unattractive to women, it is also a partial measure of the *unwillingness of others to accept women in certain sociopathic roles*. A young woman without a physical handicap is seldom a professional beggar chiefly because most men who encountered her in such a role would treat her as a prostitute, as would the police." (p. 82, emphasis added)

The relationship between sex roles, criminal behavior, and psychopathology is complex. This chapter examines these relationships and describes some of the mechanisms by which sex role stereotypes influence our perception and understanding of criminal behavior.

Cathy Spatz Widom • Departments of Forensic Studies and Psychology, Indiana University, Bloomington, Indiana 47405.

1.1. Representation of Females in Crime Statistics

Regardless of age, race, or social class, men have more consistently been found to be socially deviant than women. Statistics on both criminality and personality disorder reflect the predominance of males over females. Historically, women have been perceived as petty, second-class criminals, limited in their repertoire to a few offense categories, or as exceedingly deviant and disturbed, committing an occasional bizarre murder or infanticide.

In national *arrest* statistics (U.S. Department of Justice, 1980), males outnumber females 5:1. Although women represent 25% of arrests for Crime Index Offenses, they are rarely arrested for certain offenses. Only 1% of females arrested are arrested as accomplices in rape, and they are infrequently arrested for robbery (7%) or burglary (5%). They are more likely to be involved in murder and nonnegligent manslaughter (14%) and most likely to be involved in larceny (35%).

One out of every 23 people *incarcerated* in state and federal institutions (approximately 4%) is female, representing more than 13,000 women. Although the number of women in state and federal institutions has increased dramatically since 1970 ($N = 5635$), the total percent of the prison population represented by women has increased just slightly (from 2.9% in 1970 to 3.9% in 1980).

Findings from national victimization surveys indicate the same predominance of males among offenders (Hindelang, 1979). Similarly, self-report comparisons of male and female involvement in illegal behavior, although primarily limited to juveniles, are consistent with official statistics indicating a higher rate of involvement for males than for females (Weis, 1976; Jensen and Eve, 1976).

Although males have, over time and across cultures, exhibited consistently higher arrest, conviction, and incarceration rates than females, the disparity between the sexes varies with the kind of crime, with time, and with the social setting (Nettler, 1978). For example, arrests for males of *crime against persons* exceeds arrests for females by almost 9:1, whereas the same ratio for *crimes against property* is less than 4:1 (U.S. Department of Justice, 1980). But men are not always more murderous than women. For example, Wolfgang (1958) found that white males were convicted of homicide eight times as frequently as white females, but the ratio for black males to females for this offense was only 4:1. This meant that black females in Philadelphia had a homicide rate three times greater than white males (Wolfgang, 1958, p. 55).

While it is true that men generally produce higher crime rates than women, the sex ratios are not constant, and certain crimes show a predominance of females. Prostitution represents an obvious offense for which women have traditionally been arrested more frequently than men. Recent information on child abuse suggests that this may be another offense in which the sex ratio reflects a predominance of women (Gelles, 1979).

1.2. Sex Roles, Criminal Behavior, and Psychopathology: A Model

Individuals engage in behaviors more characteristic of males and females in part because they are complying with societal expectations regarding appropriate sex role behavior. Gender affects our understanding of the problems of crime and deviant behavior in three ways. First, sex roles have been cited as causal factors in theories of why people engage in crime and deviant behavior. Second, assumptions and societal expectations about appropriate sex role behavior influence the diagnosis and labeling of certain actions as deviant or criminal. Finally, gender affects the response to such behaviors by society.

Figure 1 presents a schematic model of the dynamic interrelationship of factors contributing to the development and form of criminal behavior and its definition as psychopathological. This is not intended as a causal model; rather, the purpose of the figure is to delineate the complexity and interrelatedness of factors involved in criminality and psychopathology.

In Figure 1, individual predispositions interact with socialization experiences that are influenced by one's sex, personality, peers and community, and societal attitudes toward appropriate sex role behavior. These characteristics and experiences produce behaviors, some of which may be deviant, aggressive, antisocial, or criminal. Situational factors, such as opportunities or alcohol consumption, influence behavior and

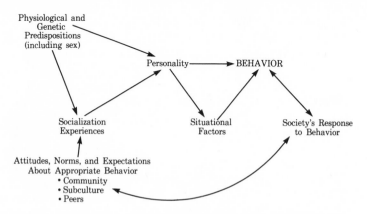

Figure 1. Schematic diagram of factors influencing criminal behavior.

are, of course, in turn influenced by peers and community, societal attitudes and expectations, sex, and socialization experiences. How one behaves influences society's response. A critical component of the model, society's response may take any of a number of forms—including labeling, diagnosis, and disposition.

This chapter examines these linkages, paying most attention to the relationship between sex roles and antisocial behavior and society's response to such behavior. In the context of this model, usage of the term *sex role* includes an individual's notion of sex role identity as well as other people's reactions, attitudes, behavior, and expectations about appropriate behavior for persons of either sex.

In the remainder of this introductory section, the components of the heuristic model shown in Figure 1 will be considered in more detail. I will then apply this framework to a discussion of theories of criminality and the influence of sex roles and will examine how societal expectations and individual predispositions are manifest in specific types of criminal activity. Finally, the influence of sex roles on psychiatric diagnosis will be discussed, with particular attention given to two personality disorders—psychopathy and hysteria.

1.2.1. Physiological and Genetic Predispositions.   The model presented in Figure 1 assumes that physiological and genetic factors produce individual differences in predispositions to criminal and antisocial behavior. Researchers have demonstrated that individuals respond differently to stimulation from birth (Thomas, Chess, and Birch, 1970). Individual differences in responsiveness to pain (Petrie, 1967) have been linked to crime, and automatic nervous system differences have been linked to psychopathy (e.g., Hare and Schalling, 1978). Finally, causal involvement of genetic factors in criminal behavior has been demonstrated (e.g., Mednick and Volavka, 1980; Ellis, 1982).

1.2.2. Personality.   Personality traits have been shown to be reliably associated with behavioral differences over time with a reasonable degree of consistency (e.g., Buss and Plomin, 1975; Dworkin, Burke, Maher, and Gottesman, 1976; Honzik, 1966). And personality characteristics have been found to be predictive of or correlated with various aspects of criminal and delinquent behavior across a variety of samples, time periods, and assessment techniques (e.g., Farley and Farley, 1972; Warren, 1979; Widom, Katkin, Stewart, and Fondacaro, 1983). Studies of both male and female prisoners have noted personality differences in comparison to noncriminal samples (e.g., Eysenck and Eysenck, 1973), differences between incarcerated males and females (e.g., Panton, 1974), and differences within same-sex prison populations (e.g., Megargee, 1979: Widom, 1978b).

1.2.3. Socialization Experiences and Community Attitudes, Norms, and Expectations. All societies have behavioral norms, and most cultures use sex as a means of assigning role. These norms presumably become known to all and are communicated during the socialization process.

Maccoby and Jacklin (1974) and others have described how socialization practices differ for boys and girls. With specific reference to criminality, "natural" socialization experiences act as a barrier, deterring girls from engaging in criminal or delinquent behavior. It is not surprising, then, that girls or women who do engage in criminal or delinquent behaviors are presumed to be improperly socialized according to society's expectations for appropriate sex role behaviors.

Boys, on the other hand, do not generally experience the same socialization barriers as girls. Stark and McEvoy (1970) found that 70% of a nationally representative sample of adults felt it was good for boys to get in a few fistfights while growing up. Since males are also more likely to leave home, enter male networks, and interact with males in other spheres (barrooms, ballparks, boardrooms), their opportunities for aggressive and criminal behavior are more extensive, and such behavior is more likely to be reinforced.

According to social learning theory, the same principles applicable to nondeviant behavior apply to criminal and delinquent behavior and reflect the individual's response to environmental contingencies. Individuals often receive tangible rewards (positive reinforcement) for engaging in delinquent and criminal behavior, particularly when no other attractive alternative is available. For example, a female may support herself on income derived from engaging in illegal behavior (e.g., prostitution). Since punishment is neither swift, sure, nor severe, the behavior continues. An individual may receive nontangible rewards such as approval by a group, social status by peers, or attention by a parent for delinquent or criminal behavior. Such nontangible—but nevertheless direct—rewards would reinforce such behavior. Vicarious reinforcement also serves to increase the likelihood that the behavior will be performed in the future. That is, watching role models in real life (i.e., parents) or in the media being reinforced and not punished may prompt individuals to behave in similar ways.

Using these general principles and applying them to a variety of backgrounds and individuals, one could explain the acquisition of deviant behavior and its maintenance. Once a person has engaged in deviant or criminal behavior, both the promise of future rewards and the threat of future punishment (i.e., getting caught) exist. However, since the probability of getting caught (arrested) is generally low and since intermittent reinforcement maintains the behavior, the criminality or delinquency is likely to persist.

1.2.4. Subcultural and Peer Influence. Subcultures may also play an important role in socialization experiences of some individuals. In our society, some forms of deviant or criminal behavior are the norm and noncriminal "straight" behavior is considered abnormal. In some cultural contexts, violence is tolerated, accepted, and even mandated.

According to Merton (1968), life in urban slums and ghettos provides an environment in which opportunities for crime are numerous, and barriers against crime are weak. Children are socialized into subcultures of deviance and crime, in which aggressive sexual and violent behavior is considered evidence of masculinity. Participation in such behavior reinforces a young man's virility or manhood in the eyes of his peers. And rather than bringing a loss of status, deviant behavior may actually increase status. For lower-class males, being "cool" is equivalent to courage, and the need to prove oneself in front of one's peers is paramount:

> "In neighborhoods where organized crime is active, its members study teenagers' street 'reps' and behavior as carefully as a professional baseball scout analyzes a sandlot player's ability to hit curve balls or hold a base runner close to the bag" (Silberman, 1978, p. 105).

In this context, role models provide first-hand knowledge of the behaviors and rewards, seldom the penalties. This description of a successful numbers operator illustrates the point:

> "He was about the biggest because everybody respected him, he always had plenty of money, he always dressed nice, and everybody always done what he wanted them to do. I dug the respect that he gave and that he got. . ." (Allen, 1977, p. 5).

1.2.5. Situational Factors. Heavy alcohol consumption is one of the most common situational factors that influences the commission of crime. For example, much interpersonal violence occurs in the context of heavy drinking at the local tavern or bar. Friday and Saturday night "beer brawls" frequently end in unplanned impulsive aggressive acts with serious bodily injuries and occasional fatalities. Robberies, generally involving little advance planning, are also frequently precipitated by heavy drinking.

Victim-precipitated crime, a concept introduced by Wolfgang (1958), illustrates another situational factor. By provoking another person, the victim may be a major precipitating cause of violence toward him/herself. Although provocation may appear to be slight, or magnified by an egocentric potential assailant, it may be sufficient to result in serious attack and bodily harm. Such crimes, then, may be precipitated by real or imagined insults and may lead to impulsive aggression on the part of the assailant.

Although crime is often associated with individuals who are psychologically disturbed, in some circumstances crime may be perceived as an instrumental or rational response, calculated to achieve some monetary or other desired goal. Consider the shoplifter whose family is going without dinner or the battered spouse who plots to kill her husband. Indeed, for certain people at certain times, criminal behavior may be a rational response to a stressful situation.

From my own work on female offenders (Widom, 1978b) and from other work with male offenders (e.g., Megargee, 1979), it is evident that not all are psychologically disturbed. We must not assume psychopathology simply because someone engages in deviant or criminal behavior or is even sentenced to spend time in prison. As Sagarin (1976) noted, the problem with such an assumption is that it infers what we *are* from what we *do* (all that can be observed). As Figure 1 illustrates, personality traits are among several antecedents to behavior. Our behavior is a product of our perceptions and responses to other people's behavior (e.g., role models), as well as a variety of environmental, genetic, and situational factors outlined in Figure 1.

1.3. Applying the Model: Assaultiveness in Women

As Figure 1 implies, it can be misleading to examine behavior in isolation from these external influences. Awareness of the interrelatedness is particularly important for those who study the behavior of criminals. Research that draws upon data collected by criminal justice institutions often fails to recognize that such data are themselves the product of discretionary decisions made by the individuals who "diagnose" criminal behavior. With respect to sex roles, this means that labeling and other societal responses to the behaviors of males and females can be as much a product of expectations about appropriate behavior as they are based on individuals' predispositions or actions.

This is illustrated by a study by Rappeport and Lassen (1966) on the dangerousness of female psychiatric hospital patients in which the authors make inferences about the characteristics of female patients based in part upon sex differences reported in the Uniform Crime Reports (UCR) published by the Federal Bureau of Investigation. The authors found that the frequency of arrest for women discharged from mental hospitals was significantly higher than for females in the general population and concluded, "We were not surprised to find that our female patients reflect the general trend in the female community of committing more aggravated assaults per capita than males" (p. 415).

This reasoning illustrates the ecological fallacy found in much research and writing on female offenders. This study also fails to recognize the way institutions, particularly the criminal justice system, respond differentially to males and females. Uniform Crime Reports (UCR) statistics are often referred to as "crimes known to police." But research has shown that many incidents that may be reported to the police are neither recorded nor formally treated as crimes by investigating officers (Maxfield, Lewis, and Szoc, 1980; Black, 1970). Crimes included in UCR data therefore include only those offenses that were reported to police, recorded as crimes by investigating officers, and retained in police records (Seidman and Couzens, 1974). This shows how the labeling of criminal behavior is in part a product of institutional response, i.e., the response of police, to that behavior. Furthermore, it is likely that these discretionary decisions made by police in turn reflect their preconceived notions about appropriate sex role behavior. Cicourel and Kitsuse (1963) have described how the social organization of justice is such that probation officers, social workers, counselors, police officers, and others process cases within the criminal justice system on the basis of normative assumptions about sex roles, male and female crime, and delinquency. These expectations, therefore, produce self-fulfilling prophecies.

Arrest data reflect not only the acts themselves but the system's response to the acts. According to UCR statistics, women are more likely to be arrested for aggravated assaults, particularly those involving family members. However, women are *overrepresented* in UCR arrest statistics for aggravated assaults relative to their representation as offenders in victimization survey results (Hindelang, 1979). Males are more often mentioned as offenders in national victim surveys, and since victimization survey data are not directly affected by the attitudes and behaviors of police, this pattern may reflect more accurately the general level of assaultive behavior in the population. Thus, women may be overrepresented in UCR *arrest* statistics, in comparison to the actual incidence of male and female aggravated assault behavior.

Furthermore, aggravated assaults, particularly involving family members, are one of the categories of crimes with the highest solution rates. Across all categories, approximately one out of five crimes known to the police is cleared by arrest. However, the percentage of aggravated assault offenses known to the police and cleared by arrest (59%) is higher than all other violent crimes, with the exception of murder (Flanagan, Alstyne, and Gottfredson, 1982).

Finally, women are more likely to be involved in *victim-precipitated* assaults. Consider the following examples:

A husband accused his wife of giving money to another man, and while she was making breakfast, he attacked her with a milk bottle, then a brick, and finally a piece of concrete block. Having had a butcher knife in hand, she stabbed him with it during the fight.

A husband threatened to kill his wife on several occasions. In this instance, he attacked her with a pair of scissors, dropping them, and grabbed a butcher knife from the kitchen. In the ensuing struggle that ended on their bed, he fell on the knife.

A husband had beaten his wife on several previous occasions. In the present instance, she insisted that he take her to the hospital. He refused, and a violent quarrel followed, during which he slapped her several times, and she concluded by stabbing him. (Wolfgang, 1958).

In these cases, the abusing males might have come to the attention of the police via previous domestic disputes. But the typical police response in such domestic violence cases is to settle the dispute with as little intrusion as possible into family matters. By the time the woman acts and the system is forced to take note of *her* actions, as these examples illustrate, the situation has often reached such extreme and violent proportions that police must intervene. This point is supported by the finding that the proportion of women offenders in victim-precipitated homicides (29%) is almost twice as high as their involvement in non-victim-precipitated slayings (14%) (Wolfgang, 1958).

With reference to Figure 1, this example shows how institutional *expectations* regarding sex roles are intimately related to the institutional response to such behavior. As the "gatekeepers" of the criminal justice system (Maxfield, 1979), police make decisions that determine which individuals in which situations will be initially labeled as offenders and which will be processed through the next stage as criminal defendants.

Studies that have examined whether a defendant's sex influences sentencing decisions have reached varying conclusions. However, a recent study (Kruttschnitt, 1982) shows that, for women, economic dependency is related to outcome of criminal prosecution. On the basis of a sample of 1034 cases of female offenders, Kruttschnitt found that sentencing disparities were related to the extent to which women were economically dependent on someone else for their daily existence. The more economically dependent the woman, the less severe her disposition.

If we are to make generalizations regarding the characteristics and motivations of offenders for different types of crimes, it is important to recognize that prior decisions restrict the flow of information about offenders. To the extent that assumptions about sex roles affect the discretionary decisions of police and other officials, our assertions about the causes and frequency of female criminality must be made with caution.

2. Sex Roles and Criminality

Our stereotypic notions about women depict them as passive, dependent, caring, and submissive—the very antithesis of how we construe criminality, particularly violent behavior. In a culture where aggressiveness is a measure of "masculinity," it is easy to argue that criminal behavior reflects an extension of the stereotypic expression of the masculine or "macho" role. This, however, represents an overly simplistic view of criminal behavior and ignores the heterogeneity of criminal activity. Criminal behavior varies as do the backgrounds, motivations, needs, and life-styles of individuals involved in crime. Certainly the bank teller who embezzles large sums of money differs from the dope addict who solicits "tricks" on the street, who in turn differs from the child molester, rapist, or hired gunman.

2.1. Traditional Assumptions Influence Theory and Research

Sex role expectations have played a prominent role in causal explanations of *female* criminality. These approaches suggest that role dissatisfaction and the frustration resulting from role demands account for female criminality and the form it takes. Female criminality represents a departure from proscribed sex role behavior.

For example, Freud (1933) believed criminal women to be neurotic, maladjusted sexual misfits who were not content with the roles of wife and mother. Their aggressive, rebellious behavior was the result of the failure to develop healthy feminine attitudes. Similarly, adolescent girls' rebellion against strict standards for sexual behavior was thought to lead to crime (Cowie, Cowie, and Slater, 1968).

An interesting contemporary variant of the deviation theories focuses on stereotypic sex roles and the opportunities, criminal and otherwise, consonant with those roles. In their general form, opportunity theories suggest that female criminality has been limited in size and form by limitations in opportunity. Shoplifting, forgery, and petty theft are thought to be "female" crimes, whereas safe-cracking, loan sharking, and robbery are "male" crimes. Women engage in shoplifting because they have more opportunities as part of their appropriate social roles as housewife and shopper. Females typically do not become involved in white-collar crime because they do not have access to the executive suites of major corporations.

Proponents of this view (e.g., Simon, 1975) have suggested that as women increase their participation in the labor force, their opportunities to commit certain kinds of crime will also increase, and crime statistics should reflect these changes. Although opportunity theories offer a partial explanation for why women have not been more heavily involved in crime, they do not provide explanations for why those who engage in crime do so. Further, given that official crime statistics (arrests and incarcerations) do not generally reflect the extent of white-collar crime, the strength of this explanation is limited.

Historically, the notion of deviant sex roles in female criminals was pervasive and often taken literally. Indeed, much of the earliest work on female criminality attempts to document "masculinity" in female offenders, including physical measurements as indicators of masculinity in physical appearance.

Believing that female offenders had a confused or deviant sex role identity, theorists offered as additional evidence the prevalence of homosexuality in incarcerated women to support their notions (e.g., Gibbens, 1971). At the same time, the lack of interest in what we must assume was (and is) a comparable percentage of homosexuality in male prisons is interesting. Recent work on the prevalence of homosexuality in female prisons suggests that the incidence and importance of this behavior has been grossly overstated (Propper, 1981) and is comparable to that found in male prisons.

Early empirical research does *not* provide strong support for a confused sex role identity or excessive masculinity in female offenders (for a review, see Widom, 1978c). Similarly, in a series of studies directly assessing masculinity and femininity as separate and independent dimensions in a number of samples of female offenders varying in geographic location, age, and level of involvement in the criminal justice system (Widom, 1981), there was little support for the deviation hypothesis. Although adult female *prisoners* (not women awaiting trial) had the highest masculinity scale scores of all the groups, they did not differ significantly from a control group of college students. Their femininity scores were also the highest of any group, suggesting (if anything) androgyny.

In a unique study of males, data were collected from prisoners within the Georgia penal system as part of a parole evaluation (Heilbrun, 1981). Sex role scales derived empirically from the California Psychological Inventory (Baucom, 1976) were used, and comparisons were made to norms developed from a sample of adult male noncriminals. The norms provide conversions of raw scores to T scores with a mean of 50 ($SD = 10$). Male prison inmates were found to be generally more masculine and less feminine than the noncriminal males (i.e., T scores greater than 50 for masculinity and less than 50 for femininity). Heilbrun then divided the sample into groups based on most serious crime committed (murder, rape, manslaughter, assault, robbery, burglary and theft) and nonviolent "victimless' crimes (drug violations, forgery, and fraud) and found the same general picture, with two exceptions. The mixed group of nonviolent prisoners had the lowest masculinity scores (44.56) and rapists had higher femininity scores (53.53). Rapists were the only group who appeared feminine relative to both other criminals and noncriminal adult males.

In addition to looking at the psychological characteristics of masculinity and femininity, one can examine the extent to which people have adopted society's standards for appropriate sex role behaviors for others and examine the social attitudes they hold about the roles and rights of men and women in society. The media have portrayed and publicized a "new breed of female offenders," the feminism of criminal women, and the notoriety of radical female offenders (e.g., Angela Davis, Susan Saxe, Patty Hearst). However, despite assertions by the media, the evidence from a variety of samples using a number of different assessment techniques suggests that the "new breed" of *feminist* female offenders may be an illusion.

In a study of a coeducational correctional facility in Massachusetts, Almy, Bravo, Burd, Chin, Cohan, Gallo, Giorgianni, Gold, Jose, and Noyes (1975) found that female inmates' attitudes on sex roles tended to be rather traditional and stereotyped (with the exception of female homosexuals). Female prisoners (Leventhal, 1977) and females awaiting trial (Widom, 1979) were found to be significantly more conservative in their attitudes toward women (less pro-feminist) than nonoffender women. Generally, these female inmates felt that women should be submissive and faithful to their husband, and should not drink, smoke, or commit crime. [I have a very vivid recollection of a large black woman awaiting trial, when asked how she felt about the statement "Women earning as much as their dates should bear equally the expense when they go out together," responding, "Hell, no!"]

As part of a national study of women's correctional programs (Glick and Neto, 1977), 1607 female inmates from 15 prisons and 42 jails were given seven items dealing with a variety of topics on stereotyped sex role behavior for males and females. Responses of the women were split, with endorsements of both traditional and nontraditional roles.

Young female offenders may indeed represent a new breed. Perhaps, the "new breed" reflects the small group of notorious, vocal, and well-educated women who may be rebelling primarily against society, and only secondarily against their sex roles. The press may be focusing on this new group of women who have recently begun to join the ranks of incarcerated women.

We have just described how research and theory on female criminality are influenced by stereotypic assumptions about females generally. There are, however, still other influences of implicit assumptions about males and females that extend beyond our discussion thus far.

Several stereotypically female and male offenses are highlighted below. With reference to Figure 1, each offense illustrates the individual's *inability or unwillingness* to meet or accept society's expectations for appropriate sex role behavior. Furthermore, these offenses illustrate how interpretations of these behaviors reflect societal expectations about appropriate behavior for males and females.

2.2. Stereotypic Female Offenses

Three offenses traditionally associated with women—prostitution, child abuse, and shoplifting—have been selected for our discussion. For females, prostitution and child abuse have been stereotypically interpreted in terms of frustration with the traditional female role. Prostitution has been viewed as an illegitimate but parallel version of traditional femininity. Having only recently come under serious empirical investigation, the phenomenon of child abuse has also been linked to the frustrations of and realities involved in traditional female roles. Finally, shoplifting has been erroneously perceived as a predominantly female offense.

2.2.1. **Prostitution.** Although prostitution is referred to as the "archetype of the traditional female role," this description is, at best, only superficially accurate. In fact, looking at the behaviors involved, apart from the question of morality, one sees that there is much in the role and behavior of prostitutes that is distinctly nontraditional. It is precisely this limitation in our thinking that clouds our understanding of these forms of behavior, and particularly since assumptions about these behaviors implicitly affect etiological considerations.

According to the UCR, arrest statistics for prostitution—traditionally a "female" crime—reflect some recent change. In 1969 approximately one-fifth of all arrests for prostitution (and commercial vice) were attributed to males. In 1979 the proportion of males had increased to almost one-third (32.5%).

However, these arrest figures are somewhat misleading for a number of reasons. They tend to reflect a higher proportion of low-status prostitutes (streetwalkers and those with drug problems). They also tend to fluctuate depending on the views of the police, prosecutors, judges, and public opinion, varying from region to region depending on local attitudes and practices. Neither do these statistics tell us what percentage of the increase is for males engaged in prostitution, in contrast to arrests of male clients of female prostitutes. Some states have recently revised criminal statutes to define prostitution as committable by males and females. The application of legal sanctions against men who patronize prostitutes is also becoming more common.

In the Victorian era, prostitution flourished simultaneously with an emphasis on women's asexuality and the chastity of married women (Laws and Schwartz, 1977). Although contemporary social norms have changed considerably since Victorian times, the same contradiction exists. Women are seldom encouraged to be blatantly sexual, although socialization experiences reinforce feelings among young girls that they are, in fact, sex objects to be valued primarily for their physical attractiveness. This illustrates once again how socialization experiences can be sex role-specific, as shown in Figure 1. However, there is a fine line between appropriate and excessive displays of sexuality. Laws and Schwartz (1977) assert that it is precisely *because* prostitutes openly display their sexuality that they are considered criminals.

This position is reminiscent of Davis's (1961) work suggesting that prostitution is simply the deviant female's attempt to adjust to the traditional feminine role in an illegitimate fashion. Such behavior served a function for the woman who had fallen from grace (seduced and abandoned) and for the woman of limited social opportunities. This is perhaps more obvious in Japan, and other countries where prostitution is an accepted way of life for girls from poor backgrounds. Daughters are often sold as prostitutes or become prostitutes out of devotion to the family and the need to help financially. As in traditionally arranged marriages, this passive acceptance of fate was entirely consistent with the traditional Japanese woman's role (Iga, 1968).

Some argue that the role of women in American society may similarly encourage the choice of prostitution. With limited options for money, independence, and status, women see few viable alternatives. Prostitution is a rational choice for some women, enabling them to acquire money, resources, and independence. The income is high and it affords women an opportunity to "earn more, buy more, and live better than would be possible by another realistic alternative" (Esselstyn, 1968). If women are socialized to regard their sexual favors as marketable and their worth as contingent on their physical attractiveness, then prostitution is a logical consequence of society's treatment of women (Rosenblum, 1975).

On the surface, prostitution has a number of parallels to caricatures of traditionally feminine roles (e.g., the comradely, warmhearted Irma La Douce). However, upon closer inspection, the picture is more complex. Considering the characteristics associated with traditional femininity, the life of the prostitute appears anything but traditionally feminine. For the streetwalker, her choice of occupation requires that she find customers, sell them a service, find a suitable place to transact business, please customers, collect money, protect herself from disease, pregnancy, and injury, and finally, avoid the police (Hirschi, 1962). Even for the higher-status, more refined call girl who stays at home, the activities involved in her profession are inappropriate and unaccustomed roles for traditional women. Furthermore, as Rosenblum (1975) pointed out, the defiant intent to show that choice of sexual partner is indiscriminate, promiscuous, and unselective—that anyone will do—is certainly contrary to "sweet womanhood."

Many early clinicians and theorists painted a picture of prostitutes as seriously in need of treatment for a variety of psychological ills (often conflicting) and pathological motivations. They have been variously described as masochistic, infantile, emotionally dangerous to men, regressed, excessively dependent, suffering from gender role confusion, frigid, aggressive, sex-crazed, and lacking in internal controls. However, there has been increasing recognition of the heterogeneity of prostitutes' needs, motivations, and psychological characteristics, as well as occupational behavior (income, method) and demographic background (e.g., Exner, Wylie, Leura, and Parrill, 1977).

> "What was a nice girl like Barbara doing in a joint like Suzette's [a Chicago brothel]?
>
> "I used to be a special-education teacher," she said, "but I couldn't help the kids as much as I wanted to and that kind of thing depressed me. I just had to get out. I was into swinging for a while and I met some people, and, well, here I am. Kinda crazy, isn't it?"
>
> Barbara, who was thirty-one and divorced, said she planned to work at Suzette's for about a year. Then she would open a house of her own somewhere else in the city. She wanted to be her own madam. (Smith and Zekman, 1979, p. 190)

In unpublished data (Widom, 1978a), women awaiting trial who were charged with prostitution showed almost the same mean scores as Bem's (1974) college students and other groups of college students on both the masculinity and femininity scales of the Bem Sex-Rose Inventory. These women also showed self-esteem scores similar to those of a group of adult female nonoffenders matched for age, race, and general socioeconomic background.

Gebhard (1969) reported that prostitutes as a group were at least as orgasmic as nonprostitute women and possibly more responsive in their sexual experiences with friends and husbands. Sixty-one percent of Gebhard's sample had no homosexual experience at all, 6% had incidental, and 9% had homosexual activity in connection with prostitution. Twenty-four percent had homosexual experiences 10 times or more for profit and of these only a few had extensive homosexual activity. Gebhard concluded that "their profession does not interfere seriously with their heterosexuality, their orgasmic capacities, or their ability to form affectional relationships with men" (p.30).

An especially intriguing recent phenomenon is the growing number of young male prostitutes in many cities. According to Coombs (1974), these young men, many of whom are associated with juvenile or youth gangs, try to appear "supermasculine" and project an image of masculinity in their speech, gait, and use of gestures. Coombs suggests that their customers insist on this exaggerated masculinity. Apparently, as long as the young male applies a financial-economic justification for his relationship with his client (an adult male), he is not defined by his peers, nor does he define himself, as homosexual. Indeed, as he grows older, he curtails this behavior and typically marries.

   2.2.2. Child Abuse. Historically and cross-culturally, women have been consistently overrepresented in statistics on infanticide. Defining violence as "an act carried out with the intention, or perceived intention, of physically injuring another person (ranging from slapping to murder), Gelles (1979) found that women were overrepresented as offenders in cases of child abuse. Sixty-eight percent of the mothers and 58% of the fathers in a national probability sample reported at least one violent act toward their children during the survey year. During that year and the period of child-rearing, mothers were more likely to throw something at the child, slap or spank the child, or hit the child with some object. Neither men nor women employed the most serious forms of violence (beating up, kicking, biting, punching, using guns or knives) very frequently. Gelles suggests that violence in the family is typically seen as legitimate, instrumental, and rational. There is a certain normative acceptability to hitting one's children. Violence and physical punishment are viewed as important for moral and character development. Parents hit children "for their own good"—to teach them not to run in the street, to keep them away from electric outlets, or to toilet-train them (Gelles, 1973).

   If violence in the family is tolerated, accepted, and even mandated under certain conditions, why should women be overrepresented? Gelles (1979) observes that the management of children is one of the only situations in which women are as likely as men to resort to violence. Yet he stresses that the explanation for the greater likelihood that mothers will use violence goes beyond the time factor, i.e., that women typically spend more time with children. He suggests that children are threats to the mother's identity and esteem more than to the father's.

   However, another possible explanation is that mothers hit their children simply because they are physically able to do this without retaliation. Individuals may come to accept hitting and violence as appropriate responses when they experience stress or frustration. But among a number of factors that inhibit people from becoming violent, despite their frustration or stress, is the likelihood of being hit back. Much of the structure of the American family and society is based on the fact that males are typically bigger and usually more powerful than females. According to this argument, just as adult males are more likely to hit adult females, adult females would themselves be more likely to hit children, with little fear of retaliation. This would not be the case were the typical adult female to attack a typical adult male. Indeed, when women do murder, it is most likely to occur when the victim's ability to strike back is seriously impaired, through being drunk, asleep, taken by surprise, etc. Our interpretations for such behaviors again relate to sex roles.

    2.2.3. Shoplifting. Shoplifting is included under the legal category of theft. It is defined by the *Random House Dictionary* as "stealing goods from a retail store while posing as a customer." The legal definition is not so simple.

    Popular stereotypes portray middle-aged and/or menopausal women as archetypal shoplifters. However, upon examination of a variety of statistics, this image appears to be erroneous. Most recent statistics indicate that males outnumber females in arrests for larceny-theft by more than two-to-one (U.S. Department of Justice, 1980).

    Between 1969 and 1979, males were apprehended more often for shoplifting than females (Griffin, 1981). In his California study of apprehensions for shoplifting in 1980, which included 853 stores and 16,946 reports, Griffin (1981) found that females were slightly overrepresented in arrests (51% vs. 49%). Adult female–male ratios for supermarket, drug store, and discount store arrests, respectively, were 52:48, 54:46, and 56:44. However, across all categories, *male juveniles* represented the largest percentage of shoplifters apprehended.

    Many authors have described the different motivations and styles of shoplifters and have called attention to the wide range of activities involved, often depending on whether the act was committed by professionals or by impulsive amateurs. However, theories of motivation for shiplifting seem to vary with the offender's sex. Women are thought to shoplift as a result of subconscious motivations and depression (Moore, 1976; Russell, 1973), or they may be low-income mothers who steal for food (Loughton, 1973). On the other hand, explanations for shoplifting in males are more likely to refer to peer pressure (Holcomb, 1973), labeling theory (Klemke, 1978), or escape from boredom and thrill-seeking (Belson, 1975).

    Since we expect women to spend more time shopping and therefore to be more exposed to opportunities to shoplift, we also expect them to be more prevalent in these statistics. As was suggested in the discussion of Figure 1, sex role expectations have a pervasive influence. However, empirical evidence on the frequency of shoplifting arrests for males and females contradicts gender-based explanations for this offense.

2.3. Stereotypic Male Offenses

Many books and articles have stressed the importance of sex roles in understanding female crime and delinquency, but few theorists have speculated on the importance of gender roles to understanding male criminal behavior. For example, Heidensohn (1968) referred to the blockage or maladjustment of instrumental roles as causes of delinquency in males, and Morris (1964) cited obstacles to economic-power status as similarly important.

Referring back to Figure 1, what happens when the normative expectations for appropriate male behavior are not met and the socialization experiences and developmental processes fail? For males, the crimes of robbery and rape often represent attempts to feel big, masculine, and powerful—to control. These forms of antisocial behavior may illustrate the opposite—the inability to legitimately fulfill societal expectations for the male role. Two other offenses committed primarily by males that do not typically involve violence (pedophilia and transvestism) may be the product of other frustrations with the male role. Pedophiliacs can be seen to lack the social skills necessary to fulfill *adult* sex roles (whether homosexual or heterosexual). And through their cross-dressing, transvestites describe the incorporation of feminine feelings, an implicit statement of the failure of traditional male roles to satisfy adequately.

2.3.1. Rape. In most states, until recently, statutory rape referred to sexual intercourse with a female under the age of consent. Few states included in their definition the situation of a young male having sexual relations with an adult female. According to UCR arrest statistics for 1969, there were no females arrested for rape. In the 10 years afterward, despite some changes in laws, females represented less than 1% of all arrests for forcible rape.

To Griffin (1973), rape is the "all-American crime," considered natural; that raping is unacceptable must be learned. Women are perceived as wanting to be raped and provoking the behavior, since "normal" heterosexual behavior involves a dominant man and a submissive woman. "Rape is simply at one end of the continuum of male-aggressive, female-passive patterns, and an arbitrary line has been drawn to mark it off from the rest of such relationships" (Medea and Thompson, 1974, pp. 11–12). Indeed, Amir (1971) found that males convicted of forcible rape had the same attitudes toward sexuality as "normal, well-adjusted males," differing only in having a greater tendency to express violence and rage.

In the context of traditional sexual socializing experiences, young girls are taught to seduce and expect to be overpowered by males. We then rationalize rape with the argument that it is understandably difficult for males to distinguish between rape and heterosexual intercourse. This belief is held despite the fact that in many other countries (e.g., Canada and Norway) rape is virtually nonexistent. Furthermore, research has shown that most rapes are *not* spontaneous but are, in fact, preplanned (Amir, 1971).

2.3.2. Robbery. Robbery—taking money or property from another by force or threat of force—is a crime committed primarily by strangers. According to Silberman (1978), robbery is the street crime *"par excellence."*

Only a small fraction of robbers are professional criminals. The majority are what Conklin (1972) calls "opportunistic robbers"—impulsive, disorganized lower-class adolescents and youths who rarely plan their crimes. Twenty-five percent of the adults and more than 40% of the juvenile robbers interviewed in northern California by Feeney and Weir (1973) had *not* intended to rob someone when they went out.

Street criminals tend to be young and poor, and a disproportionate number are members of minority groups. In 1979 nearly three-quarters (74.4%) of those arrested for robbery were under 25, and almost one-third (31.5%) were 17 or younger. Street crime is also a predominantly *male* activity. Women represented only 7.4% of those arrested for robbery in 1979 (U.S. Department of Justice, 1980).

According to Silberman (1978), almost every robber is a chronic offender, although not every chronic offender is a robber. For example, in Wolfgang's (1972) study of the Philadelphia birth cohort, 46% of the delinquents committed only a single offense. However, multiple offenders accounted for 95% of the robberies. (Two- thirds of the multiple offenders came from lower-income backgrounds and 51% were black.)

Silberman (1978) describes robbery as a group activity where participation demonstrates and reinforces a young man's virility and manhood to his peers. "People got to prove things to people. My partner didn't think I could do it" (p. 56). As an "antidote to the feelings of inadequacy and inferiority experienced by slum dwellers" (p. 55), these youths turn to robbery to prove things to themselves as well as to others. "I just like the feeling of the dude, you know . . . like if I had a .38 right now, I can make you do just about anything I wanted you to do, see, and you couldn't do nothing about it. And like just about all my life, people had been doing that to me, see . . . but now I like to get that feeling where I can make you do anything I want you to do" (p. 56).

In addition to relieving the boredom that often hangs over urban ghettos, the young robber's sense of power is enhanced when he acquires money as a result. The traditional symbolism of the gun notwithstanding, robbers feel more in command when they carry a gun. A gun is the "great equalizer." Silberman (1978) cites one robber: "You're a pretty big man standing there with your gun" (p. 58). "If you feel like you're nothing, a gun can make you feel like a king" (p. 60). By acting in illegal or rebellious ways, defying the rules and morality of middle-class society and thumbing their noses at society, in a sense they gain some control over the situation.

2.3.4. Pedophilia. As a form of sexual child abuse, pedophilia has been defined in many ways: as "expressed desire for immature sexual gratification with a prepubertal child" (Mohr, 1968), or the more explicit "post-pubertal man who has a sexual contact with a prepubertal child . . . a man who has had physical contact with a child of 13 years or under when the man was 16 years or older and at least 5 years older than the child" (Quinsey, 1977, p. 205). Legal definitions also vary according to place and time, with some laws having undergone recent changes. Those arrested for child sexual abuse (pedophilia) are overwhelmingly male. Indeed, as seen above, some definitions of pedophilia refer explicitly to males. One study (Walters, 1975) found that only 3 of 200 sexual abuse cases reported to public agencies involved female offenders with male victims.

Popular images of the pedophiliac portray the image of a "dirty old man" hanging around the schoolyard or trying to pick up little girls with enticements of candy and sweets. However, on the basis of the limited information we have at present, this picture is not accurate. Rather, child molesters are more likely known to the children, are part of the family, and do not have prior criminal records (Tobias, Danto, and Robertson, 1980)—teachers, coaches, doctors, ministers, baby-sitters, youth workers, etc. Finkelhor (1978) surveyed 800 students at six universities and found that, as children, 1/5 of the women respondents and 1/11 of the male respondents had had sexual exposure with an adult.

To explain the infrequent occurrence of child sexual abuse by adult women, researchers and theorists refer to traditional roles. According to Newton (1978), women are rarely found to be child molesters because this behavior clashes with the concept of maternal protection. Furthermore, such behavior clashes with the traditional submissiveness and passivity in the sexual role of women. Society is also more accepting of women caressing children than it is for men engaging in the same behavior.

Other theories of child molesters refer to deficiencies in social skills (e.g., Serber and Keith, 1974) or suggest that pedophiliacs demonstrate an inability to identify with adult sexual roles through either fixation at an earlier stage of development or regression to an earlier stage (Cohen, Seghorn, and Calmas, 1969).

Some have postulated that the child is a substitute sexual object, suggesting that the pedophile's wife plays an important role in causing the behavior. As a result of bad marital or sexual relationships with their wives, men are frustrated and seek out children for sexual gratification (Peters, 1976; Bastani and Kentsmith, 1980). A wife may also indirectly contribute to the abusive behavior by knowing that the husband is using children for sexual gratification and allowing and tolerating such behavior as a means of keeping him away from herself (Peters, 1976). Indeed, some go so far as to suggest that the wife is responsible for her husband's deviance by not providing him with satisfactory sexual relations (Bastani and Kentsmith, 1980).

As is the case with many other forms of criminal or deviant behavior, obtaining reliable information on the extent of such behavior or representative samples of individuals engaged in such behavior is problematic. Studies typically depend on incarcerated samples, patients in mental hospitals, or private patients in therapy. Studies of self-esteem, needs, heterosexuality/homosexuality, anxiety, religiosity, guilt, blame, etc., are confounded with the status of the individuals examined. Do the results reflect the personality of the individual or the extent to which the individuals attempt to convince doctors, police, or other institutional staff and supervisory personnel of their nondeviance, or to lay the blame elsewhere?

2.4. Transcending Sex Roles: Transvestism

Transvestism is the act of dressing in the clothes of the opposite sex and is primarily a male phenomenon. If it is confined to the privacy of one's home or to parties, masquerades, or Halloween gatherings, cross-dressing is not considered to be a violation of the law. It is, however, against the law in most places for a person to appear in public impersonating the sex of another.

Transvestism has been practiced and accepted in many cultures throughout history, and it continues to be practiced in some contemporary societies. For the ancient Greeks, "cross-dressing was believed to be a way of enhancing heterosexual potency" (Talamini, 1980, p. 4). In a study of contemporary Oaxaca, Mexico, Rymph (1974) defined transvestism as "the permanent adoption of a male of aspects of female dress and/or behavior, in accordance with customary expectations within a given society" (p. 1) and found a high frequency among men. In this Mexican city, 60% of the adult women in the sample felt that having a transvestite son was no disgrace to his parents or family and that transvestites were intelligent and hardworking. Although they joked about transvestites, males apparently did not denigrate the transvestite men.

According to Brierly (1979), transvestites cross-dress in search of feminine feelings. The process of cross-dressing involves acting the part until the feminine feelings become "instinctive." The transvestite is "preoccupied with the social female, envious of the values of the social position of women, their way of life, their mannerisms, in fact the sugar and spice and all things nice" (Brierly, 1979, p. 4). On the other hand, transvestites infrequently consider sex reassignment surgery (14%) and seldom (5%) take female hormones (Prince and Bentler, 1972).

Despite the recognized power and status of males, cases of female transvestism are extremely rare occurrences. This is in large part because our culture tolerates females dressing in male clothing. Cross-dressing by females was adaptive at times, rather than psychopathological or offensive to society. Even when acknowledged as strange (e.g., George Sand), such cross-dressing on the part of women was generally accepted.

3. Psychiatric Disorders and Criminality

Some relationship between psychiatric disorder and criminal behavior, particularly violent crime, has traditionally been part of common folk wisdom. In regard to female criminals, the relationship has moved from popular belief to explicit theorizing. Lombroso's (1903/1920) characterization that "her wickedness must have been enormous before it could triumph over so many obstacles" (p. 152) is the forerunner of more contemporary depictions.

Estimates of psychiatric disorder among criminal populations have ranged from a low of 4.6% (Petrich, 1976) to a high of 85% (Guze, 1976), depending on the nature and size of the sample and the thoroughness of psychiatric examination. It is interesting to note that in one early study, Bromberg and Thompson (1937) found that 82% of their nearly 10,000 criminals were "normal" or average individuals. Recognizing the heterogeneity of these offenders, Bromberg and Thompson described them as representing a wide spectrum of minor character difficulties. In contrast, in the more recent work of Guze and associates (Guze, 1976), 10%

of the male felons and none of the female felons were found to warrant no diagnosis.

According to Guze (1976), schizophrenia, primary affective disorders, anxiety neuroses, obsessional behaviors, and phobias are not generally associated with serious crime. The bizarre accounts of murder and violence due to schizophrenic hallucinations or delusions that appear on the front page of our newspapers describe extremely rare events. And individuals with blatant psychotic symptoms or delusions are typically diverted from the criminal justice system through incompetency hearings. Although such bizarre crimes do occur and may be linked to extreme psychiatric disorder, their relative infrequency limits their contribution to our general understanding of the relationships between criminal behavior and psychiatric disorder. Sociopathy, alcoholism, and drug dependence are the psychiatric disorders most associated with serious crime (Guze, 1976). Males are more frequently and consistently diagnosed as psychopaths or sociopaths. Epidemiological studies reveal the same pattern. In 22 out of 26 studies, the rates for personality disorders were consistently higher for males than for females, regardless of time, place, or methodological differences (Dohrenwend and Dohrenwend, 1976).

Some of the consistency in these studies is not surprising, given the nature of traditional male and female roles. Earlier studies, because they often relied on informants or official records to identify potential cases, were best suited to identifying antisocial people (disproportionately male) who left "institutional footprints"—those individuals who had the kinds of problems likely to appear in records of the police or other agents of social control in the community (Dohrenwend and Dohrenwend, 1976). Females, on the other hand, were less likely to leave behind them records of institutional contact, and therefore were more difficult to trace using methods that identify subjects from such sources.

An example of this is a provocative study focusing primarily on schizophrenia. Lewine, Strauss, and Gift (1981) found that females diagnosed as personality disorder tended to have their first admission to a psychiatric hospital earlier than males with the same diagnosis. These findings appear to suggest that antisocial behavior in females might be less tolerated in the home or community than the same behavior in males. However, despite the overall significant sex differences in admission patterns, if we look within age categories we do not find such differences. First admission for males aged 26 or below was 50% ($N = 17$), whereas the comparable figure for females was 62.5% ($N = 15$). Real divergence begins with the 27–32 age group where, the cumulative percentage for males is 64.3% and for females 91.7%.

Furthermore, the authors' sample is relatively unusual in its inclusion of women psychiatrically hospitalized for personality disorder. According to a survey by Cannon and Redick (1973), personality disorders rank among the top three disorders among male admissions to state and county mental hospitals, whereas schizophrenia, depressive disorders, and organic brain syndromes were the three leading diagnoses for female admissions. Following this line of reasoning, we might speculate that males with evidence of personality disorder would be more likely to be incarcerated at that age. Unfortunately, the data to answer such a question do not exist.*

3.1. Sex Bias in Referral and Diagnosis

Sex role standards not only influence the individual's own behavior but also affect how others view and label that behavior. Definitions of illegal and criminal behaviors reflect expectations and stereotypes about appropriate behavior for males and females. These expectations are subject to change over time, and usually correspond with changes in societal attitudes and values. In the past, female juvenile runaways were treated as criminals and were charged, booked, and frequently incarcerated in response to behavior for which their male counterparts were excused. In the same way, girls could be charged with sexual promiscuity and detained by authorities, whereas the notion of promiscuity is alien to our thinking about males.

Diagnoses are made by individuals who are part of the culture that adopts certain sex-typed standards of acceptable behavior for males and females. Hence, the person assigning the diagnosis is influenced by societal expectations for appropriate sex role behavior. Furthermore, the diagnostic criteria themselves reflect aggregate experiences that are the products of these same assumptions about how males and females can be expected to behave. When teachers, parents, and psychiatrists are asked to either interpret, diagnose, or label people exhibiting certain behaviors, they are influenced in their perceptions by their own expectations for appropriate sex role behavior.

Ten years ago, Chesler (1972) proposed that the kinds of behavior

---

*We can, however, examine the age distribution of males and females arrested and incarcerated. Despite the fact that males are incarcerated at a much higher rate than females in the United States, there does not appear to be evidence that males are incarcerated earlier. *Both* males and females aged 18–29 are vastly overrepresented among federal, state, and local correctional facilities in comparison to the general population (Flanagan *et al.*, 1982, see Table 6.15 for example). There are no significant sex differences. On the other hand, the relative proportion of women who are residents in prerelease facilities across the country is much higher than that for males in comparison to the total number of incarcerated individuals (DeJong, 1980).

considered "mad" or "criminal" were sex-specific and that individuals were labeled neurotic or psychotic in part because their behavior represented a significant departure from proscribed sex role stereotypic behaviors.

In a study by Feinblatt and Gold (1976), case records of 193 children who were referred to a child guidance clinic were examined. Children who showed behavioral characteristics inappropriate to their sex were more likely to be referred to psychiatric facilities than those showing appropriate sex role behavior. That is, more boys were referred for being emotional or passive, whereas girls were more likely to be referred if they exhibited defiant or aggressive behavior.

In two additional studies, Feinblatt and Gold had parents and psychology graduate students read hypothetical case studies in which identical behavior problems were attributed to a boy or a girl. The child described as showing inappropriate sex role behavior was seen as more severely disturbed, being more in need of treatment, and having a less successful future than the child showing behavior appropriate to his or her sex. Parents and psychology graduate students appeared to be using sex role standards as guides for their judgments about children's behavior. However, as Feinblatt and Gold point out, their findings relate to probable recommendations for treatment, not hospitalization.

Observers and trained professionals alike interpret behavior in line with expectations about sex differences. Just as individuals are socialized to adopt behavior that is appropriate for their gender, psychologists and psychiatrists are socialized to expect individuals to exhibit such behavior. Among other things, this can lead to different diagnoses of similar behavior, which is in part dependent on whether the subject is male or female. For example, Warner (1978) found that 175 mental health professionals tended to label men more frequently as antisocial personality disorder and women as hysterical personality, even when the patients had identical clinical features. When identical hypothetical clinical profiles were designated female, 76% were labeled hysterical and 22% antisocial. When designated male, 49% were labeled hysterical and 41% antisocial personality disorder. In a similar fashion, sex role expectations may cause observers to magnify any deviation from expected social roles. A rather mild strike at another child may be labeled aggressive if performed by a girl, but playful or nonaggressive if performed by a boy (Meyer and Sobieszek, 1972).

Therapists diagnose males and females through glasses filtered by sex role expectations. Stereotypes develop as the result of observed consistencies in behavior. These expectations are usually met and come to perpetuate themselves, thus continuing the cycle. Clinical diagnoses of female psychopaths are rare; male hysterics are probably even more seldom encountered. Is this because the respective traits are not often exhibited by the "wrong" sex, or because the gender of subjects produces different classifications of similar behavior?

3.2. Psychopathy and Hysteria

Boys are more likely to be antisocial in childhood than girls and more likely to develop into antisocial personality disorder as adults (Robins, 1966). To what extent are the overlapping disorders of psychopathy, sociopathy, or antisocial personality influenced by sex role expectations?

In his classic work, Cleckley (1976) listed the characteristics of the psychopath as

> superficial charm and good intelligence; absence of delusions and other signs of irrational thinking; absence of "nervousness" or other psychoneurotic manifestations; unreliability, untruthfulness, and insincerity; lack of remorse or shame; inadequately motivated antisocial behavior; poor judgment and failure to learn by experience; pathologic egocentricity and incapacity for love; general poverty in major affective reactions; specific loss of insight; unresponsiveness in general interpersonal relations; fantastic and uninviting behavior with drink and sometimes without; suicide rarely carried out; sex life impersonal, trivial, and poorly integrated, and failure to follow any life plan. (pp. 362–363)

Since Cleckley originally published his volume in 1941, many others have attempted to refine the concept and increase reliability of diagnosis. The most recent and explicit attempt is exemplified by the American Psychiatric Association's task force, which produced the *Diagnostic and Statistical Manual of Mental Disorder, Third Edition* (DSM-III). Not convinced of the usefulness of the labels psychopath or sociopath, the authors of the DSM-III chose to label the disorder Antisocial Personality Disorder and defined it in the following way:

> "The essential feature is a Personality Disorder in which there is a history of continuous and chronic antisocial behavior in which the rights of others are violated, persistence into adult life of a pattern of antisocial behavior that begins before the age of 15, and failure to sustain good job performance over a period of several years. . . . Lying, stealing, fighting, truancy, and resisting authority are typical early childhood signs. In adolescence, unusually early or aggressive sexual behavior, excessive drinking, and use of illicit drugs are frequent. In adulthood, these kinds of behavior continue, with the addition of inability to sustain consistent work performance or to function as a responsible parent and failure to accept social norms with respect to lawful behavior. After age 30 the more flagrant aspects may diminish, particularly sexual promiscuity, fighting, criminality, and vagrancy. (Spitzer, 1980, pp. 317–318)

Both sets of diagnostic criteria identify features of psychopathy and antisocial personality disorder that appear to be exaggerations of our stereotypic assumptions about appropriate behavior for males, e.g., toughness, aggressiveness, lack of concern for the feelings of others, lack of sincere emotions, and superficial interpersonal relationships— [the stereotypic image of the macho male : brutal, strong, impulsive, "love 'em and leave 'em."]

For males, occupational performance was and is an important aspect of contemporary expectations about appropriate male behavior, and failure to achieve was an index of poor social adjustment. Since women traditionally were not expected to maintain a good employment record, their failure to do so was not taken as an index of maladjustment. Different behaviors in males and females have recently been rocognized as possible manifestations of the same disorder. In diagnosing females, a history of prostitution may now be substituted for one of the DSM criteria for antisocial personality disorder.

Psychopathy is not totally absent among females. Cleckley (1976) included several case histories of female psychopaths and Robins (1966) found that 12% of the girls in her sample were later diagnosed sociopaths. Estimates of the frequency of psychopathy in female offenders range from a low of 2% (Woodside, 1962) to 6.1% (Widom, 1978b) to approximately 20% (Gibbens, Palmer, and Prince, 1971) to a high of 65% (Cloninger and Guze, 1970).

Hysteria is characterized by excitability, hyperemotionality, instability, attention seeking, immaturity, egocentricity, seductiveness, vanity, dependency, self-dramatization, and suggestibility. These traits caricature traditional notions of womanhood. Is hysteria the analogous psychiatric disorder that represents the archetypal, stereotypic woman? Several writers (e.g., Cloninger, 1978; Warner, 1978; Widom, 1978c) have suggested a link between psychopathy and hysteria.

Definitions of hysteria include many characteristics utilized to define psychopaths. For example, characteristics of the hysteric include colorful and dramatic expression, language, and appearance; ability to mimic and play the role of others; demanding dependency in interpersonal relationships; suicidal gestures; chemical dependence; and sexual problems (Engel, 1970). DSM-III criteria for Histrionic Personality Disorder include (a) behavior that is overly dramatic, reactive, and intensely expressed, as indicated by at least three of the following—self-dramatization, drawing attention to oneself, craving for activity and excitement, overreaction to minor events, and irrational, angry outbursts or tantrums; and (b) disturbances in interpersonal relationships as indicated by at least two of the following—perceived by others as shallow and lacking genuineness, even if superficially warm and charming; egocentric, self-indulgent, and inconsiderate of others; vain and demanding; dependent, helpless, constantly seeking reassurance; and prone to manipulative suicidal threats, gestures, or attempts (Spitzer, 1980, p. 315).

Both antisocial and histrionic personality disorders involve manipulative suicide attempts or threats, extreme egocentricity, exhibitionistic behavior, disturbances in interpersonal relationships, substance or chemical abuse, shallowness and superficial charm, and untruthfulness and insincerity. Histrionics have "irrational, angry outbursts or tantrums," whereas the individual labeled antisocial personality disorder suffers from "irritability and aggressiveness." The primary feature distinguishing the two disorders is dependency in the histrionics. Dependency is, of course, intricately woven into the fabric of assumptions about masculinity and femininity and is influenced by differential socialization experiences.

Empirical evidence has documented antisocial behaviors in individuals diagnosed as hysterics. For example, Robins (1966) found approximately equal numbers of antisocial symptoms in girls diagnosed as hysterical and sociopathic. Guze, Woodruff, and Clayton (1971) compared the incidence of antisocial behavior in two groups of women with hysteria and anxiety neuroses, finding that the women with hysteria had a history of more antisocial and delinquent behavior than the neurotic women. In a study of psychiatric diagnoses in convicted felons, Guze (1976) reported a greater incidence of sociopathy and hysteria in the female felons than in the general population.

There is also evidence from studies of first-degree relatives that there may be a genetic factor accounting for the overlap in the two diagnoses. For example, in an examination of the family backgrounds of male and female felons, female relatives of hysterics and sociopaths were found to have an increased prevalence of hysteria, whereas their male relatives showed a higher incidence of sociopathy and alcoholism (Cloninger and Guze, 1970). Studies of the parents of hyperactive children also show an increased prevalence of sociopathy and hysteria (Cantwell, 1972, 1978).

Clinical and behavioral observations and the findings from family studies support the hypothesis that hysteria and psychopathy may represent differential behavioral manifestations of the same underlying disorder. The similarities between the clinical descriptions of the two diagnostic categories are striking. The main difference lies in the dependency of the female hysteric. It should be obvious that this characteristic is strongly related to sex roles. Traditionally, women have been permitted and often encouraged to display dependent behaviors and to assume dependent roles, whereas they have been strongly discouraged from exhibiting antisocial or aggressive behaviors. Men, however, have traditionally been socialized to be independent, competitive, assertive, and aggressive. In addition to further research on the similarities between antisocial and histrionic personality disorders, we must examine individuals who cross these gender-related diagnostic categories.

The diagnoses of antisocial and histrionic personality disorders illustrate one possible divergent path suggested by the model in Figure 1. Despite similarities in genetic or familial components, through differential socialization experiences (including role models and peer pressures) and normative expectations, different sex-linked behaviors result. Psychopathy is primarily a disorder of men, and hysteria a disorder of women. Society not only shapes the development of the behavior but differentially responds to the behavior. That is, the process is reciprocal and reflexive. To a large extent, whether one spends time in prison labeled "psychopath" or is hospitalized labeled "hysteric" may be a function of one's sex.

4. Conclusion

Sex roles, criminality, and psychopathy are interrelated in complex, often subtle, and reflexive ways. Like other forms of behavior, criminal behavior is the result of genetic and physiological characteristics, past socialization experiences, and more current situational factors. Furthermore, definitions of behavior as criminal or psychopathological are in part the products of gender-based assumptions about what is appropriate or expected behavior for men and women. As a result, sex role stereotypes have influenced criminological and psychological theory and research in both obvious and subtle ways. Traditional sex role assumptions and expectations have explicitly formed the basis for treatises that have sought to explain female crime. Implicitly, laws, definitions of criminal behavior, clinical judgments, and both legal and mental health dispositions have been influenced by gender-based stereotypes.

It is undeniable that genetic and other biological differences account for some of the observed variation between males and females in the frequency of criminal and antisocial behavior. However, it is also important to recognize that while there may be sex-linked differences in predispositions to aggressive, violent, or criminal behavior, social and cultural factors play an important role.

Statistically, males outnumber females in most categories of criminal behavior. There are, however, some notable exceptions. The ratio of male to female criminals varies over time, across cultures, and across particular offenses. Similarly, differences in sex roles may be linked to temporal, cultural, and situational factors. While it is often tempting to call upon gender-based explanations for the predominance of, for example, females as prostitutes, it is also important to recognize that such explanations have their limits, and that they are less frequently employed to account for the criminal behavior of males.

A less obvious but no less important consequence of sex roles in seeking to understand criminal behavior is their influence on criminal justice system actors and institutions. Statistical and other information about crime is in part a product of decisions by police, prosecutors, judges, and crime victims. Since the same socialization experiences that reinforce sex roles for men and women in general also affect the behavior of individuals in the criminal justice system, these individuals may respond differently, depending on the sex of the offender and/or the victim. This affects not only the disposition of particular criminal events but aggregate information about crime as well. Thus, statistical information about the proportion of female offenders for various crimes is as much dependent on the behavior of criminal justice officials as it is on the behavior of individual women.

The diagnoses of psychopathy and hysteria illustrate many of the points discussed above. Although generally regarded as vastly different disorders with very different treatment outcomes, psychopathy and hysteria may in fact represent a common underlying disorder that, as a result of differential sex-linked socialization experiences (opportunities, models, pressures, and situational factors) is manifested differently in males and females in what happen to be sex role stereotypic ways. Thus, clinical records and the diagnoses of psychopathy and hysteria are the products of accumulated experiences that are themselves intricately linked to expectations about appropriate behavior for males and females.

Deviant behavior is defined in terms of a departure from appropriate, expected roles. Decisions are made at many points by mental health and criminal justice system personnel that determine whether one is defined as deviant, labeled as delinquent, or diagnosed as disturbed. As a result, sex role stereotypes may influence whether hospital doors are opened, or prison gates closed, for males and females. Hence, no comprehensive theory of criminality or antisocial personality is possible without understanding the influence of sex roles on the development, definition, diagnosis, and disposition of deviant and criminal behavior.

5. References

Allen, J. *Assault with a deadly weapon.* New York: Pantheon, 1977.

Almy, L, Bravo, V., Burd, L, Chin, P., Cohan, L., Gallo, F., Giorgianni, A., Gold, J., Jose, M., and Noyes, J. *A study of coeducational correctional facility.* Unpublished Master's thesis, Boston University, 1975.

American Psychiatric Association. *Diagnostic and statistical manual of mental disorder (3rd ed.).* Washington, D.C.: APA, 1980.

Amir, N. *Patterns of forcible rape.* Chicago: University of Chicago Press, 1971.

Bastani, J. B., and Kentsmith, D. K. Psychotherapy with wives of sexual deviants. *American Journal of Psychotherapy,* 1980, *34,* 20–25.

Baucom, D. H. Independent masculinity and femininity scales on the California Psychological Inventory. *Journal of Consulting and Clinical Psychology,* 1976, *44,* 876.

Belson, W. *Juvenile theft: The causal factors.* New York: Harper & Row, 1975.

Bem, S. L. The measurement of psychological androgyny. *Journal of Consulting and Clinical Psychology,* 1974, *42,* 155–162.

Black, D. J. Production of crime rates. *American Sociological Review,* 1970, *35,* 738–748.

Brierly, H. *Transvestism: A handbook with case studies for psychologists, psychiatrists, and counselors.* New York: Pergamon Press, 1979.

Bromberg, W., and Thompson, C. B. The relation of psychosis, mental defect, and personality types to crime. *Journal of Criminal Law and Criminology,* 1937, *28,* 70–89.

Buss, A. H., and Plomin, R. *A temperament theory of personality development.* New York: Wiley, 1975.

Cannon, M. S., and Redick, R. W. *Differential utilization of psychiatric facilities by men and women, U.S. 1970* (Statistical Note 81). Washington, D.C.: NIMH Biometry Branch, 1973.

Cantwell, D. P. Psychiatric illness in the families of hyperactive children. *Archives of General Psychiatry,* 1972, *27,* 414–417.

Cantwell, D. Hyperactivity and antisocial behavior. *Journal of the American Academy of Child Psychiatry,* 1978, *17,* 252–262.

Chesler, P. *Women and madness.* New York: Avon, 1972.

Cicourel, A., and Kitsuse, J. A note on the use of official statistics. *Social Problems,* 1963, *11,* 131–139.

Cleckley, H. *The mask of sanity.* St. Louis: Mosby, 1976.

Cloninger, C. R. The link between hysteria and sociopathy: An integrative model of pathogenesis based on clinical, genetic, and neuro-physiological observations. In H. S. Akiskal and W. L. Webb (Eds.) *Psychiatric diagnosis: Explorations of biological predictors.* New York: Spectrum, 1978.

Cloninger, C. R., and Guze, S. B. Female criminals; their personal, familial, and social background. *Archives of General Psychiatry,* 1970, *23,* 554–558.

Cohen, M., Seghorn, T., and Calmas, W. Sociometric study of the sex offender. *Journal of Abnormal Psychology,* 1969, *74,* 249–255.

Conklin, J. E. *Robbery and the criminal justice system.* Philadelphia: Lippincott, 1972.

Coombs, N. R. Male prostitution: A psychosocial view of behavior. *American Journal of Orthopsychiatry,* 1974, *44,* 782–789.

Cowie, J., Cowie, V., and Slater, E. *Delinquency in girls.* London: Heinemann, 1968.

Davis, K. Prostitution. In R. K. Merton and R. A. Nisbet (Eds.), *Contemporary social problems.* New York: Harcourt, 1961.

DeJong, W. *American prisons and jails, (Vol. 5): Supplemental report—Adult pre-release facilities.* Washington, D.C.: U.S. Government Printing Office, 1980.

Dohrenwend, B. P., and Dohrenwend, B. S. Sex differences and psychiatric disorders. *American Journal of Sociology*, 1976, *81*, 1447–1454.

Dworkin, R. H., Burke, B. W., Maher, B. A., and Gottesman, I. I. A longitudinal study of the genetics of personality. *Journal of Personality and Social Psychology*, 1976, *34*, 510–518.

Ellis, L. Genetics and criminal behavior. *Criminology*, 1982, *20*(1), 43–66.

Engel, G. L. Conversion symptoms. In C. M. MacBryde and R. S. Blacklow (Eds.), *Sign and symptoms: Applied pathologic physiology and clinical interpretation* (5th ed.). Philadelphia: Lippincott, 1970.

Esselstyn, T. C. Prostitution in the United States. *Annals of the American Academy of Political and Social Science*, 1968, *376*, 123–35.

Exner, J. E., Wylie, J., Leura, A., and Parrill, T. Some psychological characteristics of prostitutes. *Journal of Personality Assessment*, 1977, *41*, 474–485.

Eysenck, S. B. G., and Eysenck, H. J. The personality of female prisoners. *British Journal of Psychiatry*, 1973, *123*, 696–698.

Farley, S. H., and Farley, S. V. Stimulus-seeking motivation and delinquent behavior among institutionalized delinquent girls. *Journal of Consulting and Clinical Psychology*, 1972, *39*, 140–147.

Feeney, F., and Weir, A. (Eds.). *The prevention and control of robbery* (Vol. 1). Davis: University of California-Davis, 1973. (Mimeo)

Feinblatt, S., and Gold, A. Sex roles and the psychiatric referral process. *Sex Roles*, 1976, *2*, 109–122.

Finkelhor, S. D. Sexually victimized children and their families. *Dissertation Abstracts International*, 1978, *39* (11-A), 7006–7007.

Flanagan, T. J., Alstyne, D. J., and Gottfredson, M. R. (Eds.). *Sourcebook of criminal justice statistics—1981* (U.S. Department of Justice, Bureau of Justice Statistics). Washington, D.C.: U.S. Government Printing Office, 1982.

Freud, S. *New introductory lectures on psychoanalysis*. New York: Norton, 1933.

Gebhard, P. H. Misconceptions about female prostitutes. *Medical Aspects of Human Sexuality*, 1969, *3*, 24, 28–30.

Gelles, R. J. Child abuse as psychopathology. *American Journal of Orthopsychiatry*, 1973, *43*, 611–621.

Gelles, R. J. *Family violence*. Beverly Hills, Calif.: Sage, 1979.

Gibbens, T. C. N. Female offenders. *British Journal of Hospital Medicine*, September, 1971, 279–286.

Gibbens, T. C. N., Palmer, C., and Prince, J. Mental health aspects of shoplifting. *British Medical Journal*, 1971, *3*, 612–615.

Glick, R. M., and Neto, V. V. *National study of women's correctional programs*. Washington, D.C.: U.S. Government Printing Office, 1977.

Griffin, R. *Shoplifting in supermarkets, drug stores, discount stores: 18th annual report*. Van Nuys, California: Commercial Service Systems, 1981.

Griffin, S. *Rape: The all-American crime*. Andover, Mass: Warner Module Publications, 1973.

Guze, S. B. *Criminality and psychiatric disorders*. New York: Oxford University Press, 1976.

Guze, S. B., Woodruff, R. A., and Clayton, P. J. Hysteria and antisocial behavior: Further evidence of an association. *American Journal of Psychiatry*, 1971, *127*, 957–960.

Hare, R. D., and Schalling, D. (Eds.). *Psychopathic behavior*. London: Wiley, 1978.

Heidensohn, F. The deviance of women: A critique and an enquiry. *British Journal of Sociology*, 1968, *19*, 160–175.

Heilbrun, A. B. *Human sex-role behavior*. New York: Pergamon Press, 1981.

Hindelang, M. J. Sex differences in criminal activity. *Social Problems*, 1979, *27*, 143–156.

Hirschi, T. The professional prostitute. *Berkeley Journal of Sociology*, 1962, 7, 33–49.

Holcomb, R. *Bureau of police science* (Unpublished report). Iowa City: University of Iowa, 1973.

Honzik, M. P. Prediction of behavior from birth to maturity. In J. Rosenblith and W. Allinsmith (Eds.), *The causes of behavior* (2nd ed.). Boston: Allyn and Bacon, 1966.

Iga, M. Sociocultural factors in Japanese prostitution prevention law. *Journal of Sex Research*, 1968, 4, 127–146.

Jensen, G., and Eve, R. Sex differences in delinquency: An examination of popular sociological explanations. *Criminology*, 1976, 13, 427–448.

Klemke, L. W. Does apprehension for shoplifting amplify or terminate shoplifting activity? *Law and Society Review*, 1978, 12, 391–403.

Kruttschnitt, C. Women, crime, and dependency. *Criminology*, 1982, 19, 495–513.

Laws, J. L., and Schwartz, P. *Sexual scripts: The social construction of female sexuality.* Hinsdale, Ill.: Dryden, 1977.

Lemert, E. M. *Social pathology.* New York: McGraw-Hill, 1951.

Leventhal, G. Female criminality: Is women's lib to blame? *Psychological Reports*, 1977, 41, 1179–1182.

Lewine, R., Strauss, J., and Gift, T. Sex differences in age at first hospital admission for sex: Fact or artifact. *American Journal of Psychiatry*, 1981, 138, 440–444.

Lombroso, C. [*The female offender*] (Trans.). New York: Appleton, 1920. (Originally published, 1903.)

Loughton, M. The need to steal. *New Society*, 1973, 23, 540–41.

Maccoby, E. E., and Jacklin, C. N. *The psychology of sex differences.* Stanford: Stanford University Press, 1974.

Maxfield, M. G. *Discretion and delivery of police services: Demand, client characteristics, and street-level bureaucrats in two cities.* Doctoral dissertation, Northwestern University, 1979.

Maxfield, M. G., Lewis, D. A., and Szoc, R. Producing official crimes: Verified crime reports as measures of police output. *Social Science Quarterly*, 1980, 61(2), 221–236.

Medea, A., and Thompson, K. *Against rape.* New York: Farrar, Straus & Giroux, 1974.

Mednick, S. A., and Volavka, J. Biology and crime. In N. Morris and M. Tonry (Eds.), *Crime and justice: An annual review of research* (Vol. 2). Chicago: University of Chicago Press, 1980.

Megargee, E. I., and Bohn, M. J., Jr. *Classifying criminal offenders.* Beverly Hills, Calif.: Sage, 1979.

Merton, R. K. *Social theory and social structure.* New York: Free Press, 1968.

Meyer, J. W., and Sobieszek, B. I. Effect of a child's sex on adult interpretation of its behavior. *Developmental Psychology*, 1972, 6, 42–48.

Mohr, J. W. A child has been molested. *Medical Aspects of Human Sexuality*, 1968, 2, 43–50.

Moore, G. Publications review. *Security Management*, March 1976, 20, 60.

Morris, R. R. Female delinquency and relational problems. *Social Forces*, 1964, 43, 82–89.

Nettler, G. *Explaining crime.* New York: McGraw-Hill, 1978.

Newton, D. E. Homosexual behavior and child molesting: A review of the evidence. *Adolescence*, 1978, 13(49), 29–43.

Panton, J. H. Personality differences between male and female prison inmates (measured by the MMPI). *Criminal Justice and Behavior*, 1974, 1, 40–47.

Peters, J. J. Children who are victims of sexual assault and the psychology of offenders. *American Journal of Psychotherapy*, 1976, 30, 335–338.

Petrich, J. Rate of psychiatric morbidity in a metropolitan county jail. *American Journal of Psychiatry*, 1976, 133, 1439–1444.

Petrie, A. *Individuality in pain and suffering.* Chicago: University of Chicago Press, 1967.

Prince, C., and Bentler, P. M. Survey of 504 cases of transvestism. *Psychological Reports,* 1972, *31,* 903–917.

Propper, A. M. *Prison homosexuality—Myth and reality.* Lexington, Mass.: D. C. Heath, 1981.

Quinsey, V. L. The assessment and treatment of child molesters: A review. *Canadian Psychological Review,* 1977, *18*(3), 204–220.

Rappeport, J. R., and Lassen, G. The dangerousness of female patients: A comparison of the arrest rate of discharged psychiatric patients and the general population. *American Journal of Psychiatry,* 1966, *123,* 413–419.

Robins, L. N. *Deviant children grown up.* Baltimore: Williams and Wilkins, 1966.

Rosenblum, K. E. Female deviance and the female sex role: A preliminary investigation. *British Journal of Sociology,* 1975, *26,* 169–185.

Russell, D. Emotional aspects of shoplifting. *Psychiatric Annals,* 1973, *3,* 77–86.

Rymph, D. B. *Cross-sex behavior in an Isthmus Zapotec village.* Paper presented at the 73rd Annual Meeting of the American Anthropological Association, Mexico City, 1974.

Sagarin, E. The high personal cost of wearing a label. *Psychology Today,* 1976, *9,* 25–29.

Seidman, D., and Couzens, M. Getting the crime rate down: Political pressure and crime reporting. *Law and Society Review,* 1974, *8*(Spring).

Serber, M., and Keith, C. G. The Atascadero project: Model of a sexual retraining program for incarcerated homosexual pedophiles. *Journal of Homosexuality,* 1974, *1,* 87–97.

Silberman, C. E. *Criminal violence, criminal justice.* New York: Random House, 1978.

Simon, R. J. *The contemporary woman and crime.* Rockville, Md.: National Institute of Mental Health, 1975.

Smith, Z. N., and Zekman, P. *The mirage.* New York: Random House, 1979.

Spitzer, R. L. *Diagnostic and statistical manual of mental disorder* (3rd ed.). Washington, D.C.: American Psychiatric Association, 1980.

Stark, R., and McEvoy, J. Middle class violence. *Psychology Today,* November 1970, pp. 52–54: 110–112.

Talamini, J. T. *Cross-dressing: A socio-cultural survey.* Paper presented at the Social Science History Association meetings, Rochester, N.Y., 1980.

Thomas, A., Chess, S., and Birch, R. The origins of personality. *Scientific American,* 1970, *223,* 102–109.

Tobias, J. J., Danto, B., and Robertson, R. H. The role of the police in dealing with sexually abused children. *Journal of Police Science and Administration,* 1980, *8,* 464–473.

U.S. Department of Justice, Federal Bureau of Investigation. *Uniform crime reports, 1979.* Washington, D.C.: U.S. Government Printing Office, 1980.

Walters, D. R. *Physical and sexual abuse of children: Causes and treatments.* Bloomington: Indiana University Press, 1975.

Warner, R. The diagnosis of antisocial and hysterical personality disorder: An example of sex bias. *Journal of Nervous and Mental Disorders,* 1978, *166,* 839–845.

Warren, M. Q. The female offender. In H. Toch, (Ed.), *Psychology of crime and criminal justice.* New York: Holt, Rinehart & Winston, 1979.

Weis, J. Liberation and crime: The invention of the new female criminal. *Crime and Social Justice,* 1976, *1,* 17–27.

Widom, C. S. Unpublished data, Harvard University, 1978. (a)

Widom, C. S. An empirical classification of female offenders. *Criminal Justice and Behavior,* 1978, *5,* 35–52. (b)

Widom, C. S. Toward an understanding of female criminality. In B. A. Maher, (Ed.), *Progress in experimental personality research* (Vol. 8). New York: Academic Press, 1978. (c)

Widom, C. S. Female offenders: Three assumptions about self-esteem, sex-role identity, and feminism. *Criminal Justice and Behavior*, 1979, *6*, 365–382.

Widom, C. S. Perspectives on female criminality: A critical examination of assumptions. In A. Morris (Ed.), *Women and crime* (Cropwood Conference Series No. 13). Cambridge, England: Institute of Criminology, 1981.

Widom, C. S., Katkin, F. S., Stewart, A. J., and Fondacaro, M. *Multivariate analysis of personality and motivation in female delinquents. Journal of Research in Crime and Delinquency*, 1983, *20*, (2): 277–290.

Wolfgang, M. E. Victim-precipitated criminal homicide. *Journal of Criminal Law, Criminology, and Police Science*, 1958, *48*(1), 1–4, 6–11.

Wolfgang, M., Figlio, R. M., and Sellin, T. *Delinquency in a birth cohort*. Chicago: University of Chicago Press, 1972.

Woodside, M. Instability in women prisoners. *Lancet*, 1962, *2*, 928–930.

10

A Sex-Roles Perspective on Drug and Alcohol Use by Women

Mary Ellen Colten and Jeanne C. Marsh

Patterns of use and misuse of drugs and alcohol consistently have differed by gender. Men have exceeded women in the use of alcohol and illicit substances to such a degree that substance abuse has been seen as a male problem. Until recently, the meaning of these differential patterns and the problems of substance use and misuse by women has been virtually ignored. A decade ago, Hochschild (1973) noted that "most research in the social sciences is on male subjects; yet there are significantly different findings on males and females . . . which are often ignored. As a corrective, most sex role research is on women." This chapter offers another corrective. We believe that research in substance use and abuse has progressed so that we can go beyond describing women or describing differences between men and women to exploring what those differences tell us about substance abuse, about sex roles, and about the relationship between the two.

After documenting some of the sex differences in patterns of alcohol and drug use, noting any changes in those patterns, we will examine some of the gender differences in etiology of substance use and those factors that are thought to be antecedents of misuse or abuse, and some gender differences in the consequences of use. We will be exploring the relationship between the differing patterns of substance use in men and women and their differing social roles or sex roles with the intent of

Mary Ellen Colten • Center for Survey Research, Boston, Massachusetts 02116.
Jeanne C. Marsh • School of Social Service Administration, University of Chicago, Chicago, Illinois 60637.

identifying how knowledge about sex roles informs our understanding of substance abuse by women and how it enhances our ability to predict and prevent substance abuse in women, and to offer effective support and treatment to those women who do misuse substances.

1. Drugs and Drug Abuse

Drugs, for our purposes, are substances that are mood-modifying, altering the affective states of individuals. They may be used medicinally, socially, or recreationally, and tend to be controlled by the society. Societal regulation comes in the forms of laws, taxes, and norms or sanctions. Drug abuse in a legal sense, then, is using these substances in violation of the societal regulations—either obtaining drugs through illegal channels, using illegal drugs, or using drugs in violation of laws restricting use to certain subgroups (e.g., drinking-age laws). In a normative sense, drug abuse is using a drug, even a legal one, in excess of what is considered to be appropriate to the user's position in society. This could mean using the drug so that it interferes with performance of role functions, creates personal, psychological, or physical problems for the user, or offends the moral or normative sensibilities of observers. A dependence on a substance, either psychological or physical, also can be seen as substance abuse (Eddy, Halbach, Isbell, and Seevers, 1965). However, in the absence of interference with role functioning or of physical harm or of violation of law, dependence is not generally perceived as abuse. Thus, until the ill effects of cigarettes were uncovered, nicotine dependence was not labeled as drug abuse. We might guess that what is seen as substance abuse in women might not be identical with substance abuse in men. The National Institute on Drug Abuse monitors the nonmedical use of marijuana, cocaine, heroin, alcohol, hallucinogens, cigarettes, PCP, inhalants, and the psychotherapeutic or psychotropic drugs. These psychotropic drugs include stimulants, sedatives, tranquilizers, and analgesics (pain-killers).

Drugs can be categorized along two important dimensions. Within the dimension of *legality* there are drugs that are licit, drugs that are illicit, and drugs that are licit if prescribed by a physician and illicit if not. Another important dimension is drugs that have *medicinal* purposes and those that are used for social purposes. This dimension is complicated because medicinal drugs can be used for recreational purposes (Quaaludes and amphetamines are prime examples of this) and predominantly social drugs, such as alcohol, marijuana, and cocaine, have clear medicinal functions. When the dimensions of licit-to-illicit and social-to-medicinal are combined, the result is a characterization of substance use that Gomberg (1979) identifies as *social acceptability*. It is anchored at one end by prescribed medications and at the other end by "hard street" drugs such as heroin and cocaine. In between fall over-the-counter (OTC) drugs (pain-relievers, cold and cough medicines, tonics, some sedatives, laxatives, and antacids), licit social drugs (such as alcohol, caffeine, and nicotine) and finally, the illicit "soft" street drugs (such as marijuana).

2. Sex Differences in Drug Use

Estimating rates of drug use and ratios of male to female use of drugs is a difficult task. The errors involved are most often biases in sampling and biases in self-reports of use. In other words, it is necessary to capture *all* the right people and to get accurate information from them. These problems have long been acknowledged and present particular problems when sex ratios or sex differences in use are discussed, because the types of biases in sampling and reporting vary according to gender. For example, samples of the general population tend to underrepresent young males—they are less socially connected and more mobile, spend less time at home, are more likely to be institutionalized, and are less likely to have telephones. Similarly, studies of high school students are plagued by a higher dropout rate for males and a higher rate of absenteeism among heavy drug users (Single, Kandel, and Johnson, 1975). Since heavy drug users are more likely to be male, high school samples probably tend to underrepresent males.

On the other hand, estimates of drug and alcohol use based on accident and arrest rates most likely overrepresent males, while drug users seeking help at medical facilities may overrepresent women since women tend to seek medical help more readily. However, this may not be the case for all treatment programs since some have not been hospitable to women either by failing to meet the child care, health, and employment needs of women, by offering a sexist environment, or by placing women at risk of losing their children if they admit to a substance use problem (Anderson, 1977; Beckman and Kocel, 1982; Colten, 1982; Cuskey, Berger, and Densen-Gerber, 1977; Homiller, 1977; Levy and Doyle, 1974; Marsh, 1980; Naierman, Savage, Haskins, Lear, Chase, Marvell, and Lamothe, 1979). Thus, numbers of women in treatment also may not accurately reflect the numbers of women with problems relative to men.

Biases in reporting are probably not distributed with such striking dissimilarity between the two sexes, but underreporting could well occur according to beliefs about acceptability. Thus, we might expect women to underreport their use of illicit substances, their heavy drinking, and their nonmedical use of licit substances. Men might be likely to underreport medicinal use of substances. What we are describing, then, is the effect of sex roles on the figures we will be using to draw conclusions about sex differences in use and the relationship beween use patterns and sex roles. Our information itself is biased by sex roles.

Another factor making this difficult is that data are reported in terms of lifetime prevalences (which is the frequency with which a drug has *ever* been used), prevalence within a past specified period of time, incidence (which is the rate of new users within a given time period), or current users, with the current time period variously defined by various researchers. Reports of sex differences in use and, particularly, changes in sex differences in use obviously will be affected by which measure is applied. So, for example, comparisons of *prevalence* rates for men and women might differ from comparisons of *current use* rates. Or if a question about current use has to do with use within the past 30 days as opposed to within the past year, the figures again might look quite different.

In every comparison, male use exceeds female use for nonmedicinal, social, and recreational use of licit drugs and for all use of illicit drugs. This is true for alcohol, marijuana, inhalants, cocaine, hallucinogens, PCP, and heroin.

Since alcohol and heroin are social or recreational drugs, both of which have been the focus of considerable research and treatment activity—one representing a licit and socially acceptable drug and the other an illicit, socially unacceptable drug—the rest of this chapter will focus on these two drugs. We will also look at the psychotropic drugs since the sex differences in use of these substances are the reverse of other drugs.

2.1. Psychotropic Drugs and Over-the-Counter Medications

In general, all of the data suggest that women exceed men in the use of mood-modifying drugs that are medicinal and legal—that is, prescribed medications, tranquilizers, barbiturates and antidepressants, and over-the-counter drugs (Chambers, 1971; Cooperstock, 1976; Mellinger, Balter, Parry, Manheimer, and Cisin, 1974; Fidell, 1981; Gomberg, 1982). Over two-thirds of the prescriptions for psychotropic drugs are written for women (FDA Drug Bulletin, 1980). Other figures (Cooperstock, 1976; DAWN Report, 1976) also represent at least a 2:1 ratio of women to men in receiving prescriptions of psychotropic drugs. Yet we note that this sex ratio diminishes when we include nonmedical use of prescription drugs (that is, using a medication that has not been prescribed for the user, often to "get high") in our calculations. Balter and Levine (1972) report almost equal nonmedical and over-the-counter use for males and females. This apparently is because males exceed females in nonmedical drug use while women are greater consumers and purchasers of over-the-counter diet pills.

Females use nonprescribed licit drugs more than males and also tend to self-medicate more (Bush and Osterweis, 1978; Bush and Rabin, 1976; Rabin, 1977; Rabin and Bush, 1975; Verbrugge, 1982). Thus, for psychotropic and over-the-counter medications, it is only in the *nonmedical* use of prescription drugs that men's use tends to match or exceed that of women.

2.2. Alcohol

Although our means of determining rates of alcohol consumption and their accuracy is a subject of much debate, it is a consistent finding that men drink more frequently than women and consume more on any given drinking occasion. Men are three to four times as likely to be classified as heavy drinkers, and the rates of problem drinking in men are estimated to be considerably higher than those for women. Treatment facilities, overall, report a preponderance of male admissions. Further, it is estimated that one-third of American women are abstainers (Cahalan, Cisin and Crossley, 1969; Ference, 1980; Gomberg, 1979; Johnson, Armor, Polich, and Stambul, 1977).

Recently, attention has been directed toward women's employment status as a variable related to drinking. Johnson (1978) targeted women who are employed and married as a heavier drinking group. In other words, the interaction between employment status and marital status predicts to heavy and problem drinking. In a similar analysis, Parker, Parker, Wolz, and Harford (1980) also found employment status to be a key predictor of women's drinking, although they found no interaction with marital status.

A common belief has been that these figures indicate that male problem drinkers vastly outnumber female problem drinkers because they fail to capture incalculable numbers of middle-aged suburban housewives. These closet drinkers are presumably nursing the wounds of their "empty nest" syndrome, and since they do not drink in public and have no work-role obligations that they fail to meet, they are supposedly less exposed and can remain hidden. In fact, the evidence does not at all support this persistent myth. There is evidence to suggest that younger women and employed women abstain less and drink more (Cahalan and Cisin, 1976; Johnson *et al.*, 1977; Knupfer, 1964; Mulford, 1977).

2.3. Heroin

Most sources agree that women comprise about 20% of the heroin addict population (Martin and Martin, 1980; Prather and Fidell, 1978) and that approximately 25% of all addicts appearing for treatment are female (Mandel, Goldschmidt, and Grover 1973; Sheffet, Hickey, Duval, Millman, and Louria, 1973; Simpson, Savage, Joe, Demaree, and Sells, 1976). From 1935 through 1964, 17% of the nearly 88,000 narcotic-related admissions to the United States Public Health Services Hospitals were women. There is also evidence that heroin addition has increased at a faster rate for women than for men (Uniform Crime Reports, 1973).

Prior to the 1914 passage of the Harrison Narcotics Act, there were twice as many women addicted to opiates as men. When the use of narcotics became illegal, women's use declined significantly. In 1938 Kolb observed that women's use of opiates was to relieve "physical and mental distress." Indeed, most women's use of opiates was in tonics and in treatments for female reproductive system discomforts. Once opiates became illegal, a good deal of women's addiction was iatrogenic—an addiction following the use of morphine in medical treatment. It is noteworthy that some of the earlier studies on women identified a "pain-prone" group composed mostly of iatrogenic cases and nurses who had access to morphine through their work setting and whose initial contact was not with "street" sources (Glaser, 1966).

3. Trends and Changes in Sex Differences in Drug and Alcohol Use

For the same reasons that it is not possible to be precise about the numbers of women who drink, it is difficult to describe with precision the changes in women's drinking patterns over the years. When discussing change, we face additional obstacles. First is the margin of error we allow ourselves in description. For example, when we say 20 to 25% of alcoholics are female, that 5% difference may be quite close to the change observed. So if that estimate rises to between 25 and 30%, are we looking at a real change or one that is within our margin of error?

Change rates have many other problems. All too often, estimates of change are based upon two studies that fail to use exactly the same measure of drinking, drinking problems, or alcoholism. Or they use samples that are not comparable. So we cannot know that the change or lack of change noted is not due to a change in measurement. Even with those rare studies that appear to carefully replicate previous techniques and that document change clearly exceeding the margin of error, we cannot be sure that the change observed is an enduring one. It may be a small aberration due to a temporary convergence of social circumstances. A further problem with studies that indicate an increase in women's substance use is that we cannot be certain that what we are observing is anything more than an increased willingness to imbibe or ingest in public, to come out of the closet with the problems, or to seek treatment. Finally, some of the best studies have been done on the young. Often a change in a behavior among the young foreshadows a general social change and also represents behaviors that will endure for that age cohort. Often, however, it does not. Then we see no filtering to the larger society and may also see "maturing out" of those behaviors as the group grows up.

As a consequence of these problems, and also because we are often trying to extrapolate from a short time-span to describe long-term trends, there is considerable disagreement about what *really* is happening with patterns of women's drug use relative to that of men.

In the 1970s, many observers were endorsing the convergence hypothesis, citing evidence to indicate that men's and women's substance abuse patterns were converging due to changes in women's patterns (e.g., Chambers and Hunt, 1977; Prather and Fidell, 1978; Wechsler and McFadden, 1976). Put simply, women's drug and alcohol use was becoming more like men's. From the perspective of the 1980s, that conclusion appears to be unsupported by the data. So we will now offer our 1980s conclusions about changes in drug use patterns, noting our concurrence with Sutker (1981), who concludes that the evidence suggests that "drug abuse patterns can change quickly" (p.29).

3.1. Psychotropic Drugs

Ference and Whitehead (1980) reviewed 90 surveys of psychotropic drug use conducted during the 1970s in the United States and Canada. In order to be considered in their review, a survey had to include at least 500 respondents, have a high response rate, and be a reasonably unbiased sample. They conclude that drug use rates for drugs other than tobacco, marijuana, and cocaine have peaked. This means that rates of illicit use of barbiturates, tranquilizers, and stimulants are on the decline. We might ask, then, if some of the supposed convergence is due to different rates of decline rather than a supposed increase in women's use to match that of men. An example of this is the disappearance of a sex difference in tranquilizer use by high school students noted by Johnston, Bachman, and O'Malley (1982). A faster decline among females, who used them more than males in 1977, apparently accounts for the lack of a currently observed difference. For other drugs, the drop has been more in male use. They note that "the decline in illicit drug use among males started earlier and has been sharper than among females" (p. 47).

In no literature of the 1980s could we find support for systematic shifts in the ratio of male to female psychotropic drug use. Sex differences among the young are less marked, but there is no evidence to suggest that this difference will not increase as they enter adulthood.

3.2. Alcohol

The proportion of nonabstaining women began increasing in the 1940s and continued to increase until the 1970s, when it began to level off (Ference, 1980). Many current reports about the prevalence of alcohol use in women indicate that the rates of increase in both drinking and problem drinking among women has been greater than that of men, so that the drinking patterns of men and women are becoming more alike. These changes were most often noted among the younger age groups in the mid-1970s (Gold and Reimer, 1975; San Mateo County, 1971; Rachal, Williams, Brehm, Cavanaugh, Moore, and Eckerman, 1975; Wechsler and McFadden, 1976). Johnston et al. (1982), however, have not observed any increased convergence in the drinking patterns of male and female high school students between 1975 and 1981. They note that "frequent use of alcohol tends to be disproportionately concentrated among males." And the proportions of males and females who have ever used alcohol or have used it in the past year remained relatively stable and similar over the 6-year span of the study. Other studies do show a slight decline in sex ratios for occasional drinking. However, as frequency of drinking increases, sex ratios show sharp increases. For example, Engs (1977) reported that 75% of college women drink socially (as compared to 80% of college men), a substantial increase from the 61% reported for women in 1950, but not a substantial increase for men (up from 79%). However, Engs also reports that five times as many college men are heavy drinkers. Ference (1980), in an extensive analysis of the available data, concludes that although the rates of drinking (nonabstinence) among the young indicates convergence between males and females, the rates of heavy drinking among both the young and adult do not suggest gender convergence in patterns. So men continue to exceed women in rates of heavy and problem drinking, while abstainers remain more heavily represented among older, lower-income, and less educated women. If we accept the notion that the young and the more economically and educationally advantaged segments of the population are the leaders in social change, then it is possible that we can expect to see a considerable reduction in the gap between male nonabstainers and female nonabstainers. However, there is simply no evidence that *problem drinking* or *alcoholism* among women is currently on the rise. In 1977 Johnson *et al.* estimated the rate of "serious problem drinking" for men at between 10 and 15% and between 3 and 5% for women. Those figures remain unmodified.

We mentioned earlier that Johnson (1978, 1982) has evidence for a higher incidence of nonabstention and heavy drinking among employed women, particularly married ones. So we need to take special note of younger, educated, employed women of higher socioeconomic status because their nonabstention rates may portend changes in drinking patterns for women. Again, it is important to remember that social drinking is not heavy drinking or alcoholism, but that willingness to drink at all is a necessary condition for developing alcohol problems.

3.3. Heroin

An important characteristic of sex difference in heroin use is that women's use of opiates declined significantly relative to men's once opiate use became illegal. In the late 1960s and early 1970s a rise in heroin use among both sexes and particularly among women attracted attention and alarm. Indeed, during the 1970s heroin addiction appeared to increase at a much faster rate among women than among men. However, by the end of the decade, it became clear that heroin use had peaked, and no significant increases were to be observed in the period from 1972 to 1979 (Fishburne, Abelson, and Cisin, 1980). In 1981 Sutker interpreted drug treatment program admission data—which showed that in 1979 heroin was the primary drug for 38% of all women clients and 41% of all male clients in federally funded programs—to mean that "the differences in drug use patterns are diminishing." We suspect that this is due not to a marked increase in female heroin use but rather to a decline in treatment-seeking for other drug abuse problems. And over 60% of women in treatment in federally funded programs are not there because of heroin use. Since problem use of hallucinogens and other "street" drugs has declined and attention to the problems of tranquilizer addiction has increased, this means that most women receiving drug treatment are being treated for barbiturate, sedative, and tranquilizer use. Johnston *et al.* (1982) observe that, among the young, the prevalence of heroin use declined steadily from 1975 to 1979. The decline seems to have stopped, but absolutely no increase is detectable. Further, the sex ratio now remains stable.

3.4. Summary

Overall, it appears that women heroin addicts did increase relative to men in the early 1970s. That increase coincided with increased national attention to the problem and may well reflect a temporary convergence of circumstances. The final result is probably a slight reduction in the very large differences in male and female use.

The primary change in drug use behavior that is likely to endure, then, is in the apparent convergence in proportions of males and females who drink socially or, in other terms, the decline in the proportion of women who abstain. It is also important to note that, at this point, there is no evidence to suggest that there has been a concomitant increase in numbers of women who are problem or alcoholic drinkers. Marijuana use, incidentally, appears to be following the pattern of alcohol—initial adoption and abuse by males followed by a narrowing in the sex difference in use, but with frequent and heavy use remaining overwhelmingly male. Certain groups of women are evidencing even more marked increases in social drinking than the total population of women. They are also the groups for whom there are hints that heavy drinking or problem drinking may be on the rise. These are the young, the more educated, the working women (Johnson, 1982; Johnston *et al.*, 1982; Parker *et al.*, 1980; Wilsnack, Wilsnack, and Klassen, 1982). Models of diffusion of innovation suggest that these groups would be expected to be in the forefront of a shift in drinking patterns (Bell and Champion, 1976). These groups also have been leaders in the women's liberation movement, have been the quickest to embrace sex role changes, and, particularly in the case of the young, will lead lives that are the most profoundly affected by sex role change.

With this picture of sex differences in patterns of drug and alcohol use, we can now turn to a consideration of the relationship between sex roles and substance misuse or abuse in women.

4. Sex Roles

Roles generally refer to the functions performed by an individual in a given position within a given social context (Biddle and Thomas, 1966). Individuals occupying particular positions are socialized to understand appropriate behaviors for those positions. Within a particular context, norms and expectations develop for particular social roles. A role performance that conforms to the norms is positively evaluated and sanctioned, while a behavior that violates the norms is negatively evaluated and sanctioned. Role-related behaviors, then, can be described in terms of their (a) performance, (b) norms and expectations, and (c) evaluation and sanction (Shaw and Costanzo, 1970).

Sex roles are the different functions expected of males and females. Gender defines the social position. It is, however, also a determinant of other positions since societal allocation of tasks or functions is also based upon gender. Sex role norms and sex role socialization influence drug use behavior as expressed by different rates of substance use, different kinds of use, and the differential development of substance abuse problems.

Despite our focus on social roles and norms, we must remember that drugs and alcohol are chemical agents; thus, physiological differences between males and females may be particularly relevant to differences in use patterns. In this chapter we will confine our consideration of physiological differences to those that are most likely reflected in social roles and social behavior—specifically, the reproductive system—and will not look at other possible divergences, such as differential tolerance to drugs or differential absorption rates.

Another area that falls loosely under the rubric of sex roles is that of *sex role identity*. Sex role identity is the degree to which one experiences "the sense of one's self as masculine or feminine in social stance and behavior" (Douvan, 1978). Sex role identity conflict, then, would be a conflict between preferences or opportunities and constraints and the extent to which the individual is able to match her perception of what it is to be appropriately female.

The female sex role may influence women's substance abuse in several ways. First, the expectations related to the female sex role may serve either to precipitate drug and alcohol problems or to protect women from problems of use and misuse. Because of sex roles we might also observe differential outcomes of what appear to be the same antecedents for men and women. Second, sex roles may show their effects in the *consequences* of drug and alcohol misuse.

In the following sections we will consider the relationship between sex roles—specifically, sex role norms, gender-related roles, sex role performance, and sex role identity—and the antecedents and consequences of female substance abuse. And finally, we will speculate on what changes in sex roles might mean for women's substance use and abuse.

5. Sex Role Norms and Drug Use

A most often cited reason for the observed sex difference in the use of alcohol is that women who drink heavily encounter social disapproval, while there is actually approval, at least among some groups, for heavy drinking among men (Curlee, 1967; Gomberg, 1976, 1979). Phrases such as "to drink like a man" or "to hold your liquor like a man" are not without real social origins. There have been several studies (Knupfer, 1964; Lawrence and Maxwell, 1962) documenting the fact that both men and women condemn drunkenness in women more than they do in men.

In a study of alcoholic women in treatment, and a group of comparison women, Colten and Gomberg found that the women themselves perceive a differential social response to the drinking of men and women. Of the 301 women interviewed in 1981, 96% agreed with the statement "People find it more acceptable for a man than for a woman to be drunk," and over 91% agreed that "People look down on women problem drinkers more than they do on male problem drinkers." Alcoholic women are less likely to report that a drunk woman is worse in their own minds. Just half (50.8%) of the women agree that "a woman who is drunk is more obnoxious and disgusting than a man who is drunk." Nonalcoholic women are slightly less condemning. Of the 137 comparison women interviewed, 35.8% agreed that a drunk woman is more obnoxious and disgusting than a drunk man. Their perceptions of the norms are similar to alcoholic women: 86.1% agreed that "it is more acceptable for a man than for a woman to be drunk" and 88.3% agreed that "people look down on women problem drinkers more than they do on male problem drinkers."

There are two studies frequently cited in efforts to show that intolerance of women's drinking is no greater than that of men's drinking. Donovan and Jessor (1977) reported that among adolescents with drunkenness at least once a week, the girls reported fewer negative social consequences than the boys did. We think this finding does not at all refute the notion that there are norms against women's drinking. These findings may, in fact, be due to the more negative attitudes toward female drinking. Women are more likely to drink in nonpublic settings and, since their drinking engenders disapproval, may tend to hide it. So while a young male might be bragging about his consumption or barge boisterously into his home, the drunk young woman may be more likely to slip in quietly. Young males are, in general, more likely to encounter difficulty with the authorities and those troublemaking behaviors may well be exacerbated, or at least not as well hidden, when alcohol enters the picture.

Stafford and Petway (1977) had subjects rate the labels "alcoholic," "drunk," and "married to an alcoholic" on a variety of semantic differential descriptors for both men and women. Subjects also rated "man" or "woman" with no label preceding. They found few differences between descriptors of drunk males and females. In fact, there was a leveling of sex differences with the introduction of the labels, which may be due to a ceiling effect of a strong negative response to both male and female drunkenness. The differences between the drunk and unlabeled groups of women were larger on the selfish/unselfish and moral/immoral dimensions than they were for men. Stafford and Petway state that "drunkenness in women may be more stigmatizing than drunkenness in men." They also find that women alcoholics are rated as more *masculine* and *hard* than unlabeled women.

A similar theme runs through the literature on heroin addiction. Women addicts are seen as sicker, more deviant, more reprehensible and less treatable than male addicts. (Cuskey *et al.*, 1977; DeLeon, 1974; Olson, 1964). Indeed, we do find that drug- and alcohol-dependent women in treatment tend to report more problems than men—they are more distressed, they suffer more from low self-esteem, they experience more broken relationships, they appear to be somewhat more isolated, and they report more physical health problems.

We could assume that women are, in fact, sicker. That assumption, while sexist, is not totally preposterous. Probably the strongest evidence for it comes from the observations that fewer women ever use substances, that the norms certainly provide pressure against frequent or excessive drug use in women, and that, as we noted, the social roles occupied by women provide less access and opportunity for drug abuse. So, the logic goes, those women who exceed the limits and misuse substances must be truly disturbed and deviant. This argument is also based on observations of higher incidence in women alcoholics in treatment for psychiatric illness, suicide attempts, more apparent mental illness, and greater marital instability than in men alcoholics. Similarly, women in treatment for heroin use also report more symptoms of depression and anxiety.

These observations of greater "pathology" in women are more readily explained by the social factors that distinguish the lives of women from those of men—factors that may both influence the development of substance abuse problems and determine the nature of the consequences of the problem.

Our own data (Colten, 1979) show that both male and female addicts tend to be more disparaging about addicted women and that they most definitely feel that addicted women are subject to greater social disapproval than addicted men. Over half of addicted women (55.5%) and over two-thirds of addicted men (67.8%) in the sample agree that "women addicts are worse than men addicts." There is overwhelming agreement by both sexes (89.8% of women and 88.6% of men) that "men look down on women addicts more than they do on men addicts." Females are perceived as being somewhat less often harsh in their judgments, but still over two-thirds of both addicted women (69.2%) and men (72.8%) agree that "women look down on women addicts more than they do on men addicts."

While the norms mitigate women's use of recreational and illegal substances, they almost encourage the use of prescription and over-the-counter medications (Cooperstock, 1971; Fidell, 1981; Mellinger et al., 1974). This is an indirect sanctioning. Men are discouraged from behaviors such as the expression of emotional complaints and taking of the sick role that would lead to prescription of these drugs by physicians. The medical establishment appears to have accepted and fostered the stereotype of women as needing medications. The outcome is a convergence between physician expections and stereotypes and the demands of female patients.

Women also have been encouraged to do whatever they can to match the societal stereotype of physical attractiveness. The use of amphetamines for weight control has been common and socially sanctioned. The use of amphetamines and similar over-the-counter preparations in the form of diet pills begins in adolescence for females. And amphetamines are the only illicit substance used by as many young women as young men (Johnston et al., 1982). Their use for this purpose clearly is not recreational.

Passivity is another characteristic of women that has traditionally been the valued norm. Our society has also held a negative stereotype of the hysterical, excitable, overemotional woman. Archie Bunker repeatedly told Edith to "stifle" herself. Tranquilizers provide a handy means of stifling oneself in order to be socially acceptable and attractive to males.

A conclusion to be drawn is that certain sex role norms protect women from developing substance abuse problems. For a woman who does develop problems, however, the norms serve to make her situation worse and more uncomfortable.

What we see repeatedly is sanctioning of women's drug use according to the social roles they traditionally have been expected to fill. Control of women so that they meet the stereotypes of the roles of caretaker for children, for men, and for the sick and the elderly seems primary. The control of women's sexuality is also heavily linked to norms concerning the use of drugs and alcohol by women. Further, the responsibilities women have in the roles they fill affect their opportunities for use and access to alcohol and drugs.

6. Sex Role Performance and Drug Use

The common thread in the more negative response to women's substance use and abuse is that substance use may render women unable to carry out traditional female role functions and therefore puts them at a higher risk of violating traditional sex role norms about feminine characteristics and behaviors. The two most important areas of concern are with the female functions of caretaker and moral standard-bearers of society.

Child, Barry and Bacon (1965), in their study of cross-cultural attitudes toward drinking, note that the general social role of women makes drunkenness "more threatening in women than in men" and that "care of a field can be postponed for a day, but care of a child cannot." Knupfer (1964) also suggests that it is concern about the impairment of the traditional nurturing role of women that underlies taboos against intoxication in women. She singles out the loss of the usual sexual restraints and the loss of sensitivity to the needs of others. Similarly, LeMasters (1975) observes that the customers of the bar he studied apply two tests to alcoholic women: (1) Does the woman neglect her children and (2) does she become sexually promiscuous?

A preponderance of the literature on women and heroin has focused on the woman addict as mother and has been especially concerned with neonatal addiction. Many allege that an addicted woman cannot be an adequate mother and that "addiction must be designated as a prima facie criterion of unfitness as a parent" (Densen-Gerber and Rohrs, 1973). Entire conferences and monographs on the addicted women and her family have appeared that address only the problems of the children, with barely a mention of the mother herself. Gomberg (1979) observed an analogous situation in the response to the Fetal Alcohol Syndrome. The "discovery" of possible damage to fetuses from alcohol consumption was followed by an outpouring of research monies and warnings to women, all with moralistic overtones and to a degree that exceeded the strength of the evidence and the extent of the problem. The majority of alcoholic women are past childbearing age. As information accumulates, the panic and suggested restrictions have relaxed, but the magnitude and swiftness of the initial response is testament to the strong connection made in our society between a woman's substance use and her functioning as mother. The alarmist response to the fetal alcohol syndrome and the increased attention to neonatal addiction both may represent uneasiness about the changing status of women.

Women have been traditionally expected to fill the roles of wife and mother. The stereotypic American woman is married, has children, and is not in the labor force. Although this stereotype does not match the realities of the lives of the majority of women, it may be argued that women exist in a social system that largely operates as if it were true. Thus, we must consider the impact of these roles on the women who occupy them and also on the women who do not match the traditional roles (e.g., all nonmarried women and employed women). We should also remember that women are trained in anticipation of filling traditional adult roles, so that some characteristics may be observed even if a woman does not currently hold a particular role.

As noted previously, performance of the female sex role affords access and opportunities to a restricted set of behavior that shapes the nature of drug use for women. For example, the female's activities in the physical care of the young and the old provides her much more access to medicinal substances than to recreational substances. The relative isolation of the role of caretaker may mean she has fewer opportunities to participate in drug use with others. The passive, dependent nature of the female role suggests that she should be vulnerable to the influence of others in determining whether, when, and how to use substances.

We will now turn to a description of some of the differences between males and females with substance abuse problems that may be explained by differential role requirements. We will examine the influence of role requirements on the nature of women's use of alcohol, heroin, and psychotropic drugs.

6.1. Alcohol

The way in which women first use alcohol is consistent with the isolated nature of their social role. Women begin using alcohol later than men and tend to be introduced to it by men (Lindbeck, 1972; Rathod and Thomson, 1971). Women tend to drink less in public. They drink at home, alone, or with a spouse. Drinking women, more than men, are likely to have an alcoholic spouse (or significant other) and to drink along with him. Spouses of women appear to object less to their drinking and may even encourage it (Wanberg and Horn, 1970). However, women who drink are more likely to be divorced, and there are many reports of problem drinking women being abandoned by their spouses (Gomberg, 1979). Women, then, are more solitary drinkers.

The fact that the isolated nature of the traditional female role may contribute to the frequency and nature of women's drinking is corroborated by recent evidence of the relationship between employment and drinking in women. Johnson (1978, 1982) found that women who were the heaviest drinkers were those who were both married and employed. This may be attributed to the greater opportunities for drinking afforded to women in that role constellation. It also may be due to the stress and conflict of the two roles. The stress can arise because of role overload, since working women continue to carry the household and child care responsibilities with little, if any, additional assistance from spouses. Nieva and Gutek (1981) observed that the family roles of women intrude on their work roles to a degree that is not true for men. Work roles remain in conflict with traditional definitions and stereotypes of femininity, even though the majority of married women are employed. Parker *et al.* (1980) did not duplicate Johnson's findings in a study that used different criteria for heavy drinking and did not seek to identify drinking problems. They, however, also noted the positive relationship between employment status and drinking problems. Wilsnack *et al.* (1982) in a 1981 national survey found that never-married women, divorced women, and women in living-together-but-not-married statuses were more likely to drink than either married or widowed women. Wilsnack *et al.* suggest that these women are "in statuses that are likely to seem unpermanent and relatively unconstrained by traditional expectations of role performance." Among the married women, those who were in part-time jobs were the most likely to report drinking-related problems. Since women are much more likely than men to hold part-time jobs, the stress and problems of part-time employment and the characteristics of part-time workers are clearly sex role-and gender-related.

Women in the general population have more suicide attempts, more symptoms of depression, and more health problems than do men (Gove and Hughes, 1979; Weissman and Klerman, 1977). This pattern is repeated when alcoholic women are compared to alcoholic men. There is evidence, for example, of more liver damage in women even with less consumption and shorter duration of heavy drinking. Further, the association between depressive symptoms in alcoholic women is strong and consistently observed. Men, on the other hand, are more likely to display symptoms of character and sociopathic disorders.

Schuckit and colleagues (Schuckit, Pitts, Reich, King and Winokur, 1969) have hypothesized two groups of female alcoholics: those who exhibit alcoholism secondary to a primarily affective disorder and those who develop alcoholism independent from the affective disorder. Of course, many women may become depressed subsequent to the development of the alcoholism. There is some indication that affective disorder alcoholics have more relatives with psychiatric problems. Since the rates for depression are higher among women than among men in the general population, the preponderance of depressed women alcoholics is not surprising. It is important to note, however, that the depression can manifest itself in the form of alcoholism.

A high incidence of physical and emotional problems is consistent with the expectation that women are weak and fragile. Their recognition of these problems and willingness to seek attention for them is socially sanctioned. In their roles as caretakers, they acquire an understanding of how to acquire this attention and have opportunities to do so (Cloward and Piven, 1979).

The nature of women's use of alcohol can have serious side effects for them. Since they drink less in public, it becomes possible for them and their families to conceal their drinking problem. And for women who are unemployed, the problem can go undetected. Further, the high likelihood that women's alcoholism will be accompanied by serious health and mental health problems means that, although they may be more likely than men to seek medical attention, their drinking problems will be masked by other health and mental health problems and remain undetected (Beckman and Kocel, 1982).

6.2. Heroin

As is true with alcohol, women begin using heroin later than men and are initiated into use by men. Men also, in many cases, take the role of encouraging or helping to maintain a woman's heroin use. Women appear to have little access to heroin except through male channels, and their secondary roles in the drug-using culture also leave them dependent upon male suppliers. The entrepreneurship and hustling entailed in larger-scale drug deals has remained a male province.

Addicted women are more likely to have run away from home in adolescence. They tend not to finish high school and are more likely than male addicts to have children and also to be unemployed. They are more likely to be previously married (separated, divorced, or widowed) than male addicts, who tend more toward being currently married or never married. This means the marriages of male addicts more often stay intact. Male addicts are also more likely to be living with a partner (Douvan, 1977; Prather and Fidell, 1978; Tucker, 1979).

Thus, women addicts seem to be in more difficult circumstances than men—uneducated, unemployed, and unmarried, with dependent children. They often are forced to rely on other means—men, prostitution, welfare—for financial support. Women addicts have less social support than their male counterparts and, while not isolated, appear to have depleted social resources (Tucker 1979). Tucker (1979) and Wallace (1976) have noted the central role of the female addict's mother in providing social and practical support in lieu of other relationships. So interpersonal relations are more problematic for addicted women.

As with alcoholic women, heroin-addicted women have more problems than men in many other areas (Marsh, 1980; Tucker, 1979). Also, female addicts *feel* worse. They have lower self-esteem and more symptoms of depression and anxiety (Colten, 1979). As we noted earlier, the women are well aware of the negative view held of them. This seems to be exacerbated by participation in the male-dominated drug subculture (File, 1976; Hughes, Crawford, Barker, Schumann, and Jaffe, 1971; Levy and Doyle, 1974). Women addicts are also less assertive than men and feel that they have little control over their lives. More women than men cite "relief of personal disturbance" as the reason for initially trying heroin.

Addicted women also have more health problems than men (Andersen, 1977, 1980). Tucker (1979) found that 75% of women compared with 58% of men entering treatment reported health problems. Many of their problems center around gynecological infections and complications (Santen, Sofsky, Bilic, and Lippert, 1975; Stoffer, 1968). We suspect that women have both more health problems and more awareness of the problems.

A particular problem for women addicts is their children. Women in treatment are much more likely than men to have children and to have responsibility for their children (Colten, 1979; Tucker, 1979). They are highly invested in the mother role and are concerned and guilt-ridden about their adequacy as parents. Despite many assertions to the contrary (Densen-Gerber and Rohrs 1973), there is also evidence suggesting that women addicts do work hard at being good mothers (Colten, 1982). Most of the research on addicted mothers has focused on the physical effects of opiate on fetuses and neonates, and thus, there are almost no data available on what can be done to assist addicted women with children. We have noted before that little concern is expressed about addicted fathers. The influence of sex roles and sex role norms means that women get all the responsibility, blame, and guilt. They also get very little support. The most remarked-upon deficiency of treatment facilities is their failure to provide child care services for women or even to schedule their programs to accommodate women's child care responsibilities. Women often cannot even seek treatment for fear that their children will be taken away from them once they admit to heroin addiction.

It is often observed that female heroin addicts hold traditional values (Colten, 1979; Suffet and Brotman, 1976). Their circumstances evolve such that they become cut off from traditional social channels and sources of support. Treatment programs have notably failed to take their resultant difficulties into account, by neglecting the job training needs, child care problems, health problems, educational deficiencies, and, especially, the interpersonal and social needs of addicted women.

Again, as with alcohol, we see that gender and associated requirements of sex role protect women from initial use but more definitely
reinforce negative consequences of heavy use.

6.3. Psychotropic Drugs

While the roles of women appear to reduce the likelihood of their
using heroin and alcohol, those same roles appear to increase the probability that they will use psychotropic drugs.

We noted earlier than norms encourage women to ask for drugs and
for doctors to prescribe them. Roles and norms facilitate the development, recognition, and voicing of complaints that make the use of psychotropic drugs, either prescribed or self-medicated, seem "legitimate."
We mention these only briefly since Fidell, in Chapter 16, discusses the
relationship between sex roles and psychotropic drug use.

Although women are more vulnerable to psychotropic drug use, we
know of no evidence to suggest that the consequences of use by women
are any greater than the consequences for men. The factors that encourage the initial use of psychotropics are ones that make it easy for a
woman to continue using them.

7. Sex Role Identity and Substance Abuse

Sex role identity can be thought of as being composed of internal
psychological aspects, tendencies, or self-concepts, as distinguished
from sex role expectations or evaluations that are external to the individual. Traditionally, sex role identity has been viewed as having a
critical relationship to adjustment and adaptation. In the newer conceptualization of sex role identity, masculinity and femininity are seen as
orthogonal dimensions, so that the level of one implies nothing about
the level of the other. There has been a tendency to equate psychological
androgyny with adjustment (androgyny being defined as high in both
masculinity and femininity), but that has increasingly been called into
question (Locksley and Colten, 1979).

The possible relationship between sex role identity and substance
use can take many forms. We can think of sex role conflict caused by a
woman having either a conscious or an unconscious masculine tendency
that creates confusion or stress because it is at variance with the traditional external role demands. We could also consider intrapsychic sex
role identity conflict in which more conscious inclinations run counter to

less conscious ones. Another approach would be to consider psychological androgyny scores.

There has been very little empirical work done on the sex role identity of substance-abusing women. There has been, however, a good deal of speculation and allusion to sex role identification problems in the literature on substance-abusing women. In general, earlier work by researchers and clinicians sought to demonstrate that either the absence of femininity or the presence of masculinity was the explanation for substance abuse in women. There are two theories about female drinking—one that women drink to feel more like men and the other that women drink to feel more like women.

In general, the literature on alcoholic women suggests that they do value the traditional female role. Jones (1971) suggested that female problem drinkers escape into "ultrafemininity" as adolescents. Others have noted that many women drink because they experience a sense of failure to meet traditional standards of femininity (Fort and Porterfield, 1961; Kinsey, 1966). Gomberg (1979) has labeled this an "over-identification with traditional sexual role" in alcoholic women. She suggests that the development of alcoholism may be related to failure to succeed in that role. Others have noted that women in more masculine roles, exhibiting fewer sex-typed characteristics, are the ones prone to alcohol problems. The Wilsnacks (1978) found that rejection of traditional femininity by adolescent girls is associated with drinking more heavily, drinking more symptomatically, and experiencing more problems due to drinking.

In work on heroin-addicted women, Douvan (1979) observed that adolescence appeared to be the turning point when these young women were unable to channel their active, competitive impulses into socially acceptable channels and that traditional sex role expectations encumbered energetic young women. Colten (1979) found that heroin addicted women place greater value on traditional masculine characteristics, such as independence and assertiveness, than do nonaddicted comparison women. On the other hand, the same addicted women also more strongly endorsed traditional sex role ideology about division of labor between men and women than did the nonaddicted women. We interpret this not as an indicator of a conflict of sex role values but rather as a realistic appraisal of circumstance. In endorsing traditional sex role ideology (e.g., the fantasy of the working husband and the housewife-mother), the addicted women living quite deviant lives may be expressing a preference to live a normal life in the form of what has been held up as the American Dream. Their valuing of the more traditionally masculine characteristics of independence and less responsiveness to the feelings of others may be a recognition of the instrumental value of these characteristics in the heavily male-dominated culture inhabited by hero-in-addicted women. There is no reason to believe that the value they place on "masculine" characteristics (one that is shared by the culture) was causal in or even antecedent to their becoming addicted.

We see in the literature some evidence suggesting that women who use substances to excess either value traditional masculine characteristics, possess some traditional masculine characteristics, or value the traditional female role while simultaneously sensing that they have not been as successful at filling it as they might like. Sex role identity and placing value on the characteristics appropriate to one's gender are central to self-concept. Since gender is also linked for women with norms about substance use, substance abuse itself then constitutes a violation of traditional femininity. And when a women is able to "hold her liquor like a man" or survives in the heroin subculture, which values "masculine characteristics," then she surely must see herself as diverging from traditional standards of femininity.

It is not surprising that the sex role identity of female abusers of psychotropic medications has not been called into question, since use of psychotropics has not been viewed as a departure from traditional stereotypes of femininity. Some abusers, however, are seen as suffering from neurotic depression induced by disappointments and constraints of the female role—the "housewife syndrome" or the "empty nest syndrome."

Several studies have pointed to an intrapsychic conflict between more conscious and less conscious inclinations. The most often cited of these is the study by Wilsnack (1973) that identified a discrepancy between overt and covert identifications. Her data indicated that unconscious masculine inclinations in combination with overtly feminine compensatory behaviors might be a common theme for alcoholic women. Other studies report similar findings (Beckman, 1977; Pattison, 1975). In a replication and extension of the Wilsnack study, using sisters of alcoholic women as the comparison sample, Anderson (1980) found no difference between the two groups. Others have noted the opposite conflict, that of overt masculinity and more covert femininity (Beckman, 1978; Parker, 1972).

Scida and Vanicelli (1979) have suggested that the *magnitude* rather than the direction of the conflict may be the critical factor. In this conceptualization, some women use substances to alleviate the stress of the conflict or to express their sex role identity by engaging in behaviors that have been less traditionally feminine. We should use caution in interpreting these equivocal findings, noting that any kind of conflictual inclinations can pose difficulties for both men and women and that the available evidence does not demonstrate that sex role identity conflicts are a factor in the development of substance abuse problems. They may be a consequence or they may be unrelated. Further, we should remember that masculine characteristics and inclinations are now considered to be healthy and adaptive in women and that theories of psychological androgyny suggest that the tendency to adhere to feminine stereotypes, resulting in the absence of masculine characteristics, may be limiting and detrimental to women.

Beckman (1978) demonstrated that both alcoholic women and nonalcoholic women in treatment for psychiatric disorders were more undifferentiated and less androgynous than a control group of "normal" women. Essentially, this means that they tended to score lower on both masculine and feminine (or instrumental and expressive) characteristics. Since the traits listed in masculinity and femininity scales are generally desirable, the implication is that women in treatment (for alcoholism or emotional problems) report themselves as having fewer positive characteristics, be they labeled masculine or feminine.

Colten (1979) found that heroin-addicted women scored significantly lower on both masculinity and femininity than did a comparison of nonaddicted women. The nonaddicted women also scored higher on both subscales than did a group of addicted males. Thus, we see that both male and female heroin addicts also perceive themselves as having fewer of both expressive and instrumental skills.

Colten (1978) has shown that the effects of masculinity scores may largely be accounted for by shared variance with self-esteem. In other words, women who endorse as self-descriptive masculinity items, which attest to a sense of competence, independence, and activity, are saying that they have higher self-esteem and a surer sense of self. The resultant effect is that women who score high in masculinity, regardless of levels of femininity scores (the androgynous and masculine groups), are more likely to show signs of adjustment and coping than are women whose scores are low in masculinity (the undifferentiated and feminine groups).

Because both masculinity and femininity or instrumental and expressive skills are critical to social functioning and role performance, and because those social skills relate to many other indicators of well-being, we would expect to see impairment in these areas for those women and men who have been plagued with substance abuse problems. We have not, however, found evidence indicating that sex role identity confusion or intrapsychic conflict should be pursued as a *cause* of substance abuse. Engaging in behaviors that run counter to sex role norms may in fact be an additional stressor for both men and women and cannot be discounted.

8. Implications

Substance abuse is out-of-role behavior. It is behavior not fitting the patterns and expectations for appropriate social behavior in our society. Substance abuse by women transgresses even more social norms than abuse by men. We have documented that these norms may constitute a social shield, protecting women from becoming substance abusers. However, when women do misuse substances, the consequences may be more disruptive and damaging.

Among the correlates of drug misuse in women are more social condemnation, and more isolation, with abandonment by family, partners, and friends. Societal response may exacerbate the depression and low self-esteem that accompany women's substance misuse. Women's substance abuse is more likely to go undetected, either because their roles allow it to remain unobserved or force the women to conceal it, or because the symptoms get mistaken for those of other more acceptable ailments: depression, housewife syndrome, or empty nest syndrome.

Substance misuse is in itself a violation of the female role. Thus, a women substance abuser is seen, and sees herself, as being unable to meet the requirements of functions that have been traditionally female—wife, mother, caretaker, socioemotional leader. And she loses or relinquishes her ties in the interpersonal realm so highly valued by her.

Since it is likely that substance-abusing women are going to be more self-denigrating, discouraged, and despairing than men, the web of depression and substance abuse should be treated as a whole. They most frequently accompany one another. Too often, attention is focused only on one while the other is left to flourish.

Treatment programs also have been constrained by sex role norms, both by ignoring them and by oversubscribing to them. The needs of women often have not been seen as differing from those of men. Provisions have not been made to address the centrality of relationships in women's life and to provide services related to mother and family roles. Mechanisms to allay the guilt and sense of failure experienced by so many substance-abusing women are also often lacking in treatment.

Ironically, the other charge leveled at treatment providers is that they have neglected to meet women's needs by responding to women as though their needs were the stereotypic, traditional ones. Consequently, employment issues, problems of living alone, single parenthood, and the skills of self-sufficiency and assertiveness have been underplayed.

In the last decade there has been dramatic change in sex roles and sex role norms, reflected in the increased numbers of women in the labor force, increased acknowledgment of the substance abuse problems of women, and the greater understanding of the influence of sex roles on both the causes and consequences of substance abuse in women. With those changes have come advances in treatment for women who do develop substance abuse problems. Many claim that the previously poor prognosis for women in treatment is improving.

We have documented that the evidence does not support predictions of a drastic increase in substance misuse and substance abuse problems in women, although there may be some increase in use. Logic does tell us that if fewer women abstain, then more women are at risk of overusing or developing problems associated with that use.

Many allege that as sex roles shift, as the negative consequences of substance use in women diminish, as the barriers to use decline and access increases, not just women's *use* but women's substance *abuse* will rise. The claim is that the overload of two roles may be more stressful than the tedium of one.

We expect that, along with the sex role changes that increase the probability of use will come changes reducing stresses that may lead to abuse. We would hope that social changes will occur that buffer the pressure of dual roles, that make the workplace more hospitable to women, and that allow for more sharing of domestic tasks. Women should become freer of unrealistic sex role expectations and sex discrimination. Further, there is no reason to expect that the norms that encourage drinking among men will transfer to women. In fact, since men introduce women to drugs, a decreased dependence upon men and bolstering of ties with other women might actually reduce drinking occasions for women.

Women's overuse of psychotropics might be expected to decline, partly because of the reductions in stress and boredom afforded by sex role change. It also might decline as women have less time to go to physicians and as men share the responsibility for monitoring the physical and mental health of the family.

A cause for concern is the possibility that roles will shift in ways that only increase the multiple stresses on women, but that the changes will not extend to a redefinition of sex role expectations, and that those roles will increase substance use opportunities. At the same time, if the negative response to women who do develop substance abuse problems does not diminish, we could find ourselves with increasing numbers of women with problems and a society that exacerbates their problems by its response. Our hope and expectation is that sex role definitions will relax and that substance abuse will finally become a problem not intimately enmeshed with sex roles. Then we can begin to think of substance abuse in women in terms of real constraints and real problems and not think of it as influenced by social attitudes and stereotypes that bear no relationship to the realities and contingencies of women's lives.

9. References

Andersen, M. *Medical needs of addicted women and men and the implications for treatment: Focus on women.* National Women's Drug Research Coordinating Project Report to the National Institute on Drug Abuse, 1977.

Andersen, M. Health of heroin dependent clients: Focus on women. *Women and Health,* 1980, *5,* 22–33.

Anderson, S. C. Patterns of sex-role identification in alcoholic women. *Sex Roles,* 1980, *6,* 231–243.

Balter, M., and Levine, J. Character and extent of psychotherapeutic drug usage in the United States. In E. Brecher (Ed.), *Licit and illicit drugs.* Boston: Little, Brown, 1972.

Beckman, L. J. *Psychosocial aspects of alcoholism in women.* Paper presented at the 8th Annual Medical-Scientific Conference of the National Council on Alcoholism, San Diego, May 1977.

Beckman, L. J. Sex-role conflict in alcoholic women: Myth or reality. *Journal of Abnormal Psychology,* 1978, *87,* 408–417.

Beckman, L. J., and Kocel, K. M. The treatment-delivery system and alcohol abuse in women: Social policy implications. *Journal of Social Issues,* 1982, *38*(2), 139–152.

Bell, D. S., and Champion, R. A. *Monitoring drug use in New South Wales,* Part 3. Sydney, Australia: Division of Health Service Research, Health Commission of New South Wales, 1976.

Biddle, B. J., and Thomas, E. J. *Role theory: Concepts and research.* New York: Wiley, 1966.

Bush, P. J., and Osterweis, M. Pathways to medicine use. *Journal of Health and Social Behavior,* 1978, *19,* 179–189.

Bush, P. J., and Rabin, D. L. Who's using nonprescribed medicines? *Medical Care,* 1976, *14,* 1014–1023.

Cahalan, D., and Cisin, I. H. Drinking behavior and drinking problems in the United States. In B. Kissin and H. Begleiter (Eds.), *The biology of alcoholism* (Vol. 4). New York: Plenum, 1976.

Cahalan, D., Cisin, I. H., and Crossley, H. M. *American drinking practices: A national study of drinking behavior and attitudes.* New Brunswick, N.J.: Rutgers Center of Alcohol Studies, 1969.

Chambers, C. D. *Differential drug abuse within the New York state labor force.* Albany: New York Narcotics Central Commission, 1971.

Chambers, C. D., and Hunt, L. G., Drug abuse patterns in pregnant women. In J. L. Rementeria (Ed.), *Drug abuse in pregnancy and the neonate.* St. Louis: Mosley, 1977.

Child, I. L., Barry, H., and Bacon, M. K. A cross cultural study of drinking. *Quarterly Journal of Studies on Alcohol,* 1965, *Suppl. 3,* 49–61.

Cloward, R. A., and Piven, F. F. Hidden protest: The channeling of female innovation and resistance. *Signs,* 1979, *4,* 651–669.

Colten, M. E. *A reconsideration of psychological androgyny: Self esteem, social skills and expectations rather than sex role identification.* Unpublished doctoral dissertation, University of Michigan, 1978.

Colten, M. E. A descriptive and comparative analysis of self perceptions and attitudes of heroin addicted women. In *Addicted women: Family dynamics, self perceptions and support systems* (NIDA Services Research Monograph Series, U.S. Department of Health, Education and Welfare Publication No. ADM 80-762). Washington, D.C.: U.S. Government Printing Office, 1979.

Colten, M. E. Attitudes, experiences and self perceptions of heroin addicted mothers. *Journal of Social Issues,* 1982, *38*(2), 77–92.

Cooperstock, R. Sex differences in the use of mood modifying drugs: An explanatory model. *Journal of Health and Social Behavior,* 1971, *12,* 238–244.

Cooperstock, R. Psychotropic drug use among women. *CMA Journal,* 1976, *115,* 760–763.

Curlee, J. Alcoholic women: Some considerations for further research. *Bulletin of the Menninger Clinic,* 1967, *31,* 154–163.

Cuskey, W. R., Berger, L. H., and Densen-Gerber, J. Issues in the treatment of female addition: A review and critique of the literature. *Contemporary Drug Problems,* 1977, *6,* 307–371.

DeLeon, G. Phoenix House: Psychopathological signs among male and female drug-free residents. *Addictive Diseases: An International Journal,* 1974, *2,* 135–151.

Densen-Gerber, J., and Rohrs, O. C. Drug addicted parents and child abuse. *Contemporary Drug Problems,* 1973, *2,* 683–695.

Donovan, J., and Jessor, R. *Problem drinking among adolescents: A social-psychological study of a national sample.* Boulder: University of Colorado Institute of Behavioral Science, 1977.

Douvan, E. Introduction. Women's Drug Research Report to the National Institute on Drug Abuse, Ann Arbor, Mich., 1977.

Douvan, E. Sex role learning. In J. C. Coleman (Ed.), *The school years.* London: Methuen, 1978.

Drug Abuse Warning Network [DAWN] Report IV. Rockville, Md.: National Institute on Drug Abuse, 1977.

Eddy, N. B., Halbach, H., Isbell, H., and Seevers, M. H. Drug dependence: Its significance and characteristics. *Bulletin of the World Health Organization,* 1965, *32,* 721–733.

Engs, R. C. Drinking patterns and drinking problems of college students. *Journal of Studies on Alcohol,* 1977, *38,* 2144–2156.

FDA *Drug Bulletin.* Rockville, Md.: National Institute on Drug Abuse, Feb. 1980.

Ference, R. G. Sex differences in the prevalence of problem drinking. In O. J. Kalant (Eds), *Alcohol and drug problems in women.* New York: Plenum Press, 1980.

Ference, R. G., and Whitehead, P. C. Sex differences in psychoactive drug use. In O. J. Kalant (Ed.), *Alcohol and drug problems in women.* New York: Plenum Press, 1980.

Fidell, L. S. Sex differences in psychotropic drug use. *Professional Psychology,* 1981, *12,* 156–162.

File, K. N. Sex roles and street roles. *International Journal of the Addictions,* 1976, *11,* 263–268.

Fishburne, P. M., Abelson, H. I., and Cisin, I. *National survey on drug abuse: Main findings, 1979.* Rockville, Md.: National Institute on Drug Abuse, 1980.

Fort, T., and Porterfield, A. L. Some backgrounds and types of alcoholism among women. *Journal of Health and Human Behavior,* 1961, *2,* 283–292.

Glaser, F. B. Narcotic addiction in the pain-prone female patient: A comparison with addict controls. *International Journal of the Addictions,* 1966, *2,* 47–59.

Gold, M., and Reimer, D. J. Changing patterns of delinquent behavior among Americans 13 through 16 years old: 1967–1972. *Crime and Delinquency Literature,* 1975, *7,* 483–517.

Gomberg, E. S. Alcoholism in women. In B. Kissin and B. Begleiter (Eds.), *The biology of alcoholism.* New York: Plenum Press, 1976.

Gomberg, E. S. Problems with alcohol and other drugs. In E. Gomberg and V. Franks (Eds.), *Gender and disordered behavior.* New York: Brunner/Mazel, 1979.

Gomberg, E. S. Historical and political perspective: Women and drug use. *Journal of Social Issues,* 1982, *38*(2), 9–23.

Gove, W., and Hughes, M. Possible causes of the apparent sex differences in physical health. *American Sociological Review*, 1979, *44*, 126–146.

Hochschild, A. R. A review of sex role research. *American Journal of Sociology*, 1973, *78*, 1011–1029.

Homiller, J. D. *Women and alcohol: A guide for state and local decision makers.* Washington, D.C.: Alcohol and Drug Problems Association of North America, 1977.

Hughes, P. H., Crawford, G. A., Barker, N. W., Schumann, S., and Jaffee, J. H. The social structure of a heroin copping community. *American Journal of Psychiatry*, 1971, *128*, 551–558.

Johnson, P. B. *Working women and alcohol use: Preliminary national data.* Paper presented at the annual meeting of the American Psychological Association. Toronto, August 1978.

Johnson, P. B. Sex differences, women's roles and alcohol use: Preliminary national data. *Journal of Social Issues*, 1982, *38*(2), 93–116.

Johnson, P. B., Armor, D. J., Polich, S., and Stambul, H. *U.S. adult drinking practices: Time trends, social correlates, and sex roles.* Working note prepared for NIAAA. Santa Monica, Calif.: Rand Corporation, 1977.

Johnston, L. D., Bachman, J. G., and O'Malley, P. M. *Student drug use in America: 1975–1981.* Rockville, Md.: National Institute on Drug Abuse, 1982.

Jones, M. C. Personality antecedents and correlates of drinking patterns in women. *Journal of Consulting and Clinical Psychology*, 1971, *36*, 61–69.

Kessler, R. C., and McRae, J. A., Jr. Trends in the relationship between sex and psychological distress: 1957–1976. *American Sociological Review*, 1981, *46*, 443–452.

Kinsey, B. A. *The female alcoholic: A social psychological study.* Springfield, Ill.: Charles C Thomas, 1966.

Knupfer, G. *Female drinking patterns.* Selected papers presented at the 15th Annual Meeting of the North American Association of Alcoholism Programs, Washington, D.C., 1964.

Kolb, L. Drug addiction among women. *American Prison Association*, 1938, 349–357.

Lawrence, J. J., and Maxwell, M. A. Drinking and socioeconomic status. In D. J. Pittman and C. R. Snyder (Eds.), *Society, culture and drinking patterns.* New York: Wiley, 1962.

LeMasters, E. E. *Blue-collar aristocrats.* Madison: University of Wisconsin Press, 1975.

Levy, S., and Doyle, K. Attitudes toward women in a drug treatment program. *Journal of Drug Issues*, 1974, *4*, 428–434.

Lindbeck, V. The woman alcoholic: A review of the literature. *International Journal of the Addictions*, 1972, *7*, 567–580.

Locksley, A., and Colten, M. E. Psychological androgyny: A case of mistaken identity. *Journal of Personality and Social Psychology*, 1979, *37*, 1017–1031.

Mandel, W., Goldschmidt, P. G., and Grover, P. *Interdrug final report: An evaluation of treatment programs for drug abusers.* Baltimore: Johns Hopkins University School of Hygiene and Public Health, 1973.

Marsh, J. C. Women helping women: The evaluation of an all-female methadone maintenance program in Detroit. In A. Schecter (Ed.), *Drug dependence and alcoholism.* New York: Plenum, 1980.

Martin, C. A., and Martin, W. R. Opiate dependence in women. In O. J. Kalant (Ed.), *Alcohol and drug problems in women.* New York: Plenum Press, 1980.

Mellinger, G. D., Balter, M. B., Parry, H. J., Manheimer, D. I., and Cisin, I. H. An overview of psychotherapeutic drug use in the United States. In E. Josephson and E. E. Carroll (Eds.), *Drug use: Epidemiological and sociological Approaches.* Washington, D.C.: Hemisphere, 1974.

Mulford, H. A. Women and men problem drinkers. *Journal of Studies on Alcohol*, 1977, *38*, 1624–1639.

Naierman, N., Savage, B., Haskins, B., Lear, J., Chase, H., Marvell, K., and Lamothe, R.

Sex discrimination in health and human services. Cambridge,Mass.: Abt Associates, June 1979.

Nieva, V. T., and Gutek, B. A. *Women and work: A psychological perspective.* New York: Praeger, 1981.

Olson, R. W. MMPI sex differences in narcotic addicts. *Journal of General Psychology,* 1964, 71, 257–266.

Parker, D. A., Parker, E. S., Wolz, M. W., and Harford, T. C. Sex roles and alcohol consumption: A research note. *Journal of Health and Social Behavior,* 1980, 21, 43–48.

Parker, F. B. Sex role adjustment in women alcoholics. *Quarterly Journal of Studies on Alcohol,* 1972, 33, 647–657.

Pattison, E. M. *Personality profiles of 50 alcoholic women.* Unpublished study, University of California, Irvine, 1975.

Prather, J. E., and Fidell, L. S. Drug use and abuse among woman: An overview. *International Journal of the Addictions,* 1978, 13, 863–885.

Rabin, D. L. Prescribed and nonprescribed medicine use. In A. I. Wertheimer and P. J. Bush (Eds.), *Perspectives on medicine in society.* Washington, D.C.: Drug Intelligence Publications, 1977. pp. 55–87.

Rabin, D. L., and Bush, P. J. Who's using medicine? *Journal of Community Health,* 1975, 2, 106–117.

Rachal, J. V., Williams, J. R., Brehm, M. L., Cavanaugh, B., Moore, R. P., and Eckerman, W. C. *A national study of adolescent drinking behavior: Attitudes and correlates.* Research Triangle Park, N.C.: Research Triangle Institute, 1975.

Rathod, N. H., and Thomson, I. G. Women alcoholics: A clinical study. *Quarterly Journal of Studies on Alcohol,* 1971, 32, 45–52.

San Mateo County. *Student drug use surveys, 1968–1977.* San Mateo, Calif.: Department of Public Health and Welfare, 1971.

Santen, R. J., Sofsky, J., Bilic, N., and Lippert, R. Mechanism of action of narcotics in the production of menstrual dysfunction in women. *Fertility and Sterility,* 1975, 26, 538–548.

Schuckit, M., Pitts, F. N., Reich, T., King, L., and Winokur, G. Alcoholism I: Two types of alcoholism in women. *Archives of General Psychiatry,* 1969, 20, 301–306.

Scida, J., and Vanicelli, M. Sex-role conflict and women's drinking. *Quarterly Journal of Studies on Alcohol,* 1979, 40, 28–44.

Shaw, M. F., and Costanzo, P. R. *Theories of social psychology.* New York: McGraw-Hill, 1970.

Sheffet, A., Hickey, R. F., Duval, H., Millman, S., and Louria, D. A. A Model for drug abuse treatment program evaluation. *Preventive Medicine,* 1973, 2, 510–523.

Simpson, D. D., Savage, L. J., Joe, G. W., Demaree, R. G., and Sells, S. B. *DARP data book. Statistics on characteristics of drug users in treatment during 1969–1974* (Institute of Behavioral Research Report 76-4). Fort Worth: Texas Christian University, 1976.

Single, E., Kandel, D., and Johnson, B. D. The reliability and validity of drug use responses in a large scale longitudinal survey. *Journal of Drug Issues,* 1975, 5, 426–443.

Stafford, R. A., and Petway, J. M. Stigmatization of men and women problem drinkers and their spouses. *Journal of Studies on Alcohol,* 1977, 38, 2109–2121.

Stoffer, S. S. A gynecologic study of drug addicts. *American Journal of Obstetrics and Gynecology,* 1968, 101, 779.

Suffet, F., and Brotman, R. Female drug use: Some observations. *International Journal of the Addictions.* 1976, 11, 19–33.

Sutker, P. B. Drug dependent women. In G. M. Beschner, B. G. Reed, and J. Mondanaro (Eds.), *Treatment services for drug dependent women* (Vol. 1) (DHHS Pub. No. ADM 81-1177). Rockville, Md.: National Institute on Drug Abuse, 1981.

Tucker, M. B. A descriptive and comparative analysis of the social support structure of heroin addicted women. In *Addicted women: Family dynamics, self perceptions and support systems* (NIDA Services Research Monograph Series, U.S. Department of Health, Education and Welfare Publication No. ADM 80-762). Washington, D.C.: U. S. Government Printing Office, 1979.

Uniform Crime Reports. *Crime in the United States.* Washington, D.C.: U.S. Government Printing Office, 1973.

Verbrugge, L. Sex differences in legal drug use. *Journal of Social Issues,* 1982, 38(2), 59–76.

Wallace, N. Support networks among drug addicted women and men. W.O.M.A.N. Evaluation Project Report to the National Institute on Drug Abuse, August, 1976.

Wanberg, K. W., and Horn, J. L. Alcoholism sympton patterns of men and women: A comparative study. *Quarterly Journal of Studies on Alcohol,* 1970, 31, 40–61.

Wechsler, H., and McFadden, M. Sex differences in adolescent alcohol and drug use. A disappearing phenomenon. *Journal of Studies on Alcohol,* 1976, 37, 1291–1301.

Weissman, M. M., and Klerman, G. L. Sex differences in the epidemiology of depression. *Archives of General Psychiatry,* 1977, 34, 98–111.

Wilsnack, S. C. Sex role identity in female alcoholics. *Journal of Abnormal Psychology,* 1973, 82, 253–261.

Wilsnack, R. W., and Wilsnack, S. C. Sex roles and drinking among adolescent girls. *Journal of Studies on Alcohol,* 1978, 39, 1855–1874.

Wilsnack, R. W., Wilsnack, S. C., and Klassen, A. D. *Women's drinking and drinking problems: Patterns from a 1981 national survey.* Paper presented at the Annual Meeting of the Society for the Study of Social Problems, San Francisco, September 1982.

11

Sex Roles and Sexual Dysfunction

Wendy E. Stock

1. Introduction

1.1. General Overview

Sex roles are stereotyped norms and expectations for human behavior based on gender which are socialized from birth onward and are continually reinforced by the social environment. A complete understanding of sex roles is possible only when they are viewed in the context of the society that supports the systematic social and economic oppression of women and maintains a general imbalance of power between men and women.

Sex roles affect all relationships and interactions between women and men. They determine our self-concept as human beings as well as what expectations we bring into a sexual interaction with another. In fact, sex roles may determine, in part, the forms in which sexual dysfunction appears. Before describing the common effects of sex role expectations on sexual functioning, it is necessary to describe the more prevalent types of sexual dysfunction.

1.2. Common Sexual Dysfunctions

Low sexual desire is the absence of physical or emotional impetus to engage in sex. Clients who present for therapy with low sexual desire typically have the "want to want" syndrome. They experience a lack,

Wendy E. Stock • Department of Psychiatry and Behavioral Science, State University of New York at Stony Brook, Stony Brook, New York 11794.

and feel that they "should" desire sex with higher frequency and may, in fact, want to change. Usually, if their partner does not initiate sex, the thought of sex will not occur to them.

Impaired subjective arousal can occur at any point along the sexual response cycle. This can trigger a loss of physiological sexual arousal and impair subsequent sexual response. The cognitive activity of the brain can either augment or inhibit the sexual response cycle. Walen (1980) suggests that cognitive distortions of perception and evaluation operate in most cases of sexual dysfunction. Later, we will look specifically at those cognitions stemming from sex roles that may inhibit subjective arousal.

Vaginismus and dyspareunia are two conditions that cause painful sensation upon the introduction of any object into the vagina. Vaginismus is an involuntary spastic tightening of the pubococcygeal muscle that surrounds the opening of the vagina, such that penetration is impossible or extremely painful for the woman. Dyspareunia is any other pain experienced upon penetration and can be caused by hymenal tags, vaginal irritation, torn supporting ligaments, endometriosis, and other conditions. Primary dyspareunia, if untreated, may result in a secondary vaginismic reaction. The spastic reaction is usually present because of a learned association with pain experienced on penetration. The treatment of vaginismus involves teaching the woman to voluntarily contract and relax the pubococcygeal muscle, and the progressive introduction of a graded series of dilators or fingers as the woman relearns a new association of vaginal penetration and the absence of pain. Treatment usually works best when the woman feels that she is in control of what happens to her body.

Female orgasmic dysfunction is commonly separated into two categories—primary and secondary orgasmic dysfunction. The etiology and treatment is often different for these two dysfunctions. A woman who has never experienced an orgasm through any type of stimulation is primary inorgasmic. Treatment frequently involves teaching the client to become familiar with her anatomy and encouraging her to masturbate. Women must learn to feel that they own and control their bodies, although this is difficult to learn within the current social context. Once orgasm through masturbation is attained, transfer to partner stimulation is attempted. Secondary inorgasmia is inability to experience orgasm with a partner. Sometimes orgasm is possible only through masturbation, while sometimes a woman who is orgasmic with manual or oral stimulation and not through intercourse is defined as dysfunctional. Treatment is usually more complicated and often involves relationship-based interventions. This involves changing certain expectations for sexual performance, i.e., the goal of orgasm through intercourse, which is not possible for the vast majority of women.

Male premature ejaculation is defined as ejaculation that occurs sooner than the male would wish. The criteria for this dysfunction are considered in terms of latency to ejaculation and vary considerably. Some men ejaculate before vaginal intromission is attained; others may sustain intercourse for 10 minutes before ejaculating and consider this premature ejaculation. If female orgasm attained through penile thrusting is a goal, then premature ejaculation can be defined as any ejaculation that occurs before the female has a coital orgasm. Thus, definitions of premature ejaculation may be unrealistic at times. Standard treatment techniques exist that are highly successful. These involve gradually increasing latency to ejaculation by repeated penile stimulation until high arousal is present, then pausing until arousal decreases, then resuming stimulation, and repeating this sequence two or three times per episode (Semans, 1956).

Male erectile dysfunction may involve difficulties in achieving or maintaining erections. Organic factors including diabetes, high blood pressure, circulatory disorders, and prior history of alcohol abuse, among others, may contribute to erectile dysfunctions. However, cognitive factors often play a decisive role even when the original etiology is clearly organic. When organic factors are not reversible, most treatment approaches rely on the removal of pressure to attain an erection by encouraging the male to focus on other pleasurable sexual activity, and by stimulation of the penis with no emphasis on attaining erections. This approach is successful with organic and nonorganically based erectile dysfunction.

The treatments described above represent standard procedures used by Masters and Johnson (1970), Kaplan (1974), and LoPiccolo and LoPiccolo (1978). However, these standard behavioral treatment packages are frequently not sufficient to deal with the complexity and difficulty of cases presenting for sex therapy. Behavioral approaches represent the most basic components of treatment and are effective only when applied sensitively and in conjunction with other interventions.

Short-term sex therapy is valued for its brevity, pragmatism, mechanics, and techniques that set inherent limitations on its scope in understanding and treating more complex issues. In addition to this, the influence of medical models of sexual dysfunction has directed attention away from sex role dynamics (Seidler-Feller, 1983; Tiefer, 1981). As a result, most standard sex therapy implicitly reinforces normative sex roles and the power differential between the sexes that underlies them (Seidler-Feller, in press). A conscious awareness of the effects of sex roles and a willingness to question traditional assumptions about human sexuality is crucial in the treatment of sexual dysfunctions.

2. Sexuality and Sex Role Socialization

Rook and Hammen (1977) emphasized the effect of female sexual socialization, which differs from that of males and thus affects the meaning ascribed to arousal states. Although social norms are in the process of changing, the traditional impact of female socialization has been to constrain the range of women's sexual experiences throughout childhood and adolescence and to provide rigid norms regarding appropriate social contexts for sexual conduct. Masturbation, for example, is much less common among females than among males (Ford and Beach, 1951; Kinsey, Pomeroy, Martin, and Gebhard, 1953). Although recent research reports an increase in female masturbation, female rates remain lower than those of males. According to Rook and Hamen (1977), this difference suggests that females have relatively less experience producing and identifying states of sexual arousal. In addition, the social context of masturbation may vary for male and female children (Gagnon and Simon, 1973). Another difference in socialization involves differences in training of autonomy and initiative in sexual gratification. Male sex role experience involves more autoerotic experience and facilitates acceptance of an active independent role (Gagnon and Simon, 1973). Conversely, female sex role socialization stresses passivity and responsiveness to the needs or demands of others. A young woman may be more concerned with monitoring access to her body than in achieving sexual gratification. The male's typical role as initiator implies that the timing of specific sexual advances will be more precisely coordinated with his escalating level of sexual arousal. However, the female may link these advances to low or nonexistent levels of arousal. Rook and Hammen (1977) postulate that the repeated association of heterosexual contact with nonarousal could become problematic and perhaps lead to sexual dysfunction. Indeed, in a study of frequency of sexual dysfunction in "normal" couples (Frank, 1978), 63% of the women reported difficulty in attaining orgasm, 47% the inability to relax, and 35% disinterest. In women, difficulty becoming aroused was the dysfunction most strongly correlated with sexual dissatisfaction.

A woman's arousal is largely influenced by social scripts and ongoing social conditioning, including influences of experience; religious, parental, and peer exhortations; and modeling. Our culture has traditionally socialized women to believe that their sexual and romantic involvements should be central to their lives but, both cognitively and behaviorally, outside their locus of control (Frey, 1978). This conceptualization bears a close resemblance to Seligman's model of learned helplessness (1978), in which the subject's learning history influences his or her perception of control in a given situation. Since females have a learning history in which their sexuality is often not within their locus of control, there are obvious ramifications for their sexual behavior. Women have been taught to label sexual arousal in romantic rather than sexual terms and, until recently, not to initiate dating or sexual relations. The prohibitions against acting upon sexual arousal may have led many women to ignore, reattribute, or deny it. Women may also be less aware of their own sexual arousal; physiologically, they lack the biofeedback device, a penis, that men have. The noticeable concomitants of their arousal, i.e., nipple erection and vaginal lubrication, are not specific to arousal. Research by Heiman (1978) indicated that females have more difficulty than males in detecting their genital response. (However, males may not recognize and label their sexual arousal unless it is accompanied by an erection; this may be a limitation as well as a helpful cue.) There is an apparent need for further research on discovering the facilitators and variables associated with sexual arousal in women.

According to Ford and Beach (1951), sexuality in humans is structured and patterned by learning. Margaret Mead (1949) found that the potential for orgasm in the human female is a cultural factor. In societies that consider the orgasmic release of the female important, the essential lovemaking techniques that ensure the woman's orgasm will be learned and practiced. When female orgasm is considered unimportant or nonexistent, the members of a culture will not practice techniques essential for orgasmic release in the woman; women in these cultures are likely to be nonorgasmic.

Although orgasmic potential is an important aspect of female sexual responsiveness, it appears that traditional research has succumbed to what Messersmith (1976) calls "the tyranny of the orgasm." According to Jayne (1981), psychological response or satisfaction has been virtually ignored in research on female sexuality. Jayne reviews a number of studies concluding that women's sexual motivation cannot be attributed solely to the pursuit of orgasm. Kinsey et al. (1953), for example, found that although masturbation is the most effective means of producing orgasm in women, it is not the most frequent sexual activity engaged in. Before marriage, more women engage in coitus than in masturbation, although the likelihood of orgasm is less for this activity than for masturbation. Masters and Johnson (1966) found that the most physiologically intense orgasms occur as a result of masturbation and the lowest-intensity orgasms were found in intercourse, intensity being defined by both objective recording and subjective report. Despite the high intensity of

masturbatory orgasm, Masters and Johnson's subjects rated their satisfaction inversely to intensity, with less intense coital orgasms described
as the most satisfying. Fisher (1973) provides further confirmation of
Kinsey's data; masturbation was rated as relatively nonsatisfying while
heterosexual activity was rated as highly gratifying. It appears that
women persist in and prefer sexual activities that produce orgasm incon-
sistently, and the intensity of orgasm is not related to the amount of
satisfaction derived from it (Jayne, 1981). Specifically, those activities
most preferred and rated as most satisfying were those that included a
partner. It appears that factors other than orgasmic output must be
evaluated in order to understand what constitutes sexual satisfaction for
women. Hite (1976), for example, asked women what gave them the
greatest pleasure in sex. The most frequent response given by women
respondents was "Emotional intimacy, tenderness, a closeness, sharing
deep feelings with a loved one." This finding replicates those of Bell and
Bell (1972), who asked women, "Of all aspects of sexual activity, what
do you like best?" The most frequent response was "Closeness or feeling of oneness with partner." These findings indicate that women primarily value the emotional and interpersonal aspects of sexual activity
and derive the greatest pleasure from them.

Male sexual socialization is a complete inversion of what females
learn. Men are taught to relate to their world from a rational perspective
that discounts their own feelings and those of others as well (DeGolia,
1976). Boys are given much reinforcement to learn how to control their
environment, for "showing off" and for "proving themselves" or performing. These well-learned performance rules are clearly apparent in
sex.

Men and boys are granted unstated permission to masturbate.
However, instead of being encouraged to relate masturbation to sensual
or emotional components, men are encouraged to "jerk off." The act has
little to do with bodily sensual feeling; it is entirely goal-oriented (the
orgasm is all that counts); permission usually involves a double message, with consequent guilt (DeGolia, 1976). A result of this is the tendency to "get it over with," which often correlates with hurried sexual
contact. In addition, men are encouraged to stay emotionally in control
at all times. This is accomplished by limiting the sexual interaction to a
solely genital release without experiencing an emotional loss of control.

Litewska (1974) stresses the role that the performance norm plays in
male sexual socialization. As Zilbergeld (1978) writes: "Manhood is a
conditional attribute, and a crucial element that motivates learning is the
necessity of proving maleness. This translates into the sexual arena as
being able to perform upon desire or request. Males who don't conform
to this norm feel incomplete, unskilled, or unmanly." Littewa notes

three elements that reappear constantly in the development of male sexual learning—objectification, fixation, and conquest.

Objectification. From a young age, males are taught to objectify and generalize females to a concept and object, or a nonindividualized category. Males learn to identify females as "the other," and this is borne out by the diverging sex role behaviors required of males and females.

Fixation. Males learn as part of their sexual initiation to fixate on portions of the female's anatomy. Males learn that erections are expected and allowable in response to objectifying a female and then fixating on the parts of her body that excite.

Conquest. To conquer is a highly skilled value in our society. Litewska (1972) points out the connections between male initiation rites, e.g., sports, that require trophies, and learning to "alter the enemy into nothingness, to gain power and rule." In sexual matters, male conquest occurs when he succeeds in reducing a female from a being into a thing and achieves some form of sexual gratification. Litewska suggests that one reason men suffer from premature ejaculation is due to their fantasies, which involve fixation and conquest and are not really involved with their female partner. One implication of these socialized sexual responses is that the male sexual response often has little or nothing to do with the specific female they are with. Hite (1981) found that some men used the concept of male "sex drive" to differentiate themselves from women, and to define themselves as active and aggressive, as opposed to passive (female). For some men, this self-validation not only involved "performing" well but also included "having" or "conquering" the woman and feeling dominant and superior. Thus, the sexual socialization of males and females diverges dramatically along a number of dimensions: control versus helplessness; genitally focused sex versus generalized sensual pleasure; objectification, fixation, and conquest versus love or romantic involvement; performance versus process. It is not surprising when men and women experience difficulties in sexual communication with such differing goals and expectations.

3. Sex Role Expectations

As a function of our socialization into respective sex roles, women and men are trained to accept certain scripts. A script is defined by Berne (1964) as a life plan decided upon at an early age and based on parental and social injunctions that promote a stilted and repetitive way of acting in life. Thus, scripts diminish our changes for intimacy with others. A script can be viewed as a subcategory of general sex roles and provides a useful conceptualization of much sexual behavior. Typical women's scripts share the common theme of incompleteness, inadequacy, and dependence.

3.1. Female Sexual Scripts

The "good-girl syndrome" (Moulton, 1976) is associated with passivity, obedience, docility, and niceness. A recent study (O'Connor, 1979) finds that difficulty achieving orgasm is correlated with the good-girl syndrome. Six hundred women presenting for sex therapy were classified as orgasmic or nonorgasmic. Of the nonorgasmic group, 88% described themselves as having been "good girls" as children and teenagers. They were obedient, did well in school, and never had major conflicts with their parents. Only 30% of the orgasmic women fell into this category. The study indicates a tentative correlation between psychological independence and the ability to experience orgasm. Barbach (1975) points out that in early dating experiences, boys are expected to "get away" with anything they can, while girls are expected to stop them. A "good girl" was above sexuality, while only "loose" girls participated in and enjoyed sex, at the cost of losing male respect and marital potential. Briefly, the girl who acted on her sexual feelings would get a bad reputation, while a boy would get a better one. After years of ignoring and repressing sexual feelings, many women have difficulties becoming responsive in the context of a legitamized adult sexual relationship. Many women have difficulties fully responding and "letting go," which may inhibit orgasmic potential. Certain men are highly uncomfortable when their female partner becomes responsive, as they may suffer from the same stereotype that "nice girls" do not fully desire or enjoy sex.

Similar to the good girl syndrome is the madonna/whore dichotomy. Many women have difficulty reconciling their sexuality with other aspects of the female role, i.e., mother, wife, daughter. Often, these women have received strict religious training that negates enjoyment of sexuality separate from procreation and particularly negates the possibility of being both sexual and religious. This dichotomy places such women in a painful contradiction, the resolution of which involves either denying their sexuality or else risking being viewed by themselves and others as "whores."

"Sleeping Beauty" is a script emphasizing sexual passivity in which the woman remains totally passive, waiting for the male partner to engineer her arousal and orgasm. Typically, women who adhere to this script have difficulty initiating sex, giving feedback to partners, masturbating, knowing their own sexual needs, being sexually assertive, or taking an active role in achieving their own orgasm.

Most scripts concerning female sexuality cause women painfully ambivalent conflict about their own response. Because women have been taught to repress and control their sexuality for so long, but more recently are also expected to have the ability to respond orgasmically (in the appropriate situation), many women are confused and resentful about these competing expectations. This confusion may well be a reflection of the societal ambivalence about the expression and control of female sexuality. Sherfey (1973) believes that the entire social structure would be affected if the expression of female sexuality were allowed.

There is ample empirical evidence of the existence of cultural norms that conceptualize feminine sexuality as passive, naive, and uninterested (Kirkpatrick, 1980). The traditional view of female sexuality is stated explicitly by Freud (1950), who created the distinction between clitoral and vaginal orgasms. A clitoral or "immature" orgasm is characteristic of a masculine woman (i.e., assertive, independent), whereas a vaginal or "mature" orgasm is indicative of femininity (i.e., receptive, dependent). Freud considered all libido as masculine; by inference, to be feminine is to be asexual (Jones, 1955). Kirkpatrick (1980) argues that women have internalized these norms and regard themselves as sexually passive and naive. A "feminine sexual identification" score on the MMPI Masculinity-Femininity Scale consists of not liking to talk about sex, denial of thoughts about sex, and lack of sexual experience. Dahlstrom and Welsh (1960) and Eysenck (1971) found that sexual activity and positive attitudes toward sex were related to masculinity and unrelated to femininity. On this basis, Eysenck concluded that the sexually active and assertive male comes close to the masculine ideal stereotype, whereas a sexually active and assertive female is labeled deviant with respect to the ideal feminine stereotype.

The internalization of these expectations about female sexuality surely has an effect on female sexual satisfaction. Reiss (1956) conjectured that the double standard (i.e., sex is an acceptable pursuit for males and not for females) teaches men to think of women who have sex with them as bad, to separate sex from affection, and to regard sexual gratification as their right. Conversely, unmarried females learn to deny sexual interests and desires, to value virginity, and then expect to lose all these inhibitions within the legitimacy of marriage.

Women do learn to be passive in sex; a large number of women reportedly participate very little or not at all during foreplay activities, and even remain immobile during coitus (Kinsey et al., 1953). It has also been found that neither spouse in most marriages expects the wife to be sexually responsive (Kinsey et al. 1953) and that she may receive disapproval if she does respond (Rainwater, 1966).

Kirkpatrick (1980) notes that although many women currently feel legitimate in considering sexual satisfaction a goal and a right (Bell, 1967;

Lydon, 1970), there has been little investigation of what variables are associated with sexual satisfaction in women. Several studies suggest a variety of relevant factors. Terman (1951) found that sexually inadequate wives had less information and were less confident, more dependent, and more sensitive than the sexually adequate sample. Inadequacy was measured by orgasmic capability; although not synonymous with sexual satisfaction, it has been strongly related (Gebhard, 1966). In contrast, the sexually adequate wives saw themselves to be as passionate as men, and viewed a single standard of mortality as ideal in marriage. In keeping with this, Kinsey *et al.* (1953) found that sexually satisfied women tended to have engaged in higher rates of premarital sexual activity, were active participants in intercourse, were more orgasmic, and had higher levels of education. Other correlates of sexual satisfaction in women have included self-esteem (Maslow, 1942), dominance (DeMartino, 1963), experimentation and self-assuredness (Kaats and Davis, 1970), and use of large muscle groups (Fisher and Osofsky, 1967). The factors linked to sexual satisfaction in women reveal characteristics that are decidedly not "feminine" (Kirkpatrick, 1980). For example, such qualities as adventurousness, self-confidence, muscularity, and premarital sexual activity are in direct opposition to the qualities considered "feminine" by societal standards of mental health: passivity, timidity, virginity, and naïveté. This evidence suggests an inverse relationship between feminine sex role identification and sexual satisfaction (Kirkpatrick, 1980), which creates a serious contradiction for women. Thus, the more effectively women are socialized into the feminine role, the more likely they are required to suppress sexual feelings and interests. Kirkpatrick (1980) presents the hypothesis that the less one adopts the traditional sex role stereotype and the more one embraces a single standard of equality (feminism), the more sexually satisfied one is likely to be.

3.2. Male Sexual Scripts

Zilbergeld (1978) emphasizes that much sexual learning takes place through portrayals of sex in the media, particularly erotic literature and pornography, and through sexual humor, popular literature, movies, and television. The same sexual script for men is presented consistently as a model for male sexuality. To describe this model, Zilbergeld entitles his chapter "It's two feet long, hard as steel, and can go all night." Names given to penises in pornography reflect inhuman standards, which divorce the penis from the person, i.e., tool, weapon, rod, ramrod, battering ram, shaft, courser, and formidable machine. As a result of this myth, most men feel inadequate about their penile size and often have doubts about their own sexuality based on penile size. Zilbergeld (1978) outlines a number of components of the male sexual script. The first two are part of the general cultural model of masculinity as well as the fantasy model of sex.

1. Men should not have, or at least not express, certain feelings. Only a narrow range of feelings is permitted to men: aggressiveness, competitiveness, anger, joviality, and feelings associated with being in control. Having sexual feelings is excluded from the list. Therefore, the need for support, validation, physical affection, tenderness, and knowledge of being loved are not considered appropriately masculine.

2. In sex, as elsewhere, performance counts. The goals of intercourse and orgasm are the only important factors.

3. The man must take charge of and orchestrate sex. This myth stems from two requirements for masculinity, that men must be leading and take the active role, and that a real man needs little or nothing from a woman in terms of either information or stimulation (Zilbergeld, 1978).

4. A man always wants and is always ready to have sex. Men believe that they should always be capable of responding sexually regardless of the time, place, or emotional factors involved. Men become sex machines rather than human beings, performing "whenever the right button is pushed." Naturally, many cases of male sexual dysfunction are actually healthy reactions to this expectation of sexual performance under adverse circumstances.

5. All physical contact must lead to sex. Thus, many men refuse to engage in any physical contact unless it will lead to sex. Men are taught that it is not permissible for them to want cuddling, hugging, kissing, holding, caressing, and other types of physical affection. Again, this restricts men (and their partners) from experiencing emotional intimacy in a sexual encounter.

6. Sex equals intercourse. This is one of the most damaging aspects of the male sexual script, as the necessity for intercourse restricts other types of sexual expression and requires the presence of an erection. When men experience any difficulties in achieving or maintaining erections, they often experience a devastating sense of failure and panic. Without a hard penis, they are "not men" and they are incapable of "performing" in sex, which is the only model they know. Clinically, this is the myth that most heavily contributes to erectile dysfunction. In addition, Zilbergeld (1978) points out that this myth prevents men from discovering other forms of pleasurable stimulation, which are discounted in favor of intercourse.

7. Sex requires an erection. This myth puts tremendous pressure on men and also places them in any extremely vulnerable position. The effect of this myth are much the same as those of number 6.

To sum, the male sexual script requires that males control and orchestrate the sexual encounter, always be ready to perform, always have an erection, be free of emotional needs during sex, and always desire intercourse. The control and performance orientation of this script, if followed, limits sex to a physical act that is accomplished under great pressure. As sex role scripting produces in men an orientation toward sex as performance, which necessarily divorces it of elements of emotional intimacy and communication, in women it produces the opposite effect. While women often have less difficulty expressing themselves emotionally, or at least desiring sex in an emotional context, many have difficulty accepting their own physicality and giving reign to an unfettered response. In both cases, the conditions are not present for a relaxed, safe, and unpressured exchange: Men cannot relax and allow themselves to feel, and women cannot allow themselves to respond and often do not feel emotionally safe enough with men (who are often too busy performing to relate) to respond easily.

4. The Effects of Sex Roles in Relationships

With the above information in mind concerning the negative impact of sex role learning, scripts, and expectations on the expression of sexuality, we will now consider those effects within a relational context. Which factors contribute to sexual satisfaction and sexual dysfunction in women and men?

Among women, satisfaction with their relationship seems to be an important factor in sexual functioning. This is not surprising in light of sex role programming to value emotional intimacy. Questions about sexual performance and satisfaction are included in many measures of social or marital adjustment. Generally, these measures are concerned with the performance aspects of sex, frequency of intercourse, occurrence of orgasm, and enjoyment or satisfaction with sex. Less attention is paid to the interpersonal side of sex, which is also important for women. Kaplan (1974) notes that in contrast to the male, the female sexual response is influenced to a much greater extent by the quality of her relationship with her lover. Her sexual response is highly contingent on having positive and loving feelings toward her partner, and on her acceptance of him. If a woman evaluates her partner negatively, or if she is physically afraid of him, she may have difficulty responding to him sexually.

An example of the reciprocal relationship between marital and sexual problems is evident in studies done on female orgasm and marital happiness. On the basis of statistics complied by the Institute for Sex

Research at Indiana University, Gebhard (1966) made the following observations: Wives who reach orgasm in 90 to 100% of their marital coitus are found more commonly in very happy marriages than in any other marriages. Those wives who never reach orgasm in marital coitus are found most often in very unhappy marriages.

Another example of the importance of relationship variables to female sexual satisfaction is described by McGovern, McMullen, and LoPiccolo (1978). In a comparison of successive treatment for primary and secondary inorgasmic women, an analysis of their assessment data revealed that (1) women with both primary and secondary orgasmic dysfunction reported increased satisfaction with their sexual and marital relationships after treatment, and (2) all of the primary inorgasmic women became orgasmic in coitus, whereas the majority of the secondary inorgasmic women did not. Comparisons of pretreatment marital satisfaction scores revealed that the secondary inorgasmic women were more dissatisfied with their marital relationship prior to treatment, as were their male partners. While orgasm during coitus is not a realistic goal for most women and is overstressed in the sex therapy literature, these findings may be viewed as lending support to the importance of relationship dynamics in female sexual satisfaction.

In addition to relationship/satisfaction, another group of variables that discriminate between extreme groups of orgasm consistency in women concern early childhood experience. The most significant area associated with orgasm consistency is the father and the father/daughter relationship. Fisher (1973) found low orgasm consistency to be related to actual childhood loss or separation from the father, which includes fathers who have been emotionally unavailable to their daughters, i.e., uncommunicative, casual, or uninterested, a figure with whom the woman did not have a positive childhood relationship. Fisher's theory holds that the experience of high sexual arousal creates a more vulnerable emotional state in which the dependability of the love object becomes particularly salient. A high state of sexual arousal entails a "fade-out" of other objects, which become psychologically more vague and indistinct. This fading out may be particularly threatening to a woman highly concerned with object loss, and there might be a tendency to inhibit the fading out and, subsequently, orgasm. Orgasmic response may also be inhibited when anxiety is elevated, due to a loosening of the hold on external reality.

Fear and anxiety based on a traumatic sexual incident such as rape or incest may prevent women who have been victims of such assaults from responding sexually to their partners. A number of studies have shown a high rate of sexual dysfunction, usually in the area of 50%, among rape survivors, as well as anxiety, depression, and general disruption of life (Becker, Skinner, Abel, and Treacy, 1981; Kilpatrick, Resick, and Veronen, 1981; Ellis, Calhoun, and Atkeson, 1980; Miller, Williams, and Bernstein, 1982). In keeping with Fisher's (1973) data, many rape victims have difficulty attaining orgasm. Although they may become highly sexually aroused, the "letting go" response requires a relinquishing of control that these women find extremely threatening. In addition, Miller et al. (1982) found that serious relationship dysfunctions may continue for years after a rape; Becker et al. (1981) found that the passage of time following the assault does not appear to heal sexual fears and dysfunctions. It is interesting to consider the subtle effect that such practices have upon female sexuality in general; even if the particular woman has not been directly victimized, the threat of rape and the high frequency of sexual aggression tolerated as normative interactions may cause many women to feel constrained sexually (Riger and Gordon, 1981).

Thus, a number of relational variables exert an influence on female sexuality. These include the degree of closeness and intimacy a woman experiences in her relationships, the quality of the relationship, the childhood father/daughter relationship, and the presence of threat of traumatic sexual experiences. It is likely that relational variables both teach and reinforce sex role learning in the area of sexuality and that they can be useful in understanding the etiology and maintenance of female sexual dysfunction. Again, the interaction between male and female sex roles in the area of love, intimacy, and sex is an unfortunate one. This will become particularly clear once male relational variables have been discussed.

Whereas female sexual satisfaction is often tied to the quality of the relationship and the presence of intimacy, males are more focused on their sexual performance, a performance that must measure up to their own internalized role expectations and one that leaves little room for intimate interaction. Another way to describe this difference is to say that males are product-oriented, while females are process-oriented. Male product orientation in sex is functional; it maintains distance and protects men from dealing with threatening emotions, but unfortunately it deprives them of the closeness they may crave but are unable to ask for. Often sex is the only means by which males allow themselves to experience any degree of intimacy or emotional contact. Yet men have been taught not to be in touch with their feelings, not to express emotional vulnerability, and not to have to ask for anything, especially during sex. They are taught (and come to believe) that they must be in control at all times and must be able to "perform" under any circumstances regardless of how they may feel toward their partner. Goldfried and Friedman (1982) consider *male inexpressiveness* and *high instrumentality* to be characteristics of males in this society.

✴   Men feel that they must hide much of their real self from others, as well as from themselves. Their fear is that a display of emotional vulnerability will cause others to view them as inadequate and inferior. According to Jourard (1971), the inexpressive role consumes energy, imposes stress, and makes men less sensitive to internal cues from their bodies. Men who try to meet this image are uncomfortable with self-disclosure and typically display less insight and less empathy than women. The fear of self-disclosure is a realistic one; Derlaga and Chaikin (1976) found that males who did not disclose information about a personal problem were rated as better adjusted than men who did disclose. As a result of inexpressiveness, men are more reluctant to make themselves known to another person and are more difficult to love, experience more difficulty loving others, and find it difficult to love themselves (Goldfried and Friedman, 1972).

✴ Males are trained to be product- or goal-oriented, although they pay a high price in fulfilling this role. Highly instrumental behavior is characterized by an excessive competitive drive, an intense striving for achievement, a persistent overcommitment of responsibilities, easily provoked impatiences, high physical tension, and an excessive drive and hostility. This behavior pattern is associated with the traditional male sex role, and males are rewarded more than women for engaging in such typical behaviors as competition, aggressiveness, and ambition. Many men find it very difficult to accept the fact that there may be situations over which they have no control or situations in which accepting the relaxation of control is positive.

Inexpressiveness and instrumentality show up strikingly in men's sexual interactions with women. Men often seek nonemotional involvement, as intimacy and dependency with women is seen as "unmasculine" and also involves a loss of power in the relationship. Peplau and Cochran (1980) found two sex differences in values concerning love relationships: Males valued power while females valued emotional expressiveness. Unger (1980) points out that women behave as lower-status people in heterosexual relationships. While they tend to fear the loss of the relationship, which makes them more vulnerable emotionally, men fear the loss of power in the relationship. Shaef (1981) points out that when men engage themselves in a committed relationship, they feel they have given up something, while women have gained something. Elizabeth and Stock (1982) have developed a model based on intimacy, status, and power (see Figure 1). Males, usually of higher status, derive reinforcement from their external environment— from work-related activities, higher-paying jobs, etc. Females have traditionally looked to their male partners to confer status, power, and intimacy on them. However, intimacy cannot occur without emotional equality. Thus, males must compromise in relationships, balancing their

NEED FOR INTIMACY VERSUS LOSS OF POWER

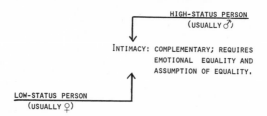

Figure 1. Dimensions of power. From Elizabeth and Stock, 1982.

need for intimacy with their fear of loss of power. This would result in males being more cautious and reluctant to approach intimacy, while females, having only to gain from this interaction, place higher value on intimacy.

According to Fasteau (1974), most men today can readily acknowledge and satisfy sexual need, but the masculine stereotype puts Eros beyond their reach. Rollo May (1969) writes that the performance ethic of sexuality is self-defeating and prevents intimacy: "The excessive concern with technical performance in sex is actually correlated with a reduction of sexual feeling . . . the more he views himself as a machine to be turned on, adjusted, and steered, the less feeling he has for either himself or his partner, and the less feeling, the more he loses genuine sexual appetite and ability. The upshot of this self-defeating pattern is that, in the long run, *the lover who is most efficient will also be the one who is impotent.*"

Men, Fasteau writes, are concerned with their technical proficiency and their partner's response, but ultimately their concern is with themselves. They desire to see ecstasy in the faces of their partners, but only to "assure themselves of their manhood, not to mingle that ecstasy with their own."

Much of sex therapy with male dysfunctions is focused on teaching men to feel again. Specifically, this involves teaching men to give themselves permission to be passive during sexual interactions, to allow themselves to receive pleasure without needing to remain in control of the sexual interaction and simultaneously be concerned with their partner, and to feel sensation over their entire body rather than focusing solely on the penis. Many cases of dysfunction are easily treated once the instrumental, product-oriented, performance aspects of the male sex role are challenged. In addition, relational skills must often be trained, and underlying defenses against intimacy must be addressed in the course of sex therapy. Men also need permission and practice in experiencing emotional closeness during sex—this may be very threatening to those men who have always maintained a distanced, controlling attitude. Naturally, couple's relationships often require restructuring, which usually dovetails with sexually based interventions.

5. Marriage, Sex Roles, and Sexual Dysfunction

This section is devoted specifically to marriage because in no other institution are sex roles so reinforced and structured. It is within marriage that the influences of sexual socialization, sex role scripting, expectations, and the relational dynamics discussed above combine with traditional institutional expectations to produce a virulent environment for healthy sexual functioning. According to Munjack and Oziel (1980), Masters and Johnson estimate that at least one-half of all marriages in this country are plagued by some form of sexual inadequacy. Empirical support exists for this assertion. In a study of 100 stable married couples who identified themselves as happily married, Frank et al. (1978) found that 63% of the women and 40% of the men had sexual dysfunctions. Half of the women had more than one dysfunction.

Bernard (1972) has presented ample evidence that the institution of marriage has a negative impact upon the mental health of women. Symonds (1971) has written about the mental disorders that often develop after marriage, "when a young woman who is apparently independent, self-sufficient, and capable, changes after marriage and develops phobias or other signs of constriction of self. These changes invariably cause her to become excessively dependent and helpless." Statistics suggest that the social institution of marriage raises the risk of disorder for women but offers protection for men (Bernard, 1972). Married women who are not employed are at the highest risk for psychological disorder. They have the highest rates of entry into psychiatric treatment of any occupational group; they request (and receive) the greatest quantity of prescribed mood-modifying drugs (New York Narcotic Addiction Control Commission, 1971); they report the highest incidence of psychogenetic symptoms such as nervousness, nightmares, dizziness, and headaches (Lief, 1975).

In contrast to comparisons between married and unmarried women, married men are significantly better off than unmarried men on various measures (Bernard, 1972). Married men are happier, less depressed, and less passive; show fewer symptoms of psychological distress including nervous breakdowns, nervousness, trembling hands, nightmares, and insomnia; show less impairment of mental health generally; make more money; and commit suicide less.

It has become increasingly apparent in the field of sex therapy that most sexual problems interact with relationship problems. Consequently, most effective sex therapy involves treating the relationship as well as sexual dysfunction. LoPiccolo (1975) considers the most important area of assessment to be the couple's interpersonal relationship, and has outlined several interpersonal factors that maintain sexual dysfunctions. One such factor is the couple's life-style or general level of mutuality in their relationship. When sex roles are divided strictly along stereotypic lines where the husband is responsible for the family's financial support while the wife handles domestic duties, she may be feeling some resentment toward her husband, not only for forgoing a career of her own but also for having a work day that extends well beyond her husband's schedule. LoPiccolo has found this to be a consistent pattern in cases of secondary female orgasmic dysfunction. Usually the woman feels comfortable being sexually responsive and orgasmic through masturbation, but she is resistent toward sharing her response with a man for whom she feels little emotional or practical support. Another area to assess is the manner in which couples order their priorities. Couples who always place job, children, dinner, house, lawn, sports, neighbors, and television before their sex life are setting the conditions for poor lovemaking. Although they are physically tired, mentally exhausted, and emotionally drained, they are often puzzled that their sex life is disappointing and frustrating. In the Frank et al. (1978) study of the frequency of sexual dysfunction in "normal" couples, 77% of the women reported sexual difficulties related to a lack of interest or inability to relax; 50% of the men reported such difficulties. The higher number of sexual difficulties (e.g., partner chooses inconvenient time, inability to relax, lack of interest, and too little foreplay) reported by the women, as compared with the men, supports the notion that women require more emotional sensitivity accompanying the sexual act, or are at least more aware of the absence of such amenities (Frank et al., 1978). In addition, the majority of women work the equivalent of two full-time jobs, balancing home- and job-related responsibilities. Seidler-Feller (1983) contends that the development of sexual dysfunctions in women may involve "a dispute or strike over working conditions." Men also may work long hours in work that is both alienating and dehumanizing, and may have few emotional resources left for their relationships.

It is also important to assess the extent to which the couple's communication problems affect other areas of their relationship beyond the sexual sphere. Peplau and Cochran (1980) found striking sex differences in what men and women value in relationships in the area of communication. Women gave greater emphasis to equality in making decisions. The area of power distribution in a relationship may crucially affect the type of problems presented in therapy. Men and women seem to be at higher risk for types of psychological disorders that dovetail with masculine and feminine stereotypes, respectively. Women are at heightened risk for disorders marked by symptoms of low self-esteem, self-punishment, passivity, guilt, depression, and social withdrawal. These symptoms could easily lead to helplessness, apathy, and inhibition of activity; such experiences may exacerbate powerlessness (Marecek, 1976). Research on conjugal power distribution indicates that decision areas in married life are sex-typed (Raven, 1974). Some recent work demonstrates that the power bases women tend to adopt have a negative impact on their self-esteem (Johnson, 1976). The data suggest the strong influence of sex role socialization: Women learn to deny certain forms of power and competence (except in sex-stereotypic areas like housekeeping and childbearing). Since the power bases women use tend to be covert, "soft" women frequently deny locus of control and causality to themselves and are denied by others. This imbalance of power affects the expression of sexuality, as well as most other relationship areas. As Jakubowski (1977) writes, attempts to use Masters and Johnson's (1970) sexual shaping therapy are unsuccessful when women cannot be assertive enough to tell the man what they find sexually stimulating, irritating, etc., to refuse sex when they are not sufficiently aroused, or to ask for tenderness after sex. Frequently, the underlying issues involve the woman's right to refuse sex, and her fear of hurting the man if she tells him that she is not being sexually satisfied. Kaplan (1974) writes that of the specific pathogenic factors that contribute to female sexual dysfunctions, primary are women's attitudes of helplessness, passivity, and dependence upon the man, which lead to fears of being abandoned and rejected by him. The dysfunctional woman often comes to realize in therapy the enormous extent to which her behavior is governed by the fear of losing her husband or his approval. Kaplan also points out that a woman's reluctance to express her needs is not always based on "cultural paranoia." The woman may run a real risk of displeasing her husband if she becomes more assertive sexually.

Since powerlessness has negative psychological consequences, we might expect sex and marital therapists to be concerned with ways of helping clients regain power. Assertiveness training is often used as an adjunct to sex and marital therapy and can have some impact on the balance of power in the relationship system. However, it is important to consider the economic realities of the marriage, which combine with the societal structure to prevent women from being independent from male power. It is apparent that powerlessness in women is not simply a matter of faulty socialization, and that it is very difficult to counter these effects by teaching assertion when the external society reinforces and maintains women's powerlessness and dependence. Urging women, as Kaplan does, to "abandon themselves sexually without fearing rejection" may be somewhat difficult to manage, given women's position.

Much empirical and clinical observation indicates that power plays an important role in marital relationships. Hatfield, Utne, and Traupmann (1979) have developed a theory that stresses the importance of equity in relationships. In the case of sexual relationships, Hatfield *et al.* (1979) conjecture that men and women who feel underbenefited may find that their anger makes it difficult for them to respond sexually to their partners. They may begin to respond sadistically or passive-aggressively to sexual advances, while the overbenefited may suffer guilt and find it difficult to receive pleasure from their partners. Much of the clinical literature associates such feelings with primary and secondary impotence, or orgasmic dysfunction (Barbach, 1975; Heiman, LoPiccolo, and LoPiccolo, 1976; Kaplan, 1974; Masters and Johnson, 1970; Zilbergeld, 1978).

Hatfield (1982) has produced some empirical data relating equity theory to sexual satisfaction in recently married couples. Couples in equitable relationships were found to be more content with the relationships and were more satisfied with their sexual relationships overall than were other couples. Further support for equity theory was found by Rainwater (1966); women's reports of satisfaction with sexual relations were found to vary as a function of social class. Spouses' reports of equal enjoyment of sex varied as a function of class, with the middle class reporting equality more frequently than the lower-class subjects. Lower-lower-class subjects were more likely to report that the husband enjoyed sex more than the wife. Rainwater views the relationship between social class and satisfaction as mediated by the variable of conjugal role organization, which varies with social class as well. In middle-class couples, joint relationships involving a more egalitarian partnership were the most common. In the lower-lower class, segregated sex role organization is the more predominant pattern.

Stock and Roberts (1982) compared two groups in which either the male or the female partner in the couple presented for therapy with a sexual dysfunction. The data indicated that wives who are directly contesting the balance of power in their relationships have husbands who are opposing their challenge indirectly by developing a sexual dysfunction. An example from the clinical literature speaks directly to this issue. In an article entitled "The Impotent King," Jacobs (1977) writes:

> . . . secondary impotence occurs within the context of the husband's narcissistic rage, elicited by the wife's unwillingness to pay continued tribute to them. The women react with mounting anger as the men refuse to respond to their increasingly more clearly voiced needs for closeness, equality, and

intimacy. . . . The development of impotence often results in a lessening of the wife's challenges to her husband's dominance. . . . She becomes less demanding which naturally reinforces his sexual difficulty which then becomes an interpersonal strategy for him to hold on to his special position with his wife. . . . Treatment of such a form of impotence may be more effective if it moves the couple toward greater equality.

The profile for wives with sexual dysfunctions indicates that they do not want to acknowledge the presence of power conflict, but their husbands consider them overly passive. As Kaplan (1974) notes, "sexual responsiveness to the other may become a symbol of compliance. It is not surprising if a women is inorgasmic when unconsciously orgasm represents submission to her father/husband. Unconsciously, she would rather relinquish orgastic pleasure than give satisfaction to her 'adversary.'" Therapy for sexual dysfunctions in which a power conflict dynamic is operating usually involves the realignment of power structure in the relationship. In addition, therapy is directed at making the dysfunctional spouse conscious of the power conflict, and encouraging him/her to take more responsibility to approach this through the use of direct power strategies.

Sex roles interact with and contribute to power conflict in relationships. The issue of power cuts across most traditional sex role behaviors and is central in many sexual and marital problems. Women typically are in a less objectively powerful position and are trained to behave in a powerless manner. They respond by conforming to this and by remaining helpless across situations, including the achievement of sexual satisfaction, or else develop manipulative and indirect strategies to gain power in the relationship that are often destructive to the relationship and, ultimately, to self-esteem. Women most often develop sexual dysfunctions because they are not familiar with their bodies, are ambivalent about being both female and sexual, are afraid to ask for the type of stimulation they require to achieve orgasm, are unwilling or unable to "let go" and relinquish control in a situation they perceive as threatening, or are using a withdrawal of sex and affection to gain leverage in the relationship. Since women generally have only affectional sources of reward at their disposal, sex then becomes one of the few areas of reinforcement that they have under their control. Sometimes withholding access to sex is not possible, as in the case of marital rape (Gelles, 1977). Women may withhold their enjoyment or active participation in sex either in order to punish their partner or because exchanging sexual pleasure has become totally incomprehensible within the context of their relationship. Seidler-Feller (1983) suggests that female dysfunction may be viewed as a "general status protest" of the power differential between the sexes. In particular, she cites the proprietary interest of the male for the female body, his sense of ownership and entitlement. Thus, female sexual dysfunctions may represent struggles concerning sexual access and a challenge of the rules regarding male sexual rights (Seidler-Feller, 1983).

Men typically have more objective bases of power in their environments but pay a high emotional price for maintaining this degree of control, which evidences itself in a performance-oriented attitude toward sexuality, and the associated loss of intimacy and emotional contact. Men often develop sexual dysfunctions based on the threat of "female power" or, more precisely, the loss of control in the relationship. Men may also be threatened by women's clearly expressed desire for sexual satisfaction. Instead of this being perceived as a cooperative goal to achieve together, it is considered another demand for which they feel totally responsible and by which they may feel intimidated. Men may withhold their sexuality from their partners in ways similar to those of women. They may respond to threats to enactment of their sex role by developing premature ejaculation, erectile dysfunction, or low sexual desire. Sex role issues are certainly not the sole cause of sexual dysfunction, but they are frequently among those observed clinically, and they enter into the etiology and maintenance of sexual dysfunctions.

6. Directions toward Change

A number of therapeutic interventions have been discussed that indirectly address sex role issues and attempt to alter behavior that is clearly related to sex role socialization. For women, such interventions include teaching sexual assertiveness, communication, acceptance of sexuality, masturbation training, and any interventions that foster women taking responsibility for their sexual satisfaction. For men, interventions that allow a relaxation of the performance orientation, focusing techniques designed to enhance total body awareness, and training communication and emotional expression are common treatment techniques. Naturally, these do not preclude the standard sex therapy approaches that are specific to treatment of type of sexual dysfunction (Masters and Johnson, 1970; LoPiccolo and LoPiccolo, 1978; Kaplan, 1974). Relationship-oriented interventions are based on fostering emotional intimacy and communication and breaking down rigid sex role expectations that partners have for themselves and for each other. It is often beneficial to address the sharing of power and locus of control in the relationship, particularly in the area of power conflict, when the sexual arena becomes a battleground for other conflicts and unmet needs in the relationship.

There are few clinical interventions explicitly based on the direct alteration of sex role-related behaviors. Clinicians have become increasingly aware that there are strong environmental factors that may constrain men and women from learning to behave in nonstereotypic ways. In fact, the larger social system both elicits and reinforces certain problems and works against the maintenance of new behavior patterns. Although men and women may experience positive consequences as they learn more intimate, expressive, and assertive ways of relating to others, there are potential drawbacks. Berger (1979) has written that "it is hard to live outside the old social forms without support and not feel crazy." The consciousness-raising group format is one intervention that has been recognized recently as providing the social support and validation necessary to accomplish these changes. Goldfried and Friedman (1982) stress the importance of consciousness-raising groups in helping men to become more aware of what it means to be male in our society and to provide the necessary social support to encourage change away from restrictive stereotypes. However, Farrell (1974) and Vanacek (1980) both emphasize that certain modifications in the format of consciousness-raising are required, particularly the involvement of a trained leader in groups for men. Men find it difficult to explore the limitations of sex role stereotypes on their own and are not nearly as motivated to do so as women. A leader becomes crucial in helping men overcome the patterns of competitiveness and inexpressiveness that can undermine the goals of consciousness-raising.

Historically, consciousness-raising groups originated from the needs of women to challenge their sex role conditioning and to reevaluate their experience of being women in the society. The group approach incorporating standard sex therapy with aspects of consciousness-raising has been used successfully in treating primary and secondary inorgasmic women (Barbach and Flaherty, 1980; Leiblum and Hershfield-Ersner, 1977; Wallace, 1974). The group process allows women to identify common myths and stereotypes that they learned as they developed sexually, and to question these beliefs and grow beyond them in a supportive context. Kirkpatrick (1980) provides some empirical basis for changing traditional notions of female sexuality. Data collected from a sample of 199 couples revealed a positive association between sexual satisfaction and feminism. Interestingly, the larger the disagreement between the two partners on the feminism items, the greater their sexual dissatisfaction. It was found that women who scored high as feminists masturbate more, are more orgasmic in masturbation, and are more aroused by erotic stimuli. It appears that certain behaviors and attitudes associated with being a feminist enhance sexual satisfaction. This is the first direct evidence regarding the relationship between changing traditional sex roles and sexual satisfaction in women.

Therapeutically, it may be advantageous to make both clients and therapists conscious of the sex role stereotypes and behaviors that exert a negative influence on their sexuality. Sex roles derive from a system based on inequality between the sexes and are consequently difficult to change within this context. Theorists such as Reich (1945) have argued that unfettering sexuality would require a fundamental change in the social structure and that it is in the interests of the *status quo* to maintain rigid sex roles. Certainly, the current political climate is shaped by forces that would maintain sex roles at the cost of personal freedom in the service of supporting traditional social and economic institutions. Therapeutically, it may be more effective to educate clients to the systemic inequalities that affect them rather than allow the internalization of conflict by overlooking these realities. Awareness of oppressive external contingencies and how these relate to individual behavior provide the basis for strategies directed toward change.

7. References

Barbach, L. *For yourself: The fulfillment of female sexuality.* Garden City: Doubleday, 1975.
Barbach, L., and Flaherty, M. Group treatment of situationally orgasmic women. *Journal of Sex and Marital Therapy,* Spring 1980, *6*, 19–29.
Becker, J. V., Skinner, L. J., Abel, G. G., and Treacy, E. C. *Incidence and types of sexual dysfunctions in rape and incest survivors.* Research Grant MH-32982-02 from the National Institute of Mental Health, 1981.
Bell, R. Some emerging sexual expectations among women. *Medical Aspects of Human Sexuality,* 1972, *6*, 136–144.
Bell, R. B., and Bell, P. L. Sexual satisfaction among married women. *Medical Aspects of Human Sexuality,* 1972, *6*, 136–144.
Berger, M. Men's new family roles: Some implications for therapists. *Family Coordinator,* 1979, *28*, 638–646.
Bernard, J. *The future of marriage.* New York: World, 1972.
Berne, E. *Games people play.* New York: Grove Press, 1964.
Dahlstrom, W., and Welsh, G. (Eds.). *Am MMPI handbook: A guide to use in clinical practice and research.* Minneapolis: University of Minnesota Press, 1960.
DeGolia, R. Thoughts on men's oppression. In H. Wyckoff (Ed.), *Love, therapy, and politics.* New York: Grove Press, 1976.
DeMartino, M. Dominance–feeling, security–insecurity, and sexuality in women. In M. DeMartino (Ed.), *Sexual behavior and personality characteristics.* New York: Grove Press, 1963.
Derlaga, V. J., and Chaikin, A. L. Norms affecting self-disclosure in men and women. *Journal of Consulting and Clinical Psychology,* 1976, *44*, 376–380.
Elizabeth, P., and Stock, W. E. *A model of power, intimacy, and status.* Personal communication, 1982.
Ellis, E. M., Calhoun, K. S., and Atkeson, B. M. Sexual dysfunction in victims of rape: Victims may experience a loss of sexual arousal and frightening flashbacks even one year after the assault. *Women and Health,* 1980, *5*, 39–47.
Eysenck, H. Masculinity–femininity, personality and sexual attitudes. *Journal of Sex Research,* 1971, *7*, 83–88.

Farrell, W. T. *The liberated man.* New York: Random, 1974.

Fasteau, M. F. *The male machine.* New York: McGraw-Hill, 1974.

Fisher, S. *The female orgasm.* New York: Basic Books, 1973.

Fisher, S., and Osofsky, H. Sexual responsiveness in women. *Archives of General Psychiatry,* 1967, *17,* 214–226.

Ford, C., and Beach, F. *Patterns of sexual behavior.* New York: Paul Hoeber, 1951.

Frank, E., Anderson, C., and Rubenstein, M. Frequency of sexual dysfunction in "normal" couples. *New England Journal of Medicine,* 1978, *299,* 111–115.

Freud, S. *Collected papers* (Vol. 5, E. Jones, Ed.). London: Hogarth Press, 1950.

Frey, M. Dissertation in preparation, SUNY at Stony Brook, 1978.

Gagnon, J., and Simon, W. *Sexual conduct: The social sources of human sexuality.* Chicago: Aldine, 1973.

Gebhard, D. Factors in marital orgasm. *Journal of Social Issues,* 1966, *22,* 88–95.

Gelles, R. J. Power, sex, and violence: The case of marital rape. *Family Coordinator,* 1977, 339–347.

Goldfried, M. R., and Friedman, J. M. Clinical behavior therapy and the male sex role. In K. Solomon and N. B. Levy (Eds.), *Men in transition: Theory and therapy.* New York: Plenum, 1982.

Hatfield, E., Greenberger, D., Traupmann, J., and Lambert, P. Equity and sexual satisfaction in recently married couples. *Journal of Sex Research,* 1982, *18*(1), 18–32.

Hatfield, E., Utne, M., and Traupman, J. Equity theory and intimate relationships. In R. Burgess and T. L. Huston (Eds.), *Social exchange in developing relationships.* New York: Academic Press, 1979.

Heiman, J. Uses of psychophysiology in the assessment and treatment of sexual dysfunction. In J. LoPiccolo and L. LoPiccolo (Eds.), *Handbook of sex therapy.* New York: Plenum, 1978.

Heiman, J., LoPiccolo, L., and LoPiccolo, J. *Becoming orgasmic: A sexual growth program for women.* New Jersey: Prentice-Hall, 1976.

Hite, S. *The Hite report.* New York: Macmillan, 1976.

Hite, S. *The Hite report on male sexuality.* New York: Knopf, 1981.

Jacobs, L. J. The impotent king: Secondary impotence refractory to brief sex therapy. *American Journal of Psychotherapy,* 1977, *31*(1), 97–104.

Jayne, C. A two-dimensional model of female sexual response. *Journal of Sex and Marital Therapy,* Spring 1981, *7*(1), 3–30.

Jones, E. *The life and work of Sigmund Freud.* New York: Basic Books, 1955.

Jourard, S. *The transparent self.* New York: Van Nostrand Reinhold, 1971.

Kaats, G., and Davis, K. The dynamics of sexual behavior of college students. *Journal of Marriage and Family,* 1970, *32,* 390–399.

Kaplan, H. S. *The new sex therapy.* New York: Brunner/Mazel, 1974.

Kilpatrick, D. G., Resick, P. A., and Veronen, L. J. Effects of rape experience: A longitudinal study. *Journal of Social Issues,* 1981, *37*(4), 105–122.

Kinsey, A., Pomeroy, W., Martin, C., and Gebhard, P. *Sexual behavior in the human female.* Philadelphia Saunders, 1953.

Kirkpatrick, C. S. Sex roles and sexual satisfaction in women. *Psychology of Women Quarterly,* 1980, *4,* 444–459.

Leiblum, S., and Hershfield-Ersner, R. Sexual enhancement groups for dysfunctional women: An evaluator. *Journal of Sex and Marital Therapy,* Summer 1977, *3*(2), 139–152.

Lief, H. I. Sexual counseling. In S. L. Romney, J. J. Gray, A. B. Little, J. A. Merrill, E. J. Quilligan, and R. Stander (Eds.), *Gynecology and obstetrics: The health care of women.* New York: McGraw-Hill, 1975.

Litewska, J. The socialized penis. *Liberation,* 1974, *18*(7).

LoPiccolo, J., and LoPiccolo, L. (Eds.). *Handbook sex therapy*. New York: Plenum Press, 1978.

LoPiccolo, J., and Miller, V. A program for enhancing the sexual relationship of normal couples. *Counseling Psychologist*, 1975, *5*(1), 41–45.

Lydon, S. The politics of orgasm. In R. Morgan (Ed.), *Sisterhood is powerful*. New York: Vintage Press, 1979. Pp. 197–204.

Maracek, J. Powerlessness and women's psychological disorders. *Voices*, Fall 1976, 50–54.

Maslow, A. Self-esteem and sexuality in women. *Journal of Social Psychology*, 1942, *16*, 259–294.

Masters, W., and Johnson, V. *Human sexual response*. Boston: Little, Brown, 1966.

Masters, W., and Johnson, V. *Human sexual inadequacy*. Boston: Little, Brown, 1970.

May, R. *Love and will*. New York: Norton, 1969.

McGovern, K. B., McMullen, R. S., and LoPiccolo, J. Secondary orgasmic dysfunction; analysis and strategies for treatment. In J. LoPiccolo and L. LoPiccolo (Eds.), *Handbook of Sex Therapy*, New York: Plenum Press, 1978.

Mead, Margaret. *Male and female: A study of the sexes in a changing world*. New York: Laurel Editions, Bell Publishing, 1949.

Messersmith, C. E. Sex therapy and the marital system. In D. Olson (Ed.), *Treating relationships*. Lake Mills, Iowa: Graphic Publishing, 1976.

Miller, W. R., Williams, A. M., and Bernstein, M. H. The effects of rape on marital and sexual adjustment. *American Journal of Family Therapy*, Spring 1982, *10*(1), 51–58.

Moulton, R. *Some effects of the new feminism*. Paper presented to the Joint Meeting of the American Academy of Psychoanalysis and the American Psychiatric Association, 1976.

Munjack, D. J., and Oziel, L. J. *Sexual medicine and counseling in office practice*. Boston: Little, Brown, 1980.

New York Narcotic Addiction Control Commission. *Differential drug use within the New York State Labor Force: An assessment of drug use within the general population*, Albany, 1971.

O'Connor, D. Good girls and orgasms. *Newsweek*, October 22, 1979.

Peplau, L. A., and Cochran, S. D. *Sex differences in values concerning love relationships*. Paper presented at the Annual Meeting of the American Psychological Association, Montreal, September 1980.

Rainwater, L. Some aspects of lower-class sexual behavior. *Journal of Social Issues*, 1966, *22*, 96–108.

Raven, B. H. The comparative analysis of power and power preference. In J. R. Tedeschi (Ed.), *Perspectives on social power*. New York: Aldine-Atherton, 1974.

Reich, W. *The sexual revolution*. New York: Doubleday, 1945.

Reiss, I. The double standard in premarital sexual intercourse: A neglected concept. *Social Forces*, 1956, *34*, 224–230.

Riger, S., and Gordon, M. T. The fear of rape: A study in social control. *Journal of Social Issues*, 1981, *37*(4), 71–92.

Rook, K., and Hammen, C. A cognitive perspective on the experience of sexual arousal. *Journal of Social Issues*, 1977, *33*(2), 7–27.

Seidler-Feller, D. A feminist critique of sex therapy. In L. B. Rosewater, L. E. Walker, and P. G. Webbink (Eds.), *Feminist therapy: A coming of age*. New York: Springer, 1983.

Seligman, M. Depression and learned helplessness. In R. Friedman and M. Katz (Eds.), *The psychology of depression: Contemporary theory and research*. Washington, D.C.: Winston-Wiley, 1978.

Semans, J. Premature ejaculation, a new approach. *Southern Medical Journal*, 1956, *49*, 353–358.

Shaef, A. W. *Women's reality*. Winston Press, 1981.

Sherfey, M. J. *The nature and evolution of female sexuality*. New York: Random House, 1973.

Stock, W. E., and Roberts, C. W. Power conflict in sexually dysfunctional couples. In *New developments in sex therapy*. Symposium presented at the meeting of the American Psychological Association, Anaheim, California, August 26, 1983.

Symonds, A. Phobias after marriage: Women's declaration of dependence. *American Journal of Psychoanalysis*, 1971, *31*(2), 144–152.

Terman, L. M. Correlates of orgasmic adequacy in a group of 556 wives. *Journal of Psychology*, 1951, *32*, 115–172.

Tiefer, L. The context and consequences of contemporary sex research: A feminist perspective. In S. Cox (Ed.), *Female psychology: The emerging self* (2nd ed.). New York: St. Martin's Press, 1981.

Unger, R. K. (Discussant). *Symposium: Female-male differences in close relationships*. Presented at the Annual Meeting of the American Psychological Association, Montreal, 1980.

Vanacek, F. R. *Men's awareness training*. Unpublished manuscript, 1980.

Walen, S. R. Cognitive factors in sexual behavior. *Journal of Sex and Marital Therapy*, 1980, *6*(2), 87–101.

Wallace, D., and Barbach, L. G. Preorgasmic group treatment. *Journal of Sex and Marital Therapy*, 1974, *1*(2), 146–154.

Zilbergeld, B. *Male sexuality*. Boston: Little, Brown, 1978.

IV

Age-Related Disorders

12

Sex-Role Stereotypes and the Epidemiology of Child Psychopathology

Robert F. Eme

Introduction

Although the sex differences in adult psychopathology have been the subject of several examinations, there have been only a few systematic explorations of sex differences in child psychopathology. The most widely cited has been that of the sociologist Walter Gove (1979; Gove and Herb, 1974). Unfortunately, his work is limited since he superficially addresses the topic of the origin and development of sex differences, as is evident from his omission of any reference to the Maccoby and Jacklin (1974) landmark tome, and to many other writings on the origins and development of sex differences. These deficiencies have been corrected in more recent expositions (Eme, 1979; Al-Issa, 1982) and will, one hopes, be more fully rectified in the present examination.

My earlier article (Eme, 1979) incorporated as much of the relevant psychological literature on child sex differences as possible in its examination of sex differences in the rates of child psychopathology. I will utilize these developmental findings in the context of the commonly accepted assumption that psychopathological behavior is on a continuum with normal development and essentially represents a developmental deviance (cf., for example, Achenbach, 1982; Wynne and O'Connor, 1979). The present chapter represents an updated and more seasoned view of the earlier presentation.

Robert F. Eme • Clinical psychologist, Forest Hospital and Foundation, Des Plaines, and private practice, 731 Grey Street, Evanston, Illinois 60202.

2. Methodological Problems

Since this chapter reflects the bringing together of problems in three areas, methodological difficulties are magnified and reflect problems in the psychology of sex differences, in the classification of psychopathology, and in epidemiology. However, since it is beyond the scope of this review to engage in a detailed analysis of all these problems areas, the reader is advised to consult Anastasi (1979), Block (1976), Jacklin (1979a), Maccoby and Jacklin (1974), or Sherman (1978) for a discussion of general problems in the psychology of sex differences, and Achenbach and Edelbrock (1978), Cantwell (1980), Hobbs (1975), Quay (1979), or Rutter (1977a) for problems in classification. As for the epidemiological issues, some discussion here is necessary.

2.1. Epidemiological Problems

Methodological problems involved in diagnosing psychological disorders in epidemiological studies of adult populations have been described by Dohrenwend and Dohrenwend (1969, 1974) and Gould, Wunsch-Hitzig, and Dohrenwend (1981) as centering on the validity and reliability of the measures used to assign cases to the various categories. One of the more conspicuous examples in the child literature has been presented by Conger and Coie (1975) in their critique of the Langer, Gersten, Greene, Eisenberg, Herson, and McCarthy (1974) study of the prevalence of serious psychological disorder among random cross-sectional samples of 1034 Manhattan families and 1000 Manhattan families receiving welfare. Almost twice as many welfare children as children from the cross-sectional sample of families were found to be seriously impaired. However, Conger and Coie pointed out that almost twice as many welfare children as cross-section children also appeared in the psychologically healthy category, and they suggested that this illustrated a problem of validity as well as problems with second-person accounts (mothers describing the problems of their children).

Different concepts and methods of assessment have led to vastly different estimates of rates of psychopathology. Moreover, according to Dohrenwend and Dohrenwend (1969, 1974), there is no way to choose a subset of studies where more valid procedures have been employed. Rather, they suggest that consistent relationships among various social variables and types of disorder exist in spite of methodological differences (e.g., consistent relationships with social class, with rural versus urban location, and, more recently, with sex differences) and represent the most meaningful findings. If, as prior works suggest (Eme, 1979; Gove, 1979), there are consistent relationships between gender and child psychopathology from study to study, then, as with the adult literature, epidemiological investigations present meaningful findings worthy of attention.

A major limitation of the childhood literature is the relative paucity of sampling untreated cases. (Compare, for example, the Gould *et al.* (1981) review of the child literature with Dohrenwend and Dohrenwend's, 1969, 1974, of the adult literature.) Ideally, a case should not be defined in terms of treatment, since such data, confounded as they are with factors affecting the decision to seek treatment, may present a specious picture of the true prevalence of cases in a population. Hence, the scarcity of prevalence studies of untreated psychological disorders in children makes conclusions about sex differences somewhat tenuous, although Graham (1979) noted that the sex ratio of clinic referrals generally mirrors the picture in the total population. Thus, although the data base for studying sex differences in child psychological disorders is limited in comparison to the adult literature, it seems sufficient to warrant preliminary examination.

2.2. Sex Bias

Adding to the difficulties previously enunciated in deciding what is a "case," there is the further difficulty of what Maccoby and Jacklin term "observer bias," i.e., the extent to which sex stereotypes prejudice an observer's determination as to what constitutes a "case."

Observer bias, which has been examined almost exclusively in the adult literature, has essentially two facets, the first of which revolves around the issue of sex bias in the data based upon treatment statistics. This subject has evoked polar opinions, with Dohrenwend and Dohrenwend (1977) contending that treated rates can be expected to give a picture of excess pathology among women because women are more likely than men to avail themselves of help for personal problems from professionals in general, to admit distress, to define their problems in mental health terms, and to have relatively favorable attitudes toward psychiatric treatment. On the other hand, Gove (1979, 1980) steadfastly denies these biases and asserts that, if anything, mental disorder is more readily recognized among males and more severely reacted to, and hence, men are more subject than women to selective control through hospitalization.

Regardless of which position is correct, it is instructive to note the paradoxical consensus that, indeed, treatment statistics are marked by a sex bias, in the direction of either less personal tolerance of symptoms on the part of women or less societal tolerance of the symptoms manifested by men. Hence, the implication for the present review is obvious.

Data based on treatment statistics must be carefully scrutinized for such bias and buttressed by studies of untreated populations that, though alleged to suffer from the same malady, are, as we shall see, far more robust than is popularly believed.

The second facet pertains to statistics based upon untreated populations and concerns itself with the extent to which clinicians have different standards of mental health for men and women—standards that reflect the cultural sex role stereotypes—and hence evaluate cases in a prejudiced fashion. Since, in the large majority of epidemiological investigations, cases are defined by applying clinical judgments to symptom data collected mainly on the basis of personal interviews (Dohrenwend and Dohrenwend, 1974) or data garnered by lay interviewers (though a growing number of investigations are employing objectively scored measures of psychopathology), this is a potentially serious source of sex bias.

Fortunately, four current comprehensive reviews concur in concluding that sex bias in clinical judgment investigated by means of analogue studies (and this kind of study constitutes the bulk of the empirical evidence) has received a resoundingly negative verdict (Abramowitz and Docecki, 1977; Davidson and Abramowitz, 1980; Smith, 1980; Zeldow, 1978). Moreover, all agree that naturalistic data (which have admittedly notorious drawbacks, Davidson and Abramowitz, 1980) have likewise failed to support claims of widespread sex bias but have nonetheless whetted suspicions that sex role attributes affect clinical decisions. While some, such as Davidson and Abramowitz, would elevate these suspicions to such a status they induce an "empirical deadlock" with analogue studies and fuel the skepticism that sexism is not as rare as analogue studies would indicate, others such as Zeldow and Smith (present author included) would conclude that evidence of sex bias in clinical assessment is largely anecdotal and hence not of sufficient merit to generate a deadlock, however ominous or titillating one's suspicions might be.

Thus, though this problem cannot be cavalierly dismissed, it evidently does not have enough empirical support to date to warrant its being considered a serious confound. Moreover, since the most current review to date, i.e., Davidson and Abramowitz, could find only two studies that addressed this problem in clinical judgments of children, and since these studies themselves yielded inconsistent results, one is on an even firmer foundation in affirming that the evidence of sex bias in the clinical diagnosis of children is at best speculative. Ergo, while this possibility must always be considered in discussing sex differences in prevalence rates of psychopathology among children, such rates are best characterized as innocent of the charge of sexual bias until proven guilty.

2.3. Classification System

Like Dohrenwend and Dohrenwend (1974), I am defining psychopathology as those types of problematic childhood behaviors described by the DSM-III and operationalized by the various epidemiological investigators. Spitzer and Cantwell (1980) indicate that these disorders (which are subsumed under the DSM-III classification of "Disorders Usually First Evident in Infancy, Childhood or Adolescence") can be separated into five major groups based on the predominant area of disturbance: (1) intellectual (mental retardation, specific developmental disorder); (2) adjustment (any maladaptive reaction to an identifiable psychosocial stress); (3) behavioral (attention deficit disorder, conduct disorder); (4) emotional (anxiety disorders); (5) developmental (pervasive developmental disorders).*

Although this classification system is not without its shortcomings (Achenbach and Edelbrock, 1978; Quay, 1979; Rutter and Shaffer, 1980), Achenbach (1980) has indicated that there is a reasonably good correspondence between it and more empirically derived categories. More specific justification for this classification system is present in subsequent sections of this chapter.

3. Intellectual Disorders

3.1. Sex Differences in Diagnosis

Although there is general agreement on those disorders labeled intellectual, only the DSM-III (American Psychiatric Association, 1980) provides major subcategories of mental retardation and specific developmental disorders. DSM-III is employed in the present discussion since this subcategorization has received support from several sources (e.g., Rie, 1980). It should also be noted here that specific developmental disorders are also found under the labels "learning disability" and "minimal brain dysfunction" (Rie, 1980) and will be treated here as synonymous with them.

As indicated in DSM-III, mental retardation is defined as significantly subaverage general intellectual functioning, with concurrent deficits in adaptive behavior, whose onset occurs before age 18. Despite the vagaries in the application of this definition (e.g., Mercer (1973)), males

---

*The sequence in which these disorders will be considered reflects the DSM-III sequence except for the following changes, which were made in order to facilitate the discussion of sex differences: (1) Specific developmental disorders are considered under the rubric of intellectual rather than developmental disorders; (2) adjustment disorders are considered a subcategory of childhood disorders rather than a distinct diagnostic class.

have been found to predominate unequivocally. Whether one looks at comprehensive reviews of treated rates of this disorder, i.e., children identified in the school system or institutionalized (Tudor, Tudor, and Gove, 1980), or at the untreated rates arrived at through community studies (Lehrke, 1978), one finds remarkable agreement in this regard.

This same pattern of males outnumbering females repeats itself with respect to specific developmental disorders ("learning disability" or "minimal brain dysfunction"), defined by the DSM-III as significantly subaverage performance in reading, arithmetic, language, etc., not explained by mental retardation, impaired vision or hearing, inadequate schooling, or emotional disturbance. Again, regardless of the fact that the actual diagnosis of specific developmental disorder is subject to even more unreliability than that of mental retardation (Rie, 1980; Schere, Richardson, and Bialer, 1980; Torgesen, 1979), males clearly exceed females whether one considers comprehensive reviews of treated rates (Rutter and Yule, 1977) or untreated rates (Belmont, 1980).

Hence, virtually everyone accepts that males are more likely to be diagnosed as having an intellectual disorder. What is less commonly accepted is the extent to which this greater prevalence in both treated and untreated disorders reflects "true" prevalence. Some have contended that because males are expected to be more intellectually competent than females, societal reaction to males who have an apparent intellectual disorder is more prompt and severe (Tudor *et al.*, 1980). Hence, males are more likely to be diagnosed as having an intellectual disorder.

While few would quarrel with the contention that methodological problems may "partially," "to some extent," and so on, inflate male prevalence rates, especially for the more mildly impaired, this clearly is not the real issue. The thrust of those espousing this position is to explain a large portion (if not all) of the greater male prevalence in this fashion, despite occasional hints of more modest intentions (Anastasi, 1972; Nance and Engel, 1972; Tudor *et al.*, 1980). To evaluate the magnitude of this alleged bias, two aspects need consideration. First, the contention that male children are expected to be more intellectually competent than female children must be examined. And second, to the extent that this expectation exists, its putative biasing effects must be assessed.

With regard to the first contention, Block's (1976, 1978, 1979) reviews offer good support for the premise that parents and teachers place a greater emphasis on cognitive achievement for males than for females. Support for this premise, however, should not be construed to mean that parents and teachers have sex-biased attitudes in their evaluation of intellectual disorders in boys and girls.

Therefore, it becomes crucial to carefully evaluate the second aspect of the alleged sex bias, namely, the extent to which parental and teacher expectation of greater intellectual competence in males can be linked to sex-biased judgments of intellectual disorders. Tudor *et al.* forthrightly acknowledge the dearth of data on this issue when they report that they have been able to find only one analogue study (Guskin, 1963) that directly dealt with this subject. Moreover, this study, though it did find evidence for sex bias, involved not parents or teachers but the ubiquitous college student. Since there is agreement that analogue studies are absolutely necessary for the establishment of internally valid findings (Abramowitz and Docecki, 1977; Smith, 1980), it would appear that little more could be said other than concluding that the topic has not been adequately researched. Undaunted, however, by this dearth, Tudor *et al.* as well as others have turned exclusively to the genre of studies variously termed "naturalistic," "corelational," or "archival" and unanimously judged as frought with internal validity problems (Abramowitz and Docecki, 1977; Smith, 1980). Because of these intractable problems, equivocality of interpretation is the inevitable net result, as Lehrke's (1972a, 1972b, 1978) analyses have indicated.

Thus, the following points should be clear. First, even the most ardent proponents of the sex bias explanation for the greater male prevalence in intellectual disorders are reluctant to apply this interpretation to the greater male prevalence among the more severely impaired (Tudor *et al.*, 1980). Second, the allegation of sex bias in the diagnosis of intellectual disorders in children has scarcely been investigated in analogue studies. Third, while there does exist a body of naturalistic data that some find persuasive in implicating sex bias, such data, bereft of supporting analogue studies, are exceedingly vulnerable to countervailing interpretations and can scarcely be deemed compelling.

3.2. Biological Influences

Having suggested that the substantial male preponderance in intellectual disorders is reflective of the "true" prevalence in the population, a consideration of biological and environmental influences is in order. Although expository convenience dictates a discussion of these factors separately, the author considers these influences to operate not in isolation but in a complexly interactive fashion. An attempt will be made to determine, wherever possible, their *modus operandi* (Anastasi, 1979).

Since it is apparent from the literature that intellectual ability is subject to genetic influences (DeFries and Plomin, 1978; Hendersen, 1982; Willerman, 1979b), it is not unreasonable to postulate that the mentally retarded and those with specific developmental disorders, as a subsample of all intellectual traits, would also be influenced by genetic factors. Hence, an examination of possible genetic contributions provides a logical starting point for the consideration of biological factors in general.

With respect to mental retardation, two major hypotheses have been put forth, the first of which is termed the sex-modified threshold hypothesis. This hypothesis suggests that since males are more susceptible to mental retardation than females, and retarded mothers have an excess of retardation among their children when compared with retarded fathers, affected females have a more extreme threshold and need a greater "dose" of deleterious genes in order to develop retardation (Willerman, 1979a). This theorizing leads to several testable predictions. First, the sons of affected mothers should be the most frequently affected, while the daughters of affected fathers should be the least frequently affected.

This prediction was supported by Pauls (1979) in his analysis of data provided by the most complete family investigation of mental retardation to date (Reed and Reed, 1965). One cannot, however, rule out alternative environmental hypotheses by examining only the children of retarded individuals. It is possible that the excess of retardation among children of retarded mothers could be due either to the effects of the prenatal environment on the children or to the postnatal environment, since mothers, because they are undoubtedly more involved in child-rearing (Baumrind, 1980), presumably would have a greater effect on the child's intelligence.

Several weaknesses of the alternative environmental hypotheses exist. First, while an adverse prenatal environment could partially explain why retarded women have more retarded offspring than retarded men (for example, Bessman, 1980, provides an excellent discussion of how some mothers, who because they are heterozygous for phenylketonuria, are deficient in the delivery of appropriate amino acid nutrition to their fetus), it is unclear why males would be more adversely affected by an unfavorable prenatal environment (remember that male offspring of retarded women have the highest frequency of retardation). One would have to gratuitously hypothesize an interactive effect whereby this environment, because it has an impact on a generally more vulnerable male organism (evidence for which will be adduced in subsequent discussion), would be more deleterious. In addition, the postnatal environmental impact of mothers is rendered suspect when one considers that reviews of parent–offspring resemblance in IQ find children no more likely to resemble one parent or another, nor is there any greater similarity when the sex of parent and offspring are the same (McAskie and Clarke, 1976; Bouchard and McGue, 1981). Hence, if mothers do have a greater impact on a child's intellectual development, one wonders why maternal–offspring resemblance in IQ is not greater than paternal–offspring resemblance. Nor could this hypothesis conveniently explain the greater frequency of retardation among sons of retarded mothers, since, if identification theory has any relevance in this regard, one would expect it would be the daughters who were more frequently affected.

The most damaging case against the alternative environmental hypotheses, however, stems from the finding of a pattern of retardation among first- (other than parents), second-, and third-degree relatives similar to the pattern found among parents and offspring. Pauls (1979) indicates that the sex-modified threshold hypothesis would predict that the relatives of the least frequently retarded sex (females) should be at higher risk than the relatives of the more frequently retarded sex (males). This would be so since one would predict that the presumably heavier dosage of genes needed for the manifestation of retardation in females would have as its corollary a higher frequency of retardation among the relatives who would be, to some extent, sharing these genes, and vice versa for the relatives of the presumably less heavily dosed males. This is precisely the result Pauls reports, thus nicely fitting the threshold hypothesis and providing an embarrassment to the environmental hypotheses for which this pattern can only be deemed a discomfiting peculiarity in the data.

Last, it should be pointed out that Freire-Maia, Freire-Maia, and Morton (1974), in an analogous analysis of some of the Reed and Reed (1965) data, similarly find support for the threshold hypothesis, leaving no discrepancy for which the maternal–environmental hypothesis need be invoked.

With regard to learning disabilities in particular, the threshold hypothesis has recently been employed by Pennington and Smith (1983) in their sweeping examination of the genetic influences on learning disabilities. They concluded that it was clear that some forms of learning disability are transmitted genetically and, more important, that the greater male prevalence did not appear to be due to a sex-linked disorder but was more likely due in part to a normal, genetically based sex difference in language skills. That is, if there is a sex difference unfavorable to males in language ability (an hypothesis for which there is ample support as will be discussed) then it is theorized that other genetic and/or environmental factors would interact with this lower threshold to produce more learning-disabled males.

The second major genetic explanation that has been proposed to account in part for the greater male prevalence of retardation takes as its premise the alleged fact of a biologically based greater male variability. A current application of this principle to mental ability comes from Lehrke's (1972a, 1972b, 1978) X-linked theory of intellectual traits.

Lehrke maintains that males are more frequently represented at the extremes of the range of general intelligence. Furthermore, he proposes that this greater male variability is best explained by assuming that there are recessive genes for intelligence on the X-chromosome, which would explain this finding in the following fashion: Since females have two X-chromosomes, it is less likely that an extreme manifestation of any gene of the X-chromosome would appear since the effect of a particularly deviant allele would probably be moderated by that of the homologous gene remaining active in the corresponding X-chromosome. However, males lack this moderating influence (since the Y-chromosome is homologous for little, if any, of the genetic material on the X-chromosome); thus, they would be more likely to manifest the effects of a deviant allele whether for good (genius) or bad (retardation).

Though several have found this theory less than persuasive (Anastasi, 1972; Nance and Engel, 1972; Wittig, 1976), striking physical evidence has recently been accumulating from chromosome culture studies that would suggest that the X-linked theory possesses far more merit than heretofore suspected, albeit in a modified form. These studies (Gerald, 1980; Turner, Brookwell, Daniel, Selikowitz, and Zilbowitz, 1980) have found that among some male and female retardates there exist certain cytogenetic abnormalities in the X-chromosome (termed "the fragile X syndrome") whose result is retardation in males, but only partial expression for some female carriers because of what is termed Lyonization of the X-chromosome.

Thus, Lehrke's theory, albeit in a modified form, would seem to have a measure of validity. X-linked mental retardation seems firmly enough established, though the retardation is due to a chromosomal abnormality rather than to a genetic recessive pattern in inheritance. Moreover, its frequency in the population may be such that it could account for all of the excess of males who are affected with nonspecific (with no definite biochemical, chromosomal, or environmental cause) mental retardation (Herbst and Miller, 1980).

Another biological factor that doubtlessly contributes to the greater male prevalence in intellectual disorders is the commonly accepted fact that from the moment of conception, the male organism appears to be more vulnerable to a host of pre-, peri-, and postnatal stresses (Birns, 1976; Maccoby and Jacklin, 1974; Rutter, 1970; Willerman, 1979a).

McMillen's (1979) analysis has recently corroborated the previously established finding of more male fetal deaths prenatally. These deaths are highest from months 3 to 5, lower in months 6, 7, 8, and increase at term, yielding an excess of male mortality on the order of 6 to 13%. An intriguing corollary datum is that while the male–female ratio at conception is 120:100 (McMillen, 1979), in the lowest socioeconomic class this greater number of male deaths actually results in a greater proportion of female births (Willerman, 1979a). This greater male prenatal mortality rate persists through infancy and into adulthood, with males succumbing more frequently to the pernicious effects of stress and disease (Garai and Scheinfeld, 1968; Willerman, 1979a).

Peri- and postnatally, males suffer more complications of pregnancy and childbirth (Rutter, 1970), are more often born with congenital malformations (Willerman, 1979a), and more often die or are hospitalized because of accidents (Block, 1979; Willerman, 1979a). Moreover, males are more likely to be affected by a given pre-, peri-, or postnatal insult than are females. For example, with regard to prematurity, Braine, Heimer, Wortis, and Freedman (1966) reported that in a sample of 346 preterm infants, males did significantly less well than females of the same birth weight on the Cattell Infant Scale at 13½ months, whereas no sex difference was found in the full-term control infants. Concerning the effects of perinatal anoxia, Gottfried (1973) in his review pointed out that sex differences have been noted in the early years, with males being more likely to be at a disadvantage in intellectual, physical, and neurological development. They are also more likely to suffer ill effects from malnutrition (Tanner, 1970, 1978) and radiation (Rutter, 1970).

The reasons commonly cited for this greater male vulnerability are greater male immaturity and greater susceptibility to sex-linked diseases (Rutter, 1970) and lesser resistance to infectious diseases in general because of the lack of the second X-chromosome, which is thought to confer certain immunological advantages (Carter, 1978) and more complex prenatal development with the concomitant greater opportunity for error (Reinisch, Gandelman, and Spiegal, 1979).

Once the commonly accepted finding of a greater male vulnerability to a variety of pre-, peri-, and postnatal insults has been documented, its contribution to explaining the greater male prevalence in intellectual disorders is obvious. These and other stresses are implicated, as being likely etiological agents, in standard works on mental retardation, e.g., Ingalls (1978), and specific developmental disorders, e.g., Martin (1980), Pirozzolo, Campanella, Christensen, and Lawson-Kerr (1981), and Rourke (1978). Hence, greater male vulnerability to these stresses predisposes them to greater likelihood of incurring intellectual disorders.

A less commonly known finding is that males are more likely to suffer deleterious sequelae as a result of these stresses. Thus, Knopp and Parmelee (1979) report in their authoritative review of prenatal and postnatal stresses that while both sexes showed more evidence of school problems as compared with controls, the percentage of males with difficulties was generally greater than that of females. Further corroboration of this is found in the Kauai longitudinal study of infants who were judged to be "at risk" because of perinatal stress (Werner and Smith, 1979). These authors reported that while there were no sex differences in the proportion of surviving boys and girls who had been exposed to moderate and severe perinatal complications, twice as many boys as girls were considered in need of placement in learning-disability classes by age 10.

The third and final biological factor to be considered, and the one most commonly cited as contributing to the greater male prevalence in the intellectual disorders (e.g., Gove and Herb, 1974; Gove, 1979), is that of the greater immaturity of the male organism. In the most extensive review to date of sex-related differences in maturation, Waber (1979) argues that this is a well-established difference, easily observable in such somatic features as bone length, and demonstrated to occur in the maturation of the central nervous system in terms of neuromotor functions, motor sequencing, and linguistic functions. From the middle of the fetal period onward, the average girl is ahead of the average boy, and this difference is such that in terms of physical maturation, girls are ahead of boys by 1 year at school entrance, 1½ years at age 9, and 2 years at the onset of puberty (Garai and Scheinfeld, 1968; Tanner, 1978). Tanner (1970) hypothesized that the male maturational lag is probably due, indirectly, to the action of the genes on the Y-chromosome. Thus, children with the abnormal chromosome constitution XXY (Klinefelter's syndrome) have a skeletal maturity indistinguishable from that of the normal male, and children with the chromosome constitution XO (Turner's syndrome) have a skeletal maturity approximating that of the normal female XX constitution.

This earlier physical and central nervous system maturation of females appears to be paralleled by a greater intellectual maturation. Although Bayley (1956) indicated that physical growth, as measured by height and skeletal maturity, is positively correlated with IQ scores, in individual cases, physical growth (as measured by percentage of mature height achieved) is not correlated with IQ measured in terms of percentage of 21-year-old intelligence scores achieved. However, Bayley clearly indicated that this lack of correlation pertains only to individuals. Sherman (1978) suggested that although physical growth spurt might not correlate with mental growth spurt within individuals, groups could differ, with both the physical and mental growth spurts coming earlier in females. Support for this observation is found in Tanner's (1970, 1978) review of the relationship between physical maturation and mental ability, where he recorded that the more physically mature scored higher on mental tests in North American and European populations at all ages tested, going back as far as 6½ years. He thus concluded that in age-linked examinations, more physically mature children have a significantly better chance than less mature children.

Though this theory enjoys widespread support, there are some who would demur. For example, Bank, Biddle, and Good (1980) in their literature review of sex roles, classroom instruction, and reading achievement argue that the immaturity hypothesis cannot account for the fact that males excel in math or for the cross-cultural research findings showing that males in some cultures outperform females.

These difficulties, however, are not that formidable. First, it should be noted that Bank *et al.* (1980) would more accurately cite Maccoby and Jacklin (1974) in regard to greater male math excellence if they indicated that this superiority does not begin to emerge until sometime around puberty. Subsequent research has confirmed this finding, except in gifted samples (Meece, Parsons, Kazala, Goff, and Futterman, 1982). Second, as Waber (1979) has made clear, puberty is a critical developmental marker with regard to sex-related differences in cognitive ability, i.e., the decline of motor and linguistic advantages of females, prominent during childhood, and the emergence of greater male spatial ability that has been found to undergird greater male math ability (McGee, 1979; Sherman, 1978, 1980). Hence, it is likely that a reorganization of brain functions occurs as part of the pubertal maturational spurt in the CNS, and that sex-related maturational variations are implicated in this reorganization.

In an encyclopedic review of the literature on sex differences in cerebral asymmetry, Levy (1981) convincingly argued that there is a decided maturational advantage of the left hemisphere in girls and of the right hemisphere in boys. This advantage would help explain the sex difference in the earlier emerging verbal-communicative functions (mediated by the left hemisphere) in girls and spatial-schematic functions (mediated by the right hemisphere) in boys. These earlier developing processes would then be hypothesized to gain a guiding role over subsequent maturation of functions, either because of inbuilt maturational programs or because the earlier developing capacities would have prior access to environmental reinforcement, or, more likely, both, which would reach fruition in puberty.

With regard to the cross-cultural finding, Jacklin (1979a) has aptly pointed out that these studies are few in number and methodologically suspect because of the likelihood of differential attrition of underachieving males.

3.3. Environmental Influences

Now that we have discussed the more probable biological factors involved in the greater male prevalence of the intellectual disorders, an analysis of the more commonly hypothesized environmental factors is in order. One such factor (which would be a corollary of the foregoing account) is that boys experience a greater difference between their ability and the expectations of others (i.e., parents and teachers) than do girls, and hence experience more stress with its concomitant deleterious effect on performance. Further elaboration on this hypothesis is contained in the work of McGuinness (1976, 1979), who contends that, especially in the early school years, the focus is on teaching skills that favor the more developmentally mature females. For example, the greater female facility in linguistic and fine-motor functioning translates into greater proficiency in such areas as reading, expressive and receptive communication skills, writing, drawing, pasting, painting, etc., while their greater attentional capacity would further enhance their superiority in these and numerous other areas. These, along with the many other examples that she furnishes, add further weight to the contention that schools may unwittingly contribute to the greater male prevalence in intellectual disorders because of the lack of adaptation to the greater immaturity of the male.

Other environmental factors influencing the differential prevalence in intellectual disorder have been recently reviewed and evaluated by Bank et al. (1980). Since the majority of primary teachers in the United States are women, writers as early as 1909 have suggested that female teachers may be prejudiced against boys, may discriminate against them in the classroom, are insensitive to male interests, or create an environment in which the accomplishments of girls are more often encouraged. However, studies that have compared the effects of male and female teachers have found weak and contradictory evidence concerning the effects of teachers' sex on the achievement of males and females (Bank et al., 1980; Good and Brophy, 1977), and female teacher bias has yet to be substantiated (Serbin, 1980).

4. Adjustment Disorder of Childhood

4.1. Sex Difference in Diagnosis

The essential feature of an adjustment disorder of childhood is maladaptive reaction to an identifiable psychosocial stressor that occurs within 3 months after the onset of the stressor. Hence, the disturbance can include virtually any symptom as long as it is not merely an instance of a pattern of overreaction to a stressor or an exacerbation of an existing mental disorder (DSM-III).

While it is clear that in studies of treated cases males exceed females (Anthony, 1970; Gove, 1979), in studies of untreated cases the picture becomes somewhat muddled, since the specific diagnosis of adjustment disorder is rarely formally employed. However, if one assumes that sex differences in adjustment disorders are reflected in sex differences in overall rates of psychopathology, then here also males outnumber females in ratios of about two to one (Gould, *et al.*, 1981; Graham, 1979).

4.2. Biological Influences

The first factor to be considered is that of temperament. This concept, *ipso facto*, contains no inference as to either biologic or environmental etiology (Thomas, 1976), and knowledge of the origins of temperamental differences is extremely fragmentary. Nonetheless, Rutter (1982a) and Bates (1980) conclude that the differences are certainly due in part to genetic factors, and to an important but uncertain extent to physical and psychosocial factors as well. Hence, its consideration under the rubric of biological factors is simply meant to indicate that it has a constitutional basis and not that it is unaffected by environment (cf., for example, Sameroff, 1978).

The relevance of this factor to the present discussion stems from two sets of findings. The first, based upon Rutter's (1977c) review, indicates that there is good evidence that individual temperamental differences play an important role in the development of psychological problems. A child thought to be especially at risk was characterized as one who is emotionally tense, who is slow to adapt to new situations, whose behavior is difficult to change, who has irregular eating, sleeping, and bowel habits, who tends to be irritable and negative in mood, and who is unusually tolerant of messiness and disorder.

Rutter (1977b) found that children with these temperamental characteristics were more likely than other children to be the subjects of parental criticism and scapegoating and hence at greater psychiatric risk. This theory suggests that when parents are depressed and irritable, they do not "pick on" each of their children to the same extent; they are more likely to take it out on the child with "difficult" tempermental features.

Second, males may be more apt to possess at least some characteristics of the "difficult" child and/or more likely to elicit an adverse reaction to those characteristics than may the female. The evidence for this is mixed and stems from findings such as those of Moss (1974), who, in summing up 10 years of his work with infants, consisting of several independent studies, concluded that males were generally more irritable than females. However, if one reviews studies that have attempted to establish standardization data on temperament (e.g., Carey, 1970; Kronstadt, Oberklaid, Berg, and Swartz, 1979; Persson-Blennow and McNeil, 1979), then one would have to conclude that only minor and inconsistent sex differences have been found for specific categories, and none for overall categorization of "easy" or "difficult."

The evidence is similarly mixed when the possibility of a sex-related difference in the maternal threshold for male "difficultness" is evaluated. While support for this possibility is found in Osofsky and Connor's (1979) extensive review of mother–infant interaction, countervailing data is evidenced in studies by Bates, Freeland, and Lounsbury (1979); Cameron (1978); Kronstadt, Oberklaid, Berg, and Swartz (1979); and Scholom, Zucker and Stollak (1979). In short this is an area that has only begun to be explored (Rutter, 1982a).

However, the possibility of significant sex differences cannot be satisfactorily assessed if reference is not also made to the previously discussed findings of greater male central nervous system immaturity and greater susceptibility to brain dysfunction and other handicapping conditions. These factors would clearly seem to place the male at a greater risk of developing a "difficult" temperament (Bates, 1980; Parsons, 1980; Rutter, 1977c; Thomas and Chess, 1975; Werry, 1979a) and hence of incurring adjustment problems. Since the preceding normative studies of temperament such as the now-classic New York longitudinal study have tended to exclude children suspected of having any kind of physical or neurological abnormality, they would be somewhat limited in their ability to detect the sex difference in question.

In sum, while the findings that would support alleged sex difference in temperament are hardly robust, there would seem to be sufficient evidence to suggest that the contribution of temperament to a greater male prevalence in adjustment disorders warrants further study.

4.3. Environmental Influences

Rutter (1970) has hypothesized that, analagous to the greater male vulnerability to biological stress, there exists a greater susceptibility to psychological stress as well.

Research relevant to this hypothesis can be loosely grouped in two categories: studies cognate to Rutter's initial research on adjustments to marital discord and related studies, e.g., reaction to adoption.

Rutter (1970) conducted a study of 200 families and matching controls in which one of the parents was a psychiatric patient. The sample contained an equal number of male and female psychiatric patients who had one or more children under the age of 15. Information about the families was obtained by psychiatric interview of the parents and information about the children's psychiatric state was obtained by teacher questionnaire. Discord and disruption in the home was found to be consistently and strongly associated with antisocial disorder in boys, but not in girls. No consistent associations were found between family characteristics and neurosis in either boys or girls. Nor did the sex of the parent bear a relation to the likelihood of the children's developing a psychiatric disorder. Rutter considered and dismissed a number of methodological biases as alternate explanations for this provocative sex difference in preadolescent children and concluded that, though the evidence is surprisingly meager, males appeared to be more vulnerable to adverse effects of family discord and disruption.

Subsequent research has tended to support Rutter's findings. In a comprehensive review of the relation between marital discord and problem behavior in children, Emery (1982) concluded that marital turmoil is more strongly related to boys' than to girls' obviously maladaptive behavior. He cautioned, however, that it is possible that girls may be just as troubled by marital discord as boys are, but they may demonstrate their feelings in a manner that is more appropriate to their sex role, namely, by becoming anxious, withdrawn, or perhaps very well behaved.

Other relevant studies focus on reactions to separation and deprivation, adoption, divorce, and maternal employment.

In his review of the literature on maternal deprivation, Rutter (1972a) pointed out that findings on sex differences were somewhat contradictory and nonexistent in many studies. However, where there has been a difference, the male has usually been found to be the more vulnerable. Rutter's (1979) more recent review of this literature reached essentially the same conclusion. Bowlby (1973) arrived at a similar conclusion in his review of the literature on separation anxiety. Of five studies, three found no sex difference and two found that males showed greater separation anxiety than females. Maccoby and Jacklin (1974) reported several studies of children aged 10 months to 3 years in which males exhibited greater resistance to separation, as indicated by greater distress at separation or greater likelihood of quickly following the departed figure. More recent studies have yielded the same results; i.e., infant boys are more distressed than girls upon separation (Lewis, 1979), although there are exceptions (Ainsworth, Blehar, Waters, and Wall, 1978).

A related group of studies focuses on adopted children. In a review of this literature, Hersov (1977a) concluded that these and other stresses place adopted children at greater risk for the development of psychiatric disorder, and in the few studies with a control group, males have been found to be more at risk than females.

With regard to divorce, comprehensive reviews by Heatherington (1979) and Kurdek (1981) indicated that there was substantial evidence that sons of divorced parents experience more problems in the areas of cognitive, emotional, and social development and more specific divorce adjustment difficulties than do daughters of divorced parents or children from intact families.

A similar pattern emerges from recent reviews of the effects of nonmaternal care on children. Rutter's (1981) conclusion, which is consonant with those of Etaugh (1980) and Hoffman (1979), indicated that the effects of day care on boys is congruent with other research indicating a greater male vulnerability to psychological stress.

Research findings that have accumulated since Rutter's initial finding of a greater male vulnerability to psychological stress are far less meager than a decade ago. And as Lewis (1979) indicated, these findings run contrary to the male stereotype but fit a more general biological pattern of greater male susceptibility to stress.

5. Behavior Disorders

5.1. Sex Difference in Diagnosis

Both DSM-III and the empirical approaches are in agreement in positing a category of disorders whose predominant area of disturbance is overt, externalized, and undercontrolled, reflecting conflict with the environment (Achenbach, 1980; Spitzer and Cantwell, 1980). Almost by definition this category includes conduct disorders and attention deficit disorders.

Whether hyperactivity and conduct disorder are essentially the same psychopathological disturbance constitutes one of the most heated controversies in the literature today (Barkley, 1982) and most certainly will not be resolved in the present discussion. Rather it is sufficient to note that since an empirical scheme to enable the clinician to arrive at a reliable differential diagnosis has yet to be devised (Herbert, 1982), these disorders have undoubtedly been conflated in epidemiological studies and hence can justifiably be grouped together for the purposes of the present exposition.

Thus, what will be examined are sex-related differences in the prevalence of those disorders whose common factor is aggression, either physical or verbal, and whose manifestations include fighting, hitting, assaultive; temper tantrums; disruptive, interrupts, disturbs; negative, refuses directions; hyperactive, distractible; steals; lies; negative, refuses direction; restless; boisterous, noisy; irritability, "blows up easily"; etc. (Quay, 1979).

The most unequivocal sex-related difference is the decisive male preponderance in aggressive behavior (Block, 1976, 1978, 1979; Feshbach, 1970; Garai and Scheinfeld, 1968; Maccoby and Jacklin, 1974, 1980; Terman and Tyler, 1954) and activity level (Maccoby and Jacklin's conclusion notwithstanding). As Block (1976, 1979) pointed out, Maccoby and Jacklin not only erred in their interpretation of some studies but they also omitted other relevant studies, all of which reported a higher activity level for males. This finding is further reflected in the fact that mortality figures among children aged 1–4 show that boys are much more likely than girls to die from accidents, a difference present around age 1 (Willerman, 1979a).

This difference in aggression and activity level is equally unequivocal in those cases where its manifestation is judged to take the form of a conduct disorder (Graham, 1979; Wolff, 1977), an attention deficit disorder (Cantwell, 1977; Ross and Pelham, 1981; Weiss and Hechtman, 1979), or miscellaneous externalizing symptoms (Anthony, 1970). The extent of those differences has been estimated as 3:1 in the conduct disorders (Graham, 1979) and from 4:1 to 9:1 in the attention deficit disorders (Cantwell, 1978; Weiss and Hechtman, 1979).

Having demonstrated that males predominate in the behavior disorders, what remains to be established is the likelihood that this preponderance reflects true prevalence and not sex-biased diagnoses. In this regard it seems satisfactory to note that while factors have been identified as moderating this difference (Caplan, 1979; Frodi, Macaulay, and Thome, 1977), no one contends that the greater male prevalence in aggressive behavior is not valid.

5.2. Biological Influences

The first hypothesis is reminiscent of the sex-modified threshold hypothesis that was discussed in regard to the greater male prevalence in mental retardation. As articulated by Maccoby and Jacklin (1974, 1980), this hypothesis suggests that because of the Y-chromosome's role in the secretion of androgen, males have a lower threshold for instigator stimuli, resulting in greater "ease of learning" of aggression than females. This role is hypothesized to be in evidence prenatally when androgen has an "organizing" influence on the central nervous system and postnatally when it has an "activating" function on concurrent behavior.

The activating function of androgen is not especially relevant for the study of sex differences in aggression during childhood since after about age 3 months, and until puberty, there is very little difference between boys and girls in the circulating level of this hormone, and the level itself is very low (Maccoby and Jacklin, 1980). Moreover, the whole issue of correlating testosterone levels in males with contemporaneous hostile or violent tendencies has recently been examined by Maccoby and Jacklin (1980), Rubin, Reinisch, and Haskett (1981), and Tieger (1980), who deemed the data suggestive but far from conclusive.

Hence, if androgen is an important factor during childhood, it is more likely to be via its organizing function, which occurs during prenatal development. And it is precisely in this latter circumstance that persuasive evidence has accumulated for a greater male predisposition toward aggression. More precisely, the evidence converges toward establishing a disposition toward a higher activity level, which in turn would then be hypothesized to be the precursor of a higher level of aggression (Patterson, Littman, and Bricker, 1967).

Several research reviews of the animal literature have documented the contribution of androgen as a predisposition to aggression. Erhardt and Meyer-Bahlburg (1979, 1981), Hart (1974), Maccoby and Jacklin (1974, 1980), Money and Erhardt (1972), Quadagno, Briscoe, and Quadagno (1977), and Tieger (1980) have all concluded that whereas the male of the vertebrate species is the more aggressive in both laboratory and natural situations, the perinatal administration of the hormone to females (thus mimicking what typically takes place in males because of the Y chromosome) results in levels of rough-and-tumble play and/or aggression approximating that of male animals.

Analogous findings have been reported in samples of fetally androgenized human females for physical energy expenditure, rough-and-tumble play, and aggressive potential (Erhardt, 1979; Erhardt and Meyer-Bahlburg, 1979, 1981; Meyer-Bahlburg and Erhardt, 1982; Reinisch, 1981). When combined with the parallels from animal research, these findings strongly suggest the predisposing role of prenatal androgens. Moreover, criticisms that these studies have not been sufficiently replicated (McGuire, Ryan and Omenn, 1975) or can be interpreted in terms of parental attitude (Quadagno et al., 1977) are not compelling.

In response to the former criticism, it should be noted that the replication attempt differed in medical and psychological assessment (Erhardt and Meyer-Bahlburg, 1979), and though its findings were not significant, they were in the expected direction, i.e., toward a higher level of physical energy expenditure in fetally androgenized females as compared with controls.

With regard to the latter criticism, while it is true that the cortisone therapy that females received whose fetal androgenization was caused by congenital andrenal hyperplasia may have fueled differential parental expectations, and hence affected the findings, this could not account for those females whose syndrome was progestin-induced and hence not in need of such treatment.

Moreover, Reinisch and Karow (1977) in their review of the effects of prenatal exposure to synthetic progestins and estrogens on human development concluded that it seemed unlikely that the fact that the parent knew the child was treated had a significant effect on the rearing of the offspring. If anything, Erhardt and Meyer-Bahlburg (1981) indicated that parents tended to oppose rather than encourage those temperamental characteristics of their daughters that appeared to be the sequelae of their specific prenatal hormone condition: e.g., if concerned about tomboyism, they tended to encourage femininity.

The second hypothesis that is commonly cited is the generally greater male body size, muscular strength, and speed and coordination of gross bodily movements (Anastasi, 1979) that would seem to be both logically and empirically related to aggression. Those differences, however, do not become that significant until puberty (Tanner, 1978; Willerman, 1979a), and hence this hypothesis would seem to have but minimal relevance for explaining the childhood sex difference in aggression.

The third hypothesis relates to the greater central nervous system immaturity of the male (due to the Y-chromosome). In comprehensive reviews of psychophysiological research with hyperactive children, Hastings and Barkley (1978) and Ross and Pelham (1981) concluded that some of these children are probably underreactive to environmental stimulation or "underarousable." One interpretation of this "underarousability" would be to postulate nervous system immaturity (Hastings and Barkley, 1978), or "developmental lag" (Kenny, 1980), as a likely etiological factor, though all recognize the need for more research.

The fourth hypothesis is based upon the greater prevalence of brain damage among males and its relationship to the hyperkinetic syndrome. It is commonly believed that some type of subtle central nervous system dysfunction is involved in an unknown number of cases (Cantwell, 1977; Ross and Pelham, 1981; Werry, 1979a), though the exact mechanisms that generate this association are still largely speculative (Rutter, 1977b, 1982b). Hence, since males are more likely to sustain neurological impairment, they can be expected to be more apt to develop externalizing symptoms.

5.3. Environmental Influences

Traditionally, authors such as Bardwick (1971), Feshbach (1970), Mischel (1966), and Mussen (1969) have argued that direct socialization pressure, largely mediated by the process of differential reinforcement, adequately depicted the environmental contribution to the sex-related difference in aggression, until, that is, the appearance of Maccoby and Jacklin's landmark book in 1974. Contrary to scholarly and popular opinion alike, Maccoby and Jacklin concluded that direct socialization pressure was clearly insufficient to account for the difference. This rude affront to conventional theorizing was reaffirmed in 1980 by them and endorsed by other theorists such as Lewis (1979).

Having duly noted the current skepticism with regard to the role of differential reinforcement, it should likewise be understood that the case has undoubtedly been overstated. Block (1976, 1978, 1979), for example, has painstakingly underlined the conceptual, sampling, and methodological problems characterizing many of the studies that provided the empirical base for the foregoing revisionist position. When these problems are addressed, she finds convincing evidence to support the position that, for males, agentic interests (i.e., competitive, aggressive, egocentric) tend to be differentially reinforced.

What other processes are involved? One answer that immediately suggests itself, of course, is modeling theory. Maccoby and Jacklin, however, have found several reasons to be dissatisfied with this theory. Principally, their reviews indicate that children have not been shown to resemble closely the same-sex parent in their behavior, nor do they characteristically select the model whose sex matches their own.

Lewis (1979) has disputed this conclusion by pointing out that Maccoby and Jacklin's own data suggest that children between the ages of 3 and 5 tend to imitate same-sex parents. He indicated, as was shown with the reinforcement literature by Block, that several factors may have contributed to a similar lack of clarity in the modeling literature, with the most important factor being the task to be modeled. Nevertheless, it would appear that Maccoby and Jacklin have correctly concluded that the explanatory power of this theory has been exaggerated with regard to aggression.

Disenchantment with the sufficiency of the two traditional foregoing theories has spawned interest in a third process that was first systematically enunciated by Kohlberg (1966). Simplistically stated, he proposed that a child gradually develops the concepts of "masculinity" and "femininity," and when he has understood what his own sex is, he attempts to match his behavior to his concepts. Stressing the inadequacy of the traditional theories, it was precisely this process that Maccoby and Jacklin have endorsed as providing the most satisfying socialization explanation for the sex difference in aggression. Since then, other theorists such as Lewis (1979) and Martin and Halverson (1981) have more fully articulated this kind of theorizing.

This model holds to the principle that it is the development of gender identity that, for the most part, controls the acquisition and development of sex role behavior. Through verbal behavior and various activities, discriminable features that differentiate the genders and define appropriate behavior for that culture are generated. It is then proposed that stereotypes are generated that function as schemas to organize and structure information and influence behavior.

In conclusion, while none will find it revelatory that differential socialization is undoubtedly a factor in explaining the greater male prevalence in the behavior disorders, it is illuminating to learn that not only direct socialization for aggression but also, and perhaps even more so, the male child's active identification with the role of the male as the aggressor is the environmental process that generates this sex-related difference.

6. Emotional Disorders

6.1. Sex Difference in Diagnosis

DSM-III and empirical approaches are in agreement in positing a category of disorders whose predominant area of disturbance is emotional, internalized, reflecting a problem primarily within the self (Achenbach, 1980; Spitzer and Cantwell, 1980). As Quay (1979) indicated, while the labels have varied, the meaning that is conveyed is that of withdrawal rather than attack, of isolation rather than active engagement, and of subjectively experienced anxiety rather than the apparent freedom from anxiety characterizing the behavioral or externalizing disorders.

The principal features of this classification are as follows: anxious, fearful, tense; shy, timid, bashful; withdrawn, seclusive, friendless; depressed, sad, disturbed; etc. (Quay, 1979), as well as a variety of somatic complaints that would be labeled psychophysiological disorders (Achenbach, 1980; Achenbach and Edelbrock, 1978).

In contrast to the other categories examined in this review, there is no consensus with regard to the sex ratio. Reviews by Hersov (1977b) and Graham (1979) combined with the results of the largest and most comprehensive epidemiological survey ever undertaken—the British National Child Development Study (Scott, 1978)—would indicate that the sex ratio is approximately equal. However, the review by Rutter and Garmezy (1983) along with the findings of the best-designed epidemiological study to date for comparing behavior problems for treated and untreated populations (Achenbach and Edelbrock, 1981), would indicate that females exceed males in emotional disorder. This lack of consensus stands in stark contrast to the decisive male preponderance in all the other major classifications of child psychopathology that have and will be discussed, and to the equally pronounced excess of females in the adult emotional disorders (see other chapters in this volume). The most likely explanation for these conflicting findings would seem to be, as Links (1983) recently noted, that prevalence estimates are heavily dependent on the manner in which the symptoms or disorder (a collection of symptoms) are defined. Furthermore, he notes that the frequency of individual symptoms may be quite high, but the prevalence of specific disorders will be much less, indicating that the prevalence studies of childhood neurosis offer an especially striking example of this fact.

Accordingly, it may be that the sex ratio depends on how one defines emotional disorder. A careful reading of the conflicting reviews and studies suggests that the sex ratio is judged approximately equal when the definition of neurosis is one of "disorder" but is judged to indicate a greater female prevalence when the definition is more one of "symptom." Thus a broader definition may yield a sex difference whereas a narrower definition would not.

Whatever the reason for this state of affairs, the ambiguity of the findings in childhood yields to clear-cut findings in adulthood, and this change would seem to involve more than a simple change in diagnostic rigor, since there is no evidence that adult diagnoses are appreciably more reliable than child diagnoses (Eysenck, Wakefield, and Friedman, 1983).

Last, it should be noted that the question of sex bias in the diagnosis of emotional disorders in children was addressed earlier in section 2.2, and it is evident that what meager data do exist are contradictory and certainly provide no reasonable grounds for rejecting the essential parity in the childhood sex ratio.

6.2. Explanations

Block (1978) in her review of the socialization literature provides the key to understanding this change when she indicates that socialization becomes more sex-differentiated with the increasing age of the child, reaching a maximum in the high school years. Hence, the hypothesis is generated that males become increasingly more likely to externalize their response to stress, and females to internalize, with the resultant clear excess of females in the adult emotional disorders.

This notion receives support in a study by Cramer (1979) on defense mechanisms in adolescence, using an objective instrument called the Defense Mechanism Inventory. According to Cramer, while studies of adults have found consistent sex differences, with males tending to use defenses that externalized conflict and females dealing with conflict internally, younger age groups had not been studied. In this study, adolescents generally showed a sex-related pattern of defense choice similar to that found in adults, and this choice became stronger during the adolescent period.

Furthermore, there is clinical speculation that because of the cultural proscription against male emotionality (Block, 1979), males may learn to mask the neurotic expression of their problems in much the same way that Kagan and Moss (1972) have suggested that they mask expressions of dependency. For example, Toolan (1962) and Glaser (1967) have both indicated that many of the acting-out symptoms of adolescents may camouflage underlying depression.

For example, although Weissman and Klerman (1977) concluded that alcohol abuse and criminal behavior cannot facilely be considered as the male equivalent of depressive disorders, they warned that the hypothesis that a substantial portion of depressed men appear under the diagnostic rubric of alcoholism or criminality cannot be ruled out. This may explain why Edelbrock and Achenbach (1980), in one of the most sophisticated factor-analytic studies to date of syndromes derived from parental report of clinic-attending children (aged 6–16 years), indicated that all samples, except the 12- to 16-year-old male sample, yielded a factor labeled depression. Not surprisingly, Graham and Rutter (1977) indicated that whereas boys with disturbances of conduct are likely to be referred to a psychiatrist, these same personality disturbances or criminal behaviors are likely to be dealt with in other ways when they get older.

In conclusion, the "altered" sex ratio in the emotional disorders that becomes increasingly clear in adolescence (Graham, 1979) would seem to be due in part to the increasingly greater likelihood of females to internalize and of males to externalize their reactions to stress. In childhood, however, one would hypothesize that the sex-differentiated socialization processes that foster these modes of reacting are appreciably less pronounced, with the result that a sex difference is more problematic.

7. Pervasive Developmental Disorders

7.1. Diagnosis

Children with severe impairments of social interaction, abnormalities of language development involving both speech and gesture, and a behavioral repertoire mainly of repetitive, stereotyped activities beginning from birth, or within the first years of life, have been described by a number of writers who have traditionally termed this pattern of impairments "childhood psychosis," "childhood autism," or "childhood schizophrenia" (Wing and Gould, 1979). More recently, however, there has been a general recognition that the term *childhood psychosis* is no longer useful since it may mislead one into assuming an association between this condition and adult psychotic disorders, a possibility that appears more and more remote (DeMyer, Hingtgen, and Jackson, 1981). Reflecting this attitude, DSM-III uses the term *pervasive developmental disorder* and includes infantile autism as one category under this general classification. Schizophrenia in childhood, on the other hand, is classified under the same categories used for the adult schizophrenias. In contrast to the foregoing distinction between infantile autism and childhood schizophrenia, for which there exists widespread support (Rutter, 1977d; Schopler, 1979), other categories such as "symbiotic psychosis," "autistic psychopathy," etc., are primarily of historical interest, being bereft of replicated empirical data (Schopler, 1979).

As autism is the pervasive developmental disorder most characteristic of childhood (Rutter, 1977d), it, along with childhood schizophrenia, will provide the focus for the following discussion. The multitude of other categories, which DSM-III would subsume under the rubric of "childhood onset, pervasive developmental disorder," will not be considered because of the previously mentioned dearth of data (Schopler, 1979).

7.2. Autism: Diagnosis and Sex Difference

DSM-III has defined autism as a syndrome whose onset occurs before 30 months and whose principal features are (1) pervasive lack of responsiveness to other people, (2) gross deficits in language development, (3) bizarre responses to various aspects of the environment, (4) absence of delusions, hallucinations, loosening of associations, and incoherence, as in schizophrenia.

As regards the sex ratio, there is universal agreement that males outnumber females by about 4:1 (DeMyer *et al.*, 1981; Ritvo and Freeman, 1978; Rutter, 1978; Schopler, 1978; Werry, 1979b). The magnitude of this disparity, coupled with the consensus that among severely impaired children the effect of sex bias in diagnosis is unremarkable (Tudor *et al.*, 1980), dictates that a discussion of this difference is mandated.

7.3. Explanation of the Sex Difference

Concerning etiology there is little support for environmental causation, particularly in the form of parental pathology, since parents of autistic children have been found to be no different from parents of other children with organic brain disorders and hence do not contribute in some unique and sufficient manner to the development of the disorder (DeMyer et al., 1981; Werry, 1979b).

There is a consensus, however, that autism is best explained as a physical dysfunction of the central nervous system, the exact nature and type of which has yet to be determined (DeMyer et al., 1981; Ritvo and Freeman, 1978; Rutter, 1978; Schopler, 1978; Werry, 1979b). Piggot (1979) and DeMyer et al. (1981) have provided the best reviews to date on the various organic hypotheses and have concluded that the accumulated evidence does indeed implicate a variety of organic disturbances, though to what degree these disturbances are unique to autism or are also involved in a variety of other developmental deviations remains uncertain.

Hence, if one adopts the position that autism is best explained as a central nervous system dysfunction whose chronic, severe nature most allies itself with a developmental disorder, then it would seem that the greater male prevalence is best explained by the same factors that were offered to explain the greater male prevalence in developmental disorders such as mental retardation and the specific developmental disorders. Namely, males are more vulnerable to a host of pre-, peri-, and postnatal stresses and genetic anomalies that contribute not only to disorders such as mental retardation or the specific developmental disorders but also to autism as well (Finnegan and Quarrington, 1979).

Finally, in contrast to earlier negative findings (Hanson and Gottesman, 1976), recent research has accumulated implicating a genetic factor in some cases of autism ("Autism: It May Be a Genetic Defect," 1981; Folstein and Rutter, 1977), although at present such evidence can only be deemed weak (DeMyer et al., 1981). Insofar as this is so, data has been adduced similar to that which was presented in the intellectual disorders, implicating both a sex-modified threshold hypothesis (Lord, Schopler, and Revicki, 1982; Tsai, Stewart, and August, 1981) and X-linked (fragile-X syndrome) factors (Brown et al., 1982; Meryash, Szymanski, and Gerald, 1982).

7.4. Childhood Schizophrenia: Diagnosis and Sex Difference

DSM-III prescribes that a diagnosis of childhood schizophrenia is to be made if a child manifests symptoms that are similar to those of adult schizophrenia, i.e., delusions, hallucinations, loosening of associations, etc. And regardless of the criteria employed, males outnumber females. This is the conclusion of literature reviews that do not distinguish between autism and schizophrenia (Hingtgen and Bryson, 1972; Marsh, 1977) and of those that do so (Al-Issa, 1982; Rutter, 1977d).

In view of the clear sex difference, it might seem somewhat surprising that genetic theories implicating a sex-mediated differential threshold or sex linkage have yet to be seriously explored with regard to childhood schizophrenia. This is most probably due to the fact that it is commonly held that there is no obvious sex difference in the overall rate of schizophrenia, though there is an earlier onset for males (Achenbach, 1982; Al-Issa, 1982; Lewine, 1982; Mayo, 1976) which thereby results in a greater rate of schizophrenia among young males.

Two main competing models, which can profitably be applied to childhood schizophrenia, have emerged to account for this sex difference in onset: a timing model and a subtype model (Lewine, 1981).

The timing model would hold that schizophrenia is essentially the same disorder in both sexes, but because it has an earlier onset in males, there is a greater male prevalence in childhood. Why men tend to develop schizophrenia earlier than women is not known, though both Mayo and Lewine speculate that genetically predisposed males are particularly vulnerable because sex role expectations are more stressful for them: e.g., the demand for autonomy may occur earlier for men than for women in such areas as leaving home, obtaining a job, and so on.

This explanation, when applied to the finding of a greater male prevalence in childhood schizophrenia, is especially noteworthy. For example, Baumrind (1980) and Ullian (1981) have both theorized that there exists a greater developmental discontinuity in male sex role functioning that might lead to a heightened vulnerability on the part of the male child. For Baumrind this discontinuity resides in viewing the male gender role as a differentiation from a female matrix, whereas for Ullian the discontinuity lies in the discrepancy between present physical attributes (male smallness and relative powerlessness) and desired future traits (superior size and strength). This discontinuity may account for the asymmetry in the socialization pressure put on boys to conform to sex stereotypes (Baumrind, 1980).

Hence, analogous to the theorizing of Lewine and Mayo for adults, it is hypothesized that genetically predisposed male children are particularly vulnerable to developing schizophrenia because the developmental discontinuities in sex role acquisition proposed by Baumrind and Ullian result in more stressful sex role expectations. Thus, although the sexes may be equally vulnerable to schizophrenia, male children, because of more stressful sex role expectations and lower psychosocial stress tolerance (see discussion on the adjustment disorders as well as the study by Mednick, Schulsinger, Teasdale, Schulsinger, Venables, and Rock, 1978, which is particularly relevant to schizophrenia), would be more likely to succumb to this disorder than females.

The subtype model would posit that the sexes exhibit different types of schizophrenia with males exhibiting more typical symptoms (and hence characteristics of poor premorbid competence and early onset) and females exhibiting more atypical symptoms (and hence characteristics of good premorbid competence and late onset). Lewine (1983) partly attributes the typicality of schizophrenic symptomatology in males to the greater presence organic abnormalities.

As applied to childhood schizophrenia, Goldfarb (1970) also reports that males are more likely to exhibit organic abnormalities than females. Hence the sex difference in subtype which Lewine indicates exists in adulthood is simply hypothesized to also occur in childhood, with the concomitant characteristic of early onset and hence greater prevalence.

8. Summary and Conclusions

Recognizing the absence of a universally accepted taxonomy for use in diagnosing psychopathology in children, the present review chose to examine sex-related differences in the prevalence of child psychopathology by focusing on those broad-band categories that were in accord with both clinically derived (DSM-III) and multivariate statistical approaches. The review revealed a markedly greater male preponderance in the intellectual, behavioral, and pervasive developmental disorders and parity in the emotional disorders. Reasons for these variations in childhood sex ratios were examined in light of what is currently known about the differential endowments and experiences of the sexes.

Perhaps the most obvious implication of this review is that being "male" in childhood places one at risk for incurring a mental disorder. Hence, it would be wise for those engaged in primary prevention programs to take cognizance of this and direct their efforts accordingly. In their review of the literature on prevention, Barclay and Frank (1979) indicated that while most prevention programs are geared to "target" groups of disadvantaged, deprived, poor, or "at risk" infants and children, there is an emerging trend toward the evaluation of the developmental needs of all children. This new emphasis is on competence and how well a child has met, and now meets, expectations of society for an individual of his/her age group. Insofar as such an orientation becomes implemented, it would behoove those involved in such programs to pay special attention to the needs of the male, since he, more than his distaff peer, would seem to require safeguarding so as to ensure his reaching mature functioning at a maximum level of development.

9. References

Abramowitz, S., and Docecki, R. The politics of clinical judgment: Early empirical returns. *Psychological Bulletin*, 1977, *84*, 460–476.

Achenbach, T. DSM-III in light of empirical research on the classification of child psychopathology. *Journal of the American Academy of Child Psychiatry*, 1980, *19*, 395–412.

Achenbach, T. *Developmental psychopathology*. New York: Wiley, 1982.

Achenbach, T., and Edelbrock, C. The classification of child psychopathology: A review and analysis of empirical efforts. *Psychological Bulletin*, 1978, *85*, 1275–1301.

Achenbach, T., and Edelbrock, C. Behavioral problems and competencies reported by parents of normal and disturbed children aged 4 through 16. *Monographs of the Society for Research in Child Development*, 1981 46, Serial No. 188.

Ainsworth, M., Blehar, M., Waters, E., and Wall, S. *Patterns of attachment: A psychological study of the strange situation*. New York: Erlbaum, 1978.

Al-Issa, I. Gender and child psychopathology. In I. Al-Issa (Ed.). *Gender and psychopathology*. New York: Academic Press, 1982.

American Psychiatric Association. *Diagnostic and statistical manual of mental disorders* (DSM-III). Washington, D.C.: 1980. American Psychiatric Association, 1980.

Anastasi, A. Four hypotheses with a dearth of data: Response to Lehrke's "A theory of X-linkage of major intellectual traits." *American Journal of Mental Deficiency*, 1972, *76*, 620–622.

Anastasi, A. Sex differences: Historical perspectives and theoretical implications. *Catalogue of Selected Documents in Psychology*, 1979, *10*, 2 (Ms. No. 1999).

Anthony, J. Behavior disorders. In P. Mussen (Ed.), *Carmichael's manual of child psychology* (Vol. 2). New York: Wiley, 1970.

Autism: It may be a genetic defect. *Newsweek*, July 27, 1981, p. 63.

Bank, B., Biddle, B., and Good, T. Sex roles, classroom instruction, and reading achievement. *Journal of Educational Psychology*, 1980, *72*, 119–132.

Barclay, M., and Frank, C. Prevention: The clinical psychologist. In M. Rosenzweig and L. Porter (Eds.), *Annual review of psychology*. Palo Alto, Calif.: Annual Reviews, 1979.

Bardwick, J. *Psychology of women: A study of bio-cultural conflicts*. New York: Harper & Row, 1971.

Bates, J. The concept of difficult temperament. *Merrill-Palmer Quarterly*, 1980, *26*, 299–317.

Bates, J., Freeland, C., and Lounsbury, M. Measurement of infant difficultness. *Child Development*, 1979, *50*, 594–603.

Baumrind, D. New directions in socialization research. *American Psychologist*, 1980, *35*, 639–652.

Bayley, N. Individual patterns of child development. *Child Development*, 1956, *27*, 45–74.

Becker, J. *Affective disorders*. Morristown, N.J.: General Learning Press, 1977.

Belmont, L. Epidemiology. In H. Rie and E. Rie (Eds.), *Handbook of minimal brain dysfunction*. New York: Wiley, 1980.

Bessman, S. Sex effect on the risk of mental retardation. *Behavior Genetics*, 1980, *10*, 327–329.

Birns, B. The emergence and socialization of sex differences in the earliest years. *Merrill-Palmer Quarterly*, 1976, *22*, 229–250.

Block, J. Issues, problems and pitfalls in assessing sex differences: A critical review of "The psychology of sex differences." *Merrill-Palmer Quarterly*, 1976, *22*, 283–308.

Block, J. Another look at differentiation in the socialization behaviors of mothers and fathers. In F. Denmark and J. Sherman (Eds.), *Psychology of women: Future direction of research*. New York: Psychological Dimensions, 1978.

Block, J. *Socialization influences on personality development in males and females.* Paper presented at the meeting of the American Psychological Association, New York, September 1979.

Bouchard, T., and McGue, T. Familial studies of intelligence: A review. *Science,* 1981, *212,* 1055–1059.

Bowlby, J. *Attachment and loss: II. Separation.* New York: Basic Books, 1973.

Braine, M., Heimer, C., Wortis, H., and Freedman, A. Factors associated with impairment of the early development of prematures. *Monographs of the Society for Research in Child Development,* 1966, *31*(4, Serial No. 106).

Brown, T., Jenkins, E., Friedman, E., Brooks, J., Wisniewski, K., Ragutho, S., and French, J. Autism is associated with the Fragile-X syndrome. *Journal of Autism and Developmental Disorders,* 1982, *12,* 303–308.

Cameron, J. Parental treatment, children's temperament, and the risk of childhood behavior problems. *American Journal of Orthopsychiatry,* 1978, *48,* 140–147.

Cantwell, D. Hyperkinetic syndrome. In M. Rutter and L. Hersov (Eds.), *Child psychiatry.* Oxford, England: Blackwell Scientific, 1977.

Cantwell, D. Hyperactivity and antisocial behavior. *Journal of the American Academy of Child Psychiatry,* 1978, *17,* 252–262.

Cantwell, D. The diagnostic process and diagnostic classification in child psychiatry, DSM-III. *Journal of the American Academy of Child Psychiatry,* 1980, *19,* 345–355.

Caplan, P. Beyond the box scores: A boundary condition for sex differences in aggression and achievement. In B. Maher (Ed.), *Progress in experimental personality research* (Vol. 9). New York: Academic Press, 1979.

Carter, C. Sex differences in the distribution of physical illness in children. *Social Science and Medicine,* 1978, *12B,* 163–166.

Conger, A., and Coie, J. Who's crazy in Manhattan: A reexamination of "Treatment of psychological disorders among urban children." *Journal of Consulting and Clinical Psychology,* 1975, *43,* 179–182.

Cramer, P. Defense mechanisms in adolescence. *Developmental Psychology,* 1979, *15,* 476–477.

Davidson, C., and Abramowitz, S. Sex bias in clinical judgment: Later empirical returns. *Psychology of Women Quarterly,* 1980, *4,* 377–395.

DeFries, J., and Plomin, R. Behavior genetics. In M. Rosenzweig and L.Porter (Eds.), *Annual review of psychology* (Vol. 29). Palo Alto, Calif.: Annual Reviews, 1978.

DeMyer, K., Hingtgen, J., and Jackson, R. Infantile autism reviewed: A decade of research. *Schizophrenia Bulletin,* 1981, *7,* 381–450.

Dohrenwend, B., and Dohrenwend, B. *Social status and psychological disorder.* New York: Wiley, 1969.

Dohrenwend, B., and Dohrenwend, B. Social and cultural influences on psychopathology. In M. Rosenzweig and L. Porter (Eds.), *Annual review of psychology* (Vol. 25). Palo Alto, Calif.: Annual Reviews, 1974.

Edelbrock, C., and Achenbach, T. A typology of child behavior profile patterns: Distributions and correlates for disturbed children aged 6–16. *Journal of Abnormal Child Psychology,* 1980, *8,* 441–470.

Ehrhardt, A. *Biological sex differences: A developmental perspective.* Paper presented at the meeting of the American Psychological Association, New York, September 1979.

Ehrhardt, A., and Meyer-Bahlburg, F. Prenatal sex hormones and the developing brain: Effects on psychosexual differentiation and cognitive functioning. In W. Creger (Ed.), *Annual review of medicine* (Vol. 30). Palo Alto, Calif.: Annual Reviews, 1979.

Ehrhardt, A., and Meyer-Bahlburg, F. Effects of prenatal sex hormones on gender-related behavior. *Science,* 1981, *177,* 1312–1318.

Eme, R. Sex differences in childhood psychopathology: A review. *Psychological Bulletin*, 1979, *86*, 574–595.

Emery, R. Interpersonal conflict and the children of discord and divorce. *Psychological Bulletin*, 1982, *92*, 310–330.

Etaugh, C. Effects of non-maternal care on children. *American Psychologist*, 1980, *35*, 309–319.

Eysenck, H., Wakefield, J., and Friedman, A. Diagnosis and clinical assessment. In M. Rosenzweig and L. Porter (Eds.), *Annual review of psychology* Vol. 34, Palo Alto, Calif.: Annual Reviews Inc., 1983.

Feshbach, S. Aggression. In P. Mussen (Ed.), *Carmichael's manual of child psychology* (Vol. 2). New York: Wiley, 1970.

Finnegan, J., and Quarrington, B. Pre-, peri-, and neonatal factors in infantile autism. *Journal of Child Psychology and Psychiatry*, 1979, *20*, 119–128.

Folstein, S., and Rutter, M. Genetic influences and infantile autism. *Nature*, 1977, *204*, 726–728.

Freire-Maia, A., Freire-Maia, C., and Morton, N. Sex effect on intelligence and mental retardation. *Behavior Genetics*, 1974, *4*, 269–272.

Frodi, A., Macaulay, J., and Thome, P. Are women always less aggressive than men? A review of the experimental literature. *Psychological Bulletin*, 1977, *84*, 634–660.

Garai, J., and Scheinfeld, A. Sex differences in mental and behavioral traits. *Genetic Psychology Monographs*, 1968, *77*, 169–229.

Gardner, B. The relationship between childhood neurotic symptomatology and later schizophrenia in males and females. *Journal of Nervous and Mental Disease*, 1967, *144*, 97–100.

Gerald, P. X-linked mental retardation and an X-chromosome marker. *New England Journal of Medicine*, 1980, September, 696–697.

Glaser, K. Masked depression in children and adolescents. *American Journal of Psychotherapy*, 1967, *21*, 565–574.

Goldfarb, W. Childhood psychosis. In P. Mussen (Ed.) *Carmichael's manual of child psychology* (Vol. 2) New York: Wiley, 1970.

Good, T., and Brophy, J. *Educational psychology: A realistic approach.* New York: Holt, Rhinehart & Winston, 1977.

Gottfried, A. Intellectual consequences of perinatal anoxia. *Psychological Bulletin*, 1973, *80*, 231–242.

Gould, M., Wunsch-Hitzig, R., and Dohrenwend, B. Estimating the prevalence of childhood psychopathology. *Journal of the American Academy of Child Psychiatry*, 1981, *20*, 462–476.

Gove, W. Sex differences in the epidemiology of mental disorder. In E. Gomberg and V. Franks (Eds.), *Gender and disordered behavior: Sex differences in psychopathology.* New York: Brunner/Mazel, 1979.

Gove, W. Mental illness and psychiatric treatment among women. *Psychology of Women Quarterly*, 1980, *4*, 345–361.

Gove, W., and Herb, T. Stress and mental illness among the young: A comparison of the sexes. *Social Forces*, 1974, *53*, 256–265.

Graham, P. Epidemiological studies. In H. Quay and J. Werry (Eds.), *Psychopathological disorders of childhood.* New York: Wiley, 1979.

Graham, P., and Rutter, M. Adolescent disorders. In M. Rutter and L. Hersov (Eds.), *Child psychiatry.* Oxford, England: Blackwell Scientific, 1977.

Guskin, S. Social psychologies of mental deficiency. In N. Ellis (Ed.), *Handbook of mental deficiency.* New York: McGraw-Hill, 1963.

Hanson, D., and Gottesman, I. The genetics, if any, of infantile autism and childhood schizophrenia. *Journal of Autism and Childhood Schizophrenia*, 1976, *6*, 209–234.

Hart, B. Gonadal androgen and sociosexual behavior of male mammals. *Psychological Bulletin*, 1974, *81*, 383–400.

Hastings, J., and Barkley, P. A review of the psychophysiological research with hyperkinetic children. *Journal of Abnormal Child Psychology*, 1978, *6*, 413–417.

Heatherington, M. Divorce: A child's perspective. *American Psychologist*, 1979, *34*, 851–858.

Hendersen, N. Human behavior genetics. In M. Rosenzweig and L. Porter (Eds.), *Annual review of psychology*. (Vol. 33). Palo Alto, Calif.: Annual Reviews, 1982.

Herbert, M. Conduct disorders. In B. Lahey and A. Kazdin (Eds.), *Advances in clinical child psychology* (Vol. 4). New York: Plenum, 1982.

Herbst, D., and Miller, J. Nonspecific X-linked mental retardation: The frequency in British Columbia. *Journal of Medical Genetics*, 1980, *7*, 461–469.

Hersov, L. Adoption. In M. Rutter and L. Hersov (Eds.), *Child psychiatry*. Oxford, England: Blackwell Scientific, 1977. (a)

Hersov, L. Emotional disorders. In M. Rutter and L. Hersov (Eds.), *Child psychiatry*. Oxford, England: Blackwell Scientific, 1977. (b)

Hingtgen, J., and Bryson, C. Recent developments in the study of early childhood psychoses: Infantile autism, childhood schizophrenia and related disorders. *Schizophrenia Bulletin*, 1972, *5*, 8–53.

Hobbs, N. *Issues in the classification of children* (Vol. 1). San Francisco: Jossey-Bass, 1975.

Hoffman, L. Maternal employment: 1979. *American Psychologist*, 1979, *34*, 859–965.

Ingalls, R. *Mental retardation: The changing outlook*. New York: Wiley, 1978.

Jacklin, C. *Sex-related differences in cognitive development*. Paper presented at the meeting of the American PsychologicalAssociation, New York, September 1979. (a)

Jacklin, C. Epilogue. In M. Wittig and A. Petersen (Eds.), *Sex-related differences in cognitive functioning*. New York: Academic Press, 1979. (b)

Kagan, J., and Moss, H. *Birth to maturity*. New York: Wiley, 1972.

Keith, S., Gunderson, J., Reifman, A., Buschbaum, S., and Mosher, L. Special report: Schizophrenia, 1976. *Schizophrenia Bulletin*, 1976, *4*, 509–565.

Kenny, T. Hyperactivity. In H. Rie and E. Rie (Eds.), *Handbook of minimal brain dysfunction*. New York: Wiley, 1980.

Knopp, C., and Parmelee, A. Prenatal and perinatal influences on infant behavior. In J. Osofsky (Ed.), *Handbook of infant development*. New York: Wiley, 1979.

Kohlberg, L. A cognitive-developmental analysis of children's sex-role concepts and attitudes. In E. Maccoby (Ed.), *The development of sex-differences*. Stanford, Calif.: Stanford University Press, 1966.

Kronstadt, D., Oberklaid, F., Berg, T., and Swartz, J. Infant behavior and maternal adaptation in the first six months of life. *American Journal of Orthopsychiatry*, 1979, *49*, 454–464.

Kurdek, L. An integrative perspective on children's divorce adjustment. *American Psychologist*, 1981, *36*, 856–866.

Langer, T., Gersten, J., Greene, E., Eisenberg, J., Herson, J., and McCarthy, E. Treatment of psychological disorders among urban children. *Journal of Clinical and Consulting Psychology*, 1974, *42*, 170–179.

Lehrke, R. A theory of X-linkage of major intellectual traits. *American Journal of Mental Deficiency*, 1972, *76*, 611–631. (a)

Lehrke, R. Response to Dr. Anastasi and to Drs. Nance and Engel. *American Journal of Mental Deficiency*, 1972, *76*, 626–631. (b)

Lehrke, R. Sex linkage: A biological base for the greater male variability in intelligence. In R. Osbourne, C. Noble, and N. Weyl (Eds.), *Human variation*. New York: Academic Press, 1978.

Levy, J. Lateralization and its implications for variation in development. In E. Gollin (Ed.),

Developmental plasticity: Behavioral and biological aspects of variation in development. New York: Academic Press, 1981.

Lewine, R. Sex differences in schizophrenia: Timing or subtype. *Psychological Bulletin,* 1981, *90,* 432–444.

Lewis, M. *Self-knowledge: A social-cognitive perspective on gender identity and sex-role development.* Paper presented at the meeting of the American Psychological Association, New York, September 1979.

Links, P. Community surveys of the prevalence of childhood psychiatric disorders: A review. *Child Development,* 1983, *54,* 531–548.

Loney, J. Hyperkinesis comes of age. *American Journal of Orthopsychiatry,* 1980, *50,* 28–42.

Lord, C., Schopler, E., and Revicki, D. Sex differences in autism. *Journal of Autism and Developmental Disorders* 1982, *12,* 317–330.

Maccoby, E., and Jacklin, C. *The psychology of sex differences.* Stanford, Calif.: Stanford University Press, 1974.

Maccoby, E., and Jacklin, C. Sex differences in aggression: A rejoinder and reprise. *Child Development,* 1980, *51,* 964–980.

Marsh, R. The diagnosis, epidemiology, and etiology of childhood schizophrenia. *Genetic Psychological Monographs,* 1977, *95,* 267–330.

Martin, H. Nutrition, injury, illness and minimal brain dysfunction. In H. Rie and E. Rie (Eds.), *Handbook of minimal brain dysfunction.* New York: Wiley, 1980.

Martin, L., and Halverson, C. A schematic processing model of sex typing and stereotyping in children. *Child Development,* 1981, *52,* 1119–1134.

Mayo, P. Sex differences and psychopathology. In B. Lloyd and J. Archer (Eds.), *Exploring sex differences.* London: Academic Press, 1976.

McAskie, M., and Clarke, A. Parent–offspring resemblances in intelligence: Theories and evidence. *British Journal of Psychology,* 1976, *67,* 243–273.

McGee, M. Human spatial abilities: Psychometric studies and environmental, genetic, hormonal, and neurological influences. *Psychological Bulletin,* 1979, *86,* 889–918.

McGuinness, D. Sex differences in the organization of perception and cognition. In B. Lloyd and J. Archer (Eds.), *Exploring sex differences.* New York: Academic Press, 1976.

McGuinness, D. How schools discriminate against boys. *Human Nature,* 1979, February, *2,* 82–88.

McGuire, L., Ryan, K., and Omenn, G. Congenital adrenal hyperplasia II. Cognitive and behavioral studies. *Behavior Genetics,* 1975, *5,* 175–188.

McMillen, M. Differential mortality by sex in fetal and neonatal deaths. *Science,* 1979, *204,* 89–91.

Mednick, J., Schulsinger, F., Teasdale, T., Schulsinger, H., Venables, P., and Rock, O. Schizophrenia in high-risk children: Sex differences in predisposing factors. In G. Serbin (Ed.), *Cognitive deficits in the development of mental illness.* New York: Brunner/Mazel, 1978.

Meece, J., Parsons, J., Kaczala, C., Goff, S., and Futterman, R. Sex differences in math achievement: Toward a model of academic choice. *Psychological Bulletin,* 1982, *91,* 324–348.

Mercer, J. *Labelling the mentally retarded.* Berkeley: University of California Press, 1973.

Meryash, D., Szymanski, D., and Gerald, P. Infantile autism associated with the Fragile-X syndrome. *Journal of Autism and Developmental Disorders.,* 1982, *12,* 295–301.

Meyer-Bahlburg, H., and Ehrhardt, A. Prenatal sex hormones and human aggression. *Aggressive Behavior,* 1982, *8,* 39–62.

Mischel, W. A social-learning view of sex-differences in behavior. In E. Maccoby (Ed.), *The development of sex differences.* Stanford, Calif.: Stanford University Press, 1966.

Money, J., and Erhardt, A. *Man and women, boy and girl.* Baltimore: Johns Hopkins University Press, 1972.

Moss, H. Early sex differences and mother–infant interaction. In R. Friedman, R. Richard, and R. Vande Wiele (Eds.), *Sex differences in behavior.* New York: Wiley, 1974.

Mussen, P. Early sex role development. In D. Goslin (Ed.), *Handbook of socialization theory and research.* Chicago: Rand McNally, 1969.

Nance, W., and Engel, E. One X and four hypotheses: Response to Lehrke's "A theory of X-linkage of major intellectual traits." *American Journal of Mental Deficiency,* 1972, *76,* 623–625.

Osofsky, J., and Connors, K. Mother–infant interaction: An integrative view of a complex system. In J. Osofsky (Ed.), *Handbook of infant development.* New York: Wiley, 1979.

Parsons, J. Psychosexual neutrality: Is anatomy destiny? In J. Parson (Ed.), *The psychology of sex differences and sex roles.* New York: Hemisphere, 1980.

Patterson, G., Littman, R., and Bricker, W. Assertive behavior in children: A step towards a theory of aggression. *Monographs of the Society for Research in Child Development,* 1967, *32*(4, Serial No. 113).

Pauls, D. Sex effect on the risk of mental retardation. *Behavior Genetics,* 1979, *9,* 289–295.

Pennington, B., and Smith, S. Genetic influences on learning disabilities and speech and language disorders. *Child Development,* 1983, *54,* 369–387.

Piggot, L. Overview of selected basic research in autism. *Journal of Autism and Development Disorders,* 1979, *9,* 199–216.

Piggot, L., and Simson, C. Changing diagnosis of childhood psychosis. *Journal of Autism and Childhood Schizophrenia,* 1975, *5,* 239–245.

Pirozzolo, F., Campanella, P., Christensen, K., and Lawson-Kerr, K. Effects of cerebral dysfunction on neurolinguistic performance in children. *Journal of Consulting and Clinical Psychology,* 1981, *49,* 792–806.

Porter, B., and O'Leary, P. Marital discord and childhood behavior problems. *Journal of Abnormal Child Psychology,* 1980, *8,* 287–295.

Quadagno, D., Briscoe, R., and Quadagno, J. Effect of perinatal gonadal hormones on selected non-sexual behavior patterns: A critical assessment of the non-human and human literature. *Psychological Bulletin,* 1977, *84,* 62–80.

Quay, H. Classification. In H. Quay and J. Werry (Eds.), *Psychopathological disorders of childhood.* New York: Wiley, 1979.

Reed, E., and Reed, S. *Mental retardation: A family study.* Philadelphia: Saunders, 1965.

Reinisch, J. Prenatal exposure to synthetic progestins increase potential for aggression in humans. *Science,* 1981, *211,* 1171–1173.

Reinisch, J., and Karow, W. Prenatal exposure to synthetic progestins and estrogens: Effect on human development. *Archives of Sexual Behavior,* 1977, *6,* 257–288.

Reinisch, J., Gandelman, R., and Spiegal, F. Prenatal influences on cognitive abilities. In M. Wittig and A. Petersen (Eds.), *Sex-related differences in cognitive functioning.* New York: Academic Press, 1979.

Rie, H. Definitional problems. In H. Rie and E. Rie (Eds.), *Handbook of minimal brain dysfunction.* New York: Wiley, 1980.

Ritvo, E., and Freeman, B. The National Society for Autistic Children's definition of the syndrome of autism. *American Academy of Child Psychiatry,* 1978, *17,* 564–575.

Ritvo, E., Ritvo, E., and Brothers, A. Genetic and immunohematologic factors in autism. *Journal of Autism and Developmental Disorders,* 1982, *12,* 109–113.

Ross, A., and Pelham, W. Child psychopathology. In M. Rosenzweig and L. Porter (Eds.), *Annual review of psychology* (Vol. 32). Palo Alto, Calif.: Annual Reviews, 1981.

Rourke, B. Neuropsychological research in reading retardation: A review. In A. Benton and D. Pearl (Eds.), *Dyslexia.* New York: Oxford University Press, 1978.

Rubin, R., Reinisch, J., and Haskett, R. Postnatal gonadal steroid effects on human behavior. *Science*, 1981, *211*, 1318–1324.

Rutter, M. Sex differences in children's responses to family stress. In E. Anthony and C. Koupernik (Eds.), *The child in his family*. New York: Wiley, 1970.

Rutter, M. *Maternal deprivation reassessed*. Hammondsworth, England: Penguin Books, 1972. (a)

Rutter, M. Relationships between adult and child psychiatric disorders. *Acta Psychiatrica Scandinavica*, 1972, *48*, 3–21. (b)

Rutter, M. Classification. In M. Rutter and L. Hersov (Eds.), *Child psychiatry*. Oxford, England: Blackwell Scientific, 1977. (a)

Rutter, M. Brain damage syndrome in childhood: Concepts and findings. *Journal of Child Psychology and Psychiatry*, 1977, *18*, 1–21. (b)

Rutter, M. Individual differences. In M. Rutter and L. Hersov (Eds.), *Child psychiatry*. Oxford, England: Blackwell Scientific, 1977. (c)

Rutter, M. Infantile autism and other child psychoses. In M. Rutter and L. Hersov (Eds.), *Child psychiatry*. Oxford, England: Blackwell Scientific, 1977. (d)

Rutter, M. Diagnosis and definition of childhood autism. *Journal of Autism and Childhood Schizophrenia*, 1978, *8*, 139–161.

Rutter, M. Maternal deprivation, 1972–1978: New findings, new concepts, new approaches. *Child Development*, 1979, *50*, 283–305.

Rutter, M. *Changing youth in a changing society*. Cambridge, Mass.: Harvard University Press, 1980.

Rutter, M. Socio-emotional consequences of day care for preschool children. *American Journal of Orthopsychiatry*, 1981, *51*, 4–28.

Rutter, M. Temperament: concepts, issues and problems. In M. Rutter (Ed.), *Temperamental differences in infants and young children*. London: Pittman, 1982. (a)

Rutter, M. Syndromes attributed to "minimal brain dysfunction" in childhood. *American Journal of Psychiatry*, 1982, *139*, 21–33. (b)

Rutter, M., and Garmezy, N. Developmental psychopathology. In P. Mussen and M. Hetherington (Eds.), *Handbook of child psychology* (Vol. 4). New York: Wiley, 1983.

Rutter, M., and Shaffer, D. DSM-III. *American Academy of Child Psychiatry*, 1980, *19*, 371–394.

Rutter, M., and Yule, W. Reading difficulties. In M. Rutter and L. Hersov (Eds.), *Child psychiatry*. Oxford, England: Blackwell Scientific, 1977.

Sameroff, A. Infant risk factors in developmental deviance. In J. Anthony, C. Koupernik, and C. Chiland (Eds.), *Vulnerable children*. New York: Wiley, 1978.

Schere, R., Richardson, E., and Bialer, I. Toward operationalizing a psychoeducational definition of learning disabilities. *Journal of Abnormal Child Psychology*, 1980, *8*, 5–20.

Scholom, A., Zucker, R., and Stollak, G. Relating early child adjustment to infant and parent temperament. *Journal of Abnormal Child Psychology*, 1979, *7*, 297–308.

Schopler, E. National Society for Autistic Children: Definition of the syndrome of autism. *Journal of Autism and Childhood Schizophrenia*, 1978, *8*, 162–169.

Schopler, E. Editorial: Change of journal scope and title. *Journal of Autism and Development Disorders*, 1979, *9*, 1–11.

Scott, D. Epidemiological indicators of the origins of behavior disturbances as measured by the Bristol social adjustment scales. *Genetic Psychology Monographs*, 1978, *97*, 127–159.

Serbin, L. Sex-role socialization. In B. Lahey and A. Kazdin (Eds.), *Advances in clinical child psychology* (Vol. 3) New York: Plenum, 1980.

Sherman, J. *Sex related cognitive differences: An essay on theory on evidence*. Springfield, Ill.: Charles C Thomas, 1978.

Sherman, J. Mathematics, spatial visualization and related factors: Changes in girls and boys, grades 8–11. *Journal of Educational Psychology*, 1980, *72*, 476–482.

Smith, M. Sex bias in counseling and psychotherapy. *Psychological Bulletin*, 1980, *87*, 392–407.

Spitzer, R., and Cantwell, D. The DSM-III classification of the psychiatric disorders in infancy, childhood and adolescence. *American Academy of Child Psychiatry*, 1980, *19*, 356–370.

Tanner, J. Physical growth. In P. Mussen (Ed.), *Carmichael's manual of child psycholgoy* (Vol. 1). New York: Wiley, 1970.

Tanner, J. *Fetus into man: Physical growth from conception to maturity*. Cambridge, Mass.: Harvard University Press, 1978.

Terman, L., and Tyler, L. Psychological sex differences. In L. Carmichael (Ed.), *Manual of child psychology*. New York: Wiley, 1954.

Thomas, A. Behavioral individuality in children. In A. Kaplan (Ed.), *Human behavior genetics*. Springfield, Ill.: Charles C Thomas, 1976.

Thomas, A., and Chess, S. A longitudinal study of three brain damaged children: Infancy to adolescence. *Archives of General Psychiatry*, 1975, *32*, 457–462.

Tieger, T. On the biological basis of sex differences in aggression. *Child Development*, 1980, *51*, 943–963.

Toolan, J. Depression in children and adolescents. *American Journal of Orthopsychiatry*, 1962, *32*, 404–415.

Torgesen, J. What shall we do with psychological processes? *Journal of Learning Disabilities*, 1979, *8*, 16–23.

Tsai, L., Stewart, M., and August, G. Implication of sex differences in the familial transmission of infantile autism. *Journal of Autism and Developmental Disorders*, 1981, *11*, 165–173.

Tudor, W., Tudor, J., and Gove, W. The effect of sex role differences on the societal reaction to mental retardation. *Social Forces*, 1980, *57*, 871–884.

Turner, G., Brookwell, R., Daniel, A., Selikowitz, M., and Zilbowitz, M. Heterozygous expression of X-linked mental retardation and X-chromosome maker. *New England Journal of Medicine*, 1980, (303) September, 662–664.

Ullian, D. Why boys will be boys: A structural perspective. *American Journal of Orthopsychiatry*, 1981, *51*, 493–501.

Waber, D. Cognitive abilities and sex-related variations in the maturations of the cerebral cortical functions. In M. Wittig and A. Petersen (Eds.), *Sex-related differences in cognitive functioning*. New York: Academic Press, 1979.

Watt, N., Fryer, J., Lewine, R., and Prentsky, R. Toward longitudinal conceptions of psychiatric disorder. In B. Maher (Ed.), *Progress in experimental personality research* (Vol. 9). New York: Academic Press, 1979.

Weiss, G., and Hechtman, L. The hyperactive child syndrome. *Science*, 1979, *205*, 1354–1354.

Weissman, M., and Klerman, G. Sex differences and the epidemiology of depression. *Archives of General Psychiatry*, 1977, *43*, 98–111.

Werner, E., and Smith, R. An epidemiologic perspective on some antecedents and consequences of childhood mental health problems and learning disabilities. *Journal of Child Psychiatry*, 1979, *18*, 292–300.

Werry, J. Organic factors. In H. Quay and J. Werry (Eds.), *Psychopathological disorders in childhood*. New York: Wiley, 1979. (a)

Werry, J. The childhood psychoses. In H. Quay and J. Werry (Eds.), *Psychopathological disorders in childhood*. New York: Wiley, 1979. (b)

Willerman, L. *The psychology of individual differences.* San Francisco: Freeman, 1979. (a)

Willerman, L. The effects of families on intellectual development. *American Psychologist,* 1979, *34,* 923–929. (b)

Wing, L., and Gould, J. Severe impairments of social interaction and associated abnormalities in children: Epidemiology and classification. *Journal of Autism and Developmental Disorders,* 1979, *9,* 1–29.

Wittig, M. Sex differences in intellectual functioning: How much of a difference do genes make? *Sex Roles,* 1976, *2,* 63–74.

Wolff, S. Non delinquent disturbance of conduct. In M. Rutter and L. Hersov (Eds.), *Child psychiatry.* Oxford, England: Blackwell Scientific, 1977.

Wynne, M., and P. O'Connor. *Exceptional children: A developmental view.* Lexington, Mass.: Heath, 1979.

Zeldow, P. Sex differences in psychiatric evaluation and treatment. *Archives of General Psychiatry,* 1978, *38,* 89–93.

13

Sex-Role Stereotypes and the Development of Eating Disorders

Gloria R. Leon and Stephen Finn

In this chapter, we explore ways in which cultural sex role stereotyping may influence the development of eating disorders. Previous reports (Boskind-Lodahl, 1976; Bruch, 1978; Chernin, 1981; Leon, 1976; Wooley and Wooley, 1980) have considered the probable etiological role of cultural attitudes regarding women for certain abnormal eating patterns. However, the relationship involving sex role attitudes, sex role identification, sex role behavior, and the development of abnormal eating patterns has not been directly studied. Therefore, one is obliged to draw conclusions about the etiological role of sex role attitudes on eating disorders through integrating the available scientific knowledge about sex role stereotypes with findings from epidemiological and other studies of eating disorders.

We begin with a review of studies of the relationship between particular demographic variables and the incidence and nature of anorexia nervosa, bulimia, and obesity. The purpose of this review is to provide a background for our theoretical formulations of the mechanisms through which the cultural roles for each gender have an influence on the development of these three eating disorders.

Gloria R. Leon and Stephen Finn • Department of Psychology, University of Minnesota, Minneapolis, Minnesota 55455.

1. Epidemiology of Eating Disorders

1.1. Sex Differences in Incidence and Topography

Anyone doing research or clinical work in the area of eating disorders is struck by the importance of biological gender in defining the epidemiology of these disorders. The ratio of females to males in the incidence of anorexia nervosa has been estimated as approaching 9:1 (Bemis, 1978). Furthermore, the topography of the disorder does not appear to be the same across the two genders. Male anorexics have been described as exhibiting a greater degree of psychopathology than female anorexics, and to have a generally poorer treatment prognosis (Crisp, Kalucy, Lacey, and Harding, 1977). Among other factors, Crisp *et al.* have speculated that the disorder develops in males in the context of severe gender identity problems and prior massive obesity.

Bulimia, like anorexia nervosa, is a problem primarily manifested in adolescent girls and adult women. In the most extensive treatment and follow-up report on this disorder to date, Russell (1979) reported only 2 cases of bulimia in males in his sample of 30 patients. Boskind-Lodahl (1976) indicated that she treated only 4 male bulimics in a series of 138 patients with this disorder. However, neither Russell nor Boskind-Lodahl mentions differences in symptomatology between male and female bulimics.

Obesity, unlike anorexia nervosa and bulimia, does not show substantial differences in incidence *per se*. The prevalence of obesity in women is somewhat higher than in men, and this is related in part to the greater amount of adipose tissue present in females (Seltzer and Mayer, 1965). However, the overwhelming number of persons attending weight-loss programs in the United States are women (Leon, 1976). Also, most persons undergoing jejunoileal bypass surgery for massive obesity are women (Leon, Eckert, Teed, and Buchwald, 1979). Like anorexia nervosa, obesity in men and women may have different associated symptoms. For example, Bruch (1957) has commented that clinical depression may be a more frequent or severe concomitant of obesity in females than in males. However, one should recall that in general, depression has a significantly higher prevalence in females.

Although there may be biological bases for gender differences in the incidence and topography of eating differences, such bases have not yet been documented. Alternatively, one may postulate that sociocultural factors are involved in these differences. Sex role attitudes seem an obvious place to look in explaining gender differences in abnormal eating patterns.

1.2. Cultural Differences in Incidence

Overeating and underexercising resulting in obesity, as well as refusing and misusing food leading to anorexia nervosa or bulimia, are
luxuries of an affluent society. In nations and cultures in which food is
scarce, obesity is not considered an eating disorder. In India, for example, being obese is considered a sign of prestige, i.e., an affirmation that
one has enough wealth to consume a plentiful amount of food. The
previous Aga Khan used to receive his weight in precious jewels each
year. Conversely, the attitude that an exceedingly slender body appearance is the ideal of physical attractiveness for women often occurs in
those countries where food is plentiful and finding enough to eat is not
for many a daily issue of survival. Studies in urban centers in the United
States and Great Britain have demonstrated that the incidence of obesity
is markedly higher among women and girls of lower as compared to
upper socioeconomic class status (Moore, Stunkard, and Srole, 1962;
Silverstone, Gordon, and Stunkard, 1969; Stunkard, d'Aquili, Fox, and
Filion, 1972). Further, obesity is more prevalent in the affluent, highly
industrialized countries in the world, and conversely, epidemiological
studies as well as case reports indicate that anorexia nervosa is extremely rare in underdeveloped countries. The highest incidence of
cases of anorexia nervosa has been reported among Caucasian (Galdston, 1974) and upper socioeconomic groups in the United States, the
industrialized countries of the British Commonwealth such as Great
Britain, Canada, Australia, and New Zealand, and the Scandinavian
countries (Crisp et al., 1977).

A recent epidemiological study of a county in New York State that
evaluated all hospitalizations over a 16-year period confirmed the preponderance of anorexia nervosa among higher SES females (Jones, Fox,
Babegian, and Hutton, 1980). Further, Jones et al., to the best of our
knowledge, documented the first case of anorexia nervosa in a black
female in the United States.

1.3. Generational Differences in Incidence

A final area of epidemiological importance in the area of eating
disturbances concerns changes in the frequency of these disorders over
time. The incidence of anorexia nervosa appears to be increasing in our
culture in a proportion far greater than that which can be explained by
an enhanced awareness of the symptoms of this disorder. Although
previous estimates of the prevalence suggested it was an extremely rare
disorder, more recent research findings contradict this. Nylander (1971)

estimated that anorexia nervosa is present in severe form in one in every 150 adolescent females in Sweden. A study by Crisp, Palmer, and Kalucy (1976) in London, consisting of a clinical interview investigation surveying a relatively large school population, indicated a prevalence rate for anorexia nervosa of 1 in 100 cases of girls aged 16 and over. Jones *et al.* (1980) found an increase in the incidence of patients hospitalized with a diagnosis of anorexia nervosa from the period of 1960–1969 to 1970–1976.

As with anorexia nervosa, a recent increase in the number of individuals diagnosed as bulimic has challenged the notion that bulimia is a relatively rare phenomenon. However, in the case of bulimia, it is unclear whether the increase in women seeking treatment for the disorder represents a true increase in incidence or simply an increase in the awareness of the general population regarding abnormal eating patterns. At the present time, a great deal of media coverage has been devoted to the disorder of bulimia, and a strikingly large number of women have come forward to seek treatment for their uncontrolled eating behavior. A number of these women have indicated that they have engaged in binging and vomiting or purging for a number of years but did not realize that this disorder had a name or that it was not as uncommon a practice as they had thought.

2. "Direct" Influences of Sex Roles on Eating Habits

2.1. Eating in Public and Table Manners

> "Ef you doan care 'bout how folks talks 'bout dis fambly, Ah does," she rumbled. . . . "Ah has tole you an' tole you dat you kin allus tell a lady by dat she eat lak a bird. . . ." "Mother is a lady and she eats," countered Scarlett. "W'en you is mahied, you kin eat, too," retorted Mammy. . . . "Young misses whut eats heavy mos' gener'ly doan never ketch husbands."
> (Margaret Mitchell, *Gone with the Wind*)

Though the days of Twelve Oaks, lace petticoats, and the graceful South are for the most part long gone, some of the social conventions described by Margaret Mitchell persist to this day in the United States. Among these is the notion that it is somehow "shameful" or "unladylike" for women to eat large or even adequate amounts of food in the presence of others. The girl or young woman who demonstrates a healthy appetite before friends or guests may be chastised by parents, or at least viewed as "tomboyish" and unconventional. This may be true even if the girl is not at all overweight. For males, however, the opposite message is given: The amount that one eats is somehow seen as a measure of one's masculinity, power, and strength. The fact that a boy can eat several portions instead of just one is viewed with approval by many mothers as a sign of the fact that he is a "good eater" and becoming a "man."

Surprisingly, there has been little mention in the research or clinical literature on eating disorders of this social equation between the amount eaten and perceived power or traits of masculinity/femininity. It is likely, however, that such cultural attitudes have a role in the development of abnormal eating patterns. We call this path of influence a *direct* influence, as the sex role stereotype in question directly bears on eating and/or body size.

There are several ways in which sex role stereotypes regarding appropriate eating patterns may be involved in the development of eating disorders. The extreme shame and disgust experienced by bulimics following a binge episode may be related in part to the fact that the binging *per se* (apart from its much-feared consequences in terms of weight gain) is viewed as unfeminine behavior. This attitude would also appear to be a factor contributing to why many bulimics binge surreptitiously. For both males and females, however, the affect experienced after a binge episode seems importantly related to the experience of loss of control as well as the perception of gluttony.

Cultural attitudes regarding appropriate eating habits for males and females may also play a role in the development of some cases of male adolescent obesity. The "eating contests" held by fraternities are an example of one message given to adolescent males by peer and family: It is somehow seen as masculine and as a sign of one's prowess to be able to eat huge amounts of food. A boy who feels insecure about his masculinity might, in spite of cultural attitudes about obesity, eat huge amounts of food in an attempt to prove his prowess to himself and others and eventually become obese.

The perceived or anticipated social evaluations of the amount of food consumed appears to be a strong societal influence and also seems to be a factor in the eating patterns of many individuals without eating disorders. Several of our female therapy clients with definitely normal eating patterns and normal weights have reported being acutely aware of the amounts they consume in public. They will stop eating at a certain point, although they may wish to consume more, because they are afraid of others' evaluations their eating behavior. To what extent these ideas are held, and whether they apply equally to men and women, remains to be demonstrated empirically.

2.2. Sex Differences in Ideal Body Shape

There is considerable research indicating sex differences in ideal body shape. Jourard and Secord (1955) found that smallness was an important factor in defining preferred body shape for women. The ideal figure was described as "smaller than you are in all dimensions except bust." In a study by Kurtz (1969), tall, thin women were the ones who rated their bodies as best liked by themselves. In another study by Jourard and Secord (1954), men stated that for the ideal man, large body size was desirable. In the Kurtz study, it was found that the men with mesomorphic builds—large muscular men—rated their bodies as best liked by selves.

It may, however, be misleading to summarize data regarding standards of ideal body build across a large period of time, as there is evidence of a shift in standards of ideal body shape in recent years, at least for females. This is clearly illustrated in a recent (although somewhat offbeat) study. The body dimensions of centerfold models in *Playboy* magazine were obtained over the period of 1959–1978, as well as the height, weight, and age data of the winners of the Miss America Beauty Pageant over that time interval (Garner, Garfinkel, Schwartz, and Thompson, 1980). The percentage of average weight and various shape changes over the 20-year period were calculated, and the results indicated a gradual but consistent shift in the ideal body standard toward a thinner size. Further, height and waist dimensions showed an increase while hips and bust size exhibited a mean decrease over the 20-year period, suggesting a more "tubular" body form. Garner *et al.* also demonstrated that this trend is in contrast to actuarial statistics indicating that average women of similar age have been getting heavier. As one might expect from these conflicting trends, dieting articles in popular women's magazines have shown a marked increase over this time period. One clearly sees the untenable situation in which women find themselves, trying to resolve the cultural demands for unrealistic thinness and the constant societal stimuli to eat.

At least one feminist critic of the "American preoccupation with slimness" (Chernin, 1981) has related these changes in ideal female body shape to the changing roles of women in America. Chernin points out the psychological equation of size with power and hypothesizes that our male-dominated culture requires that women be slender in order to symbolically limit their power. This is in contrast to earlier times, when women were clearly subordinated in other ways, and men therefore allowed women to have fuller body shapes. Women accepted the current prejudices about the ideal female figure, says Chernin, because of their own unconscious role conflicts. By emulating the male angular figure, women symbolically attempt to secure social rights that are traditionally seen as male. Chernin points out that this is analogous to George Sand's having donned male garb in order to gain acceptance in the male society in the early 1800s. The new slender body type is also seen as a rejection of earlier female forms and their associated roles. As such, hypothesizes Chernin, this body form also serves as an unconscious expression of hostility by modern women toward mothers and other generations of women who did not break out of their accepted social roles.

Bruch (1973), Chernin (1981), Leon (1981), and others have stated that sex differences in standards of ideal body shape may be implicated in the large sex differences in the incidence of anorexia nervosa and bulimia. They have also suggested that the recent cultural changes in idealizing lower body weights for women may be responsible for the apparent increase in the incidence of anorexia nervosa and bulimia since the 1960s. One of the few studies that attempted to directly link standards of ideal body shape to eating disorders (Garner and Garfinkel, 1980) demonstrated the effect of the pressures for extreme thinness on the incidence of eating disorders in professional dance and modeling students. The investigators, through questionnaire evaluation and follow-up interview, found an overrepresentation of anorexia nervosa and excessive dieting concerns in both groups of students. In fact, 12 females (6.5%) in the dance group were diagnosed as suffering from primary anorexia nervosa, with those students from the most competitive dance school environments exhibiting the relatively greatest frequency of the disorder. Four cases (7%) of anorexia nervosa were identified in the sample of modeling students. A comparison was carried out with music school students, a group in which thinness would not be a criterion for success. There were no cases of anorexia nervosa or a significant degree of thinness in the latter female group.

One of us (G. R. L.) treated a case of obesity in an adolescent male that was obviously tied to cultural standards regarding ideal male body shape. This 16-year-old young man, who was quite overweight when seen, came to the clinic at the insistence of his mother. He possessed an endomesomorphic build rather than a clear endomorphic shape. His obesity was particularly difficult to treat because he communicated that he was unwilling to give up the power and sense of masculinity that he equated with his body build. Although he was the butt of a great deal of peer teasing about his size, he had also received extensive social and self-reinforcement for his weight over a period of years because of his involvement in athletics. He stated that he enjoyed intimidating others by his large size. As can be imagined, he was quite an effective football lineman! It is unlikely that a female would have experienced the same cultural reinforcements for her large size.

2.3. Sex Differences in the Importance of Physical Traits

Besides the differences in ideal body weight and shape between men and women, other differences exist in the differentiation of body image between the two sexes. Women appear to have a more clearly defined body concept than do men, and this begins in childhood or adolescence (Fisher, 1964). This is reflected in a greater awareness of body size and function, as well as in the more intense cathexis of body parts than is seen in males of the same age. Fisher emphasizes the earlier maturation of females and the development of menstruation in explaining this phenomenon. Murphy (1972) emphasizes other factors in explaining this discrepancy, suggesting that females devote more attention to their bodies than do males, in part because the body is more linked to their cultural role and to social definitions of their worth: "Woman more nearly equates self with body. Man's role and status has typically been defined in terms of his achievement, rather than in terms of body attributes" (p. 620).

Whatever the reasons for the greater importance of physical traits for defining self-concept among females, this fact has been cited by some writers as an explanation for sex differences in the prevalence of eating disorders. Boskind-Lodahl (1976) has presented a formulation of the etiology of eating disorders as related to issues of ideal body image, femininity, and societal attitudes about female self-worth. She used the term *bulimarexia* to denote a cycle of food restriction interspersed with binging followed by vomiting and purging. According to Boskind-Lodahl, bulimarexia is an obsessive pursuit of thinness due to an acceptance of the cultural attitude that physical appearance is the most important factor in determining a female's worth to herself and to others. The eating disorder is seen as developing because of a disproportionate desire to please others, particularly men. Bulimarexic women lack a sense of self-worth and personal power; they rely on others and prove their worth by accommodating to the stereotype of thinness. Food restriction thus becomes perceived by these women as representing the struggle for control over oneself and others. However, when the expectations about how this control will affect other aspects of their lives are unfulfilled, a binge episode ensues and intense pleasure is achieved through being out of control. Inevitably, shame and disgust follow the binging episode, and control is reasserted through vomiting and purging. The bulimic then becomes preoccupied with the fear of being fat in a culture in which this body state brings about male rejection. The solution is fasting, which results in a struggle that eventually leads to a further binge episode. The cycle then repeats itself. Because men are less likely than women to define their self-worth primarily in terms of physical appearance, Boskind-Lodahl believes that they are less at risk for developing bulimarexia.

2.3.1. Adolescent-Onset Obesity. Sex differences in the importance of physical traits may have special significance in determining the clinical characteristics of individuals with juvenile-onset obesity. In our culture, the state of obesity can be considered as a deviation from a norm of physical attractiveness just as any other physical aberration is a deviation from that norm. Particularly during the adolescent years when aspects of one's body development are so painfully important, being obese would seem to result in psychological consequences similar to that of having any other type of physical handicap. Thus, depression, low self-esteem, and a generalized negative self-concept become associated with adolescent obesity (Hammar, Campbell, Campbell, Moores, Sareen, Gareis, and Lucas, 1972).

There is evidence that some individuals with juvenile-onset obesity may show signs of psychological disturbance, as compared to individuals with obesity developing in other periods of their lives. Stunkard and Burt (1967) found that obese adolescent girls exhibited strikingly negative body evaluations that were not found in an obese preadolescent female group. Furthermore, massively obese persons with juvenile-onset obesity hospitalized for weight reduction exhibited a greater degree of psychological disturbance and a greater permanence in their body image of themselves as fat than did massively obese individuals with adult-onset obesity (Glucksman and Hirsch, 1969; Grinker, Hirsch, and Levin, 1973). Our own clinical experience has been that some obese persons, most usually with obesity beginning during adolescence, will indicate that although they have succeeded in losing weight, their mental image of themselves is still that of a fat person. They often report that when catching a reflection of themselves in a store window, they feel surprised to discover that their objective body state is actually much thinner than the way they perceive themselves. Given this continued cognitive view of themselves as fat and unattractive, one can see why the self-consciousness, poor self-image, and other effects of having been obese would continue to be psychologically influential.

Sex differences in the importance of physical traits can mean that adolescent females are even more likely than adolescent males to receive negative feedback for obesity. For example, Canning and Mayer (1966, 1967) found that obese adolescent college applicants were rejected at a higher rate than nonobese applicants with similar qualifications, and that this was particularly true for female obese applicants. This differential valuation of physical traits on the basis of one's sex can also be reflected in the self-concepts of these obese adolescent females. In our clinical work, we have noted that females with adolescent-onset obesity can be quite difficult to treat. This seems in part to be due to the extremely poor self-attitudes manifested by these women and also due to their history of repeated failure of weight loss attempts. Bruch (1957) has also noted that the perception of failure becomes a self-fulfilling prophecy that dooms many of those attempting to lose weight. This process seems particularly insidious in females with adolescent-onset obesity.

2.4. Cultural Differences in Standards of Physical Attractiveness for Females

Cultural standards regarding female beauty differ across certain societies (Beller, 1977). This class of culturally transmitted sex role stereotypes concerning ideal body shape and physical attractiveness for males and females may have a direct influence on the development of eating disorders. This point has been made by Bruch (1973) and others, who have cited the "American preoccupation with slimness" as an important factor in the development of anorexia nervosa. Again, though there is little research that directly links cultural attitudes about ideal shape to abnormal eating patterns, there is evidence that both males and females equate slenderness in women with the ideal of female attractiveness (Huenemann, Shapiro, Hampton, and Mitchell, 1966; Leon, Carroll, Chernyk, and Finn, 1983). These attitudes parallel the sex differences in the epidemiology of eating disorders. Further, Huenemann *et al.* (1966) demonstrated that normal-weight black adolescent females are less likely than their Caucasian peers to designate an extremely slim body appearance as desirable. This finding seems significant in light of the fact that anorexia nervosa and bulimia are extremely rare or nonexistent among black females.

Lerner and colleagues have carried out a series of investigations of preferred body image evaluating American cultural standards as well as those of Japan and Mexico. U.S. kindergarten children (Lerner and Gellert, 1969; Lerner & Schroeder, 1971) expressed a consistent aversion to photographs of same-sex chubby children. In contrast, Mexican adolescents (Lerner and Pool, 1972), Japanese adolescents (Lerner and Iwawaki, 1975), and Japanese university students (Iwawaki and Lerner, 1976) exhibited negative attributions toward both endomorphic *and* ectomorphic body builds for males and for females. Again, these findings seem significant in view of the low incidence of anorexia nervosa in these two countries. There are only a few case reports of anorexia nervosa from Japan, and one from Mexico (Espinosa-Campos, Robles, Gual, & Perez-Palacios, 1974).

2.5. Dieting Patterns

Another cultural phenomenon that seems quite important when discussing modes of social influence on eating patterns is the current national obsession with dieting. Chernin (1981) quotes the Harvard Medical School Health Letter as estimating that 20 million Americans are on a "serious" diet at any given moment. A 1975 national survey of consumer knowledge regarding nutrition found that 47% of respondents considered themselves overweight (U.S. Department of Agriculture, 1975). Another national survey performed by the FDA in 1974 found that 55% of the households interviewed had at least one person who was attempting to gain or lose weight, with the vast majority trying to lose weight. Unfortunately, sex comparisons were not reported.

Of course, this "dietmania," as it was termed in a recent *Medical Times* report (Dietmania; 1979), has both real and metaphorical costs. Many women only somewhat overweight continually subject themselves to unhealthy diet regimens and continually cycle between gaining and losing weight. They are extremely unhappy about their physical appearance because they are probably trying to attain a weight level that is physiologically too low for them (Keesey, 1978). Chernin (1981) estimates that $10 billion a year is spent in America alone on diet-related services and products. The majority of this money goes to spas and "health farms," but a substantial portion is also spent on nonprescription diet aids, prescription appetite-suppressant medications, and diet books. As Wooley and Wooley (1980) have pointed out, perhaps the greatest cost of "dietmania" cannot easily be estimated in terms of dollars and cents. These other costs include the worry, effort, and restriction of social activities that often accompanies serious dieting. In some cases, the costs are even more serious. The expected annual death rate for patients reducing weight is slightly under 2 per 100,000. The death rate for women using the liquid protein diet in 1977 and 1978 was estimated at 59 per 100,000 (Robson, 1979).

An examination of sex differences in current dieting practices in the United States will soon convince any reader that it is women who bear the brunt of our current national obsession. Chernin (1981) quotes representatives of weight loss organizations who estimate that 95% of their members are women. Balter (1974) reported that 85% of amphetamine prescriptions were given to women before regulations were tightened in 1972. A 1978 national telephone survey by the Center for Disease Control estimated that 98,000 Caucasian women used the liquid protein diet for at least 1 month in that year (Robson, 1979).

Of course, all of these statistics would mean nothing if it could be shown that indeed so many women need to lose weight. However, several clinicians have reported (Wooley and Wooley, 1980) that half of the applicants to weight loss programs may be within normal weight limits by existing standards (i.e., within 15–20% of average weight). Also, many experts (Gubner, 1974; Wooley and Wooley, 1980) are now suggesting that current standards for defining obesity are too stringent, and that the popularly used height and weight tables should be redone to reflect this. (Of interest is the fact that the Metropolitan Life Insurance Company has recently undertaken a revision of their widely used actuarial tables.)

We have been impressed by the fact that many families do not become concerned about the anorexic's dieting patterns until the weight loss has reached an extreme level. This appears in part to be due to a cultural predisposition to view serious dieting in females as normal. Beuf (1976) mentions the case of Sue, the 19-year-old daughter of a physician. This girl's parents were aware of her bulimic pattern of binging, severe dieting, and self-induced vomiting, but did not view this pattern as abnormal. Her father even commented that his "baby girl" set a perfect example for his patients (especially those who might become heart attack victims) as to how they should be eating.

3. Other Mental Health Ramifications

In the preceding section we pointed out ways in which sex role stereotypes concerning public eating behavior, ideal body shape, the importance of physical traits, and dieting may have an etiological role in the development of abnormal eating patterns. Though the major focus of this chapter is on eating disorders, we would like to point out that these sex role attitudes may also play a role in the development of other forms of psychopathology.

The combination of more stringent weight standards for women and the suggested greater importance of physical attributes in the attitudes toward women appears to have created a situation in which a majority of females over a wide age range in the United States are greatly dissatisfied with their bodies. For example, none of the women in the Jourard and Secord study (1955) rated all parts of their bodies positively. Exactly comparable data for males are lacking; however, it is known that more women than men rated parts of their bodies in a negative manner (Secord and Jourard, 1953). Clifford (1971) found that females in the 11–19 age range rated their own bodies as less satisfactory than did males in the same age group. Further, Douty, Moore, and Hartford (1974) reported that 59% of the females in a college sample rated themselves as low on "satisfaction with figure."

The implications of these findings of general dissatisfaction among females about their bodies for the overall mental health and self-esteem of women in this country seem important to consider. Secord and Jourard (1953), among others, have reported substantial negative correlations between measures of satisfaction with one's body and measures of anxiety and self-esteem. It is well known that large sex differences exist in the number of persons seeking mental health services, with a large preponderance of females to males requesting psychotherapy (Pendergrass, 1974). Also, other disorders besides anorexia nervosa and bulimia, such as clinical depression, show a much higher incidence in females than in males (Radloff, 1980). It seems possible that cultural attitudes regarding ideal female body shape and the importance of physical appearance have significance in explaining these statistics, as well as the high proportion of women manifesting eating disorders.

4. "Indirect" Influences of Sex Roles on Eating Disorders

In the next section we will discuss certain sex-stereotypic attitudes that we believe to have an "indirect" influence on the development of anorexia nervosa, bulimia, and obesity. The possibility exists that such attitudes are general factors implicated in many forms of psychopathology, including chemical abuse and depression. We mention these factors because they have played a major role, at times, in the theorizing about eating disorders.

4.1. Emotional Expression

It indeed seems evident from the research literature as well as from an array of clinical reports that many obese persons consume foods as a means of dealing with emotional arousal (McKenna, 1972; Meyer and Pudel, 1972). Obese persons (predominantly women) who regained the weight they had previously lost in a weight-reduction program reported a greater frequency of eating in response to a variety of both positive and negative emotional states than did persons who maintained the weight they had lost 1 year previously (Leon and Chamberlain, 1973).

For many individuals with weight problems, the taking in of food becomes a learned response for dealing with the emotions generated in a variety of interpersonal situations. This may be particularly true for women, however, in that the cultural stereotypes of appropriate emotional expression can function to reinforce noneffective responses to interpersonal situations requiring assertive behaviors. Thus, in a variety of social and vocational situations that might provoke anger, women are not encouraged to or may even be punished for expressing the anger. Similarly, if one does not know how to or is afraid of asserting oneself and expressing one's realistic feelings about a difficult situation, a possible means of coping with feelings is through the consumption of food. While food intake may not necessarily result in the reduction of emotional arousal, consuming food may temporarily interfere with these unpleasant emotional feelings and thus function as a response that is incompatible with anxiety, anger, or other affective states. The encouragement of dependent attitudes and behaviors in women might in this way tend to provide strong social pressures to eat rather than openly express feelings when emotionally aroused.

A strong social pressure or expectation that women will be either hysterical in emotional expression (a nonspecific and nonfunctional emotional response to life events) or dependent and nonassertive obviously does not encourage adaptive coping behaviors. Given particular learning experiences in relation to food and perhaps certain biological predispositions as well, some women will overeat and gain weight as part of coping with various stressful events in their life. Unfortunately, the strong pressures to eat in these circumstances are contrary to equally strong societal pressures to be as thin as possible.

Difficulties in emotional expression have also been suggested by some writers to be implicated in the etiology of anorexia nervosa (Bruch, 1978; Leon, 1979). In our clinical work, we have noted that many of the anorexic youngsters we have had contact with have been described by their parents and by themselves as good, conscientious, and obedient youngsters. The preanorexic behavior pattern very often was characterized as that of a dependent, nonassertive young girl who usually did what she was told (Warren, 1968). The stubbornness and intractibility of the self-starvation pattern of anorexia nervosa is in sharp contrast to this behavioral description. The lengths to which these youngsters go to refrain from eating, or to vomit or purge themselves of the food they have just consumed, is striking. The generally compliant and unobtrusive behavior pattern that hospitalized anorexics exhibit in areas other than food consumption is also quite notable.

4.2. Sexual Conflicts

Some authors have postulated that sexual conflicts underlie many abnormal eating patterns (Cobb, 1950; Crisp, 1967; Gifford, Murawski, and Pilot, 1970; Meyer, 1971). Such theoretical formulations have usually pointed to the individual as the center of the conflict; specifically, women with eating disorders have been viewed as having disturbed or immature attitudes regarding sexuality and the feminine role.

In the case of obesity, it has been postulated that certain individuals develop a "wall of fat" to protect themselves from the possibility of engaging in sexual activity (Orbach, 1978). Our clinical experience indicates that, in general, highly overweight individuals have a less active sex life than do normal weight individuals. In some persons, however, it is unclear whether this reduced sexual activity is actually some sort of defense on the part of the individual, the result of social repudiation of obese persons, or the result of an aversion to physical exertion. It has been reported that many of the recipients of jejunoileal bypass operations for massive obesity show, among other positive clinical indicators, increased sexual activity and self-esteem (Bray, 1979). The increased availability of sexual partners postoperatively is apparently viewed by these individuals not as conflictual but, on the contrary, as desirable and welcomed. The enhancement of self-esteem and feelings of sexual attractiveness with weight loss suggests that the body weight *per se* strongly inhibited interpersonal and sexual relationships (Leon *et al.*, 1979).

Sexual concerns have also been cited in the development of anorexia nervosa and bulimia, particularly in the context of the adolescent girl's anxiety about assuming adult sexual roles. This concern is demonstrated in our ongoing investigation as well as in the data of others. As an example, a significant proportion of the anorexics in our study indicated that they were either unconcerned or pleased that their menstrual periods stopped or never started because of their severe weight loss (Leon *et al.*, 1980). Anorexia nervosa has also been conceptualized as a "disorder of shape" in terms of a phobic avoidance centering around the pubertal weight threshold (Crisp *et al.*, 1977). Bruch (1978) also discussed the onset of anorexia nervosa as due in part to sexual concerns associated with general expectations of growing up and acting as a mature adult.

Given the continued existence in our society of a double standard of sexual behavior (albeit more liberalized in recent years), the timid, obedient young girl who already might have some concerns about eating and body appearance could find the self-starvation pattern a reinforcing one in order to avoid problems and expectations related to heterosexual activity. A physically obvious result of the semistarvation is the markedly young appearance of anorexics. This look of immaturity is due to the absence of breast development and other secondary sexual characteristics with weight loss. Looking younger, then, enables one to avoid the sexual and general societal expectations of maturity that one would have for someone whose physical appearance was more commensurate with his or her age. These speculations are strengthened by the recent findings of Beaumont, Abraham, and Simson (1981) on the psychosexual histories of adolescent and young adult anorexic patients. Interviews indicated that a significant number felt that sexual problems such as anxiety and guilt feelings about heterosexual activities precipitated their illness or maintained their anorexic behavior pattern.

An interesting report by Crisp, Harding, and McGuinness (1974) suggests that sexual concerns may indeed be implicated in the development of anorexia nervosa, but that these concerns may be related to parental conflicts about sexuality. Crisp *et al.* reported that as the anorexic's weight improved in treatment and she began to exhibit a more postpubertal appearance, the parents became significantly more anxious and depressed. These parental mood changes were found to be associated with long-standing marital difficulties in terms of the parents' sexual relationship with each other as well as other areas of difficulty. Thus, being confronted with a female child who was obviously maturing sexually was a threatening aspect to the parents because of their own problems with each other. In this situation, the sexual concerns of the parents of the anorexic were projected onto her and then became part of the youngster's own concerns.

5. Overview

We have attempted to summarize the theories and empirical evidence suggesting that culturally defined sex roles are involved in the development of anorexia nervosa, bulimia, and obesity. We considered the relationship of sex role stereotyping to beliefs about appropriate eating behaviors, influences in ideal body shape and dieting, attitudes about emotional expression, and expectations regarding sexual behavior. These various cultural values as well as the family environment the youngster grows up in and the attitudes and eating practices of one's immediate peers can all be viewed as factors influencing the development and expression of eating disorders. In addition, biological variables related to endocrine functioning and hypothalamic regulatory factors might also influence the development of an eating disturbance. These cultural and biological factors could operate in a complex interaction with each other in determining the clinical manifestations of anorexia nervosa, bulimia, and obesity.

6. Implications for Clinical Intervention

An acceptance that sex role attitudes may have a place in the etiology of eating disorders has implications for possible treatment paradigms. Treatment programs including or emphasizing feminist values have been described by Boskind-Lodahl (1976), Flack and Grayer (1975), and Wooley, Wooley, and Dyrenforth (1979). At this point, we would like to discuss the elements of these programs that are related to the material presented earlier.

The strategy of including assertiveness training as a component of clinical intervention seems to follow directly from the evidence that eating disorders can result from difficulties in emotional expression. In the case of anorexia nervosa, bulimia, and obesity, learning to deal with interpersonal concerns in ways other than through food-related behaviors is a crucial treatment goal. It seems that only through more adaptive interpersonal functioning will persons with eating disorders be able to overcome these disturbances and function in a generally more adequate manner.

An additional area that seems important to explore in therapy is the tendency for women to define their self-worth in terms of their weight and physical appearance. Boskind-Lodahl (1976) stated that examining the ramifications of this attitude about self-worth was essential to her group treatment approach to bulimarexia. However, we disagree with Boskind-Lodahl's tendency to attribute cultural definitions of female attractiveness as a phenomenon entirely imposed on women by men. As Chernin (1981) has pointed out, the reasons why women have themselves fostered the "tyranny of slimness" need to be considered as well.

Perhaps one of the most obvious conclusions following from a consideration of clinical interventions for eating disorders is that the American public could benefit from large-scale public health education efforts. As discussed earlier, before the recent flux of media reports on bulimia, numerous women engaging in these behaviors did not see this pattern as abnormal or know of the physical risks of continued binging and purging. Many more women may yet be uninformed about the risks associated with this syndrome. It is also obvious that a great number of women with relatively normal eating patterns are obsessed with obtaining a weight that physiologically is too low for them. Not only the general public but also health care professionals need to be informed about the realistic standards for normal weight so they do not unwittingly contribute to unnecessary dieting or weight loss. Before a practitioner recommends a particular treatment regimen, a careful evaluation of whether the individual is truly overweight is strongly warranted (Leon, 1981).

7. Research Priorities

As we noted at the beginning of this chapter, there is little research that directly investigates the relationship between sex role stereotyping and eating behavior. As a result, it has been necessary to draw conclusions about the etiological role of sex role attitudes on eating disorders through indirect means, i.e., by observing parallels between sex role stereotypes and epidemiological trends in eating disorders in that culture. If the influence of social values on abnormal eating patterns is to be clearly understood and documented, research needs to be undertaken that directly assesses the relationship between these two sets of factors. We suggest that, initially, the following paradigms may be useful: (1)

comparisons of the sex role attitudes, sex role identities, and family role histories of individuals with eating disorders to those of individuals seeking psychiatric and psychological treatment for other problems and to nontreatment controls, (2) correlational studies with nonclinical populations assessing the relationship between sex role attitudes and issues of body cathexis, ideal body shape, self-esteem, dieting practices, and eating behavior, (3) detailed case reports on males suffering from bulimia and anorexia nervosa, with special emphasis given to sex role attitudes, gender identity, and sexual preference.

Another important area of research concerns the development of more effective treatment programs for eating disorders. Outcome studies in the area of obesity point to the continued ineffectiveness of most intervention programs when looked at from the perspective of the long-term maintenance of the weight reduction. Similarly, the outcome literature surveying the treatment of anorexia nervosa points to continued eating and psychological difficulties for a substantial number of the persons treated. In addition, there are no systematic psychotherapy outcome studies that have been reported for treating bulimics. Given the high incidence of this latter disorder, the development of effective intervention programs and their systematic evaluation is an acute priority.

The development of intervention programs that incorporate an examination of the clients' sex role attitudes and definitions of self-worth as a part of treatment (e.g., Boskind-Lodahl's approach) seems important. However, these programs need to be systematically compared to other programs to determine the specific relevance of these various treatment components. It clearly is an empirical question whether "feminist" treatment approaches are effective with all clients or only with those with certain class backgrounds and value structures.

A demonstration that feminist treatment strategies are effective in alleviating the symptoms of various eating disorders would not itself prove that sex role stereotyping plays an etiological role in the development of these problems. This finding would, however, serve as one piece of information in assessing the construct validity of such a hypothesis and would provide important information about the treatment of persons with eating disorders.

8. References

Balter, M. Extent and character of amphetamine use. In L. Lasagna (Ed.), *Obesity: Causes, consequences, and treatment.* New York: Medcom, 1974.

Beller, A. S. *Fat and thin: A natural history of obesity.* New York: Farrar, Straus & Giroux, 1977.

Bemis, K. Current approaches to the etiology and treatment of anorexia nervosa. *Psychological Bulletin*, 1978, *85*, 593–617.

Beuf, A. *Anorexia nervosa: A sociocultural approach*. Unpublished manuscript, University of Pennsylvania, 1976.

Beumont, P. J. V., Abraham, S. F., and Simson, K. G. The psychosexual histories of adolescent girls and young women with anorexia nervosa. *Psychological Medicine*, 1981, *11*, 131–140.

Boskind-Lodahl, M. Cinderella's stepsisters: A feminist perspective on anorexia nervosa and bulimia. *Signs: Journal of Women in Culture and Society*, 1976, *2*, 341–356.

Bray, G. A. A look at diets and other treatments for obesity. *Medical Times*, 1979, *107*, 51–55.

Bruch, H. *The importance of overweight*. New York: Norton, 1957.

Bruch, H. *Eating disorders: Obesity, anorexia, and the person within*. New York: Basic Books, 1973.

Bruch, H. *The golden cage. The enigma of anorexia nervosa*. Cambridge, Mass.: Harvard University Press, 1978.

Canning, H., and Mayer, J. Obesity—Its possible effect on college acceptance. *New England Journal of Medicine*, 1966, *275*, 1172–1174.

Canning, H., and Mayer, J. Obesity: An influence on high school performance? *American Journal of Clinical Nutrition*, 1967, *20*, 352–354.

Chernin, K. *The obsession: Reflections on the tyranny of slenderness*. New York: Harper & Row, 1981.

Clifford, E. Body satisfaction in adolescence. *Perceptual and Motor Skills*, 1971, *33*, 119–125.

Cobb, S. *Emotions and clinical medicine*. New York: Norton, 1950.

Crisp, A. H., Harding, B., and McGuinness, B. Anorexia nervosa: Psychoneurotic characteristics of parents: Relationship to prognosis. *Journal of Psychosomatic Research*, 1974, *18*, 167–173.

Crisp, A. H. Anorexia nervosa. *Hospital Medicine*, 1967, *1*, 713–718.

Crisp, A. H., Kalucy, R. S., Lacey, J. H., and Harding, B. The long-term prognosis in anorexia nervosa: Some factors predictive of outcome. In R. A. Vigersky (Ed.), *Anorexia nervosa*. New York: Raven Press, 1977.

Crisp, A. H., Palmer, R. L., and Kalucy, R. S. How common is anorexia nervosa? A prevalence study. *British Journal of Psychiatry*, 1976, *128*, 549–554.

Dietmania. *Medical Times*, 1979, *107*, 31–34.

Douty, H. I., Moore, J. B., and Hartford, D. Body characteristics in relation to life adjustment, body image, and attitudes of college females. *Perceptual and Motor Skills*, 1974, *33*, 119–125.

Espinosa-Campos, J., Robles, C., Gual, C., and Perez-Palacios, G. Hypothalamic, pituitary and ovarian function assessment in a patient with anorexia nervosa. *Fertility and Sterility*, 1974, *25*, 453–458.

Fisher, S. Sex differences in body perception. *Psychological Monographs*, 1964, *78*, 1–22.

Flack, R., and Grayer, E. D. A consciousness-raising group for obese women. *Social Work*, 1975, *20*, 484–486.

Food and Drug Administration. *Food and nutrition: Knowledge and beliefs, a nationwide study among food shoppers by response analysis*. Washington: U.S. Government Printing Office, March 1974.

Galdston, R. Mind over matter: Observations on 50 patients hospitalized with anorexia nervosa. *American Academy of Child Psychiatry Journal*, 1974, *13*, 246–263.

Garner, D. M., and Garfinkel, P. E. Socio-cultural factors in the development of anorexia nervosa. *Psychological Medicine*, 1980, *10*, 647–656.

Garner, D. M., Garfinkel, P. E., Schwartz, D., and Thompson, M. Cultural expectations of thinness in women. *Psychological Reports*, 1980, *47*, 483–491.

Gifford, S., Murawski, B. J., and Pilot, M. Anorexia nervosa in one of identical twins. *International Psychiatry Clinics*, 1970, 7, 139–228.

Glucksman, M. L., and Hirsch, J. The response of obese patients to weight reduction: III. The perception of body size. *Psychosomatic Medicine*, 1969, 131, 1–7.

Grinker, J., Hirsch, J., and Levin, B. The affective responses of obese patients to weight reduction: A differentiation based on age at onset of obesity. *Psychosomatic Medicine*, 1973, 35, 57–63.

Gubner, R. Overweight and health: Prognostic realities and therapeutic possibilities. In L. Lasagna (Ed.), *Obesity: Causes, consequences, and treatment*. New York: Medcom, 1974.

Hammar, S. L., Campbell, M. M., Campbell, V. A., Moores, N. L., Sareen, C., Gareis, F. J., and Lucas, B. An interdisciplinary study of adolescent obesity. *Journal of Psychiatry*, 1972, 80, 373–383.

Huenemann, R. L., Shapiro, L. R., Hampton, M. C., and Mitchell, B. W. A longitudinal study of gross body composition and body conformation and their association with food and activity in a teen-age population: Views of teen-age subjects on body conformation, food and activity. *American Journal of Clinical Nutrition*, 1966, 18, 325–338.

Iwawaki, S., and Lerner, R. M. Cross-cultural analyses of body-behavior relations: III. Developmental intra- and inter-cultural factor congruence in the body build stereotypes of Japanese and American males and females. *Psychologica: An International Journal of Psychology in the Orient*, 1976, 19, 67–76.

Jones, D. J., Fox, M. M., Babigian, H. M., and Hutton, H. E. Epidemiology of anorexia nervosa in Monroe County, New York: 1960–1976. *Psychosomatic Medicine*, 1980, 42, 551–558.

Jourard, S. M., and Secord, P. F. Body size and body-cathexis. *Journal of Consulting Psychology*, 1954, 18, 184.

Jourard, S. M., and Secord, P. F. Body-cathexis and the ideal female figure. *Journal of Abnormal Social Psychology*, 1955, 50, 243–246.

Keesey, R. E. Set-points and body weight regulation. *Psychiatric Clinics of North America*, 1978, 1, 523–543.

Kurtz, R. Your body image: What it tells about you. *Science Digest*, 1969, 66, 52–55.

Leon, G. R. Current directions in the treatment of obesity. *Psychological Bulletin*, 1976, 86, 557–578.

Leon, G. R. Cognitive-behavior therapy for eating disturbances. In P. Kendall and S. Hollon (Eds.), *Cognitive-behavioral interventions: Theory, research, and procedures*. New York: Academic Press, 1979.

Leon, G. R. Personality and behavioral correlates of obesity. In B. Wolman (Ed.), *Psychological aspects of obesity. A handbook*. New York: Van Nostrand Reinhold, 1981.

Leon, G. R., and Carroll, K. *The bulimia vomiting disorder within a generalized substance-abuse pattern*. Paper presented at the annual meeting of the Association for the Advancement of Behavior Therapy, Toronto, November 1981.

Leon, G. R., and Chamberlain, K. Emotional arousal, eating patterns, and body image as differential factors associated with varying success in maintaining a weight loss. *Journal of Consulting and Clinical Psychology*, 1973, 40, 474–480.

Leon, G. R., Eckert, E. D., Teed, D., and Buchwald, H. Body image, personality, and life event changes after jejunoileal bypass surgery for massive obesity. *Journal of Behavioral Medicine*, 1979, 2, 39–55.

Leon, G. R., Carroll, K., Chernyk, B., and Finn, S. *Binge eating and associated habit patterns within college student and identified bulimic populations*. Manuscript submitted for publication, 1983.

Leon, G. R., Lucas, A. R., Colligen, R. C., Ferdinande, R. J., and Kamp, J. *Body image, sexual attitudes, and interpersonal behavior patterns in anorexia nervosa*. Manuscript submitted for publication, 1983.

Lerner, R. M., and Gellert, E. Body identification, preference, and aversion in children. *Developmental Psychology*, 1969, *1*, 456–462.

Lerner, R. M., and Iwawaki, S. Cross-cultural analyses of body-behavior relations: II. Factor structure of body build stereotypes of Japanese and American adolescents. *Psychologia: An International Journal of Psychology in the Orient*, 1975, *18*, 83–91.

Lerner, R. M., and Pool, K. B. Body build stereotypes: A cross-cultural comparison. *Psychological Reports*, 1972, *31*, 527–532.

Lerner, R. M., and Schroeder, C. Physique identification, preference, and aversion in kindergarten children. *Developmental Psychology*, 1971, *5*, 538.

McKenna, R. J. Some effects of anxiety level and food cues on the eating behavior of obese and normal subjects: A comparison of the Schachterian and psychosomatic conceptions. *Journal of Personality and Social Psychology*, 1972, *22*, 311–319.

Meyer, J. E. Anorexia nervosa of adolescence: The central syndrome of anorexia nervosa group. *British Journal of Psychiatry*, 1971, *118*, 539–542.

Meyer, J. E., and Pudel, B. Experimental studies on food intake in obese and normal weight subjects. *Journal of Psychosomatic Research*, 1972, *16*, 305–308.

Moore, M. E., Stunkard, A., and Srole, L. Obesity, social class, and mental illness. *Journal of the American Medical Association*, 1962, *181*, 962–966.

Murphy, R. L. Body image development in adulthood. *Nursing Clinics of North America*, 1972, *7*, 617–630.

Nylander, I. The feeling of being fat and dieting in a school population: An epidemiologic interview investigation. *Acta Sociomedica* Scandinavica, 1971, *3*, 17–26.

Orbach, S. *Fat is a feminist issue*. New York: Berkley, 1978.

Pendergrass, V. Women as clinicians in private practice. *American Psychologist*, 1974, *29*, 533–535.

Radloff, L. S. Risk factors for depression: What do we learn from them? In M. Guttentag, S. Salasin, and D. Belle (Eds.), *The mental health of women*. New York: Academic Press, 1980.

Robson, J. R. Obesity—An overview. *Medical Times*, 1979, *107*, 49–50.

Russell, G. Bulimia nervosa: An ominous variant of anorexia nervosa. *Psychological Medicine*, 1979, *9*, 429–448.

Secord, P. F., and Jourard, S. M. The appraisal of body cathexis: Body-cathexis and the self. *Journal of Consulting Psychology*, 1953, *17*, 343–347.

Seltzer, C. C., and Mayer, J. A simple criterion of obesity. *Postgraduate Medicine*, 1965, *38*, A-101–A-107.

Silverstone, J. T., Gordon, R. P., and Stunkard, A. J. Social factors in obesity in London. *Practitioner*, 1969, *202*, 682–688.

Stunkard, A., and Burt, V. Obesity and the body image: II. Age at onset of disturbances in the body image. *American Journal of Psychiatry*, 1967, *123*, 1443–1447.

Stunkard, A., d'Aquili, E., Fox, S., and Filion, R. D. L. Influence of social class on obesity and thinness in children. *Journal of the American Medical Association*, 1972, *221*, 579–584.

United States Department of Agriculture. Homemakers food and nutrition knowledge, practices, and opinions. *Home Economics Research Report*, No. 39, Washington: U.S. Government Printing Office, 1975.

Warren, W. A study of anorexia nervosa in young girls. *Journal of Child Psychology and Psychiatry*, 1968, *9*, 27–40.

Wooley, S. C., and Wooley, O. W. Eating disorders: Obesity and anorexia. In A. Brodsky and R. Hare-Musten (Eds.), *Women and psychotherapy*. New York: Guilford Press, 1980.

Wooley, S. C., Wooley, O. W., and Dyrenforth, S. R. Theoretical, practical and social issues in behavioral treatments of obesity. *Journal of Applied Behavior Analysis*, 1979, *12*, 3–25.

14

Senescence, Sex Roles, and Stress
Shepherding Resources into Old Age

Linda Holt and Nancy Datan

1. Depression or Death? An Overview of Gender and Aging

In old age, breakdown is generally manifested in depression for women and death for men. We maintain that the key to this sex difference lies, at least in part, in the sex role histories accumulated over a lifetime, since sex roles expose individuals to different types of stress and do not grant the same access to coping resources for both genders. The influence of sex differences on the problems encountered during senescence is the impetus for this chapter.

We begin with a review of sex roles and stress in adulthood and old age. We will suggest an alternative to the traditional pathogenic model and its focus on disease, proposing instead that coping and stress can more usefully be studied by employing the *salutogenic* model of Aaron Antonovsky. This model asks, simply, how, if life is so hard and the bugs are so smart, do any of us manage to stay healthy? We will apply the salutogenic model to a consideration of gender differences and the accumulated stresses and resources acquired by women and men over a lifetime.

Emotional problems are more prevalent among women of all ages. For example, Pearlin (1975) notes that there is quite an accumulation of

Linda Holt • Department of Psychology, West Virginia University. Nancy Datan • Department of Psychology and Gerontology Center, West Virginia University, Morgantown, West Virginia 26506.

evidence that women suffer more from psychological impairment and maintains that it is a result of the different social experiences of men and women. Gender is one of the primary ascribed characteristics that determines one's experiences throughout life, and it seems that simply on the basis of sex, women are exposed to greater stress-provoking situations and are denied equal access to resistance resources, those personal or environmental characteristics that enable one to cope with stress and manage tension effectively (Antonovsky, 1979). In Pearlin's survey (1975) of 2300 people in Chicago (aged 18 to 65), women rated higher on measures of psychogenic illness, the use of psychotropic drugs, rates of cognitive disturbances (e.g., memory and concentration problems), anxiety, and depression. Further analysis showed that the same circumstances underlie both anxiety and depression, with depression being the most prevalent form of psychological breakdown. In addition, when the degree of depression was analyzed, the highest two categories contained almost 20% more women than men (Pearlin, 1975). A thorough analysis of the literature by Weissman (1980) supports Pearlin's contention that the preponderance of depression among females is not an artifact of measurement, which Pearlin based on the responses to a denial scale that he included in his questionnaire.

In speculating on reasons for these findings, Pearlin noted Bernard's contention (1971, cited in Pearlin, 1975) that women who were not employed outside the home lacked a significant source of gratification and were more prone to psychological breakdown; i.e., they have less access to resistance resources. However, Pearlin found no difference in depression when he compared employed women to full-time homemakers. Instead, he found that the amount of role strain was the primary stressor correlated with depression, with role strain increasing as the number of children at home increases and as the age of the youngest child at home decreases (Pearlin, 1975). Further analysis showed that role strain did cause depression, rather than the reverse. The implications are that strain from this source would decrease as women aged, since children would leave home. Although this study does not indicate that outside employment increases the abilities of women to cope with stress, neither does it imply that employment increases role strain and depression. Motherhood, not work, appears to be the source of most of the stress these women experience, and the area in which resistance resources are needed.

In Pearlin's analysis of employed women, he found that they were more likely to be depressed than employed men only when they suffered more problems and greater strains than men. When occupational strain is equal for men and women, the men are actually more likely to suffer depression (Pearlin, 1975). This could be due to women's greater access to other resources, such as family and other social supports. A job may be a man's sole resource, whereas a working woman probably has other resources on which to rely. Most women do have difficulties integrating a job with their family roles, however. The conflict hinges on several intertwining factors. The first is the association of job involvement and maternal conflict, especially among middle-class women. For working-class women, conflict is negatively correlated with the age of their youngest child at home. This also seems to account for age differences in experienced conflict. Younger women have younger children and thus have higher levels of conflict and correspondingly high levels of depression (Pearlin, 1975).

Consistent with Pearlin's findings (1975), depression was the most common form of breakdown found in a study by Lowenthal, Chiriboga, and Thurnher (1975) that involved 216 subjects from four different age groups: high school seniors, aged 16 to 18; newlyweds, aged 20 to 38; middle-aged parents, mean age of 50; and preretirees, mean age of 60. Depression comprised one-fifth of the problems reported, with family problems, phobias, feelings of inferiority, and "nervous breakdowns" also being mentioned. Overall, more women than men reported symptoms of psychological dysfunction, with sex differences particularly pronounced in the two older age groups. Among the newlyweds, men tended to report more symptoms than women, but this difference was not significant. When the context and feelings associated with the symptoms were psychiatrically evaluated, sex differences were still more prominent, with high school, middle-aged, and preretirement women all rated higher on symptomatology than their male peers. Altogether, four-fifths of the reports of depression came from the two younger groups of subjects, nearly half of whom reported severe depression at some time in their lives, and from the middle-aged women, consistent with Pearlin's study (1975).

As these studies have shown, depression is overwhelmingly more prevalent among women than among men, and it tends to rise with age. What is depression, and why is it epidemic among women and the elderly? The answer may lie in part in a lack of resistance resources. The traditional feminine role seems to offer fewer resistance resources than the masculine role, although neither is complete. For example, in a study of women by Cherry and Zarit (1978, cited in Zarit, 1980), women who rated as higher in masculinity on the Bem androgyny scale were also lower in depression and anxiety in comparison to women with low masculinity scores. Thus, there appears to be a relationship between some qualities of traditional masculinity and lower incidence of depression. There also seems to be a relationship between depression and powerlessness, which is common to women and the elderly. For example, Stewart and Salt (1981) point out that, although women have higher rates of depression and use health care facilities more frequently than men, their physical illnesses tend to be relatively minor and they have a longer life expectancy then men. The researchers hypothesize that women's depression stems from learned helplessness and is a "response to the powerlessness inherent in the traditional female role" (1981, p. 1064). With this premise, Stewart and Salt investigated the relationship of stress, life-style, and symptomatology in women. Their subjects were 33-year-old females that were categorized into four groups: (1) married career women with children, (2) married career women without children, (3) married women with children (no career), and (4) single career women without children.

The results of the study showed that, for single career women, stress in the occupational role was a significant predictor of physical illness but not depression, similar to the results of previous research on men. Stress in family roles was significantly correlated with depression for housewives, although the actual level of stress experienced was equivalent for all groups. It seems that the housewives' relative lack of control over stressors led to helplessness and depression in response to these life changes that were externally imposed. On the other hand, the single woman's lack of interpersonal supports places burdens on her that parallel the burdens of the traditional male role of provider. Her response is physical illness rather than depression, the typically masculine pattern. The two groups exposed to a mixture of the two types of stressors do not seem especially vulnerable to either (Stewart and Salt, 1981), which is surprising when the number of stressors involved is considered. From the viewpoint of the salutogenic model and its emphasis on resistance resources, however, the finding is more reasonable. The social-interpersonal support from the family role appears to interact with the economic (and other) resources provided by the work role. The combination of the resources from the two roles seems to facilitate coping, even if the number of roles—and so, the number of stressors—increases. Traditionally, however, men have more access to the resistance resources that accompany work, whereas women have more social support resources. As people age, their access to both these resources declines, which may help to explain the rise in psychopathology with old age. We will now take a closer look at the salutogenic model and its explanation of sex roles, senescence, and psychopathology.

2. Salutogenesis and Senescence: Growing Old and Liking It

Senescence is the period of gradual physical and psychological decline that eventually ends in death. Most of the current research has focused on the diseases specific to old age. It is our contention, however, that senescence may be better understood by investigating the origins of good health, not the etiology of disease. Research based on a *salutogenic* model, proposed by Antonovsky (1979), that asks "why health?" rather than "why disease?" may be better able to distinguish inevitable aspects of decline from those that can be prevented. Most important for this discussion, Antonovsky's salutogenic model provides a new framework for considering sex differences in the health of the elderly and their relationship to the sex role standards maintained throughout life and especially during old age.

We will describe the prevailing pathogenic model, Antonovsky's proposed salutogenic model, and the implications of the latter for sex differences in susceptibility to stress and disease. Of particular importance are the sex differences in access to resistance resources and the relationship to acceptance of the traditional masculine and feminine roles. We believe that the traditional roles do not allow women sufficient resources for coping with stress, as evidenced by the higher rates of most psychopathology among women of all ages (Gove, 1980).

2.1. Pathogenic Model

The pathogenic model essentially asks the question of why an individual succumbs to disease or, more specifically, why an individual succumbs to disease A rather than disease B or rather than remaining healthy. It suggests that most people are healthy most of the time, primarily because research based on this model focuses on a particular disease or set of diseases. This assumption is questionable, however, since "at any one time at least one third and quite possibly a majority of the population of any modern industrial society is characterized by some morbid condition, by any reasonable definition of the term" (Antonovsky, 1979, p. 15). Another, perhaps stronger, tenet of the pathogenic model is that health and disease form a dichotomy. This is useful for research purposes and treatment of pathology, but problems arise from conceptualizing the two as totally dichotomous. How much disease must one have in order to be classified as diseased? Is absolute health possible, other than in theory? A state of disease could be defined as occurring when a person's functioning is impaired, but how much impairment is necessary before an individual is defined as diseased? Fanshel (1972, cited in Antonovsky, 1979) maintains that health consists of a person's ability to perform his/her usual daily activities. That seems to assume that the person generally functions at a healthy and personally satisfying level, which is questionable, especially for the elderly. Our culture accepts only a narrow range of activities as appropriate in old age. When the limitations based on gender are also considered, clearly there are problems with defining health as the ability to maintain the *status quo* of activity.

2.2. Salutogenic Model

In comparison to the pathogenic model, the salutogenic model assumes that there are many degrees of disease and health, and an ease/dis-ease continuum is a better representation of reality than a dichotomy. Thus, from the salutogenic viewpoint of research, one must first locate an individual on the ease/dis-ease continuum. Disease can also be conceptualized as "breakdown," and stressors are a primary factor in the occurrence of physical and/or psychological breakdown. Generally, stressors are inevitable and omnipresent components of the internal or external environment. However, it is not clear that an absence of stressors would always result in good health. It may be that the presence of some stressors is also necessary in order to avoid breakdown or pathology.

By definition, stressors place a load or a strain on an individual, and he/she responds with a state of tension. The process of dealing with that tension is called tension management, which involves the resistance resources of the individual. The consequences of tension management may be positive, negative (pathological), or neutral. Successful tension management puts one at the health or ease pole of the ease/breakdown continuum. Poor tension management results in stress; i.e., part of the strain or tension remains after the tension management process and one moves toward breakdown or dis-ease on the continuum. To put it another way, the individual's homeostasis has not been fully restored when tension management is poor.

The notion of homeostasis is important to Antonovsky's model. There is physiological homeostasis, maintained by automatic, physical mechanisms, and social/psychological homeostasis, maintained by mechanisms that are probably learned (Antonovsky, 1979). They most likely exist in a state of reciprocal interaction and are rarely, if ever, independent. A stressor can arise from external or internal sources and causes a change that upsets the organism's homeostasis in such a way that a nonautomatic response is required to restore the balance. Note that neither the stressor's presence nor the required response is necessarily aversive in any way. In fact, the difference between stressors and nonstressful stimuli is primarily that the organism processes the latter by routine, automatic responses, whereas stressors are environmental demands that require "a nonautomatic and not readily available energy-expending action" (Antonovsky, 1979, p. 72) to restore homeostasis. It logically follows, then, that a given stimulus may be either routine or a stressor depending upon (1) its meaning to the individual and (2) his/her repertoire of available resistance resources, those mechanisms that restore the balance. Furthermore, it would seem that an individual who has successfully responded to previous stressors would be better able to respond to current stressors. To put it another way, a person who has been protected from stressors (e.g., by others) will not have the opportunity to practice resistance (or coping) responses and so has fewer routine or automatic responses in his/her repertoire. This may be the case for many traditional women who are protected from stressors by their parents until they marry and by their husbands afterward. Since they are likely to outlive their husbands, these women face not only the stress of widowhood but also the numerous daily stressors (e.g., management of finances) from which their husbands had sheltered them.

Antonovsky prefers to emphasize the stressors and resources common to the majority of human beings. He points out that the very nature of being human—physically, psychologically, and culturally—necessitates a consensus of definition for a wide range of stressors. In fact, the commonality of some stressors to a majority of people is the foundation of such research as the life change ratings done by Holmes and Rahe (1967). Their questionnaire consists of a list of 43 events that seem to require a significant life change by the individual. Although there are some important individual differences in the meaning of these items, largely there is consensus that these items measure stressors.

Some stressors most likely to be universal include "cataclysmic phenomena" (Lazarus and Cohen, 1977, cited in Antonovsky, 1979, p. 74), such as natural disasters, wars, and relocation, all of which affect large numbers of people and are not under the control of the individuals affected. A second category of universal stressors includes lack of financial resources (e.g., being fired), bereavement, terminal illness, and other extensive physical injury, all of which typically affect fewer persons than cataclysmic stressors. The third type of stressors is the daily hassles of living, in which there are probably more individual differences in meaning compared to the other two categories.

Universal stressors can also be categorized in terms of physical, emotional, or social origins. Emotional stressors may very well be inherent in the human condition. However, the ways in which individuals manage or cope with them can vary drastically. Intertwined with the emotional/psychological stressors are ones engendered by the social environment. These include personal stressors arising from stressful events that happen to significant others (an area relatively ignored by research), and the challenges that come from entering new roles as we age and grow. Some anticipatory socialization can aid in coping with the stressors of new stages and roles, but it is often inadequate and cannot do the job alone. Thus, psychosocial stressors include nonnormative as well as normative life crises, inadequate socialization for impending roles and crises, current historical events (of which today's media have made us very aware), and the "fear of [personally directed] aggression, mutilation, and destruction" (Antonovsky, 1979, pp. 89–90).

Note that the elderly are probably more prone than other age groups to stressors in each category. They are more likely to be relocated, e.g., the home of their children or a nursing home. The relocation is not usually because of war, but it is frequently against the elderly's preferences. Overall, the elderly lack financial resources and are likely to suffer more bereavement, generally losing their parents first, then close friends and spouse. In addition, they are more likely to face losing their own life through a chronic terminal illness. Interwoven with failing health and financial problems are the inevitable daily stressors, exacerbated by the more chronic stressors. For example, one of these daily problems is the fear of crime. Age, followed closely by gender, has greater impact on fear of crime than does race or family income, with women and the elderly being the most fearful. Interestingly, they are less likely to report being victims of crime, although they are more physically vulnerable. This does not mean, however, that their fears are irrational. They may be using protective tactics (Skogan and Maxfield, 1981) or resistance resources that effectively reduce their chances of being victimized.

The old are also overrepresented when we consider different forms of breakdown. They suffer more severe physical illnesses than the young, with about 86% of the elderly having at least one chronic illness. They also have a higher incidence of psychological problems than any other age group, due, at least in part, to the accumulation of "the ills of a lifetime" (Butler, 1971, p. 523). However, they receive fewer psychiatric services than almost any other age group (Zarit, 1980). More specifically, the incidence of psychosis increases significantly for those aged 65 and older (Nahemow and Pousada, 1983). Depression also rises with age (Butler, 1971), with women being prone to depression throughout the life-span. Suicide is especially high for the elderly, who constitute 10% of the general population but account for 25% of the suicides, with white men in their 80s having the highest rate (Butler, 1971). In addition, "elderly widowers have the highest rate of alcoholism of all age groups" (Butler, 1971, p. 534).

2.2.1. Generalized Resistance Resources. The high incidence of breakdown is due not only to the frequency with which women and the elderly are exposed to stressors but also to the availability of resistance resources. As with stressors, Antonovsky is mainly concerned with those resources common to the majority of human beings, which he has termed Generalized Resistance Resources (GRRs). He defines a GRR as "any characteristic of the person, the group, or the environment that can facilitate effective tension management" (1979, p. 99). They are not specific resources for a specific situation, but they do determine the extent to which specific resources are available. As there are several types of stressors, there are also several types of GRRs (Antonovsky, 1979). It is our contention that there is differential access to many of these Generalized Resistance Resources on the basis of age and, particularly, gender.

According to Antonovsky, the most fundamental resistance resource is the sense of coherence, which seems to be an intervening variable between the other GRRs and health. It is at least more highly correlated with health than any other resistance resource. The sense of coherence is related to ego identity (which, along with knowledge-intelligence, constitutes another GRR). Ego identity, based on Erikson's concept of identity, is essentially "a sense of the inner person, integrated and stable, yet dynamic and flexible; related to social and cultural reality, yet with independence" (Antonovsky, 1979, pp. 108–109). Whereas ego identity refers to a sense of oneself, however, the sense of coherence involves a sense of the world. It may be that a strong ego identity is a necessary prerequisite for a strong sense of coherence, since the latter is "a global orientation that expresses the extent to which one has a pervasive, enduring though dynamic feeling of confidence that one's internal and external environments are predictable and that there is a high probability that things will work out as well as can reasonably be expected" (Antonovsky, 1979, p. 8).

The sense of coherence is an enduring dimension of the personality that is subject to minor shifts but is basically long-lasting. It involves seeing the world as meaningful, predictable, and lawful, with affective components as well as cognitive factors. Having a sense of coherence does not mean one sees oneself as completely in control of life, although it most likely does entail the view that one has some control: "The crucial issue is not whether power to determine . . . outcome lies in our own hands or elsewhere. What is important is that the location of power is where it is legitimately supposed to be" (Antonovsky, 1979, p. 128).

Antonovsky gives credit to Erikson for the concept of ego identity, but we should probably take one further step into Erikson's theory to a concept that precedes his idea of identity. The sense of coherence seems to greatly resemble Erikson's idea of basic trust. Erikson (1963) says that "the infant's first social achievement . . . is his willingness to let the mother out of sight without undue anxiety or rage, because she has become an inner certainty as well as an outer predictability" (p. 247). From this, the sense of coherence fundamentally seems to be basic trust generalized from the primary caregiver to a more extensive philosophy. Perhaps the way this orientation becomes generalized is through ego identity, consistent with Antonovsky's speculation that ego identity is a prerequisite for a sense of coherence. Erikson gives support for this notion, stating that "consistency, continuity, and sameness of experience provides a rudimentary sense of ego identity" (1963, p. 247) in the stage of basic trust versus basic mistrust, laying the foundation for a sense of coherence. This orientation may be exemplified by Pearlin's finding (1975) that women cope successfully with the strains of homemaking and avoid depression when they hold an optimistic view of the current stressful situation as abating in the future and see their problems as similar to those of other women in the same role. According to Antonovsky, the sense of coherence seems to interact with the other Generalized Resistance Resources. How an individual develops those, however, and the extent to which they are available to members of different social groups may vary. Thus, an individual's sense of coherence may differ according to age and gender.

Another type of Generalized Resistance Resource is the macrosociocultural resistance resources. These refer to the resources provided by our culture through its definition of our place in the world, the religious or magic rituals culture provides, and other answers the social structure makes available (Antonovsky, 1979). However, the culture's definition of one's place in the world can be a tremendous stressor as well as a resistance resource. The definitions of gender- and age-appropriate behaviors are two excellent examples of this. The macrosociocultural resistance resources seem to interact directly with practically every other GRR, as is evident throughout this discussion.

The third type of Generalized Resistance Resource is "preventive knowledge, attitudes, and behavior" (Antonovsky, 1979, p. 100). The tactic of the preventive GRR is to avoid exposure to stressors. Given that the elderly have experienced a lifetime of stressors, they may have more preventive knowledge than other age groups, providing they have coped effectively with stressors in the past.

Physical and biochemical GRRs are another type of resistance resource. These constitute the physical basis for human adaptability to stressors. However, Selye pointed out that these are most effective only as a temporary holding action against stressors that also seem to be temporary. If the stressors are long-term, another resistance resource is needed (Antonovsky, 1979). These physiological resources appear to decrease with age, although part of this decrement is probably preventable. In general, then, the elderly seem to have less access to this resource than other age groups. However, in terms of gender, women have a longer life expectancy, and it may be due in part to some greater physiological resource(s), at least until menopause. This may be supported by the finding that, although women have entered the labor force at a growing rate, their death rates from occupational stress have not climbed to equal men's death rates from stress-related causes (Stewart and Salt, 1981).

The fifth type, artifactual-material GRRs, consists of access to money and other material resources. Also included in this category are the resources of interpersonal relations that involve access to or possession of power, status, and the services that correspond to such positions (Antonovsky, 1979). This is a resource that varies greatly in our culture with age and gender. Twenty-five percent of the elderly are considered to be poor. Furthermore, those who have been victims of discrimination in employment earlier in life are the ones that suffer most when they grow old (Butler, 1971). Block, Davidson, and Grambs (1981) support this finding with their conclusion that elderly women currently make up the single poorest group in our society. Not only have women generally worked for lower wages and in less prestigious positions than men throughout their working years (Block *et al.*, 1981) but they also appear to have fewer interpersonal relationships that grant access to power. Those who have worked outside the home (and, especially for the present cohort of elderly, there are many who have not) have had little access to the "old boy" network of power, and there are not very many "old girl" networks established yet. Elderly women have primarily relied on their husbands as sources of economic power and status, and since women are six times more likely than men to be widowed (Block *et al.*, 1981), they are in a precarious economic position indeed.

Valuative-attitudinal GRRs are coping styles or behavior patterns that probably vary from individual to individual as well as varying intra-individually from stressor to stressor. The more an individual's coping strategy includes the following three variables, the more effective it will be: (1) rationality, or the accurate assessment of the extent of threat by a stressor; (2) farsightedness, i.e., the ability to anticipate the response of the environment to the strategies one employs; and (3) flexibility, or the willingness to evaluate coping mechanisms, revise them if necessary, and substitute other contingency plans when needed. Thus, the more contingency plans one has available and the more open one is to new information, the greater the chance of successful coping. Some researchers have speculated that women have more flexibility because they generally experience more changes in roles than men and thus have a longer history of adaptation when they are elderly (Saul, 1974, cited in Block *et al.*, 1981). However, according to Antonovsky's definition, flexibility relies on the availability of more than one contingency plan. The number of contingency plans available to the elderly in general and to women in particular is questionable, based on the limitations in their access to other resistance resources. However, the elderly's lifetime of experience in coping with stressors may be very helpful in terms of assessing a stressor and anticipating the impact of the coping strategies that are available.

Interpersonal-relational GRRs consist of social supports, or "the extent to which one is embedded in social networks to which one is committed" (Antonovsky, 1979, p. 116). For example, Pearlin (1975) found that women with a number of social contacts outside the immediate family had more positive feelings about homemaking than women who were more isolated from outside social contacts. According to Pearlin, these social networks provide emotional support, serve as sources of information and a normative framework for problems that arise in homemaking, provide relief from daily routines, and are sources of affiliation that are lacking in the marriage role. Pearlin also found that married mothers reported less strain than did single mothers, which may be due to a husband's social support as well as his financial support. Other research also indicates that this resistance resource is an extremely important one, with some studies showing a linear relationship between social ties and death or disease. Cobb (1979) notes that social support appears to protect against depression throughout the lifespan. In addition, lack of social support has been correlated with onset of diseases such as tuberculosis, arthritis, and coronary heart disease. Cobb also cites evidence that recovery from psychological and physical illnesses is facilitated by social support. Furthermore, Berkman (cited in Cobb, 1979) has found that mortality rates decrease successively for each of the following measures of social support: marriage, contact with friends and relatives, church membership, and formal and informal group associations. These findings support Antonovsky's contention that social supports can serve as a resource only within an immediate social circle (as opposed to being a member of a nation, for example) and that the commitment must be reciprocated by other members of the social network in order for the resource to be effective.

The two genders may not have equal access to all aspects of social support, however. As previously discussed, women are much more likely to be widowed than men and are less likely to have the opportunity to remarry. (Zarit, 1980; Block et al., 1981), thus missing the support of a close marital relationship. However, older women appear to have more social support from friends than do older men. A woman's confidant is typically another woman, whereas older men usually consider their wives to be confidants and to have the responsibility for arranging social engagements (Zarit, 1980). Thus, losing a spouse seems to disrupt social support for a man more than for a woman, although a woman is more likely to suffer economically. This may have some bearing on the finding that elderly widowed men have the highest suicide rates. Although men have traditionally been more likely to work outside the home and consequently have had a greater quantity of social contacts in comparison to women, it appears that these contacts lack the quality of a social support network for men. Instead, men turn to their wives for support, and the loss of that one-person network seems to make life unbearable for many men.

3. Conclusion

We have discussed sex and age differences in the access to resistance resources. The elderly's access—or lack of it—is based in part on the culmination of a lifetime of differential access to resources and resulting psychopathologies. As we have shown, these differences are related to the sex roles and behaviors maintained throughout the life-span. In conclusion, we propose that the salutogenic model provides a useful guide for research questions in this area. Sex differences in the sense of coherence, for example, remain unclear. The powerlessness of women leads us to speculate that men may have a greater sense of coherence. However, women appear to have greater flexibility in handling different roles and live longer than men, which is surely evidence of another sort for a sense of coherence. In sum, we maintain that a change in the traditional sex roles from the masculine-feminine dichotomy to androgyny would result in a better sense of coherence and better coping throughout the life-span. This is especially important in old age, since more egalitarian access to resistance resources could partially eliminate the powerlessness that accompanies old age. As Livson pointed out in one of her last works (1981), however, early socialization patterns in traditional roles make a shift to androgyny difficult for the present cohort of elderly. An increase in age may not mean a decrease in flexibility, however, and we share Livson's hope that the elderly can rise to the challenge.

4. References

Antonovsky, A. *Health, stress, and coping.* San Francisco: Jossey-Bass, 1979.

Block, M. R., Davidson, J. L., and Grambs, J. D. *Women over forty: Visions and realities.* New York: Springer, 1981.

Butler, R. Psychiatry. In I. Rossman (Ed.), *Clinical geriatrics.* Philadelphia: Lippincott, 1971. Pp. 519–550.

Cobb, S. Social support and health through the life course. In M. W. Riley (Ed.), *Aging from birth to death: Interdisciplinary perspectives.* AAAS Selected Symposium 30. Boulder: Westview Press, 1979. Pp. 93–106.

Erikson, E. *Childhood and society* (2nd ed.). New York: Norton, 1963.

Gove, W. R. Mental illness and psychiatric treatment among women. *Psychology of Women Quarterly*, 1980, 4(3), 345–362.

Holmes, T. H., and Rahe, R. H. The social readjustment rating scale. *Journal of Psychosomatic Research*, 1967, 11(2), 213–218.

Livson, F. *Changing sex roles in the social environment of later life*. Paper presented for conference, Aging and milieu: Environmental perspectives on growing old, West Virginia University, May 21–23, 1981.

Lowenthal, M. F., Chiriboga, D., and Thurnher, M. *Four stages of life*. San Francisco: Jossey-Bass, 1975.

Nahemow, L., and Pousada, L. *Geriatric diagnostics*. New York: Springer, 1983.

Pearlin, L. Sex roles and depression. In N. Datan and L. H. Ginsberg (Eds.), *Life-span developmental psychology: Normative life crises*. New York: Academic Press, 1975. Pp. 191–207.

Skogan, W. G., and Maxfield, M. G. *Coping with crime*. Beverly Hills, Calif.: Sage, 1981.

Stewart, A. J., and Salt, P. Life stress, lifestyles, depression and illness in adult women. *Journal of Personality and Social Psychology*, 1981, 40(6), 1063–1069.

Weissman, M. W. Depression. In A. M. Brodsky and R. T. Hare-Mustin (Eds.), *Women and psychotherapy*. New York: Guilford Press, 1980. Pp. 97–112.

Zarit, S. H. *Aging and mental disorders: Psychological approaches to assessment and treatment*. New York: Free Press, 1980.

V

Societal Management and Control

15

Sex Roles, Psychological Assessment, and Patient Management

Peter B. Zeldow

The last 20 years have seen increased recognition (at least among social scientists, feminists, and feminist sympathizers) that sex roles can be restrictive and that gender considerations have exceeded their proper boundaries in many aspects of American life. These insights have been accompanied by increased scrutiny of the mental health professions for evidence of discrimination, exploitation, and oppression in the treatment of women. Two early landmarks in this effort are Chesler's (1972) book, *Women and Madness*, and the study of Broverman, Broverman, Clarkson, Rosenkrantz, and Vogel (1970) that claimed to provide the first empirical demonstration of a double standard of mental health among mental health professionals. The ensuing decade has witnessed a fair amount of empirical research aimed at determining both the nature of sex discrimination and sex role stereotyping and the extent to which they pervade the clinical practices of psychiatrists, psychologists, and other mental health professionals. The present chapter attempts to review the literature on gender differences in select aspects of psychiatric and psychological assessment (judgments of optimal mental health, severity of psychopathology, need for treatment, prognosis) and patient management (referrals, duration of treatment, prescription of medications). The effects of gender and sex roles on various diagnostic entities and on psychotherapy process and outcome are discussed elsewhere in this volume.

Peter B. Zeldow • Rush-Presbyterian-St. Luke's Medical Center, Chicago, Illinois 60612.

1. Psychological Assessment

1.1. Judgments of Mental Health

Any discussion of sex role stereotyping in clinical judgment must invariably begin with the aforementioned study by Broverman and her colleagues. One hestiates to dwell on it for long because its conclusions are well known, having been widely cited and disseminated. Yet some 15 years after the study was conducted, it still seems necessary to correct some of the mistaken impressions people have concerning what Broverman *et al.* actually found.

Broverman *et al.* (1970) instructed 79 psychologists, psychiatrists, and social workers to describe a "mature, healthy, socially competent" male, female, or adult of unspecified gender in terms of a list of known sex role stereotypes. The clinician-judges were specifically asked to indicate to which of two opposite poles (one masculine and one feminine) the object of their rating would be closer. They were asked to think in terms of direction rather than extremes of behavior. The judgments of the male and female clinicians did not differ significantly in any way and were combined for further analyses. There was also strong agreement among the clinicians in all three conditions of the study as to the behaviors and attributes generally characteristic of mental health. The remaining results form the core of the study and have been the subject of some controversy.

Twenty-seven of the items presented to the clinicians had been shown in previous research to be "male-valued" items. That is, the masculine pole represented the more socially desirable behavior or attribute. Eleven of the items were "female-valued," meaning that the female pole was more desirable. On 25 of the 27 male-valued items, the proportion of clinicians who felt males were characterized by the more desirable (read "healthy") items was greater than the proportion who felt females were so characterized. On 7 of the 11 female-valued items, the proportion of clinicians who felt females were characterized by the more desirable items was greater than the proportion who felt males were so characterized. The remaining 4 female-valued items were assigned more often to males than to females. It is from these data and from the significant chi square that they yielded that Broverman *et al.* (1970) drew their widely cited conclusion:

> On the face of it, the finding that clinicians tend to ascribe male-valued stereotypic traits more often to healthy men than to healthy women may seem trite. However an examination of the content of these items suggests . . . a powerful, negative assessment of women. For instance, among these items, clinicians are more likely to suggest that healthy women differ

> from healthy men by being more submissive, less independent, less adven-
> turous, more easily influenced, less aggressive, less competitive, more excit-
> able in minor crises . . . this constellation seems a most unusual way of
> describing any mature, healthy individual. (pp. 4–5)

I do not think it unfair or inaccurate to suggest that this and related
conclusions from the same study (concerning additional evidence of a
double standard of mental health) were welcome news to those who
were convinced of the sexist nature of the mental health professions.
Unfortunately, there are flaws in the Broverman *et al.* study, inac-
curacies in later descriptions of its results, and more recent evidence, all
of which render its original conclusions unconvincing and suggest the
need for one final effort to view the study in proper perspective.

Stricker (1977) reviewed the Broverman *et al.* study in detail and
found both semantic and statistical problems that militate against whole-
sale acceptance of its conclusions. From a semantic point of view, for
example, the conclusion that healthy women differ from healthy men by
being more submissive may not be in line with the data. Stricker suggests that a more accurate, albeit less provocative, conclusion would be
that "the proportion of those who saw healthy women as very dominant
was less than the proportion of those who saw healthy men as very
dominant" (p. 18). More important, individual items were not analyzed
statistically so there is no indication that the differences reported were
statistically significant. Yet "descriptions of the data and citations of the
study assume that significance has been established" (p. 18). In this
regard, Stricker gives examples from later review articles (Broverman,
Vogel, Broverman, Clarkson, and Rosenkrantz, 1972; Levine, Kamin,
and Levine, 1974) that represent incorrectly the actual nature of the data
and assume that a sexist double standard has been unequivocally
demonstrated.

Stricker's own conclusions, based on his review of the Broverman *et
al.* (1970) study, are widely divergent from the original:

> Although sex-role stereotyping exists as a general phenomenon, it is less
> clear that it systematically influences individuals' judgments of single pa-
> tients, and there is no indication that it is more common among male than
> female therapists. (p. 14)
> Widely cited conclusions concerning a double standard of mental health
> and negative evaluations of women are premature in light of the data. They
> may ultimately prove to be correct, but we do not have sufficient evidence at
> the present time to reach such sweeping positions. (p. 21)

Even if the Brovermans' methods and conclusions were beyond
reproach, four more recent studies raise doubts about the durability and
robustness of the phenomenon they report.

A replication by Billingsley (1976) found that the majority of clinicians do not conceptualize or employ sex role stereotypes in ways that bias their judgments of females. A large minority, 44%, however, do.

Other replications, using college students (Kravetz, 1976), school counselors (Petro and Putnam, 1979), and experienced psychotherapists (Maxfield, 1976), all provide evidence suggesting that sex role stereotypes have altered over the last decade. Kravetz (1976) found that women no longer hold different concepts of mental health for men and women corresponding to sex role stereotypes. Petro and Putnam (1979) found that only 11 of the Broverman *et al.* original 38 stereotypic items were still believed to differentiate men from women. Maxfield (1976) found no evidence that mental health stereotypes are biased toward male characteristics to the detriment of healthy women. While the increased sensitivity of clinicians to feminist concerns may have contributed to Maxfield's failure to replicate (Abramowitz and Abramowitz, 1977), the findings of Kravetz and of Petro and Putnam suggest that clinicians and laypersons alike no longer hold different concepts of mental health for men and women corresponding to sex role stereotypes.

In retrospect, and with acknowledgments to critics of Stricker (e.g., Maffeo, 1979), I must agree with Stricker's above-quoted conclusions. It is natural that mental health professionals would share the norms and values of the society in which they work. If society at large values masculine traits more than feminine traits, so will many practicing clinicians. While this must raise the possibility that sex role stereotyping will influence individual clinicians' judgments of single patients, such concern is not tantamount to proof. Indeed, social psychologists have long known that generalized attitudes will not reliably predict specific behaviors (cf. La Piere, 1934). As Stricker (1977) has observed, the rating of generic groups, such as women, provides the greatest opportunity for stereotyping to occur; the rating of specific individuals provides less opportunity.

On the other hand, there is only so much that a single study can accomplish. Whatever the ontological status of the Broverman *et al.* conclusions, their value in inspiring additional research and promoting increased awareness of the potential for sexism in clinical practice has been immense. We now turn to a number of analogue and archival studies at the opposite end of the mental health/mental illness continuum that have attempted more direct tests of evaluative bias against women.

1.2. Analogue Studies

There have been a number of studies that have investigated the effects of sex of patient on a variety of clinical judgments similar to those that mental health professionals must make when confronted with applicants for their services. These studies have been comprehensively reviewed elsewhere (Abramowitz and Docecki, 1977; Davidson and Abramowitz, 1980; Zeldow, 1978); for present purposes, it will suffice to examine a few representative analogue studies, to compare their results with results from archival studies, and, in each case, to update earlier reviews. I have chosen to begin by describing a series of my own studies (Zeldow, 1975, 1976), not out of any sense of special merit but because, in spite of any methodological weaknesses, their results seem to exemplify the results of so many others in this area.

In the first study (Zeldow, 1975), 50 male and 50 female university undergraduates were presented with 56 statements allegedly made by psychiatric patients about themselves. The students were asked to rate on a 7-point scale "how maladjusted or disturbed the patient must have been to make such a statement." Thirty-five of the statements were adopted from the MMPI and formed five separate scales of psychopathology. Half the students of each sex were asked to evaluate female patients, and half were asked to evaluate male patients. Neither sex of patient nor sex of judge, alone or in interaction, affected student judgments of psychopathology.

An additional 21 items (Zeldow, 1976) on the questionnaire were adapted from the Masculinity-femininity (Mf) and Lie (L) scales of the MMPI. Seven items from the Mf scale expressed masculine interest patterns or stereotypes, and seven expressed feminine interest patterns. The L scale items were considered "neutral" because they are not endorsed with differential frequency by men and women. All 21 items were considered nonpathological, in contrast to the obvious psychopathological nature of the other 35 items. No main effect for sex of patient or sex of judge was found. However, a three-way interaction (sex of judge × sex of patient × type of statement) revealed that a female patient, already identified as seriously disturbed, who makes a statement that is conventionally associated with the male sex role will be evaluated as more emotionally maladjusted by male lay judges than if she had described herself in terms of a female sex role stereotype. In short, female patients endorsing masculine preferences pay the price of harsher clinical judgments. Male patients can endorse feminine preferences without any such consequences (cf. Malchon and Penner, 1981).

A second study, also reported in Zeldow (1975), employed eight case histories and solicited, for each one, judgments of severity of psychiatric disturbance, need for professional help, and prognosis. Judges in this study were a heterogeneous group, all of whom either had more experience with psychiatric patients (social workers, medical students, paraprofessionals) or more formal course work in psychology (including courses in abnormal psychology or psychology of adjustment) than judges in the first study. Sex of patient did not influence any of the three ratings in any of the eight case histories, either as a main effect or in interaction with sex of judge. Sex of judge did consistently affect rating of need for professional intervention: In four of the eight cases, females perceived a greater need for intervention than did the males.*

The results of these studies parallel, in two important ways, the results of a host of other analogue studies. First, sex of patient, by itself, is rarely a factor in determining degree of psychopathology, need for professional help, or prognosis. This was confirmed for me in my own review of the literature (Zeldow, 1978), but, perhaps more convincingly, Abramowitz and Docecki (1977) reach the same conclusion in their review paper. Simple sex bias in clinical judgment is simply less pervasive a phenomenon than is sometimes claimed.

However, a second conclusion from my research appears equally well supported in the literature: Sex-related effects do occur and are embedded in complex contents. Abramowitz, Abramowitz, Jackson, and Gomes (1973) reported that politically conservative counselors attribute greater psychological maladjustment to a politically left-oriented female than to her male counterpart. Coie, Pennington, and Buckley (1974) reported that college students attribute more psychopathology to a deviant-acting female than to a male under identical circumstances. Thomas and Stewart (1971) found that high school counselors recommend therapy more often for adolescent women with nontraditional than traditional vocational goals. Hill, Tanney, Leonard, and Reiss (1977) studied university counselors and found no diagnostic or prognostic differences as a function of traditional versus nontraditional career interest. They did find complex interactions involving age of client, sex of counselor, and type of problem (personal-social versus vocational). Such findings demonstrate, not a global prejudice against women, but a variety of specific prejudices; they led me to an earlier generalization that "female patients risk harsher judgments than males when they engage in norm-deviant behavior" (Zeldow, 1978, p. 93).

The following, more recent studies also support the idea that sex-related effects occur but emphasize their situation-specific nature.

---

*An apparent limitation of these studies is their failure to use practicing clinicians as judges. The generality of analogue research findings is a complex and controversial matter (Kazdin, 1978). Certainly, had the above studies produced more widespread evidence of sex differences, replications more closely approximating actual clinical situations would have been mandatory. But if no sex differences are found among judges who bear little resemblance to trained clinicians and who are more likely than clinicians to be influenced by sex role stereotypes, then there is little reason to expect that trained clinicians would respond differently. A more serious limitation of these and other analogue studies concerns their failure to generate the affective intensity that is likely to characterize actual clinical situations (Munley, 1974; Stricker, 1977).

Tilby and Kalin (1980) presented 12 clinically normal stimulus persons to Canadian undergraduates. Half of the stimulus persons were male and half were female. Half of each sex were sex role-deviant in terms of occupation, interest, or life-style. Subjects were invited to evaluate the stimulus persons on severity of maladjustment and on likelihood of receiving psychiatric help. Not surprisingly, sex role-deviant stimulus persons were rated more negatively on both dimensions. However, sex role deviance had a greater effect on males than on females. While there are a variety of reasons why the results of this study might differ from those of Zeldow (1976), Tilby and Kalin speculate that sex role deviance may be better tolerated in successful rather than unsuccessful (or psychiatrically impaired) women. One cannot, of course, assume that actual clinicians would behave similarly.

Kelly and Kiersky (1979) investigated sex differences in judgments of psychopathology using 50 practicing psychotherapists as judges and trained actors posing as patients. Assuming that depressive symptoms are more consistent with the female patient role, and that aggression and impulse control problems are more consistent with the male patient role, it was hypothesized that clinicians would judge role-deviant patients as more severely ill than patients whose symptoms are sex-appropriate. This was indeed the case. However, the effect was limited to male clinicians and was particularly apparent in their judgments of the depressed male, whom they more often diagnosed as psychotic and for whom they more often recommended medication. While this finding was unexpected, it seems to parallel the results of a recent study by Bond (1981). Bond investigated the effects of internal (dispositional) versus external (situational) attributions of behavior that either conformed to or deviated from role expectations. Out-of-role behaviors yielded internal attributions, as predicted by attribution theory, but only when (high school student) judges observed actors of the same sex. Out-of-role behaviors of persons of the opposite sex were not interpreted as revealing the true character of the actor. Keeping problems of generalizability in mind, it is interesting to speculate that Kelly and Kiersky's results concerning male clinicians' differential evaluation of male and female patients were mediated by a similar sex-linked attributional phenomenon.

Kelly and Kiersky's results contrast with the results of a study by Stearns, Penner, and Kimmel (1978), who also examined clinical judgments as a function of patient sex and symptomatology. Practicing psychotherapists read case histories of male and female patients with symptoms of either a depressive or aggressive nature. Males were, in general, judged as having more serious problems than females; however, the sex role congruence/incongruence of the symptoms did not elicit different prognostic expectations or treatment recommendations, as it did in Kelly and Kiersky (1979).

Such studies make it difficult to maintain the generalization that norm-deviant females are the exclusive victims of evaluative prejudice. At least in some circumstances, men are at greater risk.

Attractiveness is another variable that combines with sex of patient to influence clinical judgments. Barocas and Vance (1974) found that physical attractiveness (retrospectively rated) enhanced counselor ratings of adjustment and prognosis. Schwartz and Abramowitz (1978) asked male psychology trainees to view a videotape of a female patient and to describe their reactions on a number of dimensions. In one condition the patient was made up as physically attractive; in another, she was made up to be unattractive. The trainees in the unattractive condition made fewer supportive comments and rated the patient as more likely to terminate therapy prematurely. Here is a bit of evidence in favor of sex-related countertransference suggesting that attractiveness may mediate sex differences in patient management. Of course, attractiveness can be a mixed blessing: Partisanship toward attractive persons of the opposite sex can also lead to a failure to recognize or appreciate the urgency of the request for help (Cash, Kehr, Polyson, and Freeman, 1977).

1.3. Archival Studies

Following Abramowitz and Docecki (1977), there has been a tendency to view analogue studies and archival or field-correlational studies as yielding highly divergent conclusions concerning sex bias in clinical conduct: "The relative absence of patient sex effects in clinical judgment analogues is at variance with the largely antifemale sex role stereotype and archival findings" (p. 473).

The analogue studies reviewed above, however, are overwhelmingly null only when patient sex is considered by itself. When sex of patient is considered in interaction with sex of judge, in-role versus out-role behavior, etc., numerous instances of evaluative prejudice (not always against women) are reported. Conversely, the results of archival studies are not so overwhelmingly antifemale as Abramowitz and Docecki (1977) and Davidson and Abramowitz (1980) conclude. The Masling and Harris (1969) finding of differential TAT administration by psychology interns to male and female patients was partially replicated by Siskind (1973), but not when full-fledged psychologists were studied. Hersen (1971) was unable to replicate the Masling and Harris results at all. Greenberg (1972) reported that male psychology interns obtain significantly more Rorschach responses from female than from male patients. No cross-sex differences were found either for female interns or for experienced clinicians.

Sue (1976) investigated a broad range of diagnostic and patient disposition variables as a function of various demographic characteristics in a sample of over 200 community mental health center patients. Patient sex bore no relationship to diagnosis (psychotic vs. nonpsychotic) or to other dispositions to be discussed later.

Lowinger and Dobie (1968) reported that females were seen for more psychotherapy sessions than males and were judged by their admitting residents to have a number of more positive attributes than their male counterparts. Assignment to drug treatment versus individual psychotherapy did not vary as a function of patient sex.

Haan and Livson (1973) presented data from a longitudinal personality study purportedly showing that male psychologists evaluate patients of both sexes more harshly than do female psychologists. Werner and Block (1975) observed a subtle but fundamental error in Haan and Livson's statistical calculations. Their reanalysis of the data yielded no evidence of clinician sex differences.

A recent study of the relation of psychiatric diagnosis to professional status (Wright, Meadow, Abramowitz, and Davidson, 1980) found a preponderance of psychotic diagnoses among the patients of higher-status (psychiatrist, psychologist) male professionals compared to the patients of lower-status and female professionals. Female clinicians were "strikingly disinclined" to regard female patients as psychotic. Male patients were "twice as likely" to receive more severe diagnoses independent of clinican sex.

A 2-year study of psychiatric emergency room diagnoses and dispositions shows how patient sex and race combine to influence the accuracy of clinical judgments (Gross, Herbert, Knatterud, and Donner, 1969). White women were more likely than nonwhite women to be diagnosed neurotic and referred to outpatient treatments. Nonwhite females were more likely to be diagnosed schizophrenic and to be treated solely in the emergency room. Behavior requiring hospitalization was perceived as neurotic when the patient was white, schizophrenic when the patient was nonwhite. The authors conclude that diagnoses become less accurate and dispositions less specific as social distance between (predominantly male) clinicians and patients increases.

The attempt to summarize such a plethora of studies is a sobering experience. It appears, however, that one finds in the archival data both as much and as little evidence of sex bias as can be found among the analogue studies. Sex of patient rarely influences clinical judgments alone or in interaction with sex of judge. Thus, evidence for global sex discrimination is weak. Complex and circumscribed sex-related effects are plentiful and more prejudicial, on balance, to women than to men. It would be the height of folly to deny that sex bias and sex role stereotyping in clinical assessment can occur. There now seems to be sufficient research, however, to vindicate clinicians of charges of gross evaluative discrimination against the female patient.

2. Patient Management

The next section of this chapter concerns itself with a variety of patient disposition and management variables as they are influenced by patient sex. While assessment and treatment are intimately related, a search for evidence of sex discrimination and stereotyping would be incomplete if it stopped at this point. There have been a number of studies that address the different fates of men and women in the course of seeking professional psychological or psychiatric help. Those pertaining to the disposition of patients, the duration of treatment, and the prescription of psychotropic medications will be reviewed here.

2.1. Patient Selection and Disposition

As reported earlier, Sue (1976) conducted a large-scale study of patient dispositions in a consortium of community mental health centers. Assignment to individual versus group psychotherapy, to paraprofessional versus professional therapists, and program assignments (inpatient vs. outpatient) did not vary with sex of the patient. In brief, sex bore no relationship to services received, not even in combination with other client attributes such as race.

As previously mentioned, Gross et al. (1969) found that white women were more likely to be referred for additional outpatient services, while nonwhite women were more likely to be hospitalized or treated solely in the emergency room. These results contrast sharply with those of Sue and may be attributable to differences in the settings involved.

Brodey and Detre (1972) found that intake workers at a university health service were more likely to refer female patients to individual psychotherapy and male patients to group psychotherapy.

The remaining disposition studies concern the selection of applicants for psychotherapy. Brown and Kosterlitz (1964) found that twice as many women as men sought treatment but that equal proportions of each sex were accepted. Oddly, they conclude that "the factor of sex did not appear to be important as a basis for accepting or rejecting applicants for treatment" (p. 427). Brown and Kosterlitz did recognize that marital status, which had no effect for men, strongly affected women's opportunities for treatment: Unmarried women had a higher rate of rejection than married women.

Rice (1969) examined selection criteria for individual psychotherapy as a function of patient sex at a university psychiatric clinic staffed by psychiatric residents and psychology interns. Each selected patient was matched on age, sex, and length of university enrollment with a rejected patient. While equal numbers of male and female candidates were accepted (a total of 11%), the men selected had more symptoms, more self-reported problems, and more prior treatment than males not selected. No similar differences were found among the women. Rice concludes that, in a highly selective setting, beginning therapists use more subjective criteria in selecting female patients. In a less selective college counseling center, Kirshner, Hauser, and Genack (1979) found that women were more likely than men to be selected as short-term psychotherapy patients.

An analogue study by Schwartz and Abramowitz (1975) assessed the opinion of mental health professionals as to the appropriateness of insight-oriented versus supportive psychotherapy as a function of patient sex. Therapists with traditional values tended to consider dynamic therapy less worthwhile for men than for women, whereas less traditional therapists tended to the opposite conclusion. Maracek and Johnson (1980) have observed that most (80%) of the potential respondents did not complete or return the questionnaire; those who did respond may be highly atypical, making generalization of the results difficult.

2.2. Duration of Treatment

Studies examining sex effects on length of treatment have been popular because of the simplicity of the dependent variable and because of the possibility that (male) therapists keep women in therapy longer than men (Chesler, 1972). A review of the literature by Harris (1971) concludes that, in general, sex of patient has little effect on length of therapy. More recent studies have focused on the complex contexts in which sex-related effects might occur. Abramowitz, Abramowitz, Roback, Corney, and McKee (1976) analyzed case loads and duration of treatment as a function of sex at both a psychological and a psychiatric clinic. In both clinics, there was a tendency for male psychotherapists to see female patients for a greater length of time than male patients. Additional data concerning the interaction of therapist and patient marital status and sex led to the hypothesis that male psychotherapists prolong and female psychotherapists avoid sexually arousing treatment situations.

In an attempted extension of these findings, Abramowitz, Davidson, Greene, and Edwards (1980) examined case loads and number of treatment sessions in a consortium of community mental health centers. As before, male patients were underrepresented in the case loads of female therapists, although the amount of variation explained was small. Findings regarding length of treatment were not replicated: Male psychotherapists did not offer more psychotherapy sessions to their female patients than to males. The authors suggest three equally cogent explanations for the failure to replicate. First, degree of initial impairment was controlled in the second but not the first study. Hence, the original finding may have been an artifact. Second, the therapists in the second study were more experienced than the "comparative neophytes" of the first study. Third, the relatively short-term treatment of community outpatients may provide less opportunity for covert sexual interplay. Unfortunately, no attempt was made to repeat the finer-grained analysis pertaining to the interaction of patient and therapist marital status.

Another interesting pair of studies was conducted by Del Gaudio and his colleagues. In the first (Stein, Del Gaudio, and Ansley, 1976), neurotically depressed female outpatients were offered more therapy sessions than males who were demographically, affectively, and symptomatically equivalent to the women. An attempt to generalize these findings to a more diagnostically heterogeneous group yielded no sex differences in length of treatment (Del Gaudio, Carpenter, and Morrow, 1978).

Evidently sex differences in treatment duration are relatively uncommon. When found, they are more likely to involve women remaining in treatment longer than men. Maracek and Johnson (1980) caution against assuming that the operation of some sort of bias explains these differences:

> Two conceptual problems with studies on the duration of therapy need to be mentioned. First, length of stay in therapy is not wholly determined by the therapist. Thus, it is a logical error to assume that if women remain in therapy longer than men, the reason is that therapists "keep" women in therapy longer. Women might choose to remain in therapy longer than men, possibly because they feel they are deriving more benefits from it. The point is that studies comparing the length of time that women and men remain in therapy will tell us only whether differences exist. They cannot tell us how or why such differences occur.
>
> The second conceptual issue concerns the relationship of early termination of therapy to overall duration of therapy. Early termination refers to dropping out of therapy before a therapeutic alliance has been formed. By definition, early termination is a unilateral action on the part of the client and thus, it reflects different processes than the normal termination procedure. Early termination should be treated as a separate research issue. Clients who drop out of therapy in the first few sessions should be eliminated from studies on duration of therapy, otherwise, the results of such studies may be misleading. (p. 76)

2.3. Prescription of Medications

In Schwartz and Abramowitz's (1975) analogue study, therapists were asked to prescribe psychotropic medications, electroconvulsive therapy (ECT), and various other treatment possibilities in response to care histories. Keeping in mind the questionnaire return rate problems mentioned earlier, recommendations pertaining to drugs and ECT did not vary as a function of patient sex alone. More experienced therapists rated women as better candidates for drug therapy than men.

Kelly and Kiersky (1979) found that medications were recommended more often for depressed males than for females (at least by male clinicians), probably as a function of their greater likelihood of being diagnosed as psychotic.

In the study by Stein *et al.* (1976), the neurotically depressed female outpatients were more likely than their male counterparts to be prescribed psychotropic medications. The attempted replication with a more diagnostically diverse outpatient group yielded no sex differences in drug prescriptive practices (Del Gaudio *et al.*, 1978).

This latter finding is somewhat surprising in view of the studies that have demonstrated greater prevalence of psychotropic drug use among women. Cooperstock (1978), who has carefully reviewed the literature in this area, reports that women consistently exceed men in their consumption of psychotropic drugs, in a ratio of two to one. To some extent, such sex differences are to be expected: Compared to men, women report more symptoms, are more likely to seek help, and are more likely to be depressed (Waldron, 1976; Weissman and Klerman, 1977). However, Cooperstock reports that women take more drugs than men, and receive more multiple prescriptions (especially in the 35–50 age group), even in studies where number of symptoms is controlled.

Cooperstock (1971) has provided a model for these sex differences based on a number of socially defined parameters. Basically, she argues that women are permitted greater freedom than men in expressing feelings, are more likely to perceive themselves as having personal difficulties, and are more likely to bring them to the attention of a physician. The physician, for his or her part, expects female patients to be more emotionally expressive and will more likely prescribe mood-modifying drugs. Cooperstock's model treats the sex difference somewhat ambivalently. At times, the difference is attributed to men's greater stoicism, their lack of psychological-mindedness, their greater likelihood of self-medication via alcohol and other over-the-counter and illegally acquired medications. At other times, the difference is associated with sex role stereotypes that devalue women (i.e., physicians view women as more neurotic, more self-indulgent, more vulnerable to stress).

Linn (1971) has also called attention to the possibility that physicians' prescribing habits are more related to social attitudes and values than to scientific and medical matters. The only empirical evidence that he cites pertaining to sex is a study he conducted on physician judgments of legitimacy of Librium and Dexedrine use. Although sex was not manipulated systematically, physicians did report viewing the daily use of Librium as legitimate for a housewife, but of questionable legitimacy for a student of unspecified sex. Evidently, mental alertness is not viewed as a *sine qua non* of good housewifery!

Others (King, 1980; Seidenberg, 1971) have taken a more indirect approach and have examined drug advertisements in medical and psychiatric journals; the stereotyping in the ads is clearly biased against women. King (1980), for example, found that women in psychiatric journal drug advertisements were portrayed as anxious, neurotic, with imagined and exaggerated symptoms, and in need of repair or adjustment if unable to carry out and enjoy stereotyped sex role duties. Men in need of psychotropic drugs were more likely to be depicted as having transient, situationally induced, job-related problems. More extended discussion of this topic appears in Chapter 16 by Fidell.

2.4. Summary

The study of sex bias in psychiatric and psychological dispositions and other aspects of patient management has clearly not been conducted with the same thoroughness as has the study of sex bias in assessment. Studies of psychotherapy seem to have distracted investigators from broader and equally important questions of patient management. Here is an area where more research is needed, particularly since existing studies of emergency room referral practices and drug-prescribing habits suggest that sex of patient is a potent factor, alone and combined with variables such as race, work, and marital status.

3. Conclusions and Recommendations

The 5 years that have intervened since I last reviewed the literature in this area (Zeldow, 1978) have not seen any major substantive surprises or methodological innovations. While research on sex differences in clinical judgment will undoubtedly continue, I doubt that the subject will continue to be studied so intensively and so widely. There are other, more basic and more pressing topics to investigate in the psychology of gender. While the following conclusions are by no means final, they are based on an extensive body of research, with a modest share of discernible regularities and plenty of deviations thereof. Foremost among the discernible regularities has been a shift in the attitudes of the researchers themselves. Whereas early studies were motivated by the desire to demonstrate or disconfirm the existence of sex bias and sex role stereotyping in clinical practice, later studies have recognized the inadequacy of either-or formulations and have been more concerned with improving our understanding of the conditions under which sex-related effects do and do not occur.

"By itself, sex of a patient or client is rarely a factor in determining diagnosis, prognosis, degree of psychopathology, or treatment goals" (Zeldow, 1978, p. 92). With one *major* exception, this statement remains as fair and accurate a summary statement today as when first made. The one exception concerns the various diagnostic entities (e.g., hysteria, antisocial personality, agoraphobia, alcoholism) that are discussed elsewhere in this volume and have been excluded from this review.

While patient sex rarely "acts alone," sex-related effects (i.e., patient sex combined with other patient, judge, and situational variables) are common, complex, and diverse. Norm-deviant patients seem to risk harsher judgments than patients whose behavior and symptoms conform to expectations and are sex-appropriate. Norm-deviant females may be the primary victims of this bias, but norm-deviant men are also at risk. Attractiveness and race are also likely to combine with patient sex to affect various judgments and treatment decisions. Beyond this, it is difficult to generalize from extant studies or to predict to new situations. We know that a host of variables may interact with patient sex to influence clinical judgments, but we cannot say with any precision that they will.

Certainly the most strident claims of sex discrimination at the hands of mental health professionals have been irreparably weakened by the research findings. Conversely, it can be argued that research to date has been methodologically flawed and conceptually uninspired. While I accept these characterizations, I would also point out that, taken collectively, the literature does seem to have captured some of the subtlety and complexity of the phenomenon, in spite of the inadequacies of individual studies.*

Perhaps the greatest research contribution in this area has been to

*My earlier review paper (Zeldow, 1978) contained a minor typographical error in the concluding paragraph that has been perpetuated in a quotation by Sherman (1980, p. 35). I am happy to correct it here. The statement should read: "The results of the above studies are sufficiently diverse and ambiguous as to be interpretable both as strong and weak evidence for sexism in the mental health field, depending on the point of view of the interpreter. The fairest statement that can probably be made at present is that the most compelling evidence of sex bias and sex-role stereotyping in clinical assessment and treatment is also entirely anecdotal. More systematic studies continue to demonstrate sex-related biases in diverse clinical activities, but also strongly suggest that such biases are more limited in scope and more complex in their nature than has heretofore been recognized" (Zeldow, 1978, p. 93).

sensitize mental health professionals to both the gross and subtle ways in which sexist attitudes may affect their practices. Since there is some evidence to indicate that clinicians are not now so prone to sex role stereotyping, perhaps it is not unduly optimistic to think that clinical practice has become less sexist. But it is frustrating (if not unique to this area of psychology) to review a large number of studies and to find oneself unable, in conclusion, to do more than reaffirm the incredible complexity and situation-specificity of human behavior.

My recommendations for future research are not likely to enhance our ability to predict the conditions under which sex-related biases will occur. Still, they seem worthwhile for reasons to be elaborated forthwith.

The first recommendation is that studies of sex differences in clinical judgment should be submitted to meta-analysis, as has been done in the area of psychotherapy outcome (Smith, Glass, and Miller, 1980). Such an analysis would begin with extant literature reviews, selecting for the meta-analysis those studies in which judges assess men and women on a variety of dimensions of clinical relevance. This would yield an estimate of the magnitude of sex differences across studies, something that the existing literature reviews to date have failed to do. It would also permit analysis of the extent to which effect size is related to various substantive and methodological features (e.g., sex of judge, clinician experience level, patient race, norm-deviant behavior, analogue vs. archival study). While such an undertaking would itself be subject to controversy, it would provide a new perspective and a more objective way of summarizing studies in the area than current literature reviews provide. It could also provide interested investigators with a greater awareness of lacunae in the existing literature, and with new hypotheses and promising variables for further investigation.

The second recommendation is that studies of sex-related biases in clinical practice be conducted routinely as part of the program evaluation that mental health organizations conduct. There are two reasons for this recommendation. First, if men and women are treated in systematically different ways, whether or not treatment of one group is inferior to that of the other, then it is important that the practitioners and organizations involved be aware of this fact. The frequency with which sex-related effects on patient evaluation and disposition have been reported suffices to justify a vigilant posture. Second, existing research suggests that sex-related effects, while common, are diverse and situation-specific. Thus, generalizing from studies reported in the literature to one's own setting will be of limited value. Each organization will have to investigate the possibility of sex bias by and for itself.

The last decade has seen the debunking of many myths regarding women and their alleged passivity, emotionality, intellectual inferiority, etc. Now the pendulum is swinging toward a greater interest in actual, as opposed to stereotypically perceived, sex differences. Research is beginning to explore in detail the various ways in which endowment and experience differentially shape the lives of men and women (Parsons, 1980). While I have already expressed my belief that the immediate future will not witness a surge of interest or new developments on the subject of this chapter, I do think that the above-mentioned shift in research will ultimately enrich investigations of sex bias and sex-related effects in clinical judgment. While current research has tended to search for sex differences in clinical judgment when such differential judgments are unwarranted, future studies may ironically be more concerned with judges who evaluate male and female patients identically when, in fact, they should evaluate them differently. While this is only speculation, it is certain that new developments in clinical judgment/sex bias research will be contingent upon advances in the general psychology of sex differences.

4. References

Abramowitz, C. V., and Docecki, P. R. The politics of clinical judgment: Early empirical returns. *Psychological Bulletin,* 1977, *84,* 460–476.

Abramowitz, S. I., and Abramowitz, C. V. Sex-biased researchers of sex bias in psychotherapy and impartial reviewers. *American Psychologist,* 1977, *32,* 893–894.

Abramowitz, S. I., Abramowitz, C. V., Jackson, C., and Gomes, B. The politics of clinical judgment: What nonliberal examiners infer about women who do not stifle themselves. *Journal of Consulting and Clinical Psychology,* 1973, *41,* 385–391.

Abramowitz, S. I., Abramowitz, C. V., Roback, H. B., Corney, R., and McKee, E. Sex-role related countertransference in psychotherapy. *Archives of General Psychiatry,* 1976, *33,* 71–73.

Abramowitz, S. I., Davidson, C. V., Greene, L. R., and Edwards, D. W. Sex-role related countertransference revisited: A partial extension. *Journal of Nervous and Mental Disease,* 1980, *168,* 309–311.

Barocas, R., and Vance, F. L. Physical appearance and personal judgment counseling. *Journal of Counseling Psychology,* 1974, *21,* 96–100.

Billingsley, D. *Sex-role stereotypes and clinical judgments: Negative bias in psychotherapy.* Paper presented at the meeting of the American Psychological Association, Washington, D.C., 1976.

Bond, L. A. Perceptions of sex-role deviations: An attributional analysis. *Sex Roles,* 1981, *7,* 107–115.

Brodey, J. F., and Detre, T. Criteria used by clinicians in referring patients to individual or group therapy. *American Journal of Psychotherapy,* 1972, *26,* 176–184.

Broverman, I. K., Broverman, D. M., Clarkson, F. E., Rosenkrantz, P. S., and Vogel, S. R. Sex-role stereotypes and clinical judgments of mental health. *Journal of Consulting and Clinical Psychology,* 1970, *34,* 1–7.

Broverman, I. K., Vogel, S. R., Broverman, D. M., Clarkson, F. E., and Rosenkrantz, P. S. Sex-role stereotypes: A current appraisal. *Journal of Social Issues*, 1972, *28*, 59–78.

Brown, J., and Kosterlitz, N. Selection and treatment of psychiatric outpatients. *Archives of General Psychiatry*, 1964, *11*, 425–437.

Cash, T. F., Kehr, J., Polyson, J., and Freeman, V. Role of physical attractiveness in peer attribution of psychological disturbance. *Journal of Consulting and Clinical Psychology*, 1977, *45*, 987–993.

Chesler, P. *Women and madness*. Garden City, N.Y.: Doubleday, 1972.

Coie, J. D., Pennington, B. F., and Buckley, H. H. Effects of situational stress and sex roles on the attribution of psychological disorder. *Journal of Consulting and Clinical Psychology*, 1974, *42*, 559–568.

Cooperstock, R. Sex differences in the use of mood-modifying drugs: An explanatory model. *Journal of Health and Social Behavior*, 1971, *12*, 238–244.

Cooperstock, R. Sex differences in psychotropic drug use. *Social Science and Medicine*, 1978, *12B*, 179–186.

Davidson, C. V., and Abramowitz, S. I. Sex bias in clinical judgment: Later empirical returns. *Psychology of Women Quarterly*, 1980, *4*, 377–395.

Del Gaudio, A. C., Carpenter, P. J., and Morrow, G. R. Male and female treatment differences: Can they be generalized? *Journal of Consulting and Clinical Psychology*, 1978, *46*, 1577–1578.

Greenberg, R. P. Sexual bias on Rorschach administration. *Journal of Personality Assessment*, 1972, *36*, 336–339.

Gross, H., Herbert, M., Knatterud, G., and Donner, L. The effect of sex on the variation of diagnosis and disposition in psychiatric emergency rooms. *Journal of Nervous and Mental Diseases*, 1969, *148*, 638–642.

Haan, N., and Livson, N. Sex differences in the eyes of expert personality assessors: Blind spots? *Journal of Personality Assessment*, 1973, *37*, 486–492.

Harris, S. L. The influence of patient and therapist sex in psychotherapy. *Comments on Contemporary Psychiatry*, 1971, *1*, 17–27.

Hersen, M. Sexual aspects of TAT administration: A failure at replication with an inpatient population. *Journal of Consulting and Clinical Psychology*, 1971, *36*, 20–22.

Hill, C. E., Tanney, M. F., Leonard, M. M., and Reiss, J. A. Counselor reactions to female clients: Type of problem, age of client, and sex of counselor. *Journal of Counseling Psychology*, 1977, *24*, 60–65.

Kazdin, A. E. Evaluating the generality of findings in analogue therapy research. *Journal of Consulting and Clinical Psychology*, 1978, *46*, 673–686.

Kelly, K., and Kiersky, S. *Psychotherapists and sexual stereotypes: A study of bias in diagnostic interviews employing videotape simulations.* Paper presented at the meeting of the New York State Psychological Association, Saratoga, N.Y., 1979.

King, E. Sex bias in psychoactive drug advertisements. *Psychiatry*, 1980, *43*, 129–137.

Kirshner, L. A., Hauser, S. T., and Genack, A. Effects of gender on short-term psychotherapy. *Psychotherapy: Theory, Research and Practice*, 1979, *15*, 158–167.

Kravetz, D. F. Sex-role concepts of women. *Journal of Consulting and Clinical Psychology*, 1976, *44*, 437–443.

LaPiere, R. T. Attitudes vs. actions. *Social Forces*, 1934, *13*, 230–237.

Levine, S. V., Kamin, L. E., and Levine, E. L. Sexism and psychiatry. *American Journal of Orthopsychiatry*, 1974, *44*, 327–336.

Linn, L. S. Physician characteristics and attitudes toward legitimate use of psychotherapeutic drugs. *Journal of Health and Social Behavior*, 1971, *12*, 132–140.

Lowinger, P., and Dobie, S. The attitude of the psychiatrist about his patient. *Comprehensive Psychiatry*, 1968, *9*, 627–632.

Maffeo, P. A. Thoughts on Stricker's "Implications of research for psychotherapeutic treatment of women." *American Psychologist,* 1979, *34,* 690–695.

Malchon, M. J., and Penner, L. A. The effects of sex and sex-role identity on the attribution of maladjustment. *Sex Roles,* 1981, *7,* 363–378.

Maracek, J., and Johnson, M. The influence of gender on the process of therapy: A review. In A. M. Brodsky and R. T. Hare-Mustin (Eds.), *Women and psychotherapy.* New York: Guilford Press, 1980.

Masling, J., and Harris, S. Sexual aspects of TAT administration. *Journal of Consulting and Clinical Psychology,* 1969, *33,* 166–169.

Maxfield, R. B. *Sex-role stereotypes of psychotherapists.* Unpublished doctoral dissertation, Adelphi University, 1976.

Munley, P. H. A review of counseling analogue research. *Journal of Counseling Psychology,* 1974, *21,* 320–330.

Parsons, J. E. *The psychobiology of sex differences and sex roles.* New York: Hemisphere, 1980.

Petro, C. S., and Putnam, B. A. Sex-role stereotypes: Issues of attitudinal changes. *Sex Roles,* 1979, *5,* 29–39.

Rice, D. Patient sex differences and selection for individual therapy. *Journal of Nervous and Mental Disease,* 1969, *148,* 124–133.

Schwartz, J. M., and Abramowitz, S. I. Value-related effects on psychiatric judgment. *Archives of General Psychiatry,* 1975, *32,* 1525–1529.

Schwartz, J. M., and Abramowitz, S. I. Effects of client physical attractiveness on clinical judgment. *Psychotherapy: Theory, Research and Practice,* 1978, *15,* 251–256.

Seidenberg, R. Drug advertisements and perception of mental illness. *Mental Hygiene,* 1971, *55,* 21–31.

Sherman, J. A. Therapist attitudes and sex-role stereotyping. In A. M. Brodsky and R. T. Hare-Mustin (Eds.), *Women and psychotherapy.* New York: Guilford Press, 1980.

Siskind, G. Sexual aspects of Thematic Apperception Test administration. *Journal of Consulting and Clinical Psychology,* 1973, *401,* 20–21.

Smith, M. L., Glass, G. V., and Miller, T. I. *The benefits of psychotherapy.* Baltimore: Johns Hopkins University Press, 1980.

Stearns, B. S., Penner, L. A., and Kimmel, E. B. *An experimental investigation of sexism among practicing psychotherapists.* Paper presented at the meeting of the American Psychological Association, Toronto, 1978.

Stein, L. S., Del Gaudio, A. C., and Ansley, M. Y. A comparison of female and male neurotic depressives. *Journal of Clinical Psychology,* 1976, *32,* 19–21.

Stricker, G. Implications of research for psychotherapeutic treatment of women. *American Psychologist,* 1977, *32,* 14–22.

Sue, S. Clients' demographic characteristics and therapeutic treatment: Differences that make a difference. *Journal of Consulting and Clinical Psychology,* 1976, *44,* 864.

Thomas, A. N., and Stewart, N. R. Counselor response to female clients with deviate and conforming career goals. *Journal of Counseling Psychology,* 1971, *18,* 352–357.

Tilby, P. J., and Kalin, R. Effects of sex-role deviant lifestyles in otherwise normal persons on the perception of maladjustment. *Sex Roles,* 1980, *6,* 581–592.

Waldron, I. Why do women live longer than men? *Social Science and Medicine,* 1976, *10,* 349–362.

Weissman, M. M., and Klerman, G. L. Sex differences and the epidemiology of depression. *Archives of General Psychiatry,* 1977, *34,* 98–111.

Werner, P. D., and Block, J. Sex differences in the eyes of expert personality assessors: Unwarranted conclusions. *Journal of Personality Assessment,* 1975, *39,* 110–113.

Wright, C. T., Meadow, A., Abramowitz, S. I., and Davidson, C. V. Psychiatric diagnosis as a function of assessor profession and sex. *Psychology of Women Quarterly*, 1980, *5*, 240–254.

Zeldow, P. Clinical judgment: A search for sex differences. *Psychological Reports*, 1975, *37*, 1135–1142.

Zeldow, P. Effects of nonpathological sex-role stereotypes on student evaluations of psychiatric patients. *Journal of Consulting and Clinical Psychology*, 1976, *44*, 304.

Zeldow, P. B. Sex differences in psychiatric evaluation and treatment: An empirical review. *Archives of General Psychiatry*, 1978, *35*, 89–93.

16

Sex Roles in Medicine

Linda S. Fidell

The extent to which the seeking and receiving of medical care are influenced by social factors is probably underestimated by the general public. Although current medical practice has many of the trappings of science, it, like the law and education, is still practiced in a social milieu in which cultural beliefs abound.

For example, although medical diagnoses appear to be objective, and in many cases may be so, they also represent an attempt at cognitive labeling of a set of symptoms and signs that may or may not readily fit into preestablished diagnostic categories. However, the diagnoses that are rendered by physicians have considerable social, as well as medical, implications for patients, depending on the seriousness and legitimacy of perceived illnesses. Rights and obligations of patients and others (families, friends, insurance companies, employers) are determined in part, by how a particular set of symptoms is defined. When categorizing symptoms into diagnoses, physicians exercise considerable social, economic, and political power (Freidson, 1971).

For another example, within the medical profession social factors influence the power and prestige of specialists. Shortell (1974) reports that the prestige of specialists is related directly to the amount of control exerted by the physician over the patient—the greater the autonomy of the physician (e.g., surgeon), the higher his prestige. Physicians who must depend on the cooperation of patients (e.g., psychiatrists) tend to have lower prestige.

Both Ehrenreich (1974) and Fidell (1980) have summarized historical differences in medical beliefs about men and women. In general, wom-

Linda S. Fidell • Department of Psychology, California State University, Northridge, California 91330. This chapter is a revised and updated version of Fidell (1980).

en have been viewed historically as alien, different from men, beset by reproductive health problems, and given to psychosomatic and neurotic complaints. Historically, medical treatment of women has frequently been paternalistic and guided by superstition rather than by objective data. There is some evidence (mentioned, in part, below) that current medical practice is not yet divorced from past beliefs concerning sex differences in health.

Some of the current drive toward more naturalistic health care, particularly among women, represents a growing awareness of the limitations of standard medical practice. However, I am also concerned with some aspects of the naturalistic health movement. The message sometimes seems to be that if you would only adjust your thinking or find the right combination of yogurt and vitamins, then health-related problems would disappear. This message, like that in rape, seems to me to be a case of blaming the victim. Most people most of the time, in my opinion, are reasonably objective in assessment of their health problems, which are more often physiologically based than the current development of medical diagnosis can reveal. I am not saying that meditation, exercise, and the like, are unhelpful in correcting problems, but rather that medicine is simply unable to diagnose and correct many problems. And when diagnosis and therapy are unavailable, it may be advantageous to the medical professional to define the problem as psychosomatic, for which physicians are not responsible. The naturalistic health movement may unwittingly feed into this attitude.

The purpose of this chapter is to examine the potential impact of the sex role stereotype on health, medical behavior, and medical treatment. Two alternative hypotheses are suggested. The first is that women truly have greater emotional instability than do men so that certain differences in medical treatment of women and men are warranted, i.e., more frequent prescribing to women of psychotropic drugs such as Valium, or a tendency to ascribe psychogenic illness to women and organic illness to men. On the other hand, if the differences in treatment are a function of the operation of certain aspects of the sex role stereotypes, then the differences are not warranted and changes need to be instituted in medical education.

1. Sex Differences in Health

One of the most perplexing sex differences in the health field is the difference between morbidity and mortality. Morbidity statistics reflect the extent to which persons are required to curtail activities or use drugs for health-related problems. Mortality statistics present death rates by age category. Although morbidity statistics suggest that women are less healthy than men, mortality statistics suggest the reverse. Men die more